The repoze.bfg Web Application Framework

Version 1.2

Chris McDonough

CONTENTS

Front Matter

COPYRIGHT, TRADEMARKS, AND ATTRIBUTIONS

The repoze.bfg Web Application Framework, Version 1.2

by Chris McDonough

Copyright © 2008-2010, Agendaless Consulting.

ISBN-10: 0615345379

ISBN-13: 978-0-615-34537-6

First print publishing: February, 2010

Internal proof number: 3

All terms mentioned in this book that are known to be trademarks or service marks have been appropriately capitalized. However, use of a term in this book should not be regarded as affecting the validity of any trademark or service mark.

Every effort has been made to make this book as complete and as accurate as possible, but no warranty or fitness is implied. The information provided is on as "as-is" basis. The author and the publisher shall have neither liability nor responsibility to any person or entity with respect to any loss or damages arising from the information contained in this book. No patent liability is assumed with respect to the use of the information contained herein.

Attributions

Foreword: Paul Everitt

Technical Reviewer: Andrew Sawyers

Cover Designer: Nat Hardwick of Electrosoup (http://www.electrosoup.co.uk).

Used with permission: The *Request and Response Objects* (pp. 143) chapter is adapted, with permission, from documentation originally written by Ian Bicking.

Print Production

The print version of this book was produced using the Sphinx (http://sphinx.pocoo.org/) documentation generation system and the LaTeX (http://www.latex-project.org/) typesetting system.

Contacting The Publisher

Please send documentation licensing inquiries, translation inquiries, and other business communications to Agendaless Consulting (mailto:webmaster@agendaless.com). Please send software and other technical queries to the repoze-dev maillist (http://lists.repoze.org/listinfo/repoze-dev).

HTML Version and Source Code

An HTML version of this book is freely available via http://bfg.repoze.org (http://bfg.repoze.org).

The source code for the examples used in this book are available within the `repoze.bfg` software distribution, always available via http://bfg.repoze.org (http://bfg.repoze.org).

Errata

Errata for this book will be placed at *http://bfg.repoze.org/book_errata.*

TYPOGRAPHICAL CONVENTIONS

Literals, filenames and function arguments are presented using the following style:

```
argument1
```

Warnings, which represent limitations and need-to-know information related to a topic or concept are presented in the following style:

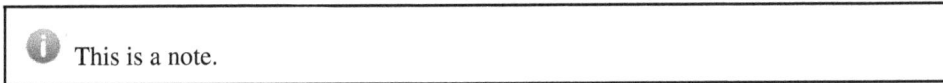

> ⚠ This is a warning.

Notes, which represent additional information related to a topic or concept are presented in the following style:

> ⓘ This is a note.

We present Python method names using the following style:

```
Python.method_name()
```

We present Python class names, module names, attributes and global variables using the following style:

```
Python.class_module_or_attribute.name
```

References to glossary terms are presented using the following style:

Repoze

URLs are presented using the following style:

Repoze (http://repoze.org)

References to sections and chapters are presented using the following style:

Traversal (pp. 61)

Python code blocks are presented in the following style:

```
1  def foo(abc):
2      pass
```

Blocks of XML markup are presented in the following style:

```
1  <root>
2    <!-- ... more XML .. -->
3  </root>
```

When a command that should be typed on one line is too long to fit on a page, the backslash \ is used to indicate that the following printed line should actually be part of the command:

```
c:\bigfntut\tutorial> ..\Scripts\nosetests --cover-package=tutorial \
      --cover-erase --with-coverage
```

A sidebar, which presents a concept tangentially related to content discussed on a page, is rendered like so:

This is a sidebar

Sidebar information.

In printed versions of this book, Python modules classes, methods, functions, and attributes that are part of the `repoze.bfg` module are referenced in paragraph text. These are contracted to omit the `repoze.bfg` prefix to reduce redundancy and increase readability. Therefore, where you might expect:

```
repoze.bfg.configuration.Configurator.add_view (pp. XXX)
```

Instead a contracted version will be rendered:

```
configuration.Configurator.add_view (pp. XXX)
```

FOREWORD

A Foreword By Paul Everitt

Paul Everitt is a principal at *Agendaless Consulting*. Before his time at Agendaless, he was the co-founder of *Digital Creations*, which later became *Zope Corporation*. He has been a widely respected member of the Python community since 1994.

Fortunate.

As I reflect upon the BFG web framework and this book by Chris to document it, I keep coming back to the same word. Certainly the conventional wisdom is clear: "Don't we have too many web frameworks, paired with outdated books?" Yes we do, but to the contrary and for that very reason, we are fortunate to have this book and this framework.

Chris McDonough first came to work with us at Digital Creations almost a decade ago, just after there existed a Zope. We were all pioneers: the first open source application server, one of the first open source web companies to get serious investment, and entrants in nearly every book and article about the open source space. Zope wasn't just a unique business model, though. It really was, as quoted at the time, one of the places where open source delivered fresh ideas in design and architecture.

Then a decade happened. Bubbles burst and the new new thing became the old new thing, many times in succession. All of us changed jobs, worked on a variety of endeavors, and big dreams yielded to small realities. Somehow, though the trajectory was unforeseen, we have orbited back to the same spot. Older, wiser, but with similar ideas and familiar faces. Back to dream again.

We are fortunate to have BFG. It really does carve out a unique spot in the Python web frameworks landscape. It permits the core good ideas from Zope, while not requiring them. Moreover, the reason you'll love it has less to do with Zope and more to do with the old fashioned stuff:

- A superb commitment to outstanding and constantly updated documentation

- An equal commitment to quality: test coverage, performance, and documented compatibility

- Adult supervision and minimalism in the design, with "pay only for what you eat" simplicity

For those of us from the Zope world, BFG permits our still-unique ideas while teleporting us into the modern world of Python web programming. It is fascinating, liberating, and rejuvenating. We are able to cast off old sins and legitimately reclaim the title of best damn game in town. Quite a coup: whether you considered Zope but turned away, or became an adopter, you'll find BFG the new new new thing.

We are also fortunate to have this book. We never had such a resource in Zope, even though we funded the writing of the first book a decade ago. In retrospect, the answer is obvious: a second group tried to retrofit a book onto code created by the first group. The true magic in BFG is that the top-notch documentation is written by the same person as the top-notch code, a person with equal passion and commitment to both. Rarely are we so fortunate.

Which brings us to the final point. We are fortunate to have Chris. I personally consider myself lucky to have worked with him and to be his friend this past decade. He has changed my thinking in numerous ways, fundamentally improving the way I view many things. He's the best person I know in the world of open source, and I get to be in business with him. Fortunate indeed.

I very much hope you enjoy this book and get involved with BFG. We use it for applications as small as "hello world" demos up to scalable, re-usable, half-a-million-dollar projects. May you find BFG, and the book, to be a high-quality, honest, and durable framework choice for your work as well.

AUTHOR INTRODUCTION

Welcome to "The `repoze.bfg` Web Application Framework". In this introduction, I'll describe the audience for this book, I'll describe the book content, I'll provide some context regarding the genesis of `repoze.bfg`, and I'll thank some important people.

I hope you enjoy both this book and the software it documents. I've had a blast writing both.

Audience

This book is aimed primarily at a reader that has the following attributes:

- At least a moderate amount of *Python* experience.

- A familiarity with web protocols such as HTTP and CGI.

If you fit into both of these categories, you're in the direct target audience for this book. But don't worry, even if you have no experience with Python or the web, both are easy to pick up "on the fly".

Python is an *excellent* language in which to write applications; becoming productive in Python is almost mind-blowingly easy. If you already have experience in another language such as Java, Visual Basic, Perl, Ruby, or even C/C++, learning Python will be a snap; it should take you no longer than a couple of days to become modestly productive. If you don't have previous programming experience, it will be slightly harder, and it will take a little longer, but you'd be hard-pressed to find a better "first language."

Web technology familiarity is assumed in various places within the book. For example, the book doesn't try to define common web-related concepts like "URL" or "query string." Likewise, the book describes various interactions in terms of the HTTP protocol, but it does not describe how the HTTP protocol works in detail. Like any good web framework, though, `repoze.bfg` shields you from needing to know most of the gory details of web protocols and low-level data structures. As a result, you can usually avoid becoming "blocked" while you read this book even if you don't yet deeply understand web technologies.

Book Content

This book is divided into four major parts:

Narrative Documentation

> This is documentation which describes `repoze.bfg` concepts in narrative form, written in a largely conversational tone. Each narrative documentation chapter describes an isolated `repoze.bfg` concept. You should be able to get useful information out of the narrative chapters if you read them out-of-order, or when you need only a reminder about a particular topic while you're developing an application.

Tutorials

> Each tutorial builds a sample application or implements a set of concepts with a sample; it then describes the application or concepts in terms of the sample. You should read the tutorials if you want a guided tour of `repoze.bfg`.

API Reference

> Comprehensive reference material for every public API exposed by `repoze.bfg`. The API documentation is organized alphabetically by module name.

ZCML Directive Reference

> Comprehensive reference material for every *ZCML directive* provided by `repoze.bfg`. The ZCML directive documentation is organized alphabetically by directive name.

The Genesis of `repoze.bfg`

I wrote `repoze.bfg` after many years of writing applications using *Zope*. Zope provided me with a lot of mileage: it wasn't until almost a decade of successfully creating applications using it that I decided to write a different web framework. Although `repoze.bfg` takes inspiration from a variety of web frameworks, it owes more of its core design to Zope than any other.

The Repoze "brand" existed before `repoze.bfg` was created. One of the first packages developed as part of the Repoze brand was a package named `repoze.zope2`. This was a package that allowed Zope 2 applications to run under a *WSGI* server without modification. Zope 2 did not have reasonable WSGI support at the time.

During the development of the `repoze.zope2` package, I found that replicating the Zope 2 "publisher" – the machinery that maps URLs to code – was time-consuming and fiddly. Zope 2 had evolved over many years, and emulating all of its edge cases was extremely difficult. I finished the `repoze.zope2` package, and it emulates the normal Zope 2 publisher pretty well. But during its development, it became clear that Zope 2 had simply begun to exceed my tolerance for complexity, and I began to look around for simpler options.

I considered using the Zope 3 application server machinery, but it turned out that it had become more indirect than the Zope 2 machinery it aimed to replace, which didn't fulfill the goal of simplification. I also considered using Django and Pylons, but neither of those frameworks offer much along the axes of traversal, contextual declarative security, or application extensibility; these were features I had become accustomed to as a Zope developer.

I decided that in the long term, creating a simpler framework that retained features I had become accustomed to when developing Zope applications was a more reasonable idea than continuing to use any Zope publisher or living with the limitations and unfamiliarities of a different framework. The result is what is now `repoze.bfg`.

It is immodest to say so, but I believe `repoze.bfg` has turned out to be the very best Python web framework available today, bar none. It combines all the "good parts" from other web frameworks into a cohesive whole that is reliable, down-to-earth, flexible, speedy, and well-documented.

Thanks

This book is dedicated to my grandmother, who gave me my first typewriter (a Royal), and my mother, who bought me my first computer (a VIC-20).

Thanks to the following people for providing expertise, resources, and software. Without the help of these folks, neither this book nor the software which it details would exist: Paul Everitt, Tres Seaver, Andrew Sawyers, Malthe Borch, Carlos de la Guardia, Chris Rossi, Shane Hathaway, Daniel Holth, Wichert Akkerman, Georg Brandl, Simon Oram and Nat Hardwick of Electrosoup, Ian Bicking of the Open Planning Project, Jim Fulton of Zope Corporation, Tom Moroz of the Open Society Institute, and Todd Koym of Environmental Health Sciences.

Thanks to Guido van Rossum and Tim Peters for Python.

Special thanks to Tricia for putting up with me.

Part I

Narrative Documentation

REPOZE.BFG INTRODUCTION

If they are judged only by differences in user interface, most web applications seem to have very little in common with each other. For example, a web page served by one web application might be a representation of the contents of an accounting ledger, while a web page served by another application might be a listing of songs. These applications probably won't serve the same set of customers. However, although they're not very similar on the surface, both a ledger-serving application and a song-serving application could be successfully be written using repoze.bfg.

repoze.bfg is a very general open source Python web *framework*. As a framework, its primary job is to make it easier for a developer to create an arbitrary web application. The type of application being created isn't really important; it could be a spreadsheet, a corporate intranet, or an "oh-so-Web-2.0" social networking platform. repoze.bfg is general enough that it can be used in a wide variety of circumstances.

Frameworks vs. Libraries

A *framework* differs from a *library* in one very important way: library code is always *called* by code that you write, while a framework always *calls* code that you write. Using a set of libraries to create an application is usually easier than using a framework initially, because you can choose to cede control to library code you have not authored very selectively. But when you use a framework, you are required to cede a greater portion of control to code you have not authored: code that resides in the framework itself. You needn't use a framework at all to create a web application using Python. A rich set of libraries already exists for the platform. In practice, however, using a framework to create an application is often more practical than rolling your own via a set of libraries if the framework provides a set of facilities that fits your application requirements.

The first release of repoze.bfg was made in July of 2008. Since its first release, we've tried to ensure that it maintains the following attributes:

Simplicity repoze.bfg attempts to be a *"pay only for what you eat"* framework which delivers results even if you have only partial knowledge. Other frameworks may expect you to understand many concepts and technologies fully before you can be truly productive. repoze.bfg doesn't force you to use any particular technology to produce an application, and we try to keep the core set of concepts you need to understand to a minimum.

A Sense of Fun Developing a repoze.bfg application should not feel "enterprisey". We like to keep things down-to-earth.

Minimalism repoze.bfg provides only the very basics: *URL to code mapping*, *templating*, *security*, and *resources*. There is not much more to the framework than these pieces: you are expected to provide the rest.

Documentation Because repoze.bfg is minimal, it's relatively easy to keep its documentation up-to-date, which is helpful to bring new developers up to speed. It's our goal that nothing remain undocumented about repoze.bfg.

Speed repoze.bfg is faster than many other popular Python web frameworks for common tasks such as templating and simple response generation. The "hardware is cheap" mantra has its limits when you're responsible for managing a great many machines: the fewer you need, the less pain you'll have.

Familiarity The repoze.bfg framework is a canonization of practices that "fit the brains" of its authors.

Trustability repoze.bfg is developed conservatively and tested exhaustively. *If it ain't tested, it's broke*. Every release of repoze.bfg has 100% statement coverage via unit tests.

Openness Like *Python*, the repoze.bfg software is distributed under a permissive open source license (http://repoze.org/license.html).

This book usually refers to the framework by its full package name, repoze.bfg. However, it is often referred to as just "BFG" (the "repoze-dot" dropped) in conversation.

1.1 What Is Repoze?

repoze.bfg is a member of the collection of software published under the *Repoze* "brand". *Repoze* software is written by *Agendaless Consulting* and a community of contributors. The Repoze website (http://repoze.org) describes the Repoze brand in more detail. Software authored that uses this brand is usually placed into a repoze namespace package. This namespace consists of a number of packages. Each package is useful in isolation. The repoze namespace package represents that the software is written by a notional community rather than representing a collection of software that is meant to be used as a unit. For example, even though repoze.bfg shares the same namespace as another popular Repoze package, repoze.who, these two packages are otherwise unrelated and can be used separately.

1.2 `repoze.bfg` and Other Web Frameworks

`repoze.bfg` was inspired by *Zope*, *Pylons* and *Django*. As a result, `repoze.bfg` borrows several concepts and features from each, combining them into a unique web framework.

Many features of `repoze.bfg` trace their origins back to *Zope*. Like Zope applications, `repoze.bfg` applications can be configured via a set of declarative configuration files. Like Zope applications, `repoze.bfg` applications can be easily extended: if you obey certain constraints, the application you produce can be reused, modified, re-integrated, or extended by third-party developers without forking the original application. The concepts of *traversal* and declarative security in `repoze.bfg` were pioneered first in Zope.

The `repoze.bfg` concept of *URL dispatch* is inspired by the *Routes* system used by *Pylons*. Like Pylons, `repoze.bfg` is mostly policy-free. It makes no assertions about which database you should use, and its built-in templating facilities are included only for convenience. In essence, it only supplies a mechanism to map URLs to *view* code, along with a set of conventions for calling those views. You are free to use third-party components that fit your needs in your applications.

The concepts of *view* and *model* are used by `repoze.bfg` mostly as they would be by Django. `repoze.bfg` has a documentation culture more like Django's than like Zope's.

Like *Pylons*, but unlike *Zope*, a `repoze.bfg` application developer may use completely imperative code to perform common framework configuration tasks such as adding a view or a route. In Zope, *ZCML* is typically required for similar purposes. In *Grok*, a Zope-based web framework, *decorator* objects and class-level declarations are used for this purpose. `repoze.bfg` supports *ZCML* and decorator-based configuration, but does not require either. See *Application Configuration* (pp. 15) for more information.

Also unlike *Zope* and unlike other "full-stack" frameworks such as *Django*, `repoze.bfg` makes no assumptions about which persistence mechanisms you should use to build an application. Zope applications are typically reliant on *ZODB*; `repoze.bfg` allows you to build *ZODB* applications, but it has no reliance on the ZODB software. Likewise, *Django* tends to assume that you want to store your application's data in a relational database. `repoze.bfg` makes no such assumption; it allows you to use a relational database but doesn't encourage or discourage the decision.

Other Python web frameworks advertise themselves as members of a class of web frameworks named model-view-controller (http://en.wikipedia.org/wiki/Model–view–controller) frameworks. Insofar as this term has been claimed to represent a class of web frameworks, `repoze.bfg` also generally fits into this class.

You Say BFG is MVC, But Where's The Controller?

The repoze.bfg authors believe that the MVC pattern just doesn't really fit the web very well. In a repoze.bfg application, there are models, which store data, and views, which present the data stored in models. However, no facility provided by the framework actually maps to the concept of a "controller". So repoze.bfg is actually an "MV" framework rather than an "MVC" framework. "MVC", however, is close enough as a general classification moniker for purposes of comparison with other web frameworks.

INSTALLING REPOZE.BFG

2.1 Before You Install

You will need Python (http://python.org) version 2.4 or better to run `repoze.bfg`.

Python Versions

As of this writing, `repoze.bfg` has been tested under Python 2.4.6, Python 2.5.4 and Python 2.6.2, and Python 2.7a1. To ensure backwards compatibility, development of `repoze.bfg` is currently done primarily under Python 2.4 and Python 2.5. `repoze.bfg` does not run under any version of Python before 2.4, and does not yet run under Python 3.X.

`repoze.bfg` is known to run on all popular Unix-like systems such as Linux, MacOS X, and FreeBSD as well as on Windows platforms. It is also known to run on Google's App Engine and *Jython*.

`repoze.bfg` installation does not require the compilation of any C code, so you need only a Python interpreter that meets the requirements mentioned.

2.1.1 If You Don't Yet Have A Python Interpreter (UNIX)

If your system doesn't have a Python interpreter, and you're on UNIX, you can either install Python using your operating system's package manager *or* you can install Python from source fairly easily on any UNIX system that has development tools.

Package Manager Method

You can use your system's "package manager" to install Python. Every system's package manager is slightly different, but the "flavor" of them is usually the same.

For example, on an Ubuntu Linux system, to use the system package manager to install a Python 2.6 interpreter, use the following command:

```
$ sudo apt-get install python2.6-dev
```

Once these steps are performed, the Python interpreter will usually be invokable via python2.6 from a shell prompt.

Source Compile Method

It's useful to use a Python interpreter that *isn't* the "system" Python interpreter to develop your software. The authors of repoze.bfg tend not to use the system Python for development purposes; always a self-compiled one. Compiling Python is usually easy, and often the "system" Python is compiled with options that aren't optimal for web development.

To compile software on your UNIX system, typically you need development tools. Often these can be installed via the package manager. For example, this works to do so on an Ubuntu Linux system:

```
$ sudo apt-get install build-essential
```

On Mac OS X, installing XCode (http://developer.apple.com/tools/xcode/) has much the same effect.

Once you've got development tools installed on your system, On the same system, to install a Python 2.6 interpreter from *source*, use the following commands:

```
[chrism@vitaminf ~]$ cd ~
[chrism@vitaminf ~]$ mkdir tmp
[chrism@vitaminf ~]$ mkdir opt
[chrism@vitaminf ~]$ cd tmp
[chrism@vitaminf tmp]$ cd tmp
[chrism@vitaminf tmp]$ wget \
      http://www.python.org/ftp/python/2.6.4/Python-2.6.4.tgz
```

```
[chrism@vitaminf tmp]$ tar xvzf Python-2.6.4.tgz
[chrism@vitaminf tmp]$ cd Python-2.6.4
[chrism@vitaminf Python-2.6.4]$ ./configure \
        --prefix=$HOME/opt/Python-2.6.4
[chrism@vitaminf Python-2.6.4]$ make; make install
```

Once these steps are performed, the Python interpreter will be invokable via
$HOME/opt/Python-2.6.4/bin/python from a shell prompt.

2.1.2 If You Don't Yet Have A Python Interpreter (Windows)

If your Windows system doesn't have a Python interpreter, you'll need to install it by
downloading a Python 2.6-series interpreter executable from python.org's download section
(http://python.org/download/) (the files labeled "Windows Installer"). Once you've downloaded it, dou-
ble click on the executable and accept the defaults during the installation process. You may also need to
download and install the Python for Windows extensions (http://sourceforge.net/projects/pywin32/files/).

After you install Python on Windows, you may need to add the C:\Python26 directory to
your environment's Path in order to make it possible to invoke Python from a command prompt
by typing python. To do so, right click My Computer, select Properties -> Advanced
Tab -> Environment Variables and add that directory to the end of the Path environment
variable.

2.2 Installing repoze.bfg on a UNIX System

It is best practice to install repoze.bfg into a "virtual" Python environment in order to obtain isolation
from any "system" packages you've got installed in your Python version. This can be done by using the
virtualenv package. Using a virtualenv will also prevent repoze.bfg from globally installing versions
of packages that are not compatible with your system Python.

To set up a virtualenv in which to install repoze.bfg, first ensure that *setuptools* is installed. Invoke
import setuptools within the Python interpreter you'd like to run repoze.bfg under:

9

```
[chrism@vitaminf bfg]$ python
Python 2.4.5 (#1, Aug 29 2008, 12:27:37)
[GCC 4.0.1 (Apple Inc. build 5465)] on darwin
Type "help", "copyright", "credits" or "license" for more information.
>>> import setuptools
```

If running `import setuptools` does not raise an `ImportError`, it means that setuptools is already installed into your Python interpreter. If `import setuptools` fails, you will need to install setuptools manually. Note that above we're using a Python 2.4-series interpreter on Mac OS X; your output may differ if you're using a later Python version or a different platform.

If you are using a "system" Python (one installed by your OS distributor or a 3rd-party packager such as Fink or MacPorts), you can usually install the setuptools package by using your system's package manager. If you cannot do this, or if you're using a self-installed version of Python, you will need to install setuptools "by hand". Installing setuptools "by hand" is always a reasonable thing to do, even if your package manager already has a pre-chewed version of setuptools for installation.

To install setuptools by hand, first download ez_setup.py (http://peak.telecommunity.com/dist/ez_setup.py) then invoke it using the Python interpreter into which you want to install setuptools.

```
$ python ez_setup.py
```

Once this command is invoked, setuptools should be installed on your system. If the command fails due to permission errors, you may need to be the administrative user on your system to successfully invoke the script. To remediate this, you may need to do:

```
$ sudo python ez_setup.py
```

2.2.1 Installing the `virtualenv` Package

Once you've got setuptools installed, you should install the *virtualenv* package. To install the *virtualenv* package into your setuptools-enabled Python interpreter, use the `easy_install` command.

```
$ easy_install virtualenv
```

This command should succeed, and tell you that the virtualenv package is now installed. If it fails due to permission errors, you may need to install it as your system's administrative user. For example:

```
$ sudo easy_install virtualenv
```

2.2.2 Creating the Virtual Python Environment

Once the *virtualenv* package is installed in your Python, you can then create a virtual environment. To do so, invoke the following:

```
$ virtualenv --no-site-packages bfgenv
New python executable in bfgenv/bin/python
Installing setuptools............done.
```

> ⚠ Using `--no-site-packages` when generating your virtualenv is *very important*. This flag provides the necessary isolation for running the set of packages required by `repoze.bfg`. If you do not specify `--no-site-packages`, it's possible that `repoze.bfg` will not install properly into the virtualenv, or, even if it does, may not run properly, depending on the packages you've already got installed into your Python's "main" site-packages dir.

> ⚠ If you're on UNIX, *do not* use `sudo` to run the `virtualenv` script. It's perfectly acceptable (and desirable) to create a virtualenv as a normal user.

You should perform any following commands that mention a "bin" directory from within the `bfgenv` virtualenv dir.

2.2.3 Installing `repoze.bfg` Into the Virtual Python Environment

After you've got your `bfgenv` virtualenv installed, you may install `repoze.bfg` itself using the following commands from within the virtualenv (`bfgenv`) directory:

11

```
$ bin/easy_install -i http://dist.repoze.org/bfg/current/simple \
      repoze.bfg
```

This command will take longer than the previous ones to complete, as it downloads and installs a number of dependencies.

2.3 Installing `repoze.bfg` on a Windows System

1. Install, or find Python 2.6 (http://python.org/download/releases/2.6.4/) for your system.

2. Install the Python for Windows extensions (http://sourceforge.net/projects/pywin32/files/). Make sure to pick the right download for Python 2.6 and install it using the same Python installation from the previous step.

3. Install latest *setuptools* distribution into the Python you obtained/installed/found in the step above: download ez_setup.py (http://peak.telecommunity.com/dist/ez_setup.py) and run it using the `python` interpreter of your Python 2.6 installation using a command prompt:

```
c:\> c:\Python26\python ez_setup.py
```

4. Use that Python's *bin/easy_install* to install *virtualenv*:

```
c:\> c:\Python26\Scripts\easy_install virtualenv
```

5. Use that Python's virtualenv to make a workspace:

```
c:\> c:\Python26\Scripts\virtualenv --no-site-packages bfgenv
```

6. Switch to the `bfgenv` directory:

```
c:\> cd bfgenv
```

7. (Optional) Consider using `bin\activate.bat` to make your shell environment wired to use the virtualenv.

8. Use `easy_install` pointed at the "current" index to get `repoze.bfg` and its direct dependencies installed:

```
c:\bfgenv> Scripts\easy_install -i \
      http://dist.repoze.org/bfg/current/simple repoze.bfg
```

2.4 Installing `repoze.bfg` on Google App Engine

Running repoze.bfg on Google's App Engine (pp. 331) documents the steps required to install a `repoze.bfg` application on Google App Engine.

2.5 Installing `repoze.bfg` on Jython

`repoze.bfg` is known to work under *Jython* version 2.5.1. Install *Jython*, and then follow the installation steps for `repoze.bfg` on your platform described in one of the sections entitled *Installing repoze.bfg on a UNIX System* (pp. 9) or *Installing repoze.bfg on a Windows System* (pp. 12) above, replacing the `python` command with `jython` as necessary. The steps are exactly the same except you should use the `jython` command name instead of the `python` command name.

One caveat exists to using `repoze.bfg` under Jython: the *Chameleon* templating engine, which is the default templating engine for `repoze.bfg` does not work on Jython.

The `jinja2` distribution provides templating for `repoze.bfg` using the *Jinja2* templating system. You may install it like so using the `easy_install` command for Jython:

```
$ easy_install repoze.bfg.jinja2
```

Once this is done, you can use this command to get started with a `repoze.bfg` sample application that uses the Jinja2 templating engine:

```
$ paster create -t bfg_jinja2_starter
```

See the chapter entitled *Creating a repoze.bfg Project* (pp. 37) for more information about the `paster create` command.

2.6 What Gets Installed

When you `easy_install repoze.bfg`, various Zope libraries, various Chameleon libraries, WebOb, Paste, PasteScript, and PasteDeploy libraries are installed.

Additionally, as shown in a following chapter, PasteScript (aka *paster*) templates will be registered that make it easy to start a new `repoze.bfg` project.

APPLICATION CONFIGURATION

Each deployment of an application written using `repoze.bfg` implies a specific *configuration* of the framework itself. For example, an application which serves up MP3s for user consumption might plug code into the framework that manages songs, while an application that manages corporate data might plug in code that manages accounting information. `repoze.bfg` refers to the way in which code is plugged in to it for a specific application as "configuration".

Most people understand "configuration" as coarse settings that inform the high-level operation of a specific application deployment. For instance, it's easy to think of the values implied by a `.ini` file parsed at application startup time as "configuration". `repoze.bfg` extends this pattern to application development, using the term "configuration" to express standardized ways that code gets plugged into a deployment of the framework itself. When you plug code into the `repoze.bfg` framework, you are "configuring" `repoze.bfg` for the purpose of creating a particular application deployment.

There are two different mechanisms you may use to configure `repoze.bfg` to create an application: *imperative* configuration and *declarative* configuration. We'll examine both modes in the sections which follow.

3.1 Imperative Configuration

Experienced Python programmers might find that performing configuration "imperatively" fits their brain best. This is the configuration mode in which a developer cedes the least amount of control to the framework; it's "imperative" because you express the configuration directly in Python code, and you have the full power of Python at your disposal as you issue configuration statements.

Here's one of the simplest `repoze.bfg` applications, configured imperatively:

```
1  from webob import Response
2  from paste.httpserver import serve
3  from repoze.bfg.configuration import Configurator
4
5  def hello_world(request):
6      return Response('Hello world!')
7
8  if __name__ == '__main__':
9      config = Configurator()
10     config.begin()
11     config.add_view(hello_world)
12     config.end()
13     app = config.make_wsgi_app()
14     serve(app, host='0.0.0.0')
```

We won't talk much about what this application does yet. Just note that the "configuration' statements take place underneath the if __name__ == '__main__': stanza in the form of method calls on a *Configurator* object (e.g. config.begin(), config.add_view(...), and config.end(). These statements take place one after the other, and are executed in order, so the full power of Python, including conditionals, can be employed in this mode of configuration.

3.2 Declarative Configuration

A repoze.bfg application can be alternately be configured "declaratively", if so desired. Declarative configuration relies on *declarations* made external to the code in a configuration file format named *ZCML* (Zope Configuration Markup Language), an XML dialect.

A repoze.bfg application configured declaratively requires not one, but two files: a Python file and a *ZCML* file.

In a file named helloworld.py:

```
1  from webob import Response
2  from paste.httpserver import serve
3  from repoze.bfg.configuration import Configurator
4
5  def hello_world(request):
6      return Response('Hello world!')
```

```
7
8   if __name__ == '__main__':
9       config = Configurator()
10      config.begin()
11      config.load_zcml('configure.zcml')
12      config.end()
13      app = config.make_wsgi_app()
14      serve(app, host='0.0.0.0')
```

In a file named `configure.zcml` in the same directory as the previously created `helloworld.py`:

```
1   <configure xmlns="http://namespaces.repoze.org/bfg">
2
3     <include package="repoze.bfg.includes" />
4
5     <view
6       view="helloworld.hello_world"
7       />
8
9   </configure>
```

This pair of files forms an application functionally equivalent to the application we created earlier in *Imperative Configuration* (pp. 15). Let's examine the differences between that code listing and the code above.

In *Imperative Configuration* (pp. 15), we had the following lines within the `if __name__ == '__main__'` section of `helloworld.py`:

```
1   if __name__ == '__main__':
2       config = Configurator()
3       config.begin()
4       config.add_view(hello_world)
5       config.end()
6       app = config.make_wsgi_app()
7       serve(app, host='0.0.0.0')
```

In our "declarative" code, we've removed the call to `add_view` and replaced it with a call to the `configuration.Configurator.load_zcml()` (pp. 378) method so that it now reads as:

```
1  if __name__ == '__main__':
2      config = Configurator()
3      config.begin()
4      config.load_zcml('configure.zcml')
5      config.end()
6      app = config.make_wsgi_app()
7      serve(app, host='0.0.0.0')
```

Everything else is much the same.

The `config.load_zcml('configure.zcml')` line tells the configurator to load configuration declarations from the file named `configure.zcml` which sits next to `helloworld.py` on the filesystem. Let's take a look at that `configure.zcml` file again:

```
1  <configure xmlns="http://namespaces.repoze.org/bfg">
2
3      <include package="repoze.bfg.includes" />
4
5      <view
6          view="helloworld.hello_world"
7          />
8
9  </configure>
```

Note that this file contains some XML, and that the XML contains a `<view>` *configuration declaration* tag that references a *dotted Python name*. This dotted name refers to the `hello_world` function that lives in our `helloworld` Python module.

This `<view>` declaration tag performs the same function as the `add_view` method that was employed within *Imperative Configuration* (pp. 15). In fact, the `<view>` tag is effectively a "macro" which calls the `configuration.Configurator.add_view()` (pp. 374) method on your behalf.

The `<view>` tag is an example of a `repoze.bfg` declaration tag. Other such tags include `<route>`, `<scan>`, `<notfound>`, `<forbidden>`, and others. Each of these tags is effectively a "macro" which calls methods of a `configuration.Configurator` (pp. 367) object on your behalf.

Essentially, using a *ZCML* file and loading it from the filesystem allows us to put our configuration statements within this XML file rather as declarations, rather than representing them as method calls to a *Configurator* object. Otherwise, declarative and imperative configuration are functionally equivalent.

18

Using declarative configuration has a number of benefits, the primary benefit being that applications configured declaratively can be *overridden* and *extended* by third parties without requiring the third party to change application code. If you want to build a framework or an extensible application, using declarative configuration is a good idea.

Declarative configuration has an obvious downside: you can't use plain-old-Python syntax you probably already know and understand to configure your application; instead you need to use *ZCML*.

3.2.1 ZCML Conflict Detection

A minor additional feature of ZCML is *conflict detection*. If you define two declaration tags within the same ZCML file which logically "collide", an exception will be raised, and the application will not start. For example, the following ZCML file has two conflicting <view> tags:

```
1  <configure xmlns="http://namespaces.repoze.org/bfg">
2
3    <include package="repoze.bfg.includes" />
4
5    <view
6      view="helloworld.hello_world"
7      />
8
9    <view
10     view="helloworld.hello_world"
11     />
12
13 </configure>
```

If you try to use this ZCML file as the source of ZCML for an application, an error will be raised when you attempt to start the application. This error will contain information about which tags might have conflicted.

3.2.2 Configuration Decorations and Code Scanning

An alternate mode of declarative configuration lends more *locality of reference* to a *configuration declaration*. It's sometimes painful to have all configuration done in ZCML, or even in imperative code, because you may need to have two files open at once to see the "big picture": the file that represents the configuration, and the file that contains the implementation objects referenced by the configuration. To avoid this, repoze.bfg allows you to insert *configuration decoration* statements very close to code that is referred to by the declaration itself. For example:

```
1  from repoze.bfg.view import bfg_view
2  from webob import Response
3
4  @bfg_view(name='hello', request_method='GET')
5  def hello(request):
6      return Response('Hello')
```

The mere existence of configuration decoration doesn't cause any configuration registration to be made. Before they have any effect on the configuration of a `repoze.bfg` application, a configuration decoration within application code must be found through a process known as a *scan*.

The `view.bfg_view` (pp. 428) decorator above adds an attribute to the `hello` function, making it available for a *scan* to find it later.

`repoze.bfg` is willing to *scan* a module or a package and its subpackages for decorations when the `configuration.Configurator.scan()` (pp. 378) method is invoked: scanning implies searching for configuration declarations in a package and its subpackages. For example:

Imperatively Starting A Scan

```
1  from paste.httpserver import serve
2  from repoze.bfg.view import bfg_view
3  from webob import Response
4
5  @bfg_view()
6  def hello(request):
7      return Response('Hello')
8
9  if __name__ == '__main__':
10     from repoze.bfg.configuration import Configurator
11     config = Configurator()
12     config.begin()
13     config.scan()
14     config.end()
15     app = config.make_wsgi_app()
16     serve(app, host='0.0.0.0')
```

ZCML can also invoke a *scan* via its `<scan>` directive. If a ZCML file is processed that contains a scan directive, the package the ZCML file points to is scanned.

Declaratively Starting a Scan

```python
 1  # helloworld.py
 2
 3  from paste.httpserver import serve
 4  from repoze.bfg.view import bfg_view
 5  from webob import Response
 6
 7  @bfg_view()
 8  def hello(request):
 9      return Response('Hello')
10
11  if __name__ == '__main__':
12      from repoze.bfg.configuration import Configurator
13      config = Configurator()
14      config.begin()
15      config.load_zcml('configure.zcml')
16      config.end()
17      app = config.make_wsgi_app()
18      serve(app, host='0.0.0.0')
```

```xml
 1  <configure xmlns="http://namespaces.repoze.org">
 2
 3    <!-- configure.zcml -->
 4
 5    <include package="repoze.bfg.includes"/>
 6    <scan package="."/>
 7
 8  </configure>
```

The scanning machinery imports each module and subpackage in a package or module recursively, looking for special attributes attached to objects defined within a module. These special attributes are typically attached to code via the use of a *decorator*. For example, the view.bfg_view (pp. 428) decorator can be attached to a function or instance method.

Once scanning is invoked, and *configuration decoration* is found by the scanner, a set of calls are made to a *Configurator* on behalf of the developer: these calls represent the intent of the configuration decoration.

In the example above, this is best represented as the scanner translating the arguments to view.bfg_view (pp. 428) into a call to the configuration.Configurator.add_view() (pp. 374) method, effectively:

21

```
config.add_view(hello)
```

3.3 Which Mode Should I Use?

A combination of imperative configuration, declarative configuration via ZCML and scanning can be used to configure any application. They are not mutually exclusive.

The `repoze.bfg` authors often recommend using mostly declarative configuration, because it's the more traditional form of configuration used in `repoze.bfg` applications, it can be overridden and extended by third party deployers, and there are more examples for it "in the wild".

However, imperative mode configuration can be simpler to understand, and the framework is not "opinionated" about the choice. This book presents examples in both styles, mostly interchangeably. You can choose the mode that best fits your brain as necessary.

CREATING YOUR FIRST
REPOZE.BFG APPLICATION

We will walk through the creation of a tiny `repoze.bfg` application in this chapter. After we're finished creating it, we'll explain in more detail how the application works.

> If you're a "theory-first" kind of person, you might choose to read *Context Finding and View Lookup* (pp. 57) and *Views* (pp. 105) to augment your understanding before diving into the code that follows, but it's not necessary if – like many programmers – you're willing to "go with the flow".

4.1 Hello World, Goodbye World (Imperative)

Here's one of the very simplest `repoze.bfg` applications, configured imperatively:

```
1  from webob import Response
2  from paste.httpserver import serve
3  from repoze.bfg.configuration import Configurator
4
5  def hello_world(request):
6      return Response('Hello world!')
7
8  def goodbye_world(request):
```

```
 9        return Response('Goodbye world!')
10
11   if __name__ == '__main__':
12        config = Configurator()
13        config.begin()
14        config.add_view(hello_world)
15        config.add_view(goodbye_world, name='goodbye')
16        config.end()
17        app = config.make_wsgi_app()
18        serve(app, host='0.0.0.0')
```

When this code is inserted into a Python script named helloworld.py and executed by a Python interpreter which has the repoze.bfg software installed, an HTTP server is started on TCP port 8080. When port 8080 is visited by a browser on the root URL (/), the server will simply serve up the text "Hello world!" When visited by a browser on the URL /goodbye, the server will serve up the text "Goodbye world!"

Now that we have a rudimentary understanding of what the application does, let's examine it piece-by-piece.

4.1.1 Imports

The above script defines the following set of imports:

```
1   from webob import Response
2   from paste.httpserver import serve
3   from repoze.bfg.configuration import Configurator
```

repoze.bfg uses the *WebOb* library as the basis for its *request* and *response* objects. The script uses the webob.Response class later in the script to create a *response* object.

Like many other Python web frameworks, repoze.bfg uses the *WSGI* protocol to connect an application and a web server together. The paste.httpserver server is used in this example as a WSGI server for convenience, as the paste package is a dependency of repoze.bfg itself.

The script also imports the Configurator class from the configuration module. This class is used to configure repoze.bfg for a particular application. An instance of this class provides methods which help configure various parts of repoze.bfg for a given application deployment.

4.1.2 View Callable Declarations

The above script, beneath its set of imports, defines two functions: one named `hello_world` and one named `goodbye_world`.

```
1  def hello_world(request):
2      return Response('Hello world!')
3
4  def goodbye_world(request):
5      return Response('Goodbye world!')
```

These functions don't do anything very taxing. Both functions accept a single argument (`request`). The `hello_world` function does nothing but return a response instance with the body `Hello world!`. The `goodbye_world` function returns a response instance with the body `Goodbye world!`.

Each of these functions is known as a *view callable*. View callables in a `repoze.bfg` application accept a single argument, `request` and are expected to return a *response* object. A view callable doesn't need to be a function; it can be represented via another type of object, like a class or an instance, but for our purposes here, a function serves us well.

A view callable is always called with a *request* object. A request object is a representation of an HTTP request sent to `repoze.bfg` via the active *WSGI* server.

A view callable is required to return a *response* object because a response object has all the information necessary to formulate an actual HTTP response; this object is then converted to text by the upstream *WSGI* server and sent back to the requesting browser. To return a response, each view callable creates an instance of the `webob.Response` class. In the `hello_world` function, the string `'Hello world!'` is passed to the `Response` constructor as the *body* of the response. In the `goodbye_world` function, the string `'Goodbye world!'` is passed.

4.1.3 Application Configuration

In the above script, the following code, representing the *configuration* of an application which uses the previously defined imports and function definitions is placed within the confines of an `if` statement:

```
1  if __name__ == '__main__':
2      config = Configurator()
3      config.begin()
4      config.add_view(hello_world)
5      config.add_view(goodbye_world, name='goodbye')
6      config.end()
7      app = config.make_wsgi_app()
8      serve(app, host='0.0.0.0')
```

Let's break this down this piece-by-piece.

4.1.4 Configurator Construction

```
1  if __name__ == '__main__':
2      config = Configurator()
```

The if __name__ == '__main__': line in the code sample above represents a Python idiom: the code inside this if clause is not invoked unless the script containing this code is run directly from the command line. For example, if the file named helloworld.py contains the entire script body, the code within the if statement will only be invoked when python helloworld.py is executed from the operating system command line.

helloworld.py in this case is a Python *module*. Using the if clause is necessary – or at least best practice – because code in any Python module may be imported by another Python module. By using this idiom, the script is indicating that it does not want the code within the if statement to execute if this module is imported; the code within the if block should only be run during a direct script execution.

The   config = Configurator()   line   above   creates   an   instance   of   the configuration.Configurator (pp. 367) class. The resulting config object represents an API which the script uses to configure this particular repoze.bfg application. Methods called on the Configurator will cause registrations to be made in a *application registry* associated with the application.

4.1.5 Beginning Configuration

```
config.begin()
```

26

The `configuration.Configurator.begin()` (pp. 368) method tells the system that application configuration has begun. In particular, this causes the *application registry* associated with this configurator to become the "current" application registry, meaning that code which attempts to use the application registry *thread local* will obtain the registry associated with the configurator. This is an explicit step because it's sometimes convenient to use a configurator without causing the registry associated with the configurator to become "current".

See *Thread Locals* (pp. 227) for a discussion about what it means for an application registry to be "current".

4.1.6 Adding Configuration

```
1  config.add_view(hello_world)
2  config.add_view(goodbye_world, name='goodbye')
```

Each of these lines calls the `configuration.Configurator.add_view()` (pp. 374) method. The `add_view` method of a configurator registers a *view configuration* within the *application registry*. A *view configuration* represents a set of circumstances related to the *request* that will cause a specific *view callable* to be invoked. This "set of circumstances" is provided as one or more keyword arguments to the `add_view` method. Each of these keyword arguments is known as a view configuration *predicate*.

The line `config.add_view(hello_world)` registers the `hello_world` function as a view callable. The `add_view` method of a Configurator must be called with a view callable object as its first argument, so the first argument passed is the `hello_world` function. This line calls `add_view` with a *default* value for the *predicate* argument, named `name`. The `name` predicate defaults to a value equalling the empty string (``''``). This means that we're instructing `repoze.bfg` to invoke the `hello_world` view callable when the *view name* is the empty string. We'll learn in later chapters what a *view name* is, and under which circumstances a request will have a view name that is the empty string; in this particular application, it means that the `hello_world` view callable will be invoked when the root URL / is visited by a browser.

The line `config.add_view(goodbye_world, name='goodbye')` registers the `goodbye_world` function as a view callable. The line calls `add_view` with the view callable as the first required positional argument, and a *predicate* keyword argument `name` with the value `'goodbye'`. The `name` argument supplied in this *view configuration* implies that only a request that has a *view name* of `goodbye` should cause the `goodbye_world` view callable to be invoked. In this particular application, this means that the `goodbye_world` view callable will be invoked when the URL /goodbye is visited by a browser.

Each invocation of the add_view method implies a *view configuration* registration. Each *predicate* provided as a keyword argument to the add_view method narrows the set of circumstances which would cause the view configuration's callable to be invoked. In general, a greater number of predicates supplied along with a view configuration will more strictly limit the applicability of its associated view callable. When repoze.bfg processes a request, however, the view callable with the *most specific* view configuration (the view configuration that matches the most specific set of predicates) is always invoked.

In this application, repoze.bfg chooses the most specific view callable based only on view *predicate* applicability. The ordering of calls to configuration.Configurator.add_view() (pp. 374) is never very important. We can register goodbye_world first and hello_world second; repoze.bfg will still give us the most specific callable when a request is dispatched to it.

4.1.7 Ending Configuration

```
config.end()
```

The configuration.Configurator.end() (pp. 368) method tells the system that application configuration has ended. It is the inverse of configuration.Configurator.begin() (pp. 368). In particular, this causes the *application registry* associated with this configurator to no longer be the "current" application registry, meaning that code which attempts to use the application registry *thread local* will no longer obtain the registry associated with the configurator.

> See *Thread Locals* (pp. 227) for a discussion about what it means for an application registry to be "current".

4.1.8 WSGI Application Creation

```
app = config.make_wsgi_app()
```

After configuring views and ending configuration, the script creates a WSGI *application* via the configuration.Configurator.make_wsgi_app() (pp. 378) method. A call to make_wsgi_app implies that all configuration is finished (meaning all method calls to the configurator which set up views, and various other configuration settings have been performed). The make_wsgi_app method returns a *WSGI* application object that can be used by any WSGI server to present an application to a requestor. *WSGI* is a protocol that allows servers to talk to Python applications. We don't discuss *WSGI* in any depth within this book, however, you can learn more about it by visiting wsgi.org (http://wsgi.org).

The `repoze.bfg` application object, in particular, is an instance of a class representing a `repoze.bfg` *router*. It has a reference to the *application registry* which resulted from method calls to the configurator used to configure it. The *router* consults the registry to obey the policy choices made by a single application. These policy choices were informed by method calls to the *Configurator* made earlier; in our case, the only policy choices made were implied by two calls to its `add_view` method.

4.1.9 WSGI Application Serving

```
serve(app, host='0.0.0.0')
```

Finally, we actually serve the application to requestors by starting up a WSGI server. We happen to use the `paste.httpserver.serve()` WSGI server runner, passing it the `app` object (a *router*) as the application we wish to serve. We also pass in an argument `host=='0.0.0.0'`, meaning "listen on all TCP interfaces." By default, the Paste HTTP server listens only on the `127.0.0.1` interface, which is problematic if you're running the server on a remote system and you wish to access it with a web browser from a local system. We don't specify a TCP port number to listen on; this means we want to use the default TCP port, which is 8080.

When this line is invoked, it causes the server to start listening on TCP port 8080. It will serve requests forever, or at least until we stop it by killing the process which runs it.

4.1.10 Conclusion

Our hello world application is one of the simplest possible `repoze.bfg` applications, configured "imperatively". We can see that it's configured imperatively because the full power of Python is available to us as we perform configuration tasks.

4.2 Hello World, Goodbye World (Declarative)

Another almost entirely equivalent mode of application configuration exists named *declarative* configuration. `repoze.bfg` can be configured for the same "hello world" application "declaratively", if so desired.

To do so, first, create a file named `helloworld.py`:

```
1  from webob import Response
2  from paste.httpserver import serve
3  from repoze.bfg.configuration import Configurator
4
5  def hello_world(request):
6      return Response('Hello world!')
7
8  def goodbye_world(request):
9      return Response('Goodbye world!')
10
11 if __name__ == '__main__':
12     config = Configurator()
13     config.begin()
14     config.load_zcml('configure.zcml')
15     config.end()
16     app = config.make_wsgi_app()
17     serve(app, host='0.0.0.0')
```

Then create a file named configure.zcml in the same directory as the previously created helloworld.py:

```
1  <configure xmlns="http://namespaces.repoze.org/bfg">
2
3    <include package="repoze.bfg.includes" />
4
5    <view
6       view="helloworld.hello_world"
7       />
8
9    <view
10      name="goodbye"
11      view="helloworld.goodbye_world"
12      />
13
14 </configure>
```

This pair of files forms an application functionally equivalent to the application we created earlier in *Hello World, Goodbye World (Imperative)* (pp. 23). Let's examine the differences between the code in that section and the code above.

In *Application Configuration* (pp. 25), we had the following lines within the if __name__ == '__main__' section of helloworld.py:

```
1  if __name__ == '__main__':
2      config = Configurator()
3      config.begin()
4      config.add_view(hello_world)
5      config.add_view(goodbye_world, name='goodbye')
6      config.end()
7      app = config.make_wsgi_app()
8      serve(app, host='0.0.0.0')
```

In our "declarative" code, we've added a call to the `configuration.Configurator.load_zcml()` (pp. 378) method with the value `configure.zcml`, and we've removed the lines which read `config.add_view(hello_world)` and `config.add_view(goodbye_world, name='goodbye')`, so that it now reads as:

```
1  if __name__ == '__main__':
2      config = Configurator()
3      config.begin()
4      config.load_zcml('configure.zcml')
5      config.end()
6      app = config.make_wsgi_app()
7      serve(app, host='0.0.0.0')
```

Everything else is much the same.

The `config.load_zcml('configure.zcml')` line tells the configurator to load configuration declarations from the `configure.zcml` file which sits next to `helloworld.py`. Let's take a look at the `configure.zcml` file now:

```
1  <configure xmlns="http://namespaces.repoze.org/bfg">
2
3      <include package="repoze.bfg.includes" />
4
5      <view
6        view="helloworld.hello_world"
7        />
8
9      <view
10       name="goodbye"
11       view="helloworld.goodbye_world"
```

```
12        />
13
14  </configure>
```

We already understand what the view code does, because the application is functionally equivalent to the application described in *Hello World, Goodbye World (Imperative)* (pp. 23), but use of *ZCML* is new. Let's break that down tag-by-tag.

4.2.1 The <configure> Tag

The `configure.zcml` ZCML file contains this bit of XML:

```
1   <configure xmlns="http://namespaces.repoze.org/bfg">
2
3      <!-- other directives -->
4
5   </configure>
```

Because *ZCML* is XML, and because XML requires a single root tag for each document, every ZCML file used by `repoze.bfg` must contain a `configure` container directive, which acts as the root XML tag. It is a "container" directive because its only job is to contain other directives.

See also *configure* (pp. 447) and *A Word On XML Namespaces* (pp. 448).

4.2.2 The <include> Tag

The `configure.zcml` ZCML file contains this bit of XML within the `<configure>` root tag:

```
<include package="repoze.bfg.includes" />
```

This self-closing tag instructs `repoze.bfg` to load a ZCML file from the Python package with the *dotted Python name* includes, as specified by its `package` attribute. This particular `<include>` declaration is required because it actually allows subsequent declaration tags (such as `<view>`, which we'll see shortly) to be recognized. The `<include>` tag effectively just includes another ZCML file, causing its declarations to be executed. In this case, we want to load the declarations from the file named `configure.zcml` within the includes Python package. We know we want to load the `configure.zcml` from this package because `configure.zcml` is the default value for another attribute of the `<include>` tag named `file`. We could have spelled the include tag more verbosely, but equivalently as:

```
1  <include package="repoze.bfg.includes"
2          file="configure.zcml"/>
```

The `<include>` tag that includes the ZCML statements implied by the `configure.zcml` file from the Python package named `includes` is basically required to come before any other named declaration in an application's `configure.zcml`. If it is not included, subsequent declaration tags will fail to be recognized, and the configuration system will generate an error at startup. However, the `<include package="includes"/>` tag needs to exist only in a "top-level" ZCML file, it needn't also exist in ZCML files *included by* a top-level ZCML file.

See also *include* (pp. 453).

4.2.3 The `<view>` Tag

The `configure.zcml` ZCML file contains these bits of XML *after* the `<include>` tag, but *within* the `<configure>` root tag:

```
1  <view
2    view="helloworld.hello_world"
3    />
4
5  <view
6    name="goodbye"
7    view="helloworld.goodbye_world"
8    />
```

These `<view>` declaration tags direct `repoze.bfg` to create two *view configuration* registrations. The first `<view>` tag has an attribute (the attribute is also named `view`), which points at a *dotted Python name*, referencing the `hello_world` function defined within the `helloworld` package. The second `<view>` tag has a `view` attribute which points at a *dotted Python name*, referencing the `goodbye_world` function defined within the `helloworld` package. The second `<view>` tag also has an attribute called `name` with a value of `goodbye`.

These effect of the `<view>` tag declarations we've put into our `configure.zcml` is functionally equivalent to the effect of lines we've already seen in an imperatively-configured application. We're just spelling things differently, using XML instead of Python.

In our previously defined application, in which we added view configurations imperatively, we saw this code:

33

```
1   config.add_view(hello_world)
2   config.add_view(goodbye_world, name='goodbye')
```

Each `<view>` declaration tag encountered in a ZCML file effectively invokes the `configuration.Configurator.add_view()` (pp. 374) method on the behalf of the developer. Various attributes can be specified on the `<view>` tag which influence the *view configuration* it creates.

Since the relative ordering of calls to `configuration.Configurator.add_view()` (pp. 374) doesn't matter (see the sidebar entitled *View Dispatch and Ordering* within *Adding Configuration* (pp. 27)), the relative order of `<view>` tags in ZCML doesn't matter either. The following ZCML orderings are completely equivalent:

Hello Before Goodbye

```
1   <view
2     view="helloworld.hello_world"
3     />
4
5   <view
6     name="goodbye"
7     view="helloworld.goodbye_world"
8     />
```

Goodbye Before Hello

```
1   <view
2     name="goodbye"
3     view="helloworld.goodbye_world"
4     />
5
6   <view
7     view="helloworld.hello_world"
8     />
```

We've now configured a `repoze.bfg` helloworld application declaratively. More information about this mode of configuration is available in *Declarative Configuration* (pp. 16) and within *ZCML Directive Reference*.

4.3 References

For more information about the API of a *Configurator* object, see `configuration.Configurator` (pp. 367) . The equivalent ZCML declaration tags are introduced in *ZCML Directive Reference*.

For more information about *view configuration*, see *Views* (pp. 105).

CREATING A REPOZE.BFG PROJECT

It's possible to create a repoze.bfg application completely manually, but it's usually more convenient to use a template to generate a basic repoze.bfg application structure.

repoze.bfg comes with templates that you can use to generate a project. Each template makes different configuration assumptions about what type of application you're trying to construct.

These templates are rendered using the *PasteDeploy* paster script, and so therefore they are often referred to as "paster templates".

5.1 Paster Templates Included with repoze.bfg

The convenience paster templates included with repoze.bfg differ from each other on two axes:

- the persistence mechanism they offer (no persistence mechanism, *ZODB*, or *SQLAlchemy*).

- the mechanism they use to map URLs to code (*traversal* or *URL dispatch*).

The included templates are these:

bfg_starter URL mapping via *traversal* and no persistence mechanism.

bfg_zodb URL mapping via *traversal* and persistence via *ZODB*

bfg_routesalchemy URL mapping via *URL dispatch* and persistence via *SQLAlchemy*

bfg_alchemy URL mapping via *traversal* and persistence via *SQLAlchemy*

Each of these project templates uses *ZCML* instead of *imperative configuration*. Each also makes the assumption that you want your code to live in a Python *package*. Even if your application is extremely simple, it is useful to place code that drives the application within a package, because a package is more easily extended with new code. An application that lives inside a package can also be distributed more easily than one which does not live within a package.

37

5.2 Creating the Project

In in *Installing repoze.bfg* (pp. 7), you created a virtual Python environment via the `virtualenv` command. To start a `repoze.bfg` *project*, use the `paster` facility installed within the virtualenv. In *Installing repoze.bfg* (pp. 7) we called the virtualenv directory `bfgenv`; the following command assumes that our current working directory is that directory.

We'll choose the `bfg_starter` template for this purpose.

```
$ bin/paster create -t bfg_starter
```

The above command uses the `paster` command to create a project using the `bfg_starter` template. The `create` version of paster invokes the creation of a project from a template. To use a different template, such as `bfg_routesalchemy`, you'd just change the last argument. For example:

```
$ bin/paster create -t bfg_routesalchemy
```

`paster create` will ask you a single question: the *name* of the project. You should use a string without spaces and with only letters in it. Here's sample output from a run of `paster create` for a project we name `MyProject`:

```
$ bin/paster create -t bfg_starter
Selected and implied templates:
  repoze.bfg#bfg  repoze.bfg starter project

Enter project name: MyProject
Variables:
  egg:      MyProject
  package:  myproject
  project:  MyProject
Creating template bfg
Creating directory ./MyProject
# ... more output ...
Running /Users/chrism/projects/repoze/bfg/bin/python setup.py egg_info
```

> ⓘ You can skip the interrogative question about a project name during `paster create` by adding the project name to the command line, e.g. `paster create -t bfg_starter MyProject`.

As a result of invoking the `paster create` command, a project is created in a directory named `MyProject`. That directory is a *setuptools project* directory from which a setuptools *distribution* can be created. The `setup.py` file in that directory can be used to distribute your application, or install your application for deployment or development.

A sample *PasteDeploy* `.ini` file named `MyProject.ini` will also be created in the project directory. You will use this `.ini` file to configure a server, to run your application, and to and debug your application.

The `MyProject` project directory contains an additional subdirectory named `myproject` (note the case difference) representing a Python *package* which holds very simple `repoze.bfg` sample code. This is where you'll edit your application's Python code and templates.

5.3 Installing your Newly Created Project for Development

Using the interpreter from the *virtualenv* you create during *Installing repoze.bfg* (pp. 7), invoke the following command when inside the project directory. The file named `setup.py` will be in the root of the paster-generated project directory. The `python` you're invoking should be the one that lives in the `bin` directory of your virtual Python environment.

```
$ ../bin/python setup.py develop
```

Elided output from a run of this command is shown below:

```
$ ../bin/python setup.py develop
...
Finished processing dependencies for MyProject==0.1
```

This will install the *distribution* representing your application's into the interpreter's library set so it can be found and run by *PasteDeploy* via the command `paster serve`.

5.4 Running The Tests For Your Application

To run unit tests for your application, you should invoke them using the `python` that lives in the `bin` directory of your virtualenv:

```
$ ../bin/python setup.py test -q
```

Here's sample output from a test run:

```
$ python setup.py test -q
running test
running egg_info
writing requirements to MyProject.egg-info/requires.txt
writing MyProject.egg-info/PKG-INFO
writing top-level names to MyProject.egg-info/top_level.txt
writing dependency_links to MyProject.egg-info/dependency_links.txt
writing entry points to MyProject.egg-info/entry_points.txt
reading manifest file 'MyProject.egg-info/SOURCES.txt'
writing manifest file 'MyProject.egg-info/SOURCES.txt'
running build_ext
..
----------------------------------------------------------------------
Ran 1 test in 0.108s

OK
```

The tests themselves are found in the `tests.py` module in your `paster create` -generated project. Within a project generated by the `bfg_starter` template, a single sample test exists.

5.5 The Interactive Shell

Once you've installed your program for development using `setup.py develop`, you can use an interactive Python shell to examine your `repoze.bfg` application *model* and *view* objects from a Python prompt. To do so, use the `paster` shell command with the `bfgshell` argument:

The first argument to `bfgshell` is the path to your application's `.ini` file. The second is the section name inside the `.ini` file which points to your *application* as opposed to any other section within the `.ini` file. For example, if your application `.ini` file might have a `[app:main]` section that looks like so:

```
1  [app:main]
2  use = egg:MyProject#app
3  reload_templates = true
4  debug_authorization = false
5  debug_notfound = false
```

If so, you can use the following command to invoke a debug shell using the name `main` as a section name:

```
[chrism@vitaminf bfgshellenv]$ ../bin/paster --plugin=repoze.bfg bfgshell \
    MyProject.ini main
Python 2.4.5 (#1, Aug 29 2008, 12:27:37)
[GCC 4.0.1 (Apple Inc. build 5465)] on darwin
Type "help" for more information. "root" is the BFG app root object.
>>> root
<foo.models.MyModel object at 0x445270>
```

> ⓘ You *might* get away without passing `--plugin=repoze.bfg` to the bfgshell command.

If you have IPython (http://en.wikipedia.org/wiki/IPython) installed in the interpreter you use to invoke the `paster` command, the `bfgshell` command will use an IPython interactive shell instead of a standard Python interpreter shell. If you don't want this to happen, even if you have IPython installed, you can pass the `--disable-ipython` flag to the `bfgshell` command to use a standard Python interpreter shell unconditionally.

```
[chrism@vitaminf bfgshellenv]$ ../bin/paster --plugin=repoze.bfg bfgshell \
    --disable-ipython MyProject.ini main
```

You should always use a section name argument that refers to the actual `app` section within the Paste configuration file that points at your `repoze.bfg` application *without any middleware wrapping*. In particular, a section name is inappropriate as the second argument to "bfgshell" if the configuration section it names is a `pipeline` rather than an `app`. For example, if you have the following `.ini` file content:

```
[app:myapp]
use = egg:MyProject#app
reload_templates = true
debug_authorization = false
debug_notfound = false

[pipeline:main]
pipeline = egg:repoze.tm2#tm
          myapp
```

The command you use to invoke the interactive shell should be:

```
[chrism@vitaminf bfgshellenv]$ ../bin/paster --plugin=repoze.bfg bfgshell \
     MyProject.ini myapp
```

If you use `main` as the section name argument instead of `myapp` against the above `.ini` file, an error will likely occur. Use the most specific reference to the application within the `.ini` file possible as the section name argument.

Press `Ctrl-D` to exit the interactive shell (or `Ctrl-Z` on Windows).

5.6 Runnning The Project Application

Once a project is installed for development, you can run the application it represents using the `paster serve` command against the generated configuration file. In our case, this file is named `MyProject.ini`:

```
$ ../bin/paster serve MyProject.ini
```

Here's sample output from a run of `paster serve`:

```
$ ../bin/paster serve MyProject.ini
Starting server in PID 16601.
serving on 0.0.0.0:6543 view at http://127.0.0.1:6543
```

By default, `repoze.bfg` applications generated from a `paster` template will listen on TCP port 6543.

During development, it's often useful to run `paster serve` using its `--reload` option. When `--reload` is passed to `paster serve`, changes to any Python module your project uses will cause the server to restart. This typically makes development easier, as changes to Python code made within a `repoze.bfg` application is not put into effect until the server restarts.

For example:

```
$ ../bin/paster serve MyProject.ini --reload
Starting subprocess with file monitor
Starting server in PID 16601.
serving on 0.0.0.0:6543 view at http://127.0.0.1:6543
```

For more detailed information about the startup process, see *Startup* (pp. 223). For more information about environment variables and configuration file settings that influence startup and runtime behavior, see *Environment Variables and .ini File Settings* (pp. 189).

5.6.1 Using an Alternate WSGI Server

The code generated by `repoze.bfg paster` templates assumes that you will be using the `paster serve` command to start your application while you do development. However, `paster serve` is by no means the only way to start up and serve a `repoze.bfg` application. As we saw in *Application Configuration* (pp. 15), `paster serve` needn't be invoked at all to run a `repoze.bfg` application. The use of `paster serve` to run a `repoze.bfg` application is purely conventional based on the output of its `paster` templates.

Any *WSGI* server is capable of running a `repoze.bfg` application. Some WSGI servers don't require the *PasteDeploy* framework's `paster serve` command to do server process management at all. Each *WSGI* server has its own documentation about how it creates a process to run an application, and there are many of them, so we cannot provide the details for each here. But the concepts are largely the same, whatever server you happen to use.

One popular production alternative to a `paster`-invoked server is *mod_wsgi*. can also use *mod_wsgi* to serve your `repoze.bfg` application using the Apache web server rather than any "pure-Python" server that is started as a result of `paster serve`. See *Running a repoze.bfg Application under mod_wsgi* (pp. 337) for details. However, it is usually easier to *develop* an application using a `paster serve` -invoked webserver, as exception and debugging output will be sent to the console.

43

5.7 Viewing the Application

Once your application is running via `paster serve`, you may visit `http://localhost:6543/` in your browser. You will see something in your browser like what is displayed in the following image:

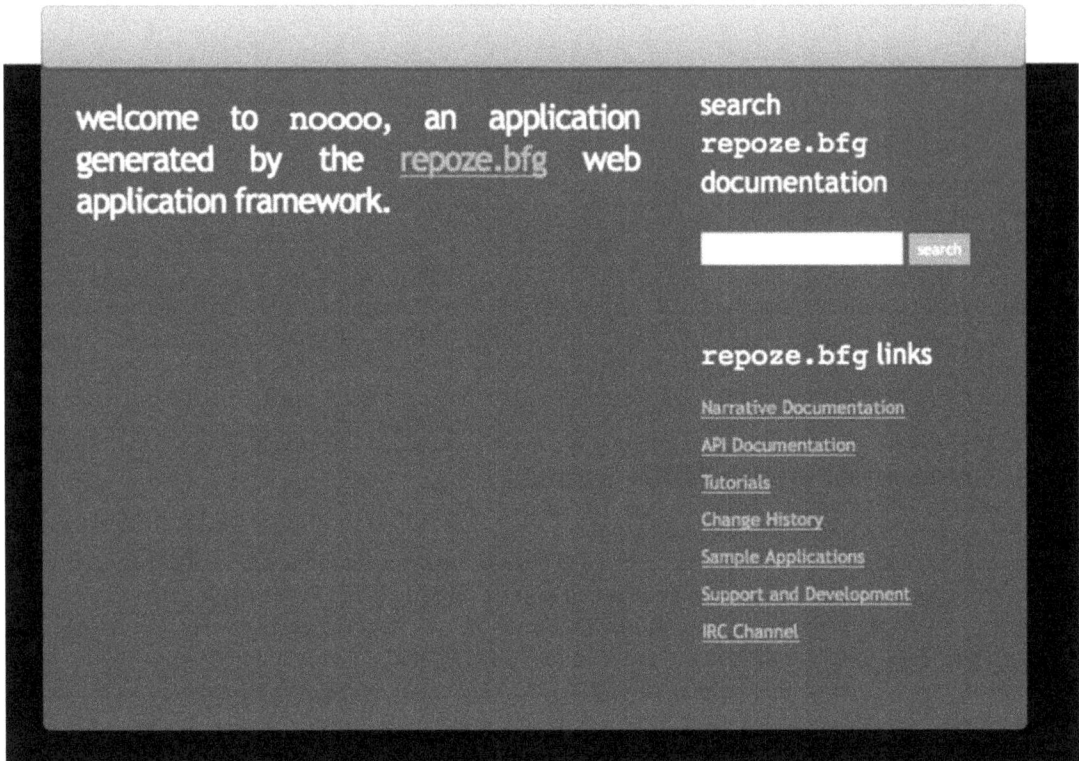

noooo, a repoze.bfg application

This is the page shown by default when you visit an unmodified `paster create` -generated `bfg_starter` application in a browser.

5.8 The Project Structure

Our generated `repoze.bfg bfg_starter` application is a setuptools *project* (named `MyProject`), which contains a Python *package* (which is *also* named `myproject`, but lowercased; the paster template generates a project which contains a package that shares its name except for case). All `repoze.bfg paster` -generated projects share a similar structure.

The `MyProject` project we've generated has the following directory structure:

```
MyProject/
|-- CHANGES.txt
|-- README.txt
|-- myproject
|    |-- __init__.py
|    |-- configure.zcml
|    |-- models.py
|    |-- run.py
|    |-- templates
|    |    |-- mytemplate.pt
|    |    `-- static/
|    |-- tests.py
|    `-- views.py
|-- MyProject.ini
`-- setup.py
```

5.9 The `MyProject` *Project*

The `MyProject` *project* is the distribution and deployment wrapper for your application. It contains both the `myproject` *package* representing your application as well as files used to describe, run, and test your application.

1. `CHANGES.txt` describes the changes you've made to the application. It is conventionally written in *ReStructuredText* format.

2. `README.txt` describes the application in general. It is conventionally written in *ReStructuredText* format.

3. `MyProject.ini` is a *PasteDeploy* configuration file that can be used to execute your application.

4. `setup.py` is the file you'll use to test and distribute your application. It is a standard *setuptools* `setup.py` file.

5.9.1 `MyProject.ini`

The `MyProject.ini` file is a *PasteDeploy* configuration file. Its purpose is to specify an application to run when you invoke `paster serve`, as well as the deployment settings provided to that application.

The generated `MyProject.ini` file looks like so:

```
[DEFAULT]
debug = true

[app:main]
use = egg:MyProject#app
reload_templates = true
debug_authorization = false
debug_notfound = false

[server:main]
use = egg:Paste#http
host = 0.0.0.0
port = 6543
```

This file contains several "sections" including [DEFAULT], [app:main], and [server:main].

The [DEFAULT] section consists of global parameters that are shared by all the applications, servers and *middleware* defined within the configuration file. By default it contains one key debug, which is set to true. This key is used by various components to decide whether to act in a "debugging" mode. repoze.bfg itself does not do anything at all with this parameter, and neither does any template-generated application.

The [app:main] section represents configuration for your application. This section name represents the main application (and it's an app -lication, thus app:main), signifying that this is the default application run by paster serve when it is invoked against this configuration file. The name main is a convention signifying that it the default application.

The use setting is required in the [app:main] section. The use setting points at a *setuptools entry point* named MyProject#app (the egg: prefix in egg:MyProject#app indicates that this is an entry point *URI* specifier, where the "scheme" is "egg").

`setuptools` Entry Points and PasteDeploy `.ini` Files

This part of configuration can be confusing so let's try to clear things up a bit. Take a look at the generated `setup.py` file for this project. Note that the `entry_point` line in `setup.py` points at a string which looks a lot like an `.ini` file. This string representation of an `.ini` file has a section named `[paste.app_factory]`. Within this section, there is a key named `app` (the entry point name) which has a value `myproject.run:app`. The *key* app is what our `egg:MyProject#app` value of the `use` section in our config file is pointing at. The value represents a *dotted Python name* path, which refers to a callable in our `myproject` package's `run.py` module. In English, this entry point can thus be referred to as a "Paste application factory in the `MyProject` project which has the entry point named `app` where the entry point refers to a `app` function in the `mypackage.run` module". If indeed if you open up the `run.py` module generated within the `myproject` package, you'll see a `app` function. This is the function called *PasteDeploy* when the `paster serve` command is invoked against our application. It accepts a global configuration object and *returns* an instance of our application.

The `use` setting is the only setting required in the `[app:main]` section unless you've changed the callable referred to by the `MyProject#app` entry point to accept more arguments: other settings you add to this section are passed as keywords arguments to the callable represented by this entry point (`app` in our `run.py` module). You can provide startup-time configuration parameters to your application by requiring more settings in this section.

The `reload_templates` setting in the `[app:main]` section is a `repoze.bfg` -specific setting which is passed into the framework. If it exists, and its value is `true`, *Chameleon* template changes will not require an application restart to be detected. See *Automatically Reloading Templates* (pp. 159) for more information.

⚠ The `reload_templates` option should be turned off for production applications, as template rendering is slowed when it is turned on.

Various other settings may exist in this section having to do with debugging or influencing runtime behavior of a `repoze.bfg` application. See *Environment Variables and .ini File Settings* (pp. 189) for more information about these settings.

The `[server:main]` section of the configuration file configures a WSGI server which listens on TCP port 6543. It is configured to listen on all interfaces (`0.0.0.0`). The `Paste#http` server will create a new thread for each request.

ⓘ In general, `repoze.bfg` applications generated from `paster templates` should be threading-aware. It is not required that a `repoze.bfg` application be nonblocking as all application code will run in its own thread, provided by the server you're using.

See the *PasteDeploy* documentation for more information about other types of things you can put into this .ini file, such as other applications, *middleware* and alternate *WSGI* server implementations.

5.9.2 setup.py

The setup.py file is a *setuptools* setup file. It is meant to be run directly from the command line to perform a variety of functions, such as testing your application, packaging, and distributing your application.

---

setup.py is the defacto standard which Python developers use to distribute their reusable code. You can read more about setup.py files and their usage in the Setuptools documentation (http://peak.telecommunity.com/DevCenter/setuptools).

Our generated setup.py looks like this:

```
import os

from setuptools import setup, find_packages

here = os.path.abspath(os.path.dirname(__file__))
README = open(os.path.join(here, 'README.txt')).read()
CHANGES = open(os.path.join(here, 'CHANGES.txt')).read()

setup(name='MyProject',
      version='0.0',
      description='MyProject',
      long_description=README + '\n\n' +  CHANGES,
      classifiers=[
        "Programming Language :: Python",
        "Framework :: BFG",
        "Topic :: Internet :: WWW/HTTP",
        "Topic :: Internet :: WWW/HTTP :: WSGI :: Application",
        ],
      author='',
      author_email='',
      url='',
      keywords='web wsgi bfg',
      packages=find_packages(),
      include_package_data=True,
      zip_safe=False,
      install_requires=[
```

```
27          'repoze.bfg',
28          ],
29      tests_require=[
30          'repoze.bfg',
31          ],
32      test_suite="myproject",
33      entry_points = """\
34  [paste.app_factory]
35  app = myproject.run:app
36      """
37      )
```

The `setup.py` file calls the setuptools `setup` function, which does various things depending on the arguments passed to `setup.py` on the command line.

Within the arguments to this function call, information about your application is kept. While it's beyond the scope of this documentation to explain everything about setuptools setup files, we'll provide a whirlwind tour of what exists in this file in this section.

Your application's name can be any string; it is specified in the `name` field. The version number is specified in the `version` value. A short description is provided in the `description` field. The `long_description` is conventionally the content of the README and CHANGES file appended together. The `classifiers` field is a list of Trove (http://pypi.python.org/pypi?%3Aaction=list_classifiers) classifiers describing your application. `author` and `author_email` are text fields which probably don't need any description. `url` is a field that should point at your application project's URL (if any). `packages=find_packages()` causes all packages within the project to be found when packaging the application. `include_package_data` will include non-Python files when the application is packaged if those files are checked into version control. `zip_safe` indicates that this package is not safe to use as a zipped egg; instead it will always unpack as a directory, which is more convenient. `install_requires` and `tests_require` indicate that this package depends on the `repoze.bfg` package. `test_suite` points at the package for our application, which means all tests found in the package will be run when `setup.py test` is invoked. We examined `entry_points` in our discussion of the `MyProject.ini` file; this file defines the `app` entry point that represents our project's application.

Usually you only need to think about the contents of the `setup.py` file when distributing your application to other people, or when versioning your application for your own use. For fun, you can try this command now:

```
$ python setup.py sdist
```

This will create a tarball of your application in a `dist` subdirectory named `MyProject-0.1.tar.gz`. You can send this tarball to other people who want to use your application.

> ⚠ By default, `setup.py sdist` does not place non-Python-source files in generated tarballs. This means, in this case, that the `templates/mytemplate.pt` file and the files in the `templates/static` directory are not packaged in the tarball. To allow this to happen, check all the files that you'd like to be distributed along with your application's Python files into a version control system such as Subversion. After you do this, when you rerun `setup.py sdist`, all files checked into the version control system will be included in the tarball.

5.10 The `myproject` *Package*

The `myproject` *package* lives inside the `MyProject` *project*. It contains:

1. An `__init__.py` file which signifies that this is a Python *package*. It is conventionally empty, save for a single comment at the top.

2. A `configure.zcml` is a *ZCML* file which maps view names to model types. Its contents populate the *application registry* when loaded.

3. A `models.py` module, which contains *model* code.

4. A `run.py` module, which contains code that helps users run the application.

5. A `templates` directory, which contains *Chameleon* (or other types of) templates.

6. A `tests.py` module, which contains unit test code for the application.

7. A `views.py` module, which contains view code for the application.

These are purely conventions established by the `paster` template: `repoze.bfg` doesn't insist that you name things in any particular way.

5.10.1 `configure.zcml`

The `configure.zcml` contains configuration statements that populate the *application registry*. It looks like so:

```
1  <configure xmlns="http://namespaces.repoze.org/bfg">
2
3    <include package="repoze.bfg.includes" />
4
5    <view
6        context=".models.MyModel"
7        view=".views.my_view"
8        renderer="templates/mytemplate.pt"
9        />
10
11   <static
12       name="static"
13       path="templates/static"
14       />
15
16 </configure>
```

1. Line 1 provides the root node and namespaces for the configuration language. `http://namespaces.repoze.org/bfg` is the default XML namespace. Add-on packages may require other namespaces.

2. Line 4 initializes `repoze.bfg` -specific configuration directives by including the `includes` package. This causes all of the ZCML within the `configure.zcml` of the `includes` package to be "included" in this configuration file's scope. Effectively this means that we can use (for this example) the `view` and `static` directives which follow later in this file.

3. Lines 6-10 register a "default view" (a view that has no `name` attribute). It is registered so that it will be found when the *context* of the request is an instance of the `myproject.models.MyModel` class. The `view` attribute points at a Python function that does all the work for this view, also known as a *view callable*. Note that the values of both the `context` attribute and the `view` attribute begin with a single period. Names that begin with a period are "shortcuts" which point at files relative to the *package* in which the `configure.zcml` file lives. In this case, since the `configure.zcml` file lives within the `myproject` package, the shortcut `.models.MyModel` could also be spelled `myproject.models.MyModel` (forming a full Python dotted-path name to the `MyModel` class). Likewise the shortcut `.views.my_view` could be replaced with `myproject.views.my_view`.

   The view declaration also names a `renderer`, which in this case is a template that will be used to render the result of the view callable. This particular view declaration points at `templates/mytemplate.pt`, which is a *relative* file specification; it's relative to the directory in which the `configure.zcml` file lives. The template file it points at is a *Chameleon* ZPT template file.

51

4. Lines 12-15 register a static view, which will register a view which serves up the files from the templates/static directory relative to the directory in which the configure.zcml file lives.

5. Line 17 ends the configure root tag.

5.10.2 views.py

Much of the heavy lifting in a repoze.bfg application comes in the form of *view callables*. A *view callable* is the main tool of a repoze.bfg web application developer; it is a bit of code which accepts a *request* and which returns a *response*.

```
1  def my_view(request):
2      return {'project':'MyProject'}
```

This bit of code was registered as the view callable within configure.zcml. configure.zcml said that the default URL for instances that are of the class myproject.models.MyModel should run this myproject.views.my_view() function.

This view callable function is handed a single piece of information: the *request*. The *request* is an instance of the *WebOb* Request class representing the browser's request to our server.

This view returns a dictionary. When this view is invoked, a *renderer* converts the dictionary returned by the view into HTML, and returns the result as the *response*. This view is configured to invoke a renderer which uses a *Chameleon* ZPT template (templates/my_template.pt, as specified in the configure.zcml file).

See *Writing View Callables Which Use a Renderer* (pp. 109) for more information about how views, renderers, and templates relate and cooperate.

ⓘ because our MyProject.ini has a reload_templates = true directive indicating that templates should be reloaded when they change, you won't need to restart the application server to see changes you make to templates. During development, this is handy. If this directive had been false (or if the directive did not exist), you would need to restart the application server for each template change. For production applications, you should set your project's reload_templates to false to increase the speed at which templates may be rendered.

5.10.3 `models.py`

The `models.py` module provides the *model* data and behavior for our application. Models are objects which store application data and provide APIs which mutate and return this data. We write a class named `MyModel` that provides the behavior.

```
1  class MyModel(object):
2      pass
3
4  root = MyModel()
5
6  def get_root(environ):
7      return root
```

1. Lines 1-2 define the MyModel class.

2. Line 4 defines an instance of MyModel as the root.

3. Line 6 is a "root factory" function that will be called by the `repoze.bfg` *Router* for each request when it wants to find the root of the object graph. Conventionally this is called `get_root`.

In a "real" application, the root object would not be such a simple object. Instead, it would be an object that could access some persistent data store, such as a database. `repoze.bfg` doesn't make any assumption about which sort of datastore you'll want to use, so the sample application uses an instance of `myproject.models.MyModel` to represent the root.

5.10.4 `run.py`

We need a small Python module that configures our application and which advertises an entry point for use by our *PasteDeploy* `.ini` file. This is the file named `run.py`:

```
1  from repoze.bfg.configuration import Configurator
2  from myproject.models import get_root
3
4  def app(global_config, **settings):
5      """ This function returns a WSGI application.
6
7      It is usually called by the PasteDeploy framework during
8      ``paster serve``.
```

```
9      """
10     config = Configurator(root_factory=get_root, settings=settings)
11     config.begin()
12     zcml_file = settings.get('configure_zcml', 'configure.zcml')
13     config.load_zcml(zcml_file)
14     config.end()
15     return config.make_wsgi_app()
```

1. Line 1 imports the *Configurator* class from `configuration` (pp. 367) that we use later.

2. Line 2 imports the `get_root` function from `myproject.models` that we use later.

3. Lines 4-13 define a function that returns a `repoze.bfg` WSGI application. This function is meant to be called by the *PasteDeploy* framework as a result of running `paster serve`.

5.10.5 `templates/mytemplate.pt`

The single *Chameleon* template exists in the project. Its contents are too long to show here, but it displays a default page when rendered. It is referenced by the `view` declaration's `renderer` attribute in the `configure.zcml` file. See *Writing View Callables Which Use a Renderer* (pp. 109) for more information about renderers.

Templates are accessed and used by view configurations and sometimes by view functions themselves. See *Templates Used Directly* (pp. 151) and *Templates Used as Renderers* (pp. 153).

5.10.6 `templates/static`

This directory contains static resources which support the `mytemplate.pt` template. It includes CSS and images.

5.10.7 `tests.py`

The `tests.py` module includes unit tests for your application.

```
1  import unittest
2
3  from repoze.bfg.configuration import Configurator
4  from repoze.bfg import testing
5
6  class ViewTests(unittest.TestCase):
7      def setUp(self):
8          self.config = Configurator()
9          self.config.begin()
10
11     def tearDown(self):
12         self.config.end()
13
14     def test_my_view(self):
15         from myproject.views import my_view
16         request = testing.DummyRequest()
17         info = my_view(request)
18         self.assertEqual(info['project'], 'MyProject')
```

This sample `tests.py` file has a single unit test defined within it. This test is executed when you run `python setup.py test`. You may add more tests here as you build your application. You are not required to write tests to use `repoze.bfg`, this file is simply provided as convenience and example.

See *Unit and Integration Testing* (pp. 193) for more information about writing `repoze.bfg` unit tests.

CONTEXT FINDING AND VIEW LOOKUP

In order for a web application to perform any useful action, the web framework must provide a mechanism to find and invoke code written by the application developer based on parameters present in the *request*.

`repoze.bfg` uses two separate but cooperating subsystems to find and invoke code written by the application developer: *context finding* and *view lookup*.

- A `repoze.bfg` *context finding* subsystem is given a *request*; it is responsible for finding a *context* object and a *view name* based on information present in the request.

- Using the context and view name provided by *context finding*, the `repoze.bfg` *view lookup* subsystem is provided with a *request*, a *context* and a *view name*. It is then responsible for finding and invoking a *view callable*. A view callable is a specific bit of code written and registered by the application developer which receives the *request* and which returns a *response*.

These two subsystems are are used by `repoze.bfg` serially: first, a *context finding* subsystem does its job. Then the result of context finding is passed to the *view lookup* subsystem. The view lookup system finds a *view callable* written by an application developer, and invokes it. A view callable returns a *response*. The response is returned to the requesting user.

What Good is A Context Finding Subsystem?

The *URL dispatch* mode of `repoze.bfg` as well as many other web frameworks such as *Pylons* or *Django* actually collapse the two steps of context finding and view lookup into a single step. In these systems, a URL can map *directly* to a view callable. This makes them simpler to understand than systems which use distinct subsystems to locate a context and find a view. However, explicitly finding a context provides extra flexibility. For example, it makes it possible to protect your application with declarative context-sensitive instance-level *authorization*, which is not well-supported in frameworks that do not provide a notion of a context.

There are two separate *context finding* subsystems in `repoze.bfg`: *traversal* and *URL dispatch*. The subsystems are documented within this chapter. They can be used separately or they can be combined. Three chapters which follow describe *context finding*: *Traversal* (pp. 61), *URL Dispatch* (pp. 73) and *Combining Traversal and URL Dispatch* (pp. 93).

There is only one *view lookup* subsystem present in `repoze.bfg`. Where appropriate, within this chapter, we describe how view lookup interacts with context finding. One chapter which follows describes *view lookup*: *Views* (pp. 105).

6.1 Should I Use Traversal or URL Dispatch for Context Finding?

URL dispatch is very straightforward. When you limit your application to using URL dispatch, you know every URL that your application might generate or respond to, all the URL matching elements are listed in a single place, and you needn't think about *context finding* or *view lookup* at all.

URL dispatch can easily handle URLs such as `http://example.com/members/Chris`, where it's assumed that each item "below" `members` in the URL represents a single member in some system. You just match everything "below" `members` to a particular *view callable*, e.g. `/members/:memberid`.

However, URL dispatch is not very convenient if you'd like your URLs to represent an arbitrary hierarchy. For example, if you need to infer the difference between sets of URLs such as these, where the `document` in the first URL represents a PDF document, and `/stuff/page` in the second represents an OpenOffice document in a "stuff" folder.

```
http://example.com/members/Chris/document
http://example.com/members/Chris/stuff/page
```

It takes more pattern matching assertions to be able to make hierarchies work in URL-dispatch based systems, and some assertions just aren't possible. Essentially, URL-dispatch based systems just don't deal very well with URLs that represent arbitrary-depth hierarchies.

But *traversal does* work well for URLs that represent arbitrary-depth hierarchies. Since the path segments that compose a URL are addressed separately, it becomes very easy to form URLs that represent arbitrary depth hierarchies in a system that uses traversal. When you're willing to treat your application models as a graph that can be traversed, it also becomes easy to provide "instance-level security": you just attach a security declaration to each instance in the graph. This is not nearly as easy to do when using URL dispatch.

In essence, the choice to use traversal vs. URL dispatch is largely religious. Traversal dispatch probably just doesn't make any sense when you possess completely "square" data stored in a relational database because it requires the construction and maintenance of a graph and requires that the developer think about mapping URLs to code in terms of traversing that graph. However, when you have a hierarchical data store, using traversal can provide significant advantages over using URL-based dispatch.

Since `repoze.bfg` provides support for both approaches, you can use either exclusively or combine them as you see fit.

TRAVERSAL

Traversal is a *context finding* mechanism. It is the act of finding a *context* and a *view name* by walking over an *object graph*, starting from a *root* object, using a *request* object as a source of path information.

In this chapter, we'll provide a high-level overview of traversal, we'll explain the concept of an *object graph*, and we'll show how traversal might be used within an application.

7.1 A Traversal Analogy

We use an analogy to provide an introduction to *traversal*. Imagine an inexperienced UNIX computer user, wishing only to use the command line to find a file and to invoke the `cat` command against that file. Because he is inexperienced, the only commands he knows how to use are `cd`, which changes the current directory and `cat`, which prints the contents of a file. And because he is inexperienced, he doesn't understand that `cat` can take an absolute path specification as an argument, so he doesn't know that you can issue a single command command `cat /an/absolute/path` to get the desired result. Instead, this user believes he must issue the `cd` command, starting from the root, for each intermediate path segment, *even the path segment that represents the file itself*. Once he gets an error (because you cannot successfully `cd` into a file), he knows he has reached the file he wants, and he will be able to execute `cat` against the resulting path segment.

This inexperienced user's attempt to execute `cat` against the file named `/fiz/buz/myfile` might be to issue the following set of UNIX commands:

```
cd /
cd fiz
cd buz
cd myfile
```

The user now know he has found a *file*, because the `cd` command issues an error when he executed `cd myfile`. Now he knows that he can run the `cat` command:

```
cat myfile
```

The contents of `myfile` are now printed on the user's behalf.

`repoze.bfg` is very much like this inexperienced UNIX user as it uses *traversal* against an object graph. In this analogy, we can map the `cat` program to the `repoze.bfg` concept of a *view callable*: it is a program that can be run against some *context* as the result of *view lookup*. The file being operated on in this analogy is the *context* object; the context is the "last node found" in a traversal. The directory structure is the object graph being traversed. The act of progressively changing directories to find the file as well as the handling of a `cd` error as a stop condition is analogous to *traversal*.

The analogy we've used is not *exactly* correct, because, while the naive user already knows which command he wants to invoke before he starts "traversing" (`cat`), `repoze.bfg` needs to obtain that information from the path being traversed itself. In *traversal*, the "command" meant to be invoked is a *view callable*. A view callable is derived via *view lookup* from the combination of the *view name* and the *context*. Traversal is the act of obtaining these two items.

7.2 A High-Level Overview of Traversal

Traversal is dependent on information in a *request* object. Every *request* object contains URL path information in the PATH_INFO portion of the *WSGI* environment. The PATH_INFO portion of the WSGI environment is the portion of a request's URL following the hostname and port number, but before any query string elements or fragment element. For example the PATH_INFO portion of the URL `http://example.com:8080/a/b/c?foo=1` is `/a/b/c`.

Traversal treats the PATH_INFO segment of a URL as a sequence of path segments. For example, the PATH_INFO string `/a/b/c` is converted to the sequence `['a', 'b', 'c']`.

After the path info is converted, a lookup is performed against the object graph for each path segment. Each lookup uses the `__getitem__` method of an object in the graph.

For example, if the path info sequence is `['a', 'b', 'c']`:

- *Traversal* pops the first element (a) from the path segment sequence and attempts to call the root object's __getitem__ method using that value (a) as an argument; we'll presume it succeeds.

- When the root object's __getitem__ succeeds it will return an object, which we'll call "A". The *context* temporarily becomes the "A" object.

- The next segment (b) is popped from the path sequence, and the "A" object's __getitem__ is called with that value (b) as an argument; we'll presume it succeeds.

- When the "A" object's __getitem__ succeeds it will return an object, which we'll call "B". The *context* temporarily becomes the "B" object.

This process continues until the path segment sequence is exhausted or a lookup for a path element fails. In either case, a *context* is found.

Traversal "stops" when it either reaches a leaf level model instance in your object graph or when the path segments implied by the URL "run out". The object that traversal "stops on" becomes the *context*. If at any point during traversal any node in the graph doesn't have a __getitem__ method, or if the __getitem__ method of a node raises a KeyError, traversal ends immediately, and that node becomes the *context*.

The results of a *traversal* also include a *view name*. The *view name* is the *first* URL path segment in the set of PATH_INFO segments "left over" in the path segment list popped by the traversal process *after* traversal finds a context object.

The combination of the *context* object and the *view name* found via traversal is used later in the same request by a separate repoze.bfg subsystem – the *view lookup* subsystem – to find a *view callable* later within the same request. How repoze.bfg performs view lookup is explained within the *Views* (pp. 105) chapter.

7.3 The Object Graph

When your application uses *traversal* to resolve URLs to code, your application must supply an *object graph* to repoze.bfg. This graph is represented by a *root* object.

In order to supply a root object for an application, at system startup time, the repoze.bfg *Router* is configured with a callback known as a *root factory*. The root factory is supplied by the application developer as the root_factory argument to the application's *Configurator*.

Here's an example of a simple root factory:

```
1  class Root(dict):
2      def __init__(self, request):
3          pass
```

Here's an example of using this root factory within startup configuration, by passing it to an instance of a *Configurator* named `config`:

```
1  config = Configurator(root_factory=Root)
```

Using the `root_factory` argument to a `configuration.Configurator` (pp. 367) constructor tells your `repoze.bfg` application to call this root factory to generate a root object whenever a request enters the application. This root factory is also known as the global root factory.

A root factory is passed a *request* object and it is expected to return an object which represents the root of the object graph. All *traversal* will begin at this root object. Usually a root factory for a traversal-based application will be more complicated than the above `Root` object; in particular it may be associated with a database connection or another persistence mechanism. A root object is often an instance of a class which has a `__getitem__` method.

> In `repoze.bfg` 1.0 and prior versions, the root factory was passed a term WSGI *environment* object (a dictionary) while in `repoze.bfg` 1.1+ it is passed a *request* object. For backwards compatibility purposes, the request object passed to the root factory has a dictionary-like interface that emulates the WSGI environment, so code expecting the argument to be a dictionary will continue to work.

If no *root factory* is passed to the `repoze.bfg` *Configurator* constructor, or the `root_factory` is specified as the value `None`, a *default* root factory is used. The default root factory always returns an object that has no child nodes.

Emulating the Default Root Factory

For purposes of understanding the default root factory better, we'll note that you can emulate the default root factory by using this code as an explicit root factory in your application setup:

```
1  class Root(object):
2      def __init__(self, request):
3          pass
4
5  config = Configurator(root_factory=Root)
```

The default root factory is just a really stupid object that has no behavior or state. Using *traversal* against an application that uses the object graph supplied by the default root object is not very interesting, because the default root object has no children. Its availability is more useful when you're developing an application using *URL dispatch*.

Items contained within the object graph are sometimes analogous to the concept of *model* objects used by many other frameworks (and `repoze.bfg` APIs often refers to them as "models", as well). They are typically instances of Python classes.

The object graph consists of *container* nodes and *leaf* nodes. There is only one difference between a *container* node and a *leaf* node: *container* nodes possess a __getitem__ method while *leaf* nodes do not. The __getitem__ method was chosen as the signifying difference between the two types of nodes because the presence of this method is how Python itself typically determines whether an object is "containerish" or not.

Each container node is presumed to be willing to return a child node or raise a KeyError based on a name passed to its __getitem__.

No leaf-level instance is required to have a __getitem__. If instances that you'd like to be leaves already happen to have a __getitem__ through some historical inequity, you should subclass these node types and cause their __getitem__ methods to simply raise a KeyError. Or just disuse them and think up another strategy.

Usually, the traversal root is a *container* node, and as such it contains other nodes. However, it doesn't *need* to be a container. Your object graph can be as shallow or as deep as you require.

In general, the object graph is traversed beginning at its root object using a sequence of path elements described by the PATH_INFO of the current request; if there are path segments, the root object's __getitem__ is called with the next path segment, and it is expected to return another graph object. The resulting object's __getitem__ is called with the very next path segment, and it is expected to return another graph object. This happens *ad infinitum* until all path segments are exhausted.

7.4 The Traversal Algorithm

This section will attempt to explain the `repoze.bfg` traversal algorithm. We'll provide a description of the algorithm, a diagram of how the algorithm works, and some example traversal scenarios that might help you understand how the algorithm operates against a specific object graph.

We'll also talk a bit about *view lookup* . The *Views* (pp. 105) chapter discusses *view lookup* in detail, and it is the canonical source for information about views. Technically, *view lookup* is a `repoze.bfg` subsystem that is separated from traversal entirely. However, we'll describe the fundamental behavior of view lookup in the examples in the next few sections to give you an idea of how traversal and view lookup cooperate, because they are almost always used together.

7.4.1 A Description of The Traversal Algorithm

When a user requests a page from your `traversal` -powered application, the system uses this algorithm to find a *context* and a *view name*.

1. The request for the page is presented to the `repoze.bfg` *router* in terms of a standard *WSGI* request, which is represented by a WSGI environment and a WSGI `start_response` callable.

2. The router creates a *request* object based on the WSGI environment.

3. The *root factory* is called with the *request*. It returns a *root* object.

4. The router uses the WSGI environment's PATH_INFO information to determine the path segments to traverse. The leading slash is stripped off PATH_INFO, and the remaining path segments are split on the slash character to form a traversal sequence.

   The traversal algorithm by default attempts to first URL-unquote and then Unicode-decode each path segment derived from PATH_INFO from its natural byte string (`str` type) representation. URL unquoting is performed using the Python standard library `urllib.unquote` function. Conversion from a URL-decoded string into Unicode is attempted using the UTF-8 encoding. If any URL-unquoted path segment in PATH_INFO is not decodeable using the UTF-8 decoding, a `TypeError` is raised. A segment will be fully URL-unquoted and UTF8-decoded before it is passed it to the `__getitem__` of any model object during traversal.

   Thus, a request with a PATH_INFO variable of /a/b/c maps to the traversal sequence [u'a', u'b', u'c'].

5. *Traversal* begins at the root object returned by the root factory. For the traversal sequence [u'a', u'b', u'c'], the root object's __getitem__ is called with the name a. Traversal continues through the sequence. In our example, if the root object's __getitem__ called with the name a returns an object (aka "object a"), that object's __getitem__ is called with the name b. If object A returns an object when asked for b, "object b"'s __getitem__ is then asked for the name c, and may return "object c".

6. Traversal ends when a) the entire path is exhausted or b) when any graph element raises a KeyError from its __getitem__ or c) when any non-final path element traversal does not have a __getitem__ method (resulting in a NameError) or d) when any path element is pre-fixed with the set of characters @@ (indicating that the characters following the @@ token should be treated as a *view name*).

7. When traversal ends for any of the reasons in the previous step, the last object found during traversal is deemed to be the *context*. If the path has been exhausted when traversal ends, the *view name* is deemed to be the empty string (''). However, if the path was *not* exhausted before traversal terminated, the first remaining path segment is treated as the view name.

8. Any subsequent path elements after the *view name* is found are deemed the *subpath*. The subpath is always a sequence of path segments that come from PATH_INFO that are "left over" after traversal has completed.

Once *context* and *view name* and associated attributes such as the *subpath* are located, the job of *traversal* is finished. It passes the back the information it obtained to its caller, the repoze.bfg *Router*, which subsequently invokes *view lookup* with the context and view name information.

The traversal algorithm exposes two special cases:

- You will often end up with a *view name* that is the empty string as the result of a particular traversal. This indicates that the view lookup machinery should look up the *default view*. The default view is a view that is registered with no name or a view which is registered with a name that equals the empty string.

- If any path segment element begins with the special characters @@ (think of them as goggles), the value of that segment minus the goggle characters is considered the *view name* immediately and traversal stops there. This allows you to address views that may have the same names as model instance names in the graph unambiguously.

Finally, traversal is responsible for locating a *virtual root*. A virtual root is used during "virtual hosting"; see the *Virtual Hosting* (pp. 181) chapter for information. We won't speak more about it in this chapter.

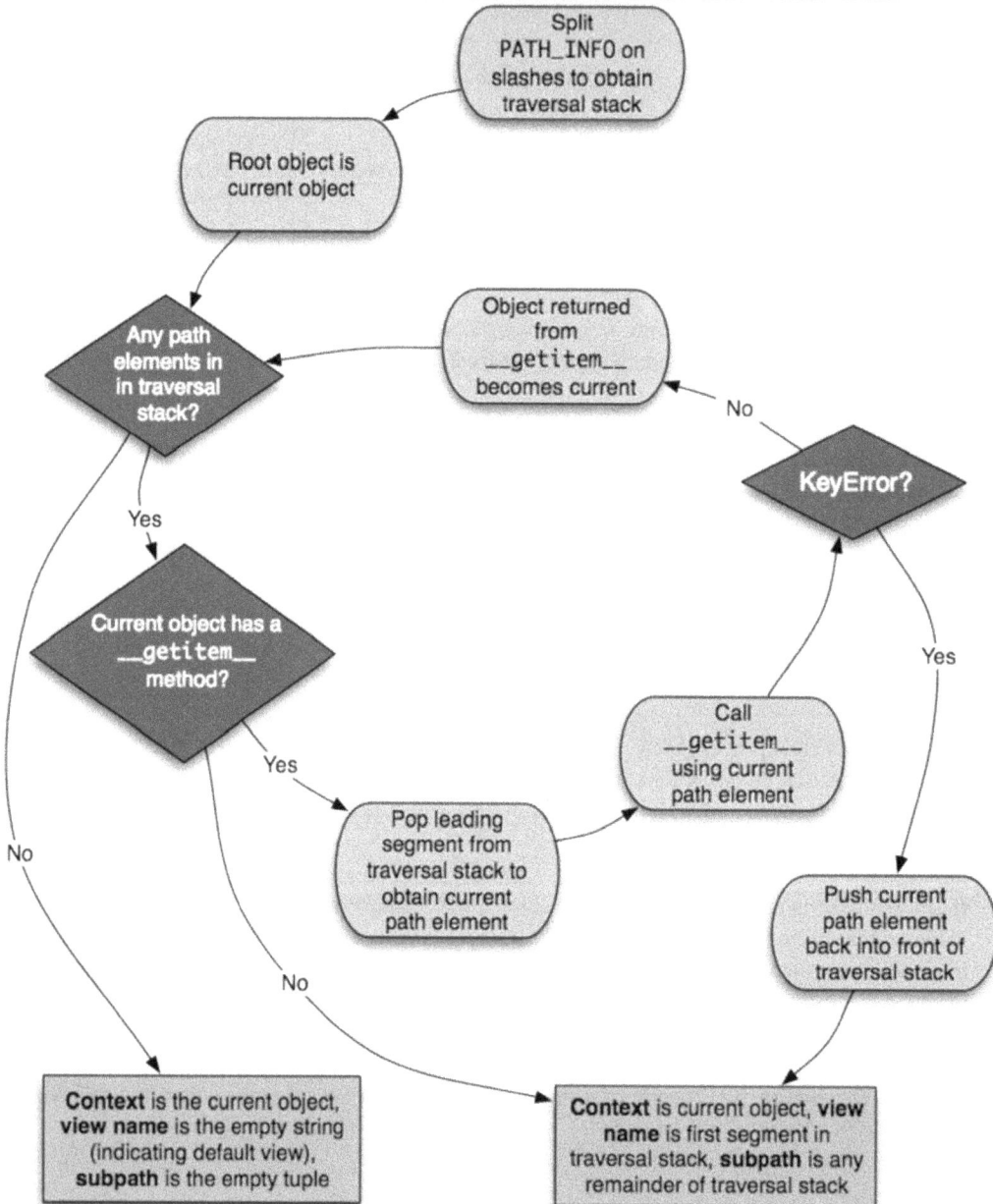

7.4.2 Traversal Algorithm Examples

No one can be expected to understand the traversal algorithm by analogy and description alone, so let's examine some traversal scenarios that use concrete URLs and object graph compositions.

Let's pretend the user asks for `http://example.com/foo/bar/baz/biz/buz.txt`. The request's `PATH_INFO` in that case is `/foo/bar/baz/biz/buz.txt`. Let's further pretend that when this request comes in that we're traversing the following object graph:

```
/--
   |
   |-- foo
       |
        ----bar
```

Here's what happens:

- `traversal` traverses the root, and attempts to find "foo", which it finds.

- `traversal` traverses "foo", and attempts to find "bar", which it finds.

- `traversal` traverses bar, and attempts to find "baz", which it does not find ("bar" raises a `KeyError` when asked for "baz").

The fact that it does not find "baz" at this point does not signify an error condition. It signifies that:

- the *context* is "bar" (the context is the last item found during traversal).

- the *view name* is `baz`

- the *subpath* is `('biz', 'buz.txt')`

At this point, traversal has ended, and *view lookup* begins.

Because it's the "context", the view lookup machinery examines "bar" to find out what "type" it is. Let's say it finds that the context is an `Bar` type (because "bar" happens to be an instance of the class `Bar`). Using the *view name* (`baz`) and the type, view lookup asks the *application registry* this question:

- Please find me a *view callable* registered using a *view configuration* with the name "baz" that can be used for the class `Bar`.

Let's say that view lookup finds no matching view type. In this circumstance, the `repoze.bfg` *router* returns the result of the *not found view* and the request ends.

However, for this graph:

```
/--
   |
   |-- foo
       |
       ----bar
            |
            ----baz
                 |
                 biz
```

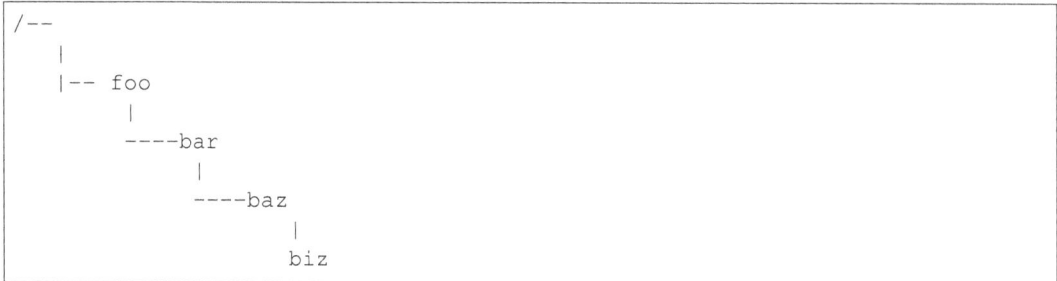

The user asks for `http://example.com/foo/bar/baz/biz/buz.txt`

- `traversal` traverses "foo", and attempts to find "bar", which it finds.

- `traversal` traverses "bar", and attempts to find "baz", which it finds.

- `traversal` traverses "baz", and attempts to find "biz", which it finds.

- `traversal` traverses "biz", and attempts to find "buz.txt" which it does not find.

The fact that it does not find "buz.txt" at this point does not signify an error condition. It signifies that:

- the *context* is "biz" (the context is the last item found during traversal).

- the *view name* is "buz.txt"

- the *subpath* is an empty sequence (`()`).

At this point, traversal has ended, and *view lookup* begins.

Because it's the "context", the view lookup machinery examines "biz" to find out what "type" it is. Let's say it finds that the context is a `Biz` type (because "biz" is an instance of the Python class `Biz`). Using the *view name* (`buz.txt`) and the type, view lookup asks the *application registry* this question:

- Please find me a *view callable* registered with a *view configuration* with the name `buz.txt` that can be used for class `Biz`.

Let's say that question is answered by the application registry; in such a situation, the application registry returns a *view callable*. The view callable is then called with the current *WebOb request* as the sole argument: `request`; it is expected to return a response.

The Example View Callables Accept Only a Request; How Do I Access the Context?

Most of the examples in this book assume that a view callable is typically passed only a *request* object. Sometimes your view callables need access to the *context*, especially when you use *traversal*. You might use a supported alternate view callable argument list in your view callables such as the `(context, request)` calling convention described in *Request-And-Context View Callable Definitions* (pp. 107). But you don't need to if you don't want to. In view callables that accept only a request, the *context* found by traversal is available as the `context` attribute of the request object, e.g. `request.context`. The *view name* is available as the `view_name` attribute of the request object, e.g. `request.view_name`. Other `repoze.bfg`-specific request attributes are also available as described in *Special Attributes Added to the Request by repoze.bfg* (pp. 145).

7.5 References

A tutorial showing how *traversal* can be used within a `repoze.bfg` application exists in *ZODB + Traversal Wiki Tutorial* (pp. 239).

See the *Views* (pp. 105) chapter for detailed information about *view lookup*.

The `traversal` (pp. 413) module contains API functions that deal with traversal, such as traversal invocation from within application code.

The `url.model_url()` (pp. 421) function generates a URL when given an object retrieved from an object graph.

URL DISPATCH

The URL dispatch feature of `repoze.bfg` allows you to either augment or replace *traversal* as a *context finding* mechanism, allowing URL pattern matching to have the "first crack" at resolving a given URL to *context* and *view name*.

Although it is a "context-finding" mechanism, ironically, using URL dispatch exclusively allows you to avoid thinking about your application in terms of "contexts" and "view names" entirely.

Many applications don't need `repoze.bfg` features – such as declarative security via an *authorization policy* – that benefit from having any visible separation between *context finding* and *view lookup*. To this end, URL dispatch provides a handy syntax that allows you to effectively map URLs *directly* to *view* code in such a way that you needn't think about your application in terms "context finding" at all. This makes developing a `repoze.bfg` application seem more like developing an application in a system that is "context-free", such as *Pylons* or *Django*.

Whether or not you care about "context", it often makes a lot of sense to use *URL dispatch* instead of *traversal* in an application that has no natural data hierarchy. For instance, if all the data in your application lives in a relational database, and that relational database has no self-referencing tables that form a natural hierarchy, URL dispatch is easier to use than traversal, and is often a more natural fit for creating an application that manipulates "flat" data.

The presence of *route* (pp. 465) statements in a *ZCML* file used by your application or the presence of calls to the `configuration.Configurator.add_route()` (pp. 369) method in imperative configuration within your application is a sign that you're using *URL dispatch*.

8.1 High-Level Operational Overview

If route configuration is present in an application, the `repoze.bfg` *Router* checks every incoming request against an ordered set of URL matching patterns present in a *route map*.

If any route pattern matches the information in the *request* provided to `repoze.bfg`, a route-specific *context* and *view name* will be generated. In this circumstance, `repoze.bfg` will shortcut *traversal*, and will invoke *view lookup* using the context and view name generated by URL dispatch. If the matched route names a *view callable* in its configuration, that view callable will be invoked when view lookup is performed.

However, if no route pattern matches the information in the *request* provided to `repoze.bfg`, it will fail over to using *traversal* to perform context finding and view lookup.

8.2 Route Configuration

Route configuration is the act of adding a new *route* to an application. A route has a *path*, representing a pattern meant to match against the `PATH_INFO` portion of a URL, and a *name*, which is used by developers within a `repoze.bfg` application to uniquely identify a particular route when generating a URL. It also optionally has a `factory`, a set of *route predicate* parameters, and a set of *view* parameters.

A route configuration may be added to the system via *imperative configuration* or via *ZCML*. Both are completely equivalent.

8.2.1 Configuring a Route Imperatively via The `add_route` Configurator Method

The `configuration.Configurator.add_route()` (pp. 369) method adds a single *route configuration* to the *application registry*. Here's an example:

```
# "config" below is presumed to be an instance of the
# repoze.bfg.configuration.Configurator class; "myview" is assumed
# to be a "view callable" function
from views import myview
config.add_route(name='myroute', path='/prefix/:one/:two', view=myview)
```

8.2.2 Configuring a Route via ZCML

Instead of using the imperative `configuration.Configurator.add_route()` (pp. 369) method to add a new route, you can alternately use *ZCML*. For example, the following *ZCML declaration* causes a route to be added to the application.

```
1  <route
2      name="myroute"
3      path="/prefix/:one/:two"
4      view=".views.myview"
5  />
```

> Values prefixed with a period (.) within the values of ZCML attributes such as the `view` attribute of a `route` mean "relative to the Python package directory in which this *ZCML* file is stored". So if the above `route` declaration was made inside a `configure.zcml` file that lived in the `hello` package, you could replace the relative `.views.myview` with the absolute `hello.views.myview` Either the relative or absolute form is functionally equivalent. It's often useful to use the relative form, in case your package's name changes. It's also shorter to type.

See *route* (pp. 465) for full `route` ZCML directive documentation.

8.2.3 Route Configuration That Names a View Callable

When a route configuration declaration names a `view` attribute, the attribute will be a value that references a *view callable*. A view callable, as described in *Views* (pp. 105), is developer-supplied code that "does stuff" as the result of a request. For more information about how to create view callables, see *Views* (pp. 105).

Here's an example route configuration that references a view callable:

```
1  <route
2      name="myroute"
3      path="/prefix/:one/:two"
4      view="mypackage.views.myview"
5  />
```

When a route configuration names a `view` attribute, the *view callable* named as that `view` attribute will always be found and invoked when the associated route path pattern matches during a request.

The purpose of making it possible to specify a view callable within a route configuration is to prevent developers from needing to deeply understand the details of *context finding* and *view lookup*. When a route names a view callable, and a request enters the system which matches the path of the route, the result is simple: the view callable associated with the route is invoked with the request that caused the invocation.

For most usage, you needn't understand more than this; how it works is an implementation detail. In the interest of completeness, however, we'll explain how it *does* work in the following section. You can skip it if you're uninterested.

Route View Callable Registration and Lookup Details

When a `view` attribute is attached to a route configuration, `repoze.bfg` ensures that a *view configuration* is registered that will always be found when the route path pattern is matched during a request. To do so:

- A special route-specific *interface* is created at startup time for each route configuration declaration.

- When a route configuration declaration mentions a `view` attribute, a *view configuration* is registered at startup time. This view configuration uses the route-specific interface as a *request* type.

- At runtime, when a request causes any route to match, the *request* object is decorated with the route-specific interface.

- The fact that the request is decorated with a route-specific interface causes the view lookup machinery to always use the view callable registered using that interface by the route configuration to service requests that match the route path pattern.

In this way, we supply a shortcut to the developer. Under the hood, `repoze.bfg` still consumes the *context finding* and *view lookup* subsystems provided by `repoze.bfg`, but in a way which does not require that a developer understand either of them if he doesn't want or need to. It also means that we can allow a developer to combine *URL dispatch* and *traversal* in various exceptional cases as documented in *Combining Traversal and URL Dispatch* (pp. 93).

8.2.4 Route Path Pattern Syntax

The syntax of the pattern matching language used by `repoze.bfg` URL dispatch in the *path* argument is straightforward; it is close to that of the *Routes* system used by *Pylons*.

The *path* used in route configuration may start with a slash character. If the path does not start with a slash character, an implicit slash will be prepended to it at matching time. For example, the following paths are equivalent:

```
:foo/bar/baz
```

and:

```
/:foo/bar/baz
```

A path segment (an individual item between / characters in the path) may either be a literal string (e.g. foo) *or* it may segment replacement marker (e.g. :foo). A segment replacement marker is in the format :name, where this means "accept any characters up to the next slash and use this as the name matchdict value." For example, the following pattern defines one literal segment ("foo") and two dynamic segments ("baz", and "bar"):

```
foo/:baz/:bar
```

The above pattern will match these URLs, generating the following matchdicts:

```
foo/1/2        -> {'baz':u'1', 'bar':u'2'}
foo/abc/def    -> {'baz':u'abc', 'bar':u'def'}
```

It will not match the following patterns however:

```
foo/1/2/       -> No match (trailing slash)
bar/abc/def    -> First segment literal mismatch
```

Note that values representing path segments matched with a :segment match will be url-unquoted and decoded from UTF-8 into Unicode within the matchdict. So for instance, the following pattern:

```
foo/:bar
```

When matching the following URL:

```
foo/La%20Pe%C3%B1a
```

The matchdict will look like so (the value is URL-decoded / UTF-8 decoded):

```
{'bar':u'La Pe\xf1a'}
```

If the pattern has a * in it, the name which follows it is considered a "remainder match". A remainder match *must* come at the end of the path pattern. Unlike segment replacement markers, it does not need to be preceded by a slash. For example:

```
foo/:baz/:bar*fizzle
```

The above pattern will match these URLs, generating the following matchdicts:

```
foo/1/2/              -> {'baz':1, 'bar':2, 'fizzle':()}
foo/abc/def/a/b/c  -> {'baz':abc, 'bar':def, 'fizzle':('a', 'b', 'c')}
```

Note that when a *stararg remainder match is matched, the value put into the matchdict is turned into a tuple of path segments representing the remainder of the path. These path segments are url-unquoted and decoded from UTF-8 into Unicode. For example, for the following pattern:

```
foo/*fizzle
```

When matching the following path:

```
/foo/La%20Pe%C3%B1a/a/b/c
```

Will generate the following matchdict:

```
{'fizzle':(u'La Pe\xf1a', u'a', u'b', u'c')}
```

78

8.2.5 Route Declaration Ordering

Because route configuration declarations are evaluated in a specific order when a request enters the system, route configuration declaration ordering is very important.

The order that routes declarations are evaluated is the order in which they are added to the application at startup time. This is unlike *traversal*, which depends on emergent behavior which happens as a result of traversing a graph.

The order that route are evaluated when they are defined via *ZCML* is the order in which they appear in the ZCML relative to each other. For routes added via the `configuration.Configurator.add_route` method, the order that routes are evaluated is the order in which they are added to the configuration imperatively.

For example, route configuration statements with the following patterns might be added in the following order:

```
members/:def
members/abc
```

In such a configuration, the `members/abc` pattern would *never* be matched; this is because the match ordering will always match `members/:def` first; the route configuration with `members/abc` will never be evaluated.

8.2.6 Route Factories

A "route" configuration declaration can mention a "factory". When that route matches a request, and a factory is attached to a route, the *root factory* passed at startup time to the *Configurator* is ignored; instead the factory associated with the route is used to generate a *root* object. This object will usually be used as the *context* of the view callable ultimately found via *view lookup*.

```
<route
 path="/abc"
 name="abc"
 view=".views.theview"
 factory=".models.root_factory"
 />
```

In this way, each route can use a different factory, making it possible to supply a different *context* object to the view related to each particular route.

Supplying a different context for each route is useful when you're trying to use a `repoze.bfg` *authorization policy* to provide declarative "context-sensitive" security checks; each context can maintain a separate *ACL*, as in *Using repoze.bfg Security With URL Dispatch* (pp. 90). It is also useful when you wish to combine URL dispatch with *traversal* as documented within *Combining Traversal and URL Dispatch* (pp. 93).

8.2.7 Route Configuration Arguments

Route configuration statements may specify a large number of arguments.

Many of these arguments are *route predicate* arguments. A route predicate argument specifies that some aspect of the request must be true for the associated route to be considered a match during the route matching process.

Other arguments are view configuration related arguments. These only have an effect when the route configuration names a `view`.

Other arguments are `name` and `factory`. These are required arguments but represent neither a predicate nor view configuration information.

Non-Predicate Arguments

name The name of the route, e.g. `myroute`. This attribute is required. It must be unique among all defined routes in a given application.

factory A reference to a Python object (often a function or a class) that will generate a `repoze.bfg` *context* object when this route matches. For example, `mypackage.models.MyFactoryClass`. If this argument is not specified, the traversal root factory will be used.

Predicate Arguments

path The path of the route e.g. `ideas/:idea`. This argument is required. See *Route Path Pattern Syntax* (pp. 76) for information about the syntax of route paths. If the path doesn't match the current URL, route matching continues.

xhr This value should be either `True` or `False`. If this value is specified and is `True`, the *request* must possess an `HTTP_X_REQUESTED_WITH` (aka `X-Requested-With`) header for this route to match. This is useful for detecting AJAX requests issued from jQuery, Prototype and other Javascript libraries. If this predicate returns `False`, route matching continues.

request_method A string representing an HTTP method name, e.g. GET, POST, HEAD, DELETE, PUT. If this argument is not specified, this route will match if the request has *any* request method. If this predicate returns False, route matching continues.

path_info This value represents a regular expression pattern that will be tested against the PATH_INFO WSGI environment variable. If the regex matches, this predicate will return True. If this predicate returns False, route matching continues.

request_param This value can be any string. A view declaration with this argument ensures that the associated route will only match when the request has a key in the request.params dictionary (an HTTP GET or POST variable) that has a name which matches the supplied value. If the value supplied as the argument has a = sign in it, e.g. request_params="foo=123", then the key (foo) must both exist in the request.params dictionary, and the value must match the right hand side of the expression (123) for the route to "match" the current request. If this predicate returns False, route matching continues.

header This argument represents an HTTP header name or a header name/value pair. If the argument contains a : (colon), it will be considered a name/value pair (e.g. User-Agent:Mozilla/.* or Host:localhost). If the value contains a colon, the value portion should be a regular expression. If the value does not contain a colon, the entire value will be considered to be the header name (e.g. If-Modified-Since). If the value evaluates to a header name only without a value, the header specified by the name must be present in the request for this predicate to be true. If the value evaluates to a header name/value pair, the header specified by the name must be present in the request *and* the regular expression specified as the value must match the header value. Whether or not the value represents a header name or a header name/value pair, the case of the header name is not significant. If this predicate returns False, route matching continues.

accept This value represents a match query for one or more mimetypes in the Accept HTTP request header. If this value is specified, it must be in one of the following forms: a mimetype match token in the form text/plain, a wildcard mimetype match token in the form text/* or a match-all wildcard mimetype match token in the form */*. If any of the forms matches the Accept header of the request, this predicate will be true. If this predicate returns False, route matching continues.

custom_predicates This value should be a sequence of references to custom predicate callables. Use custom predicates when no set of predefined predicates does what you need. Custom predicates can be combined with predefined predicates as necessary. Each custom predicate callable should accept two arguments: context and request and should return either True or False after doing arbitrary evaluation of the context and/or the request. If all callables return True, the associated route will be considered viable for a given request. If any custom predicate returns False, route matching continues. Note that the value context will always be None when passed to a custom route predicate.

View-Related Arguments

81

view A reference to a Python object that will be used as a view callable when this route matches. e.g. `mypackage.views.my_view`.

view_context A reference to a class or an *interface* that the *context* of the view should match for the view named by the route to be used. This argument is only useful if the `view` attribute is used. If this attribute is not specified, the default (`None`) will be used.

If the `view` argument is not provided, this argument has no effect.

This attribute can also be spelled as `for_` or `view_for`.

view_permission The permission name required to invoke the view associated with this route. e.g. `edit`. (see *Using repoze.bfg Security With URL Dispatch* (pp. 90) for more information about permissions).

If the `view` attribute is not provided, this argument has no effect.

This argument can also be spelled as `permission`.

view_renderer This is either a single string term (e.g. `json`) or a string implying a path or *resource specification* (e.g. `templates/views.pt`). If the renderer value is a single term (does not contain a dot `.`), the specified term will be used to look up a renderer implementation, and that renderer implementation will be used to construct a response from the view return value. If the renderer term contains a dot (`.`), the specified term will be treated as a path, and the filename extension of the last element in the path will be used to look up the renderer implementation, which will be passed the full path. The renderer implementation will be used to construct a response from the view return value. See *Writing View Callables Which Use a Renderer* (pp. 109) for more information.

If the `view` argument is not provided, this argument has no effect.

This argument can also be spelled as `renderer`.

view_attr The view machinery defaults to using the `__call__` method of the view callable (or the function itself, if the view callable is a function) to obtain a response dictionary. The `attr` value allows you to vary the method attribute used to obtain the response. For example, if your view was a class, and the class has a method named `index` and you wanted to use this method instead of the class' `__call__` method to return the response, you'd say `attr="index"` in the view configuration for the view. This is most useful when the view definition is a class.

If the `view` argument is not provided, this argument has no effect.

use_global_views When a request matches this route, and view lookup cannot find a view which has a 'route_name' predicate argument that matches the route, try to fall back to using a view that otherwise matches the context, request, and view name (but does not match the route name predicate).

8.3 Route Matching

The main purpose of route configuration is to match (nor not match) the PATH_INFO present in the WSGI environment provided during a request against a URL path pattern.

The way that repoze.bfg does this is very simple. When a request enters the system, for each route configuration declaration present in the system, repoze.bfg checks the PATH_INFO against the pattern declared.

If any route matches, the route matching process stops. The *request* is decorated with a special *interface* which describes it as a "route request", the *context* and *view name* are generated, and the context, the view name, and the resulting request are handed off to *view lookup*. This process is otherwise known as *context finding*. During view lookup, if any view argument was provided within the matched route configuration, the *view callable* it points to is called.

When a route configuration is declared, it may contain *route predicate* arguments. All route predicates associated with a route declaration must be True for the route configuration to be used for a given request.

If any predicate in the set of *route predicate* arguments provided to a route configuration returns False, that route is skipped and route matching continues through the ordered set of routes.

If no route matches after all route patterns are exhausted, repoze.bfg falls back to *traversal* to do *context finding* and *view lookup*.

8.3.1 The Matchdict

When the URL path pattern associated with a particular route configuration is matched by a request, a dictionary named matchdict is added as an attribute of the *request* object. Thus, request.matchdict will contain the values that match replacement patterns in the path element. The keys in a matchdict will be strings. The values will be Unicode objects.

> If no route URL pattern matches, no matchdict is attached to the request.

8.4 Routing Examples

Let's check out some examples of how route configuration statements might be commonly declared, and what will happen if a they are matched by the information present in a request. The examples that follow assume that *ZCML* will be used to perform route configuration, although you can use *imperative configuration* equivalently if you like.

8.4.1 Example 1

The simplest route declaration which configures a route match to *directly* result in a particular view callable being invoked:

```
<route
  name="idea"
  path="site/:id"
  view="mypackage.views.site_view"
/>
```

When a route configuration with a `view` attribute is added to the system, and an incoming request matches the *path* of the route configuration, the *view callable* named as the `view` attribute of the route configuration will be invoked.

In the case of the above example, when the URL of a request matches `/site/:id`, the view callable at the Python dotted path name `mypackage.views.site_view` will be called with the request. In other words, we've associated a view callable directly with a route path.

When the `/site/:id` route path pattern matches during a request, the `site_view` view callable is invoked with that request as its sole argument. When this route matches, a `matchdict` will be generated and attached to the request as `request.matchdict`. If the specific URL matched is `/site/1`, the `matchdict` will be a dictionary with a single key, `id`; the value will be the string `'1'`, ex.: `{'id':'1'}`.

The `mypackage.views` module referred to above might look like so:

```
from webob import Response

def site_view(request):
    return Response(request.matchdict['id'])
```

The view has access to the matchdict directly via the request, and can access variables within it that match keys present as a result of the route path pattern.

See *Views* (pp. 105) for more information about views.

8.4.2 Example 2

Below is an example of a more complicated set of route statements you might add to your application:

```
1   <route
2    name="idea"
3    path="ideas/:idea"
4    view="mypackage.views.idea_view"
5    />
6
7   <route
8    name="user"
9    path="users/:user"
10   view="mypackage.views.user_view"
11   />
12
13  <route
14   name="tag"
15   path="tags/:tag"
16   view="mypackage.views.tag_view"
17   />
```

The above configuration will allow `repoze.bfg` to service URLs in these forms:

```
/ideas/:idea
/users/:user
/tags/:tag
```

- When a URL matches the pattern /ideas/:idea, the view available at the dotted Python path-name mypackage.views.idea_view will be called. For the specific URL /ideas/1, the matchdict generated and attached to the *request* will consist of {'idea':'1'}.

- When a URL matches the pattern /users/:user, the view available at the dotted Python path-name mypackage.views.user_view will be called. For the specific URL /users/1, the matchdict generated and attached to the *request* will consist of {'user':'1'}.

- When a URL matches the pattern /tags/:tag, the view available at the dotted Python path-name mypackage.views.tag_view will be called. For the specific URL /tags/1, the matchdict generated and attached to the *request* will consist of {'tag':'1'}.

In this example we've again associated each of our routes with a *view callable* directly. In all cases, the request, which will have a matchdict attribute detailing the information found in the URL by the process will be passed to the view callable.

8.4.3 Example 3

The context object passed in to a view found as the result of URL dispatch will, by default, be an instance of the object returned by the *root factory* configured at startup time (the `root_factory` argument to the *Configurator* used to configure the application).

You can override this behavior by passing in a `factory` argument to the ZCML directive for a particular route. The `factory` should be a callable that accepts a *request* and returns an instance of a class that will be the context used by the view.

An example of using a route with a factory:

```
1  <route
2    name="idea"
3    path="ideas/:idea"
4    view=".views.idea_view"
5    factory=".models.Idea"
6    />
```

The above route will manufacture an `Idea` model as a *context*, assuming that `mypackage.models.Idea` resolves to a class that accepts a request in its `__init__`. For example:

```
1  class Idea(object):
2      def __init__(self, request):
3          pass
```

In a more complicated application, this root factory might be a class representing a *SQLAlchemy* model.

8.4.4 Example 4

It is possible to create a route declaration without a `view` attribute, but associate the route with a *view callable* using a `view` declaration.

```
1  <route
2    name="idea"
3    path="site/:id"
4    />
5
6  <view
7    view="mypackage.views.site_view"
8    route_name="idea"
9    />
```

This set of configuration parameters creates a configuration completely equivalent to this example provided in *Example 1* (pp. 84):

```
1  <route
2    name="idea"
3    path="site/:id"
4    view="mypackage.views.site_view"
5    />
```

In fact, the spelling which names a `view` attribute is just syntactic sugar for the more verbose spelling which contains separate view and route registrations.

More uses for this style of associating views with routes are explored in *Combining Traversal and URL Dispatch* (pp. 93).

8.5 Matching the Root URL

It's not entirely obvious how to use a route path pattern to match the root URL ("/"). To do so, give the empty string as a path in a ZCML `route` declaration:

```
1  <route
2      path=""
3      name="root"
4      view=".views.root_view"
5      />
```

Or provide the literal string / as the path:

```
1  <route
2      path="/"
3      name="root"
4      view=".views.root_view"
5      />
```

8.6 Generating Route URLs

Use the `url.route_url()` (pp. 423) function to generate URLs based on route paths. For example, if you've configured a route in ZCML with the `name` "foo" and the `path` ":a/:b/:c", you might do this.

```
1  from repoze.bfg.url import route_url
2  url = route_url('foo', request, a='1', b='2', c='3')
```

This would return something like the string `http://example.com/1/2/3` (at least if the current protocol and hostname implied `http:/example.com`). See the `url.route_url()` (pp. 423) API documentation for more information.

8.7 Redirecting to Slash-Appended Routes

For behavior like Django's `APPEND_SLASH=True`, use the `view.append_slash_notfound_view()` (pp. 434) view as the *Not Found view* in your application. When this view is the Not Found view (indicating that no view was found), and any routes have been defined in the configuration of your application, if the value of `PATH_INFO` does not already end in a slash, and if the value of `PATH_INFO` *plus* a slash matches any route's path, do an HTTP redirect to the slash-appended `PATH_INFO`.

Let's use an example, because this behavior is a bit magical. If this your route configuration is looks like so, and the `append_slash_notfound_view` is configured in your application:

```
1  <route
2    view=".views.no_slash"
3    path="no_slash"
4    />
```

```
5
6  <route
7    view=".views.has_slash"
8    path="has_slash/"
9  />
```

If a request enters the application with the PATH_INFO value of /no_slash, the first route will match. If a request enters the application with the PATH_INFO value of /no_slash/, *no* route will match, and the slash-appending "not found" view will *not* find a matching route with an appended slash.

However, if a request enters the application with the PATH_INFO value of /has_slash/, the second route will match. If a request enters the application with the PATH_INFO value of /has_slash, a route *will* be found by the slash appending notfound view. An HTTP redirect to /has_slash/ will be returned to the user's browser.

Note that this will *lose* POST data information (turning it into a GET), so you shouldn't rely on this to redirect POST requests.

To configure the slash-appending not found view in your application, change the application's configure.zcml, adding the following stanza:

```
1  <notfound
2    view="repoze.bfg.views.append_slash_notfound_view"
3  />
```

See *repoze.bfg.view* (pp. 427) and *Changing the Not Found View* (pp. 201) for more information about the slash-appending not found view and for a more general description of how to configure a not found view.

This feature is new as of repoze.bfg 1.1.

8.8 Cleaning Up After a Request

Often it's required that some cleanup be performed at the end of a request when a database connection is involved. When *traversal* is used, this cleanup is often done as a side effect of the traversal *root factory*. Often the root factory will insert an object into the WSGI environment that performs some cleanup when its __del__ method is called. When URL dispatch is used, however, no special root factory is required, so sometimes that option is not open to you.

Instead of putting this cleanup logic in the root factory, however, you can cause a subscriber to be fired when a new request is detected; the subscriber can do this work. For example, let's say you have a mypackage repoze.bfg application package that uses SQLAlchemy, and you'd like the current SQLAlchemy database session to be removed after each request. Put the following in the mypackage.run module:

```
from mypackage.sql import DBSession

class Cleanup:
    def __init__(self, cleaner):
        self.cleaner = cleaner
    def __del__(self):
        self.cleaner()

def handle_teardown(event):
    environ = event.request.environ
    environ['mypackage.sqlcleaner'] = Cleanup(DBSession.remove)
```

Then in the configure.zcml of your package, inject the following:

```
<subscriber for="repoze.bfg.interfaces.INewRequest"
  handler="mypackage.run.handle_teardown"/>
```

This will cause the DBSession to be removed whenever the WSGI environment is destroyed (usually at the end of every request).

Alternate mechanisms for performing this sort of cleanup exist; an alternate mechanism which uses cleanup services offered by the repoze.tm2 package is used in the SQLAlchemy-related paster templates generated by repoze.bfg and within *App Startup with run.py* (pp. 299) within the *SQLAlchemy + URL Dispatch Wiki Tutorial* (pp. 289).

8.9 Using repoze.bfg Security With URL Dispatch

repoze.bfg provides its own security framework which consults a *authorization policy* before allowing any application code to be called. This framework operates in terms of an access control list, which is

90

stored as an `__acl__` attribute of a context object. A common thing to want to do is to attach an `__acl__` to the context object dynamically for declarative security purposes. You can use the `factory` argument that points at a factory which attaches a custom `__acl__` to an object at its creation time.

Such a `factory` might look like so:

```
1  class Article(object):
2      def __init__(self, request):
3          matchdict = request.matchdict
4          article = matchdict.get('article', None)
5          if article == '1':
6              self.__acl__ = [ (Allow, 'editor', 'view') ]
```

If the route `archives/:article` is matched, and the article number is 1, `repoze.bfg` will generate an `Article` *context* with an ACL on it that allows the `editor` principal the `view` permission. Obviously you can do more generic things that inspect the routes match dict to see if the `article` argument matches a particular string; our sample `Article` factory class is not very ambitious.

> See *Security* (pp. 167) for more information about `repoze.bfg` security and ACLs.

8.10 References

A tutorial showing how *URL dispatch* can be used to create a `repoze.bfg` application exists in *SQLAlchemy + URL Dispatch Wiki Tutorial* (pp. 289).

COMBINING TRAVERSAL AND URL DISPATCH

When you write most `repoze.bfg` applications, you'll be using one or the other of two available *context finding* subsystems: traversal or URL dispatch. However, to solve a limited set of problems, it's useful to use *both* traversal and URL dispatch together within the same application. `repoze.bfg` makes this possible via *hybrid* applications.

> ⚠ Reasoning about the behavior of a "hybrid" URL dispatch + traversal application can be challenging. To successfully reason about using URL dispatch and traversal together, you need to understand URL pattern matching, root factories, and the *traversal* algorithm, and the potential interactions between them. Therefore, we don't recommend creating an application that relies on hybrid behavior unless you must.

9.1 A Review of Non-Hybrid Applications

When used according to the tutorials in its documentation `repoze.bfg` is a "dual-mode" framework: the tutorials explain how to create an application in terms of using either *url dispatch or traversal*. This chapter details how you might combine these two dispatch mechanisms, but we'll review how they work in isolation before trying to combine them.

9.1.1 URL Dispatch Only

An application that uses *url dispatch* exclusively to map URLs to code will often have declarations like this within *ZCML*:

```
1   <route
2      path=":foo/:bar"
3      name="foobar"
4      view=".views.foobar"
5      />
6
7   <route
8      path=":baz/:buz"
9      name="bazbuz"
10     view=".views.bazbuz"
11     />
```

Each *route* typically corresponds to a single view callable, and when that route is matched during a request, the view callable named by the `view` attribute is invoked.

Typically, an application that uses only URL dispatch won't perform any configuration in ZCML that includes a `<view>` declaration and won't have any calls to `configuration.Configurator.add_view()` (pp. 374) in its startup code.

9.1.2 Traversal Only

An application that uses only traversal will have view configuration declarations that look like this:

```
1   <view
2      name="foobar"
3      view=".views.foobar"
4      />
5
6   <view
7      name="bazbuz"
8      view=".views.bazbuz"
9      />
```

When the above configuration is applied to an application, the `.views.foobar` view callable above will be called when the URL `/foobar` is visited. Likewise, the view `.views.bazbuz` will be called when the URL `/bazbuz` is visited.

An application that uses *traversal* exclusively to map URLs to code usually won't have any ZCML `<route>` declarations nor will it make any calls to the `configuration.Configurator.add_route()` (pp. 369) method.

9.2 Hybrid Applications

Either traversal or url dispatch alone can be used to create a `repoze.bfg` application. However, it is also possible to combine the concepts of traversal and url dispatch when building an application: the result is a hybrid application. In a hybrid application, traversal is performed *after* a particular route has matched.

A hybrid application is a lot more like a "pure" traversal-based application than it is like a "pure" URL-dispatch based application. But unlike in a "pure" traversal-based application, in a hybrid application, *traversal* is performed during a request after a route has already matched. This means that the URL pattern that represents the `path` argument of a route must match the `PATH_INFO` of a request, and after the route path has matched, most of the "normal" rules of traversal with respect to *context finding* and *view lookup* apply.

There are only four real differences between a purely traversal-based application and a hybrid application:

- In a purely traversal based application, no routes are defined; in a hybrid application, at least one route will be defined.

- In a purely traversal based application, the root object used is global implied by the *root factory* provided at startup time; in a hybrid application, the *root* object at which traversal begins may be varied on a per-route basis.

- In a purely traversal-based application, the `PATH_INFO` of the underlying *WSGI* environment is used wholesale as a traversal path; in a hybrid application, the traversal path is not the entire `PATH_INFO` string, but a portion of the URL determined by a matching pattern in the matched route configuration's path.

- In a purely traversal based applications, view configurations which do not mention a `route_name` argument are considered during *view lookup*; in a hybrid application, when a route is matched, only view configurations which mention that route's name as a `route_name` are considered during *view lookup*.

More generally, a hybrid application *is* a traversal-based application except:

- the traversal *root* is chosen based on the route configuration of the route that matched instead of from the `root_factory` supplied during application startup configuration.

- the traversal *path* is chosen based on the route configuration of the route that matched rather than from the `PATH_INFO` of a request.

- the set of views that may be chosen during *view lookup* when a route matches are limited to those which specifically name a `route_name` in their configuration that is the same as the matched route's `name`.

To create a hybrid mode application, use a *route configuration* that implies a particular *root factory* and which also includes a `path` argument that contains a special dynamic part: either `*traverse` or `*subpath`.

9.2.1 The Root Object for a Route Match

A hybrid application implies that traversal is performed during a request after a route has matched. Traversal, by definition, must always begin at a root object. Therefore it's important to know *which* root object will be traversed after a route has matched.

Figuring out which *root* object results from a particular route match is straightforward. When a route is matched:

- If the route's configuration has a `root_factory` argument which points to a *root factory* callable, that callable will be called to generate a *root* object.

- If the route's configuration does not have a `root_factory` argument, the *global root factory* will be called to generate a *root* object. The global root factory is the callable implied by the `root_factory` argument passed to `configuration.Configurator` (pp. 367) at application startup time.

- If a `root_factory` argument is not provided to the `configuration.Configurator` (pp. 367) at startup time, a *default* root factory is used. The default root factory is used to generate a root object.

> Root factories related to a route were explained previously in within *Route Factories* (pp. 79). Both the global root factory and default root factory were explained previously within *The Object Graph* (pp. 63).

9.2.2 Using `*traverse` In a Route Path

A hybrid application most often implies the inclusion of a route configuration that contains the special token `*traverse` at the end of a route's path:

```
<route
  path=":foo/:bar/*traverse"
  name="home"
  />
```

A `*traverse` token at the end of the path in a route's configuration implies a "stararg" *capture* value. When it is used, it will match the remainder of the path segments of the URL. This remainder becomes the path used to perform traversal.

> ⓘ The `*stararg` route path pattern syntax is explained in more detail within *Route Path Pattern Syntax* (pp. 76).

Note that unlike the examples provided within *URL Dispatch* (pp. 73), the `<route>` configuration named previously does not name a `view` attribute. This is because a hybrid mode application relies on *traversal* to do *context finding* and *view lookup* instead of invariably invoking a specific view callable named directly within the matched route's configuration.

Because the path of the above route ends with `*traverse`, when this route configuration is matched during a request, `repoze.bfg` will attempt to use *traversal* against the *root* object implied by the *root factory* implied by the route's configuration. Once *traversal* has found a *context*, *view lookup* will be invoked in almost exactly the same way it would have been invoked in a "pure" traversal-based application.

The *default root factory* cannot be traversed: it has no useful `__getitem__` method. So we'll need to associate this route configuration with a non-default root factory in order to create a useful hybrid application. To that end, let's imagine that we've created a root factory looks like so in a module named `routes.py`:

```
1  class Traversable(object):
2      def __init__(self, subobjects):
3          self.subobjects = subobjects
4
5      def __getitem__(self, name):
6          return self.subobjects[name]
7
8  root = Traversable(
9          {'a':Traversable({'b':Traversable({'c':Traversable({})})})}
10         )
11
12 def root_factory(request):
13     return root
```

Above, we've defined a (bogus) graph here that can be traversed, and a `root_factory` function that can be used as part of a particular route configuration statement:

```
1  <route
2    path=":foo/:bar/*traverse"
3    name="home"
4    root_factory=".routes.root_factory"
5    />
```

The `root_factory` above points at the function we've defined. It will return an instance of the `Traversable` class as a root object whenever this route is matched. Because the `Traversable` object we've defined has a `__getitem__` method that does something nominally useful, and because traversal uses `__getitem__` to walk the nodes that make up an object graph, using traversal against the root object implied by our route statement becomes a reasonable thing to do.

> We could have also used our `root_factory` callable as the `root_factory` argument of the `configuration.Configurator` (pp. 367) constructor instead of associating it with a particular route inside the route's configuration. Every hybrid route configuration that is matched but which does *not* name a `root_factory` ` attribute will use the use global `root_factory` function to generate a root object.

When the route configuration named `home` above is matched during a request, the matchdict generated will be based on its path: `:foo/:bar/*traverse`. The "capture value" implied by the `*traverse` element in the path pattern will be used to traverse the graph in order to find a context, starting from the root object returned from the root factory. In the above example, the *root* object found will be the instance named `root` in `routes.py`.

If the URL that matched a route with the path `:foo/:bar/*traverse`, is `http://example.com/one/two/a/b/c`, the traversal path used against the root object will be `a/b/c`. As a result, `repoze.bfg` will attempt to traverse through the edges `a`, `b`, and `c`, beginning at the root object.

In our above example, this particular set of traversal steps will mean that the *context* of the view would be the `Traversable` object we've named `c` in our bogus graph and the *view name* resulting from traversal will be the empty string; if you need a refresher about why this outcome is presumed, see *The Traversal Algorithm* (pp. 66).

At this point, a suitable view callable will be found and invoked using *view lookup* as described in *View Configuration: Mapping a Context to a View* (pp. 121), but with a caveat: in order for view lookup to work, we need to define a view configuration that will match when *view lookup* is invoked after a route matches:

```
1  <route
2    path=":foo/:bar/*traverse"
3    name="home"
4    root_factory=".routes.root_factory"
5    />
6
7  <view
8    route_name="home"
9    view=".views.myview"
10   />
```

Note that the above `view` declaration includes a `route_name` argument. Views that include a `route_name` argument are meant to associate a particular view declaration with a route, using the route's name, in order to indicate that the view should *only be invoked when the route matches*.

View configurations may have a `route_name` attribute which refers to the value of the `<route>` declaration's `name` attribute. In the above example, the route name is `home`, referring to the name of the route defined above it.

The above `.views.myview` view will be invoked when:

- the route named "home" is matched
- the *view name* resulting from traversal is the empty string.
- the *context* is any object.

It is also possible to declare alternate views that may be invoked when a hybrid route is matched:

```
1  <route
2    path=":foo/:bar/*traverse"
3    name="home"
4    root_factory=".routes.root_factory"
5    />
6
7  <view
8    route_name="home"
9    view=".views.myview"
10   />
11
12 <view
13   route_name="home"
14   name="another"
15   view=".views.another_view"
16   />
```

The `view` declaration for `.views.another_view` above names a different view and, more importantly, a different *view name*. The above `.views.another_view` view will be invoked when:

- the route named "home" is matched

- the *view name* resulting from traversal is `another`.

- the *context* is any object.

For instance, if the URL `http://example.com/one/two/a/another` is provided to an application that uses the previously mentioned object graph, the `.views.another` view callable will be called instead of the `.views.myview` view callable because the *view name* will be `another` instead of the empty string.

More complicated matching can be composed. All arguments to *route* configuration statements and *view* configuration statements are supported in hybrid applications (such as *predicate* arguments).

Making Global Views Match

By default, view configurations that don't mention a `route_name` will be not found by view lookup when a route that mentions a `*traverse` in its path matches. You can make these match forcibly by adding the `use_global_views` flag to the route definition. For example, the `views.bazbuz` view below will be found if the route named `abc` below is matched and the `PATH_INFO` is `/abc/bazbuz`, even though the view configuration statement does not have the `route_name="abc"` attribute.

```
1  <route
2    path="/abc/*traverse"
3    name="abc"
4    use_global_views="True"
5    />
6
7  <view
8    name="bazbuz"
9    view=".views.bazbuz"
10   />
```

9.2.3 Using *subpath in a Route Path

There are certain extremely rare cases when you'd like to influence the traversal *subpath* when a route matches without actually performing traversal. For instance, the wsgi.wsgiapp2() (pp. 436) decorator and the view.static (pp. 433) helper attempt to compute PATH_INFO from the request's subpath, so it's useful to be able to influence this value.

When *subpath exists in a path pattern, no path is actually traversed, but the traversal algorithm will return a *subpath* list implied by the capture value of *subpath. You'll see this pattern most commonly in route declarations that look like this:

```
1  <route
2    path="/static/*subpath"
3    name="static"
4    view=".views.static_view"
5    />
```

Where .views.static_view is an instance of view.static (pp. 433). This effectively tells the static helper to traverse everything in the subpath as a filename.

9.3 Corner Cases

A number of corner case "gotchas" exist when using a hybrid application. We'll detail them here.

9.3.1 Registering a Default View for a Route That Has a view Attribute

It is an error to provide *both* a view argument to a *route configuration and* a *view configuration* which names a route_name that has no name value or the empty name value. For example, this pair of route/view ZCML declarations will generate a "conflict" error at startup time.

```
1  <route
2    path=":foo/:bar/*traverse"
3    name="home"
4    view=".views.home"
5    />
6
7  <view
8    route_name="home"
9    view=".views.another"
10   />
```

This is because the `view` attribute of the `<route>` statement above is an *implicit* default view when that route matches. `<route>` declarations don't *need* to supply a view attribute. For example, this `<route>` statement:

```
<route
  path=":foo/:bar/*traverse"
  name="home"
  view=".views.home"
  />
```

Can also be spelled like so:

```
<route
  path=":foo/:bar/*traverse"
  name="home"
  />

<view
  route_name="home"
  view=".views.home"
  />
```

The two spellings are logically equivalent. In fact, the former is just a syntactical shortcut for the latter.

9.3.2 Binding Extra Views Against a Route Configuration that Doesn't Have a `*traverse` Element In Its Path

Here's another corner case that just makes no sense.

```
<route
  path="/abc"
  name="abc"
  view=".views.abc"
  />

<view
  name="bazbuz"
  view=".views.bazbuz"
  route_name="abc"
  />
```

The above `<view>` declaration is useless, because it will never be matched when the route it references has matched. Only the view associated with the route itself (`.views.abc`) will ever be invoked when the route matches, because the default view is always invoked when a route matches and when no post-match traversal is performed.

To make the above `<view>` declaration non-useless, the special `*traverse` token must end the route's path. For example:

```
<route
  path="/abc/*traverse"
  name="abc"
  view=".views.abc"
  />

<view
  name="bazbuz"
  view=".views.bazbuz"
  route_name="abc"
  />
```

VIEWS

The primary job of any `repoze.bfg` application is is to find and invoke a *view callable* when a *request* reaches the application. View callables are bits of code written by you – the application developer – which do something interesting in response to a request made to your application.

> 🛈 A `repoze.bfg` *view callable* is often referred to in conversational shorthand as a *view*. In this documentation, however, we need to use less ambiguous terminology because there are significant differences between view *configuration*, the code that implements a view *callable*, and the process of view *lookup*.

The chapter named *Context Finding and View Lookup* (pp. 57) describes how, using information from the *request*, a *context* and a *view name* are computed. But neither the context nor the view name found are very useful unless those elements can eventually be mapped to a *view callable*.

The job of actually locating and invoking the "best" *view callable* is the job of the *view lookup* subsystem. The view lookup subsystem compares information supplied by *context finding* against *view configuration* statements made by the developer stored in the *application registry* to choose the most appropriate view callable for a specific request.

This chapter provides documentation detailing the process of creating view callables, documentation about performing view configuration, and a detailed explanation of view lookup.

10.1 View Callables

No matter how a view callable is eventually found, all view callables used by `repoze.bfg` must be constructed in the same way, and must return the same kind of return value.

Most view callables accept a single argument named `request`. This argument represents a *WebOb Request* object as represented to `repoze.bfg` by the upstream *WSGI* server.

A view callable may always return a *WebOb Response* object directly. It may optionally return another arbitrary non-Response value: if a view callable returns a non-Response result, the result must be converted into a response by the *renderer* associated with the *view configuration* for the view.

View callables can be functions, instances, or classes. View callables can optionally be defined with an alternate calling convention.

10.1.1 Defining a View Callable as a Function

The easiest way to define a view callable is to create a function that accepts a single argument named `request` and which returns a *Response* object. For example, this is a "hello world" view callable implemented as a function:

```
from webob import Response

def hello_world(request):
    return Response('Hello world!')
```

10.1.2 Defining a View Callable as a Class

> This feature is new as of `repoze.bfg` 0.8.1.

A view callable may also be a class instead of a function. When a view callable is a class, the calling semantics are slightly different than when it is a function or another non-class callable. When a view callable is a class, the class' __init__ is called with a `request` parameter. As a result, an instance of the class is created. Subsequently, that instance's __call__ method is invoked with no parameters. Views defined as classes must have the following traits:

- an __init__ method that accepts a `request` as its sole positional argument or an __init__ method that accepts two arguments: `request` and `context` as per *Request-And-Context View Callable Definitions* (pp. 107).

- a __call__ method that accepts no parameters and which returns a response.

For example:

```
from webob import Response

class MyView(object):
    def __init__(self, request):
        self.request = request

    def __call__(self):
        return Response('hello')
```

The request object passed to __init__ is the same type of request object described in *Defining a View Callable as a Function* (pp. 106).

If you'd like to use a different attribute than __call__ to represent the method expected to return a response, you can use an `attr` value as part of view configuration. See *View Configuration Parameters* (pp. 122).

10.1.3 Request-And-Context View Callable Definitions

Usually, view callables are defined to accept only a single argument: `request`. However, view callables may alternately be defined as classes or functions (or any callable) that accept *two* positional arguments: a *context* as the first argument and a *request* as the second argument.

The *context* and *request* arguments passed to a view function defined in this style can be defined as follows:

context An instance of a *context* found via graph *traversal* or *URL dispatch*. If the context is found via traversal, it will be a *model* object.

request A *WebOb* Request object representing the current WSGI request.

The following types work as view callables in this style:

1. Functions that accept two arguments: `context`, and `request`, e.g.:

```
1  from webob import Response
2
3  def view(context, request):
4      return Response('OK')
```

2. Classes that have an __init__ method that accepts `context`, `request` and a __call__ which accepts no arguments, e.g.:

```
1  from webob import Response
2
3  class view(object):
4      def __init__(self, context, request):
5          self.context = context
6          self.request = request
7
8      def __call__(self):
9          return Response('OK')
```

3. Arbitrary callables that have a __call__ method that accepts `context`, `request`, e.g.:

```
1  from webob import Response
2
3  class View(object):
4      def __call__(self, context, request):
5          return Response('OK')
6  view = View() # this is the view callable
```

This style of calling convention is most useful for *traversal* based applications, where the context object is frequently used within the view callable code itself.

No matter which view calling convention is used, the view code always has access to the context via `request.context`.

10.1.4 View Callable Responses

A view callable may always return an object that implements the *WebOb Response* interface. The easiest way to return something that implements this interface is to return a `webob.Response` object instance directly. But any object that has the following attributes will work:

status The HTTP status code (including the name) for the response. E.g. `200 OK` or `401 Unauthorized`.

headerlist A sequence of tuples representing the list of headers that should be set in the response. E.g. `[('Content-Type', 'text/html'), ('Content-Length', '412')]`

app_iter An iterable representing the body of the response. This can be a list, e.g. `['<html><head></head><body>Hello world!</body></html>']` or it can be a file-like object, or any other sort of iterable.

If a view happens to return something to the `repoze.bfg` *router* which does not implement this interface, `repoze.bfg` will attempt to use an a *renderer* to construct a response. The renderer associated with a view callable can be varied by changing the `renderer` attribute in the view's configuration. See *Writing View Callables Which Use a Renderer* (pp. 109).

10.1.5 Using a View Callable to Do A HTTP Redirect

You can issue an HTTP redirect from within a view by returning a particular kind of response.

```
from webob.exc import HTTPFound

def myview(request):
    return HTTPFound(location='http://example.com')
```

All exception types from the `webob.exc` module implement the Webob *Response* interface; any can be returned as the response from a view. See *WebOb* for the documentation for this module; it includes other response types that imply other HTTP response codes, such as `401 Unauthorized`.

10.1.6 Writing View Callables Which Use a Renderer

> 🛈 This feature is new as of `repoze.bfg` 1.1

View callables needn't always return a WebOb Response object. Instead, they may return an arbitrary Python object, with the expectation that a *renderer* will convert that object into a response instance on behalf of the developer. Some renderers use a templating system; other renderers use object serialization techniques.

109

If you do not define a `renderer` attribute in *view configuration* for an associated *view callable*, no renderer is associated with the view. In such a configuration, an error is raised when a view callable does not return an object which implements the WebOb *Response* interface, documented within *View Callable Responses* (pp. 108).

View configuration can vary the renderer associated with a view callable via the `renderer` attribute. For example, this ZCML associates the `json` renderer with a view callable:

```
<view
  view=".views.my_view"
  renderer="json"
  />
```

When this configuration is added to an application, the `.views.my_view` view callable will now use a `json` renderer, which renders view return values to a *JSON* serialization.

Other built-in renderers include renderers which use the *Chameleon* templating language to render a dictionary to a response.

If the *view callable* associated with a *view configuration* returns a Response object directly (an object with the attributes `status`, `headerlist` and `app_iter`), any renderer associated with the view configuration is ignored, and the response is passed back to `repoze.bfg` unmolested. For example, if your view callable returns an instance of the `webob.exc.HTTPFound` class as a response, no renderer will be employed.

```
from webob.exc import HTTPFound

def view(request):
    return HTTPFound(location='http://example.com') # renderer avoided
```

Views which use a renderer can vary non-body response attributes (such as headers and the HTTP status code) by attaching properties to the request. See *Varying Attributes of Rendered Responses* (pp. 113).

Additional renderers can be added to the system as necessary via a ZCML directive (see *Adding and Overriding Renderers* (pp. 114)).

10.1.7 Built-In Renderers

Several built-in "renderers" exist in `repoze.bfg`. These renderers can be used in the `renderer` attribute of view configurations.

`string`: String Renderer

The `string` renderer is a renderer which renders a view callable result to a string. If a view callable returns a non-Response object, and the `string` renderer is associated in that view's configuration, the result will be to run the object through the Python `str` function to generate a string. Note that if a Unicode object is returned by the view callable, it is not `str()`-ified.

Here's an example of a view that returns a dictionary. If the `string` renderer is specified in the configuration for this view, the view will render the returned dictionary to the `str()` representation of the dictionary:

```
1  from webob import Response
2  from repoze.bfg.view import bfg_view
3
4  @bfg_view(renderer='string')
5  def hello_world(request):
6      return {'content':'Hello!'}
```

The body of the response returned by such a view will be a string representing the `str()` serialization of the return value:

Views which use the string renderer can vary non-body response attributes by attaching properties to the request. See *Varying Attributes of Rendered Responses* (pp. 113).

`json`: JSON Renderer

The `json` renderer is a renderer which renders view callable results to *JSON*. If a view callable returns a non-Response object it is called. It passes the return value through the `json.dumps` standard library function, and wraps the result in a response object.

Here's an example of a view that returns a dictionary. If the `json` renderer is specified in the configuration for this view, the view will render the returned dictionary to a JSON serialization:

```
1  from webob import Response
2  from repoze.bfg.view import bfg_view
3
4  @bfg_view(renderer='json')
5  def hello_world(request):
6      return {'content':'Hello!'}
```

The body of the response returned by such a view will be a string representing the JSON serialization of the return value:

The return value needn't be a dictionary, but the return value must contain values serializable by `json.dumps()`.

You can configure a view to use the JSON renderer in ZCML by naming `json` as the `renderer` attribute of a view configuration, e.g.:

```
<view
    context=".models.Hello"
    view=".views.hello_world"
    name="hello"
    renderer="json"
    />
```

Views which use the JSON renderer can vary non-body response attributes by attaching properties to the request. See *Varying Attributes of Rendered Responses* (pp. 113).

**.pt* or **.txt*: Chameleon Template Renderers

Two built-in renderers exist for *Chameleon* templates.

If the `renderer` attribute of a view configuration is an absolute path, a relative path or *resource specification* which has a final path element with a filename extension of `.pt`, the Chameleon ZPT renderer is used. See *Chameleon ZPT Templates* (pp. 155) for more information about ZPT templates.

If the `renderer` attribute of a view configuration is an absolute path, a source-file relative path, or a *resource specification* which has a final path element with a filename extension of `.txt`, the *Chameleon* text renderer is used. See *Chameleon ZPT Templates* (pp. 155) for more information about Chameleon text templates.

The behavior of these renderers is the same, except for the engine used to render the template.

When a `renderer` attribute that names a Chameleon template path (e.g. `templates/foo.pt` or `templates/foo.txt`) is used, the view must return a Response object or a Python *dictionary*. If the view callable with an associated template returns a Python dictionary, the named template will be passed the dictionary as its keyword arguments, and the template renderer implementation will return the resulting rendered template in a response to the user. If the view callable returns anything but a Response object or a dictionary, an error will be raised.

Before passing keywords to the template, the keywords derived from the dictionary returned by the view are augmented. The callable object – whatever object was used to define the `view` – will be automatically inserted into the set of keyword arguments passed to the template as the `view` keyword. If the view callable was a class, the `view` keyword will be an instance of that class. Also inserted into the keywords passed to the template are `renderer_name` (the name of the renderer, which may be a full path or a package-relative name, typically the full string used in the `renderer` attribute of the directive), `context` (the context of the view used to render the template), and `request` (the request passed to the view used to render the template).

Here's an example view configuration which uses a Chameleon ZPT renderer:

```
<view
    context=".models.Hello"
    view=".views.hello_world"
    name="hello"
    renderer="templates/foo.pt"
    />
```

Here's an example view configuration which uses a Chameleon text renderer:

```
<view
    context=".models.Hello"
    view=".views.hello_world"
    name="hello"
    renderer="templates/foo.txt"
    />
```

Views with use a Chameleon renderer can vary response attributes by attaching properties to the request. See *Varying Attributes of Rendered Responses* (pp. 113).

10.1.8 Varying Attributes of Rendered Responses

Before a response that is constructed as the result of the use of a *renderer* is returned to `repoze.bfg`, several attributes of the request are examined which have the potential to influence response behavior.

View callables that don't directly return a response should set these values on the `request` object via `setattr` within the view callable to influence associated response attributes.

`response_content_type` Defines the content-type of the resulting response, e.g. `text/xml`.

113

response_headerlist A sequence of tuples describing cookie values that should be set in the response, e.g. `[('Set-Cookie', 'abc=123'), ('X-My-Header', 'foo')]`.

response_status A WSGI-style status code (e.g. `200 OK`) describing the status of the response.

response_charset The character set (e.g. `UTF-8`) of the response.

response_cache_for A value in seconds which will influence `Cache-Control` and `Expires` headers in the returned response. The same can also be achieved by returning various values in the `response_headerlist`, this is purely a convenience.

For example, if you need to change the response status from within a view callable that uses a renderer, assign the `response_status` attribute to the request before returning a result:

```
from repoze.bfg.view import bfg_view

@bfg_view(name='gone', renderer='templates/gone.pt')
def myview(request):
    request.response_status = '404 Not Found'
    return {'URL':request.URL}
```

10.1.9 Adding and Overriding Renderers

New templating systems and serializers can be associated with `repoze.bfg` renderer names. To this end, configuration declarations can be made which override an existing *renderer factory* and which add a new renderer factory.

Adding or overriding a renderer is accomplished via *ZCML* or via imperative configuration. Renderers can be registered imperatively using the `configuration.Configurator.add_renderer()` (pp. 369) API or via the *renderer* (pp. 459) ZCML directive.

For example, to add a renderer which renders views which have a `renderer` attribute that is a path that ends in `.jinja2`:

Via ZCML

```
<renderer
  name=".jinja2"
  factory="my.package.MyJinja2Renderer"/>
```

The `factory` attribute is a *dotted Python name* that must point to an implementation of a *renderer factory*.
The `name` attribute is the renderer name.

Via Imperative Configuration

```
from my.package import MyJinja2Renderer
config.add_renderer('.jinja2', MyJinja2Renderer)
```

The first argument is the renderer name.

The second argument is a reference to an to an implementation of a *renderer factory*.

Adding a New Renderer

You may a new renderer by creating and registering a *renderer factory*.

A renderer factory implementation is usually a class which has the following interface:

```
class RendererFactory:
    def __init__(self, name):
        """ Constructor: ''name'' may be an absolute path or a
        resource specification """

    def __call__(self, value, system):
        """ Call a the renderer implementation with the value and
        the system value passed in as arguments and return the
        result (a string or unicode object).  The value is the
        return value of a view.  The system value is a dictionary
        containing available system values (e.g. ''view'',
        ''context'', and ''request''). """
```

There are essentially two different kinds of renderer factories:

- A renderer factory which which expects to accept a *resource specification* or an absolute path as the name value in its constructor. These renderer factories are registered with a name value that begins with a dot (.). These types of renderer factories usually relate to a file on the filesystem, such as a template.

- A renderer factory which expects to accepts a token that does not represent a filesystem path or a resource specification in its constructor. These renderer factories are registered with a name value that does not begin with a dot. These renderer factories are typically object serializers.

115

Resource Specifications

A resource specification is a colon-delimited identifier for a *resource*. The colon separates a Python *package* name from a package subpath. For example, the resource specification `my.package:static/baz.css` identifies the file named `baz.css` in the `static` subdirectory of the `my.package` Python *package*.

Here's an example of the registration of a simple renderer factory via ZCML:

```
<renderer
  name="amf"
  factory="my.package.MyAMFRenderer"/>
```

Adding the above ZCML to your application will allow you to use the `my.package.MyAMFRenderer` renderer factory implementation in view configurations by referring to it as `amf` in the `renderer` attribute of a *view configuration*:

```
from repoze.bfg.view import bfg_view

@bfg_view(renderer='amf')
def myview(request):
    return {'Hello':'world'}
```

At startup time, when a *view configuration* is encountered which has a `name` argument that does not contain a dot, such as the above `amf` is encountered, the full value of the `name` attribute is used to construct a renderer from the associated renderer factory. In this case, the view configuration will create an instance of an `AMFRenderer` for each view configuration which includes `amf` as its renderer value. The `name` passed to the `AMFRenderer` constructor will always be `amf`.

Here's an example of the registration of a more complicated renderer factory, which expects to be passed a filesystem path:

```
<renderer
  name=".jinja2"
  factory="my.package.MyJinja2Renderer"/>
```

Adding the above ZCML to your application will allow you to use the `my.package.MyJinja2Renderer` renderer factory implementation in view configurations by referring to any `renderer` which *ends in* `.jinja` in the `renderer` attribute of a *view configuration*:

```
from repoze.bfg.view import bfg_view

@bfg_view(renderer='templates/mytemplate.jinja2')
def myview(request):
    return {'Hello':'world'}
```

When a *view configuration* which has a `name` attribute that does contain a dot, such as `templates/mytemplate.jinja2` above is encountered at startup time, the value of the name attribute is split on its final dot. The second element of the split is typically the filename extension. This extension is used to look up a renderer factory for the configured view. Then the value of `renderer` is passed to the factory to create a renderer for the view. In this case, the view configuration will create an instance of an `Jinja2Renderer` for each view configuration which includes anything ending with `.jinja2` as its `renderer` value. The `name` passed to the `Jinja2Renderer` constructor will usually be a *resource specification*, but may also be an absolute path; the renderer factory implementation should be able to deal with either.

See also *renderer* (pp. 459) and `configuration.Configurator.add_renderer()` (pp. 369).

Overriding an Existing Renderer

You can associate more than one filename extension with the same existing renderer implementation as necessary if you need to use a different file extension for the same kinds of templates. For example, to associate the `.zpt` extension with the Chameleon ZPT renderer factory, use:

```
<renderer
    name=".zpt"
    factory="repoze.bfg.chameleon_zpt.renderer_factory"/>
```

After you do this, `repoze.bfg` will treat templates ending in both the `.pt` and `.zpt` filename extensions as Chameleon ZPT templates.

To override the default mapping in which files with a `.pt` extension are rendered via a Chameleon ZPT page template renderer, use a variation on the following in your application's ZCML:

```
1  <renderer
2     name=".pt"
3     factory="my.package.pt_renderer"/>
```

After you do this, the *renderer factory* in my.package.pt_renderer will be used to render templates which end in .pt, replacing the default Chameleon ZPT renderer.

To override the default mapping in which files with a .txt extension are rendered via a Chameleon text template renderer, use a variation on the following in your application's ZCML:

```
1  <renderer
2     name=".txt"
3     factory="my.package.text_renderer"/>
```

After you do this, the *renderer factory* in my.package.text_renderer will be used to render templates which end in .txt, replacing the default Chameleon text renderer.

To associate a *default* renderer with *all* view configurations (even ones which do not possess a renderer attribute), use a variation on the following (ie. omit the name attribute to the renderer tag):

```
1  <renderer
2     factory="repoze.bfg.renderers.json_renderer_factory"/>
```

See also *renderer* (pp. 459) and configuration.Configurator.add_renderer() (pp. 369).

10.1.10 Using Special Exceptions In View Callables

Usually when a Python exception is raised within a view callable, repoze.bfg allows the exception to propagate all the way out to the *WSGI* server which invoked the application.

However, for convenience, two special exceptions exist which are always handled by repoze.bfg itself. These are exceptions.NotFound (pp. 383) and exceptions.Forbidden (pp. 383). Both is an exception class which accepts a single positional constructor argument: a message.

If exceptions.NotFound (pp. 383) is raised within view code, the result of the *Not Found View* will be returned to the user agent which performed the request.

If exceptions.Forbidden (pp. 383) is raised within view code, the result of the *Forbidden View* will be returned to the user agent which performed the request.

In all cases, the message provided to the exception constructor is made available to the view which repoze.bfg invokes as request.environ['message'].

10.1.11 Handling Form Submissions in View Callables (Unicode and Character Set Issues)

Most web applications need to accept form submissions from web browsers and various other clients. In `repoze.bfg`, form submission handling logic is always part of a *view*. For a general overview of how to handle form submission data using the *WebOb* API, see *Request and Response Objects* (pp. 143) and "Query and POST variables" within the WebOb documentation (http://pythonpaste.org/webob/reference.html#query-post-variables). `repoze.bfg` defers to WebOb for its request and response implementations, and handling form submission data is a property of the request implementation. Understanding WebOb's request API is the key to understanding how to process form submission data.

There are some defaults that you need to be aware of when trying to handle form submission data in a `repoze.bfg` view. Because having high-order (non-ASCII) characters in data contained within form submissions is exceedingly common, and because the UTF-8 encoding is the most common encoding used on the web for non-ASCII character data, and because working and storing Unicode values is much saner than working with and storing bytestrings, `repoze.bfg` configures the *WebOb* request machinery to attempt to decode form submission values into Unicode from the UTF-8 character set implicitly. This implicit decoding happens when view code obtains form field values via the *WebOb* `request.params`, `request.GET`, or `request.POST` APIs.

For example, let's assume that the following form page is served up to a browser client, and its `action` points at some `repoze.bfg` view code:

```
1  <html xmlns="http://www.w3.org/1999/xhtml">
2    <head>
3      <meta http-equiv="Content-Type" content="text/html; charset=UTF-8"/>
4    </head>
5    <form method="POST" action="myview">
6      <div>
7        <input type="text" name="firstname"/>
8      </div>
9      <div>
10       <input type="text" name="lastname"/>
11     </div>
12     <input type="submit" value="Submit"/>
13   </form>
14 </html>
```

The `myview` view code in the `repoze.bfg` application *must* expect that the values returned by `request.params` will be of type `unicode`, as opposed to type `str`. The following will work to accept a form post from the above form:

```
1  def myview(request):
2      firstname = request.params['firstname']
3      lastname = request.params['lastname']
```

But the following myview view code *may not* work, as it tries to decode already-decoded (unicode) values obtained from request.params:

```
1  def myview(request):
2      # the .decode('utf-8') will break below if there are any high-order
3      # characters in the firstname or lastname
4      firstname = request.params['firstname'].decode('utf-8')
5      lastname = request.params['lastname'].decode('utf-8')
```

For implicit decoding to work reliably, you must ensure that every form you render that posts to a repoze.bfg view is rendered via a response that has a ;charset=UTF-8 in its Content-Type header; or, as in the form above, with a meta http-equiv tag that implies that the charset is UTF-8 within the HTML head of the page containing the form. This must be done explicitly because all known browser clients assume that they should encode form data in the character set implied by Content-Type value of the response containing the form when subsequently submitting that form; there is no other generally accepted way to tell browser clients which charset to use to encode form data. If you do not specify an encoding explicitly, the browser client will choose to encode form data in its default character set before submitting it. The browser client may have a non-UTF-8 default encoding. If such a request is handled by your view code, when the form submission data is encoded in a non-UTF8 charset, eventually the WebOb request code accessed within your view will throw an error when it can't decode some high-order character encoded in another character set within form data e.g. when request.params['somename'] is accessed.

If you are using the webob.Response class to generate a response, or if you use the render_template_* templating APIs, the UTF-8 charset is set automatically as the default via the Content-Type header. If you return a Content-Type header without an explicit charset, a WebOb request will add a ;charset=utf-8 trailer to the Content-Type header value for you for response content types that are textual (e.g. text/html, application/xml, etc) as it is rendered. If you are using your own response object, you will need to ensure you do this yourself.

To avoid implicit form submission value decoding, so that the values returned from request.params, request.GET and request.POST are returned as bytestrings rather than Unicode, add the following to your application's configure.zcml:

```
<subscriber for="repoze.bfg.interfaces.INewRequest"
            handler="repoze.bfg.request.make_request_ascii"/>
```

You can then control form post data decoding "by hand" as necessary. For example, when this subscriber is active, the second example above will work unconditionally as long as you ensure that your forms are rendered in a request that has a ;charset=utf-8 stanza on its Content-Type header.

> The behavior that form values are decoded from UTF-8 to Unicode implicitly was introduced in repoze.bfg 0.7.0. Previous versions of repoze.bfg performed no implicit decoding of form values (the default was to treat values as bytestrings).

> Only the *values* of request params obtained via request.params, request.GET or request.POST are decoded to Unicode objects implicitly in repoze.bfg's default configuration. The keys are still strings.

10.2 View Configuration: Mapping a Context to a View

A developer makes a *view callable* available for use within a repoze.bfg application via *view configuration*. A view configuration associates a view callable with a set of statements about the set of circumstances which must be true for the view callable to be invoked.

A view configuration statement is made about information present in the *context* and in the *request*, as well as the *view name*. These three pieces of information are known, collectively, as a *triad*.

View configuration is performed in one of three ways:

- by adding a <view> declaration to *ZCML* used by your application as per *View Configuration Via ZCML* (pp. 126) and *view* (pp. 479).

- by running a *scan* against application source code which has a view.bfg_view (pp. 428) decorator attached to a Python object as per view.bfg_view (pp. 428) and *View Configuration Using the @bfg_view Decorator* (pp. 128).

- by using the `configuration.Configurator.add_view()` (pp. 374) method as per `configuration.Configurator.add_view()` (pp. 374) and *View Configuration Using the add_view Method of a Configurator* (pp. 133).

Each of these mechanisms is completely equivalent to the other.

A view configuration might also be performed by virtue of *route configuration*. View configuration via route configuration is performed in one of the following two ways:

- by using the `configuration.Configurator.add_route()` (pp. 369) method to create a route with a `view` argument.

- by adding a `<route>` declaration that uses a `view` attribute to *ZCML* used by your application as per *route* (pp. 465).

10.2.1 View Configuration Parameters

All forms of view configuration accept the same general types of arguments.

Many arguments supplied during view configuration are *view predicate* arguments. View predicate arguments used during view configuration are used to narrow the set of circumstances in which `view lookup` will find a particular view callable. In general, the fewer number of predicates which are supplied to a particular view configuration, the more likely it is that the associated view callable will be invoked. A greater the number supplied, the less likely.

Some view configuration arguments are non-predicate arguments. These tend to modify the response of the view callable or prevent the view callable from being invoked due to an authorization policy. The presence of non-predicate arguments in a view configuration does not narrow the circumstances in which the view callable will be invoked.

Non-Predicate Arguments

permission The name of a *permission* that the user must possess in order to invoke the *view callable*. See *Configuring View Security* (pp. 135) for more information about view security and permissions.

If `permission` is not supplied, no permission is registered for this view (it's accessible by any caller).

attr The view machinery defaults to using the `__call__` method of the *view callable* (or the function itself, if the view callable is a function) to obtain a response. The `attr` value allows you to vary the method attribute used to obtain the response. For example, if your view was a class, and the class has a method named `index` and you wanted to use this method instead of the class' `__call__` method to return the response, you'd say `attr="index"` in the view configuration for the view. This is most useful when the view definition is a class.

If `attr` is not supplied, `None` is used (implying the function itself if the view is a function, or the `__call__` callable attribute if the view is a class).

renderer This is either a single string term (e.g. `json`) or a string implying a path or *resource specification* (e.g. `templates/views.pt`) naming a *renderer* implementation. If the `renderer` value does not contain a dot `.`, the specified string will be used to look up a renderer implementation, and that renderer implementation will be used to construct a response from the view return value. If the `renderer` value contains a dot (`.`), the specified term will be treated as a path, and the filename extension of the last element in the path will be used to look up the renderer implementation, which will be passed the full path. The renderer implementation will be used to construct a *response* from the view return value.

When the renderer is a path, although a path is usually just a simple relative pathname (e.g. `templates/foo.pt`, implying that a template named "foo.pt" is in the "templates" directory relative to the directory of the current *package*), a path can be absolute, starting with a slash on UNIX or a drive letter prefix on Windows. The path can alternately be a *resource specification* in the form `some.dotted.package_name:relative/path`, making it possible to address template resources which live in a separate package.

The `renderer` attribute is optional. If it is not defined, the "null" renderer is assumed (no rendering is performed and the value is passed back to the upstream `repoze.bfg` machinery unmolested). Note that if the view callable itself returns a *response* (see *View Callable Responses* (pp. 108)), the specified renderer implementation is never called.

wrapper The *view name* of a different *view configuration* which will receive the response body of this view as the `request.wrapped_body` attribute of its own *request*, and the *response* returned by this view as the `request.wrapped_response` attribute of its own request. Using a wrapper makes it possible to "chain" views together to form a composite response. The response of the outermost wrapper view will be returned to the user. The wrapper view will be found as any view is found: see *View Lookup and Invocation* (pp. 135). The "best" wrapper view will be found based on the lookup ordering: "under the hood" this wrapper view is looked up via `view.render_view_to_response(context, request, 'wrapper_viewname')`. The context and request of a wrapper view is the same context and request of the inner view.

If `wrapper` is not supplied, no wrapper view is used.

Predicate Arguments

name The *view name* required to match this view callable. Read *Traversal* (pp. 61) to understand the concept of a view name.

If name is not supplied, the empty string is used (implying the default view).

context An object representing Python class that the *context* must be an instance of, *or* the *interface* that the *context* must provide in order for this view to be found and called. This predicate is true when the *context* is an instance of the represented class or if the *context* provides the represented interface; it is otherwise false.

If context is not supplied, the value None, which matches any model, is used.

route_name If route_name is supplied, the view callable will be invoked only when the named route has matched.

This value must match the name of a *route configuration* declaration (see *URL Dispatch* (pp. 73)) that must match before this view will be called. Note that the route configuration referred to by route_name usually has a *traverse token in the value of its path, representing a part of the path that will be used by *traversal* against the result of the route's *root factory*.

If route_name is not supplied, the view callable will be have a chance of being invoked for when the *triad* includes a request object that does not indicate it matched a route.

request_type This value should be an *interface* that the *request* must provide in order for this view to be found and called.

If request_type is not supplied, the value None is used, implying any request type.

This is an advanced feature, not often used by "civilians".

request_method This value can either be one of the strings GET, POST, PUT, DELETE, or HEAD representing an HTTP REQUEST_METHOD. A view declaration with this argument ensures that the view will only be called when the request's method attribute (aka the REQUEST_METHOD of the WSGI environment) string matches the supplied value.

If request_method is not supplied, the view will be invoked regardless of the REQUEST_METHOD of the *WSGI* environment.

request_param This value can be any string. A view declaration with this argument ensures that the view will only be called when the *request* has a key in the `request.params` dictionary (an HTTP `GET` or `POST` variable) that has a name which matches the supplied value.

If the value supplied has a = sign in it, e.g. `request_params="foo=123"`, then the key (`foo`) must both exist in the `request.params` dictionary, *and* the value must match the right hand side of the expression (`123`) for the view to "match" the current request.

If `request_param` is not supplied, the view will be invoked without consideration of keys and values in the `request.params` dictionary.

containment This value should be a reference to a Python class or term:*interface* that a parent object in the *lineage* must provide in order for this view to be found and called. The nodes in your object graph must be "location-aware" to use this feature.

If `containment` is not supplied, the interfaces and classes in the lineage are not considered when deciding whether or not to invoke the view callable.

See *Location-Aware Model Instances* (pp. 165) for more information about location-awareness.

xhr This value should be either `True` or `False`. If this value is specified and is `True`, the *WSGI* environment must possess an `HTTP_X_REQUESTED_WITH` (aka `X-Requested-With`) header that has the value `XMLHttpRequest` for the associated view callable to be found and called. This is useful for detecting AJAX requests issued from jQuery, Prototype and other Javascript libraries.

If `xhr` is not specified, the `HTTP_X_REQUESTED_WITH` HTTP header is not taken into consideration when deciding whether or not to invoke the associated view callable.

accept The value of this argument represents a match query for one or more mimetypes in the `Accept` HTTP request header. If this value is specified, it must be in one of the following forms: a mimetype match token in the form `text/plain`, a wildcard mimetype match token in the form `text/*` or a match-all wildcard mimetype match token in the form `*/*`. If any of the forms matches the `Accept` header of the request, this predicate will be true.

If `accept` is not specified, the `HTTP_ACCEPT` HTTP header is not taken into consideration when deciding whether or not to invoke the associated view callable.

header This value represents an HTTP header name or a header name/value pair.

If `header` is specified, it must be a header name or a `headername:headervalue` pair.

If `header` is specified without a value (a bare header name only, e.g. `If-Modified-Since`), the view will only be invoked if the HTTP header exists with any value in the request.

If `header` is specified, and possesses a name/value pair (e.g. `User-Agent:Mozilla/.*`), the view will only be invoked if the HTTP header exists *and* the HTTP header matches the value requested. When the `headervalue` contains a `:` (colon), it will be considered a name/value pair (e.g. `User-Agent:Mozilla/.*` or `Host:localhost`). The value portion should be a regular expression.

Whether or not the value represents a header name or a header name/value pair, the case of the header name is not significant.

If `header` is not specified, the composition, presence or absence of HTTP headers is not taken into consideration when deciding whether or not to invoke the associated view callable.

path_info This value represents a regular expression pattern that will be tested against the `PATH_INFO` WSGI environment variable to decide whether or not to call the associated view callable. If the regex matches, this predicate will be `True`.

If `path_info` is not specified, the WSGI `PATH_INFO` is not taken into consideration when deciding whether or not to invoke the associated view callable.

custom_predicates If `custom_predicates` is specified, it must be a sequence of references to custom predicate callables. Use custom predicates when no set of predefined predicates do what you need. Custom predicates can be combined with predefined predicates as necessary. Each custom predicate callable should accept two arguments: `context` and `request` and should return either `True` or `False` after doing arbitrary evaluation of the context and/or the request. If all callables return `True`, the associated view callable will be considered viable for a given request.

If `custom_predicates` is not specified, no custom predicates are used.

> This feature is new as of `repoze.bfg` 1.2.

10.2.2 View Configuration Via ZCML

You may associate a view with a URL by adding *view* (pp. 479) declarations via *ZCML* in a `configure.zcml` file. An example of a view declaration in ZCML is as follows:

```
<view
    context=".models.Hello"
    view=".views.hello_world"
    name="hello.html"
    />
```

The above maps the `.views.hello_world` view callable function to the following set of *context finding* results:

- A *context* object which is an instance (or subclass) of the Python class represented by `.models.Hello`

- A *view name* equalling `hello.html`.

Values prefixed with a period (.) for the `context` and `view` attributes of a `view` declaration (such as those above) mean "relative to the Python package directory in which this *ZCML* file is stored". So if the above `view` declaration was made inside a `configure.zcml` file that lived in the `hello` package, you could replace the relative `.models.Hello` with the absolute `hello.models.Hello`; likewise you could replace the relative `.views.hello_world` with the absolute `hello.views.hello_world`. Either the relative or absolute form is functionally equivalent. It's often useful to use the relative form, in case your package's name changes. It's also shorter to type.

You can also declare a *default view callable* for a *model* type:

```
<view
    context=".models.Hello"
    view=".views.hello_world"
    />
```

A *default view callable* simply has no `name` attribute. For the above registration, when a *context* is found that is of the type `.models.Hello` and there is no *view name* associated with the result of *context finding*, the *default view callable* will be used. In this case, it's the view at `.views.hello_world`.

A default view callable can alternately be defined by using the empty string as its `name` attribute:

```
<view
    context=".models.Hello"
    view=".views.hello_world"
    name=""
    />
```

You may also declare that a view callable is good for any context type by using the special * character as the value of the `context` attribute:

```
1  <view
2      context="*"
3      view=".views.hello_world"
4      name="hello.html"
5      />
```

This indicates that when `repoze.bfg` identifies that the *view name* is `hello.html` and the context is of any type, the `.views.hello_world` view callable will be invoked.

A ZCML `view` declaration's `view` attribute can also name a class. In this case, the rules described in *Defining a View Callable as a Class* (pp. 106) apply for the class which is named.

See *view* (pp. 479) for complete ZCML directive documentation.

10.2.3 View Configuration Using the `@bfg_view` Decorator

For better locality of reference, you may use the `view.bfg_view` (pp. 428) decorator to associate your view functions with URLs instead of using *ZCML* or imperative configuration for the same purpose.

> ⚠ Using this feature tends to slows down application startup slightly, as more work is performed at application startup to scan for view declarations. Additionally, if you use decorators, it means that other people will not be able to override your view declarations externally using ZCML: this is a common requirement if you're developing an extensible application (e.g. a framework). See *Extending An Existing repoze.bfg Application* (pp. 207) for more information about building extensible applications.

Usage of the `bfg_view` decorator is a form of *declarative configuration*, like ZCML, but in decorator form. `view.bfg_view` (pp. 428) can be used to associate *view configuration* information – as done via the equivalent ZCML – with a function that acts as a `repoze.bfg` view callable. All ZCML *view* (pp. 479) attributes (save for the `view` attribute) are available in decorator form and mean precisely the same thing.

An example of the `view.bfg_view` (pp. 428) decorator might reside in a `repoze.bfg` application module `views.py`:

```
1  from models import MyModel
2  from repoze.bfg.view import bfg_view
3  from repoze.bfg.chameleon_zpt import render_template_to_response
4
5  @bfg_view(name='my_view', request_method='POST', context=MyModel,
6            permission='read', renderer='templates/my.pt')
7  def my_view(request):
8      return {'a':1}
```

Using this decorator as above replaces the need to add this ZCML to your application registry:

```
1  <view
2   context=".models.MyModel"
3   view=".views.my_view"
4   name="my_view"
5   permission="read"
6   request_method="POST"
7   renderer="templates/my.pt"
8   />
```

Or replaces the need to add this imperative configuration stanza:

```
config.add_view(name='my_view', request_method='POST', context=MyModel,
                permission='read')
```

All arguments to bfg_view may be omitted. For example:

```
1  from webob import Response
2  from repoze.bfg.view import bfg_view
3
4  @bfg_view()
5  def my_view(request):
6      """ My view """
7      return Response()
```

Such a registration as the one directly above implies that the view name will be my_view, registered with a context argument that matches any model type, using no permission, registered against requests with any request method / request type / request param / route name / containment.

129

The mere existence of a @bfg_view decorator doesn't suffice to perform view configuration. To make repoze.bfg process your view.bfg_view (pp. 428) declarations, you *must* do one of the following:

- If you are using *ZCML*, insert the following boilerplate into your application's configure.zcml:

```
<scan package="."/>
```

- If you are using *imperative configuration*, use the scan method of a configuration.Configurator (pp. 367):

```
# config is assumed to be an instance of the
# repoze.bfg.configuration.Configurator class
config.scan()
```

Please see *Configuration Decorations and Code Scanning* (pp. 19) for detailed information about what happens when code is scanned for configuration declarations resulting from use of decorators like view.bfg_view (pp. 428).

See *repoze.bfg.configuration* (pp. 367) for additional API arguments to the configuration.Configurator.scan() (pp. 378) method. For example, the method allows you to supply a package argument to better control exactly *which* code will be scanned. This is the same value implied by the package attribute of the ZCML <scan> directive (see *scan* (pp. 471)).

@bfg_view Placement

A view.bfg_view (pp. 428) decorator can be placed in various points in your application.

If your view callable is a function, it may be used as a function decorator:

```
from repoze.bfg.view import bfg_view
from webob import Response

@bfg_view(name='edit')
def edit(request):
    return Response('edited!')
```

If your view callable is a class, the decorator can also be used as a class decorator in Python 2.6 and better (Python 2.5 and below do not support class decorators). All the arguments to the decorator are the same when applied against a class as when they are applied against a function. For example:

```python
from webob import Response
from repoze.bfg.view import bfg_view

@bfg_view()
class MyView(object):
    def __init__(self, request):
        self.request = request

    def __call__(self):
        return Response('hello')
```

You can use the `view.bfg_view` (pp. 428) decorator as a simple callable to manually decorate classes in Python 2.5 and below without the decorator syntactic sugar, if you wish:

```python
from webob import Response
from repoze.bfg.view import bfg_view

class MyView(object):
    def __init__(self, request):
        self.request = request

    def __call__(self):
        return Response('hello')

my_view = bfg_view()(MyView)
```

More than one `view.bfg_view` (pp. 428) decorator can be stacked on top of any number of others. Each decorator creates a separate view registration. For example:

```python
from repoze.bfg.view import bfg_view
from webob import Response

@bfg_view(name='edit')
@bfg_view(name='change')
def edit(request):
    return Response('edited!')
```

This registers the same view under two different names.

> ⓘ `view.bfg_view` (pp. 428) decorator stacking is a feature new in `repoze.bfg` 1.1. Previously, these decorators could not be stacked without the effect of the "upper" decorator cancelling the effect of the decorator "beneath" it.

The decorator can also be used against class methods:

```python
from webob import Response
from repoze.bfg.view import bfg_view

class MyView(object):
    def __init__(self, request):
        self.request = request

    @bfg_view(name='hello')
    def amethod(self):
        return Response('hello')
```

When the decorator is used against a class method, a view is registered for the *class*, so the class constructor must accept an argument list in one of two forms: either it must accept a single argument `request` or it must accept two arguments, `context, request` as per *Request-And-Context View Callable Definitions* (pp. 107).

The method which is decorated must return a *response* or it must rely on a *renderer* to generate one.

Using the decorator against a particular method of a class is equivalent to using the `attr` parameter in a decorator attached to the class itself. For example, the above registration implied by the decorator being used against the `amethod` method could be spelled equivalently as the below:

```python
from webob import Response
from repoze.bfg.view import bfg_view

@bfg_view(attr='amethod', name='hello')
class MyView(object):
    def __init__(self, request):
        self.request = request

    def amethod(self):
        return Response('hello')
```

> ⓘ The ability to use the `view.bfg_view` (pp. 428) decorator as a method decorator is new in `repoze.bfg` version 1.1. Previously it could only be used as a class or function decorator.

10.2.4 View Configuration Using the `add_view` Method of a Configurator

The `configuration.Configurator.add_view()` (pp. 374) method within *repoze.bfg.configuration* (pp. 367) is used to configure a view imperatively. The arguments to this method are very similar to the arguments that you provide to the `@bfg_view` decorator. For example:

```
from webob import Response

def hello_world(request):
    return Response('hello!')

# config is assumed to be an instance of the
# repoze.bfg.configuration.Configurator class
config.add_view(hello_world, name='hello.html')
```

10.2.5 Using Model Interfaces In View Configuration

Instead of registering your views with a `context` that names a Python model *class*, you can optionally register a view callable with a `context` which is an *interface*. An interface can be attached arbitrarily to any model instance. View lookup treats context interfaces specially, and therefore the identity of a model can be divorced from that of the class which implements it. As a result, associating a view with an interface can provide more flexibility for sharing a single view between two or more different implementations of a model type. For example, if two model object instances of different Python class types share the same interface, you can use the same view against each of them.

In order to make use of interfaces in your application during view dispatch, you must create an interface and mark up your model classes or instances with interface declarations that refer to this interface.

To attach an interface to a model *class*, you define the interface and use the `zope.interface.implements()` function to associate the interface with the class.

```
1  from zope.interface import Interface
2  from zope.interface import implements
3
4  class IHello(Interface):
5      """ A marker interface """
6
7  class Hello(object):
8      implements(IHello)
```

To attach an interface to a model *instance*, you define the interface and use the
zope.interface.alsoProvides() function to associate the interface with the instance.
This function mutates the instance in such a way that the interface is attached to it.

```
1  from zope.interface import Interface
2  from zope.interface import alsoProvides
3
4  class IHello(Interface):
5      """ A marker interface """
6
7  class Hello(object):
8      pass
9
10 def make_hello():
11     hello = Hello()
12     alsoProvides(hello, IHello)
13     return hello
```

Regardless of how you associate an interface with a model instance or a model class, the resulting ZCML
to associate that interface with a view callable is the same. Assuming the above code that defines an
IHello interface lives in the root of your application, and its module is named "models.py", the below
interface declaration will associate the .views.hello_world view with models that implement (aka
provide) this interface.

```
1  <view
2      context=".models.IHello"
3      view=".views.hello_world"
4      name="hello.html"
5      />
```

Any time a model that is determined to be the *context* provides this interface, and a view named `hello.html` is looked up against it as per the URL, the `.views.hello_world` view callable will be invoked.

Note that views registered against a model class take precedence over views registered for any interface the model class implements when an ambiguity arises. If a view is registered for both the class type of the context and an interface implemented by the context's class, the view registered for the context's class will "win".

For more information about defining models with interfaces for use within view configuration, see *Model Instances Which Implement Interfaces* (pp. 162).

10.2.6 Configuring View Security

If a *authorization policy* is active, any *permission* attached to a *view configuration* found during view lookup will be consulted to ensure that the currently authenticated user possesses that permission against the *context* before the view function is actually called. Here's an example of specifying a permission in a view configuration declaration in ZCML:

```
1  <view
2      context=".models.IBlog"
3      view=".views.add_entry"
4      name="add.html"
5      permission="add"
6      />
```

When an authentication policy is enabled, this view will be protected with the `add` permission. The view will *not be called* if the user does not possess the `add` permission relative to the current *context* and an authorization policy is enabled. Instead the *forbidden view* result will be returned to the client as per *Protecting Views with Permissions* (pp. 170).

10.3 View Lookup and Invocation

View lookup is the `repoze.bfg` subsystem responsible for finding an invoking a *view callable*. The view lookup subsystem is passed a *context*, a *view name*, and the *request* object. These three bits of information are referred to within this chapter as a *triad*.

View configuration information stored within in the *application registry* is compared against a triad by the view lookup subsystem in order to find the "best" view callable for the set of circumstances implied by the triad.

Predicate attributes of view configuration can be thought of like "narrowers". In general, the greater number of predicate attributes possessed by a view's configuration, the more specific the circumstances need to be before the registered view callable will be invoked.

For any given request, a view with five predicates will always be found and evaluated before a view with two, for example. All predicates must match for the associated view to be called.

This does not mean however, that `repoze.bfg` "stops looking" when it finds a view registration with predicates that don't match. If one set of view predicates does not match, the "next most specific" view (if any) view is consulted for predicates, and so on, until a view is found, or no view can be matched up with the request. The first view with a set of predicates all of which match the request environment will be invoked.

If no view can be found which has predicates which allow it to be matched up with the request, `repoze.bfg` will return an error to the user's browser, representing a "not found" (404) page. See *Changing the Not Found View* (pp. 201) for more information about changing the default notfound view.

10.3.1 `NotFound` **Errors**

It's useful to be able to debug `NotFound` error responses when they occur unexpectedly due to an application registry misconfiguration. To debug these errors, use the `BFG_DEBUG_NOTFOUND` environment variable or the `debug_notfound` configuration file setting. Details of why a view was not found will be printed to `stderr`, and the browser representation of the error will include the same information. See *Environment Variables and .ini File Settings* (pp. 189) for more information about how and where to set these values.

STATIC RESOURCES

repoze.bfg makes it possible to serve up "static" (non-dynamic) resources from a directory on a filesystem. This chapter describes how to configure repoze.bfg to do so.

11.1 Serving Static Resources Using a ZCML Directive

Use of the static ZCML directive or the configuration.configurator.add_static_view() method is the preferred way to instruct repoze.bfg to serve static resources such as JavaScript and CSS files. These mechanisms makes static files available at a name relative to the application root URL, e.g. /static.

Here's an example of a static ZCML directive that will serve files up /static URL from the /var/www/static directory of the computer which runs the repoze.bfg application.

```
<static
    name="static"
    path="/var/www/static"
    />
```

Here's an example of a static directive that will serve files up /static URL from the a/b/c/static directory of the Python package named some_package.

```
1  <static
2      name="static"
3      path="some_package:a/b/c/static"
4      />
```

Here's an example of a `static` directive that will serve files up under the `/static` URL from the `static` directory of the Python package in which the `configure.zcml` file lives.

```
1  <static
2      name="static"
3      path="static"
4      />
```

When you place your static files on filesystem in the directory represented as the `path` of the directive you, you should be able to view the static files in this directory via a browser at URLs prefixed with the directive's name. For instance if the `static` directive's name is `static` and the static directive's path is `/path/to/static`, `http://localhost:6543/static/foo.js` will return the file `/path/to/static/dir/foo.js`. The static directory may contain subdirectories recursively, and any subdirectories may hold files; these will be resolved by the static view as you would expect.

See *static* (pp. 473) for detailed information about the `static` ZCML directive.

> ⓘ The *static* (pp. 473) ZCML directive is new in `repoze.bfg` 1.1.

The `configuration.Configurator.add_static_view()` (pp. 373) method offers an imperative equivalent to the `static` ZCML directive. Use of the `add_static_view` imperative configuration method is completely equivalent to using ZCML for the same purpose.

11.1.1 Generating Static Resource URLs

When a *static* (pp. 473) ZCML directive or a call to the `add_static_view` method of a `configuration.Configurator` (pp. 367) is used to register a static resource directory, a special helper API named `static_url()` can be used to generate the appropriate URL for a package resource that lives in one of the directories named by the static registration `path` attribute.

For example, let's assume you create a set of `static` declarations in ZCML like so:

```
1  <static
2     name="static1"
3     path="resources/1"
4     />
5
6  <static
7     name="static2"
8     path="resources/2"
9     />
```

These declarations create URL-accessible directories which have URLs which begin, respectively, with `/static1` and `/static2`. The resources in the `resources/1` directory are consulted when a user visits a URL which begins with `/static1`, and the resources in the `resources/2` directory are consulted when a user visits a URL which begins with `/static2`.

You needn't generate the URLs to static resources "by hand" in such a configuration. Instead, use the `url.static_url()` (pp. 424) API to generate them for you. For example, let's imagine that the following code lives in a module that shares the same directory as the above ZCML file:

```
1  from repoze.bfg.url import static_url
2  from repoze.bfg.chameleon_zpt import render_template_to_response
3
4  def my_view(request):
5      css_url = static_url('resources/1/foo.css', request)
6      js_url = static_url('resources/2/foo.js', request)
7      return render_template_to_response('templates/my_template.pt',
8                                         css_url = css_url,
9                                         js_url = js_url)
```

If the request "application URL" of the running system is `http://example.com`, the `css_url` generated above would be: `http://example.com/static1/foo.css`. The `js_url` generated above would be `http://example.com/static2/foo.js`.

One benefit of using the `url.static_url()` (pp. 424) function rather than constructing static URLs "by hand" is that if you need to change the `name` of a static URL declaration in ZCML, the generated URLs will continue to resolve properly after the rename.

The `url.static_url()` (pp. 424) API is new in `repoze.bfg` 1.1.

11.2 Advanced: Serving Static Resources Using a View Callable

For more flexibility, static resources can be served by a *view callable* which you register manually. For example, you may want static resources to only be available when the *context* of the view is of a particular type, or when the request is of a particular type.

The `view.static` (pp. 433) helper class is used to perform this task. This class creates an object that is capable acting as a `repoze.bfg` view callable which serves static resources from a directory. For instance, to serve files within a directory located on your filesystem at `/path/to/static/dir` mounted at the URL path `/static` in your application, create an instance of the `view.static` (pp. 433) class inside a `static.py` file in your application root as below.

```
from repoze.bfg.view import static
static_view = static('/path/to/static/dir')
```

> the argument to `view.static` (pp. 433) can also be a relative pathname, e.g. `my/static` (meaning relative to the Python package of the module in which the view is being defined). It can also be a *resource specification* (e.g. `anotherpackage:some/subdirectory`) or it can be a "here-relative" path (e.g. `some/subdirectory`). If the path is "here-relative", it is relative to the package of the module in which the static view is defined.

Subsequently, you may wire this view up to be accessible as `/static` using either the `configuration.Configurator.add_view` method or the `<view>` ZCML directive in your application's `configure.zcml` against either the class or interface that represents your root object. For example (ZCML):

```
<view
    context=".models.Root"
    view=".static.static_view"
    name="static"
/>
```

In this case, `.models.Root` refers to the class of which your `repoze.bfg` application's root object is an instance.

You can also provide a `context` of `*` if you want the name `static` to be accessible as the static view against any model. This will also allow `/static/foo.js` to work, but it will allow for `/anything/static/foo.js` too, as long as `anything` itself is resolvable.

Note that you cannot use the `static_url()` API to generate URLs against resources made accessible by registering a custom static view.

> ⚠ To ensure that model objects contained in the root don't "shadow" your static view (model objects take precedence during traversal), or to ensure that your root object's `__getitem__` is never called when a static resource is requested, you can refer to your static resources as registered above in URLs as, e.g. `/@@static/foo.js`. This is completely equivalent to `/static/foo.js`. See *Traversal* (pp. 61) for information about "goggles" (`@@`).

REQUEST AND RESPONSE OBJECTS

> ⓘ This chapter is adapted from a portion of the *WebOb* documentation, originally written by Ian Bicking.

`repoze.bfg` uses the *WebOb* package to supply *request* and *response* object implementations. The *request* object that is passed to a `repoze.bfg` *view* is an instance of the `Request` class, which is a subclass of `webob.Request`. The *response* returned from a `repoze.bfg` *view renderer* is an instance of the `webob.Response` class. Users can also return an instance of `webob.Response` directly from a view as necessary.

WebOb is a project separate from `repoze.bfg` with a separate set of authors and a fully separate set of documentation (http://pythonpaste.org/webob/).

> ⚠ The following information is only an overview of the request and response objects provided by *WebOb*. See the reference documentation (http://pythonpaste.org/webob/reference.html) for more detailed API reference information. All methods in the *WebOb* documentation work against `repoze.bfg` requests and responses.

WebOb provides objects for HTTP requests and responses. Specifically it does this by wrapping the WSGI (http://wsgi.org) request environment and response status/headers/app_iter(body).

The request and response objects provide many conveniences for parsing HTTP request and forming HTTP responses. Both objects are read/write: as a result, WebOb is also a nice way to create HTTP requests and parse HTTP responses; however, we won't cover that use case in this document. The reference documentation (http://pythonpaste.org/webob/reference.html) shows many examples of creating requests.

12.1 Request

The request object is a wrapper around the WSGI environ dictionary (http://www.python.org/dev/peps/pep-0333/#environ-variables). This dictionary contains keys for each header, keys that describe the request (including the path and query string), a file-like object for the request body, and a variety of custom keys. You can always access the environ with `req.environ`.

Some of the most important/interesting attributes of a request object:

req.method: The request method, e.g., `'GET'`, `'POST'`

req.GET: A *multidict* with all the variables in the query string.

req.POST: A *multidict* with all the variables in the request body. This only has variables if the request was a `POST` and it is a form submission.

req.params: A *multidict* with a combination of everything in `req.GET` and `req.POST`.

req.body: The contents of the body of the request. This contains the entire request body as a string. This is useful when the request is a `POST` that is *not* a form submission, or a request like a `PUT`. You can also get `req.body_file` for a file-like object.

req.cookies: A simple dictionary of all the cookies.

req.headers: A dictionary of all the headers. This is dictionary is case-insensitive.

req.urlvars and req.urlargs: `req.urlvars` is the keyword parameters associated with the request URL. `req.urlargs` are the positional parameters. These are set by products like Routes (http://routes.groovie.org/) and Selector (http://lukearno.com/projects/selector/).

Also, for standard HTTP request headers there are usually attributes, for instance: `req.accept_language`, `req.content_length`, `req.user_agent`, as an example. These properties expose the *parsed* form of each header, for whatever parsing makes sense. For instance, `req.if_modified_since` returns a datetime (http://python.org/doc/current/lib/datetime-datetime.html) object (or None if the header is was not provided). Details are in the Request reference (http://pythonpaste.org/webob/class-webob.Request.html).

12.1.1 Special Attributes Added to the Request by `repoze.bfg`

In addition to the standard *WebOb* attributes, `repoze.bfg` adds the following special attributes to every request.

req.context The *context* will be available as the `context` attribute of the *request* object. It will be the context object implied by the current request. See *Traversal* (pp. 61) for information about context objects.

req.registry The *application registry* will be available as the `registry` attribute of the *request* object. See *Using the Zope Component Architecture in repoze.bfg* (pp. 231) for more information about the application registry.

req.root The *root* object will be available as the `root` attribute of the *request* object. It will be the model object at which traversal started (the root). See *Traversal* (pp. 61) for information about root objects.

req.subpath The traversal *subpath* will be available as the `subpath` attribute of the *request* object. It will be a sequence containing zero or more elements (which will be Unicode objects). See *Traversal* (pp. 61) for information about the subpath.

req.traversed The "traversal path" will be as the `traversed` attribute of the *request* object. It will be a sequence representing the ordered set of names that were used to traverse to the *context*, not including the view name or subpath. If there is a virtual root associated with request, the virtual root path is included within the traversal path. See *Traversal* (pp. 61) for more information.

req.view_name The *view name* will be available as the `view_name` attribute of the *request* object. It will be a single string (possibly the empty string if we're rendering a default view). See *Traversal* (pp. 61) for information about view names.

req.virtual_root The *virtual root* will be available as the `virtual_root` attribute of the *request* object. It will be the virtual root object implied by the current request. See *Virtual Hosting* (pp. 181) for more information about virtual roots.

req.virtual_root_path The *virtual root path* will be available as the `virtual_root_path` attribute of the *request* object. It will be a sequence representing the ordered set of names that were used to traverse to the virtual root object. See *Virtual Hosting* (pp. 181) for more information about virtual roots.

12.1.2 URLs

In addition to these attributes, there are several ways to get the URL of the request. I'll show various values for an example URL `http://localhost/app/?id=10`, where the application is mounted at `http://localhost/app`.

req.url: The full request URL, with query string, e.g., `http://localhost/app/?id=10`

req.application_url: The URL of the application (just the SCRIPT_NAME portion of the path, not PATH_INFO). E.g., `http://localhost/app`

req.host_url: The URL with the host, e.g., `http://localhost`

req.relative_url(url, to_application=False): Gives a URL, relative to the current URL. If `to_application` is True, then resolves it relative to `req.application_url`.

12.1.3 Methods

There are several methods (http://pythonpaste.org/webob/class-webob.Request.html#__init__) but only a few you'll use often:

Request.blank(base_url): Creates a new request with blank information, based at the given URL. This can be useful for subrequests and artificial requests. You can also use `req.copy()` to copy an existing request, or for subrequests `req.copy_get()` which copies the request but always turns it into a GET (which is safer to share for subrequests).

req.get_response(wsgi_application): This method calls the given WSGI application with this request, and returns a Response object. You can also use this for subrequests or testing.

12.1.4 Unicode

Many of the properties in the request object will return unicode values if the request encoding/charset is provided. The client *can* indicate the charset with something like `Content-Type: application/x-www-form-urlencoded; charset=utf8`, but browsers seldom set this. You can set the charset with `req.charset = 'utf8'`, or during instantiation with `Request(environ, charset='utf8')`. If you subclass `Request` you can also set `charset` as a class-level attribute.

If it is set, then `req.POST`, `req.GET`, `req.params`, and `req.cookies` will contain unicode strings. Each has a corresponding `req.str_*` (like `req.str_POST`) that is always `str` and never unicode.

146

12.2 Response

The response object looks a lot like the request object, though with some differences. The request object wraps a single `environ` object; the response object has three fundamental parts (based on WSGI):

response.status: The response code plus message, like `'200 OK'`. To set the code without the reason, use `response.status_int = 200`.

response.headerlist: A list of all the headers, like `[('Content-Type', 'text/html')]`. There's a case-insensitive *multidict* in `response.headers` that also allows you to access these same headers.

response.app_iter: An iterable (such as a list or generator) that will produce the content of the response. This is also accessible as `response.body` (a string), `response.unicode_body` (a unicode object, informed by `response.charset`), and `response.body_file` (a file-like object; writing to it appends to `app_iter`).

Everything else in the object derives from this underlying state. Here's the highlights:

response.content_type: The content type *not* including the `charset` parameter. Typical use: `response.content_type = 'text/html'`. You can subclass `Response` and add a class-level attribute `default_content_type` to set this automatically on instantiation.

response.charset: The `charset` parameter of the content-type, it also informs encoding in `response.unicode_body`. `response.content_type_params` is a dictionary of all the parameters.

response.request: This optional attribute can point to the request object associated with this response object.

response.set_cookie(key, value, max_age=None, path='/', ...): Set a cookie. The keyword arguments control the various cookie parameters. The `max_age` argument is the length for the cookie to live in seconds (you may also use a timedelta object). The `Expires` key will also be set based on the value of `max_age`.

response.delete_cookie(key, path='/', domain=None): Delete a cookie from the client. This sets `max_age` to 0 and the cookie value to ''.

response.cache_expires(seconds=0): This makes this response cacheable for the given number of seconds, or if `seconds` is 0 then the response is uncacheable (this also sets the `Expires` header).

response(environ, start_response): The response object is a WSGI application. As an application, it acts according to how you create it. It *can* do conditional responses if you pass `conditional_response=True` when instantiating (or set that attribute later). It can also do HEAD and Range requests.

12.2.1 Headers

Like the request, most HTTP response headers are available as properties. These are parsed, so you can do things like `response.last_modified = os.path.getmtime(filename)`.

The details are available in the extracted Response documentation (http://pythonpaste.org/webob/class-webob.Response.html).

12.2.2 Instantiating the Response

Of course most of the time you just want to *make* a response. Generally any attribute of the response can be passed in as a keyword argument to the class; e.g.:

```
from webob import Response

response = Response(body='hello world!', content_type='text/plain')
```

The status defaults to `'200 OK'`. The content_type does not default to anything, though if you subclass `Response` and set `default_content_type` you can override this behavior.

12.2.3 Exceptions

To facilitate error responses like 404 Not Found, the module `webob.exc` contains classes for each kind of error response. These include boring but appropriate error bodies.

Each class is named `webob.exc.HTTP*`, where `*` is the reason for the error. For instance, `webob.exc.HTTPNotFound`. It subclasses `Response`, so you can manipulate the instances in the same way. A typical example is:

```
from webob.exc import HTTPNotFound
from webob.exc import HTTPMovedPermanently

response = HTTPNotFound('There is no such resource')
# or:
response = HTTPMovedPermanently(location=new_url)
```

These are not exceptions unless you are using Python 2.5+, because they are new-style classes which are not allowed as exceptions until Python 2.5. To get an exception object use `response.exception`. You can use this like:

```
1  from webob.exc import HTTPException
2  from webob.exc import HTTPNotFound
3
4  def aview(request):
5      try:
6          # ... stuff ...
7          raise HTTPNotFound('No such resource').exception
8      except HTTPException, e:
9          return request.get_response(e)
```

The exceptions are still WSGI applications, but you cannot set attributes like content_type, charset, etc. on these exception objects.

12.3 Multidict

Several parts of WebOb use a "multidict"; this is a dictionary where a key can have multiple values. The quintessential example is a query string like ?pref=red&pref=blue; the pref variable has two values: red and blue.

In a multidict, when you do request.GET['pref'] you'll get back only 'blue' (the last value of pref). Sometimes returning a string, and sometimes returning a list, is the cause of frequent exceptions. If you want *all* the values back, use request.GET.getall('pref'). If you want to be sure there is *one and only one* value, use request.GET.getone('pref'), which will raise an exception if there is zero or more than one value for pref.

When you use operations like request.GET.items() you'll get back something like [('pref', 'red'), ('pref', 'blue')]. All the key/value pairs will show up. Similarly request.GET.keys() returns ['pref', 'pref']. Multidict is a view on a list of tuples; all the keys are ordered, and all the values are ordered.

TEMPLATES

A *template* is a file on disk which can be used to render dynamic data provided by a *view*. `repoze.bfg` offers a number of ways to perform templating tasks out of the box, and provides add-on templating support through a set of bindings packages.

Out of the box, `repoze.bfg` provides templating via the *Chameleon* templating library. *Chameleon* provides support for two different types of templates: *ZPT* templates and text templates.

Before discussing how built-in templates are templates are used in detail, we'll discuss two ways to render templates within `repoze.bfg` in general: directly, and via renderer configuration.

13.1 Templates Used Directly

The most straightforward way to use a template within `repoze.bfg` is to cause it to be rendered directly within a *view callable*. You may use whatever API is supplied by a given templating engine to do so.

`repoze.bfg` provides various APIs that allow you to render *Chameleon* templates directly from within a view callable. For example, if there is a *Chameleon* ZPT template named `foo.pt` in a directory in your application named `templates`, you can render the template from within the body of view callable like so:

```
from repoze.bfg.chameleon_zpt import render_template_to_response

def sample_view(request):
    return render_template_to_response('templates/foo.pt', foo=1, bar=2)
```

The `sample_view` *view callable* above returns a *response* object which contains the body of the `template/foo.pt` template. The template author will have the names `foo` and `bar` available as top-level names for replacement or comparison purposes.

Every views must return a *response* object (except for views which use a *renderer*, which we'll see shortly). The `chameleon_zpt.render_template_to_response()` (pp. 365) function is a shortcut function that actually returns a response object, but not all template APIs know about responses. When you use an template API that is "response-ignorant" you can also easily render a template to a string, and construct your own response object as necessary with the string as the body.

For example, the `chameleon_zpt.render_template()` (pp. 365) API returns a string. We can manufacture a *response* object directly, and use that string as the body of the response:

```
from repoze.bfg.chameleon_zpt import render_template
from webob import Response

def sample_view(request):
    result = render_template('templates/foo.pt', foo=1, bar=2)
    response = Response(result)
    return response
```

Because *view callable* functions are typically the only code in `repoze.bfg` that need to know anything about templates, and because view functions are very simple Python, you can use whatever templating system you're most comfortable with within `repoze.bfg`. Install the templating system, import its API functions into your views module, use those APIs to generate a string, then return that string as the body of a *WebOb Response* object.

For example, here's an example of using Mako (http://www.makotemplates.org/) from within a `repoze.bfg` *view*:

```
from mako.template import Template
from webob import Response

def make_view(request):
    template = Template(filename='/templates/template.mak')
    result = template.render(name=request.params['name'])
    response = Response(result)
    return response
```

> ℹ️ If you use third-party templating languages without cooperating BFG bindings directly within view callables, the auto-template-reload strategy explained in *Automatically Reloading Templates* (pp. 159) will not be available, nor will the template resource overriding capability explained in *Overriding Resources* (pp. 214) be available, nor will it be possible to use any template using that language as a *renderer*. However, it's reasonably easy to write custom templating system binding packages for use under `repoze.bfg` so that templates written in the language can be used as renderers. See *Adding and Overriding Renderers* (pp. 114) for instructions on how to create your own template renderer and *Available Add-On Template System Bindings* (pp. 160) for example packages.

If you need more control over the status code and content-type, or other response attributes from views that use direct templating, you may set attributes on the response that influence these values.

Here's an example of changing the content-type and status of the response object returned by `chameleon_zpt.render_template_to_response()` (pp. 365):

```
from repoze.bfg.chameleon_zpt import render_template_to_response

def sample_view(request):
    response = render_template_to_response('templates/foo.pt', foo=1, bar=2)
    response.content_type = 'text/plain'
    response.status_int = 204
    return response
```

Here's an example of manufacturing a response object using the result of `chameleon_zpt.render_template()` (pp. 365) (a string):

```
from repoze.bfg.chameleon_zpt import render_template
from webob import Response
def sample_view(request):
    result = render_template('templates/foo.pt', foo=1, bar=2)
    response = Response(result)
    response.content_type = 'text/plain'
    return response
```

13.2 Templates Used as Renderers

Instead of using templating system APIs within a the body of a view function directly to render a specific template, you may associate a template written in a supported templating language with a view indirectly by specifying it as a *renderer*.

To use a renderer, specify a template *resource specification* as the `renderer` argument or attribute to the *view configuration* of a *view callable*. Then return a *dictionary* from that view callable. The dictionary items returned by the view callable will be made available to the renderer template as top-level names.

The association of a template as a renderer for a *view configuration* makes it possible to replace code within a *view callable* that handles the rendering of a template.

Here's an example of using a `view.bfg_view` (pp. 428) decorator to specify a *view configuration* that names a template renderer:

```
from repoze.bfg.view import bfg_view

@bfg_view(renderer='templates/foo.pt')
def my_view(request):
    return {'foo':1, 'bar':2}
```

The `renderer` argument to the `@bfg_view` configuration decorator shown above is the template *path*. In the example above, the path `templates/foo.pt` is *relative*. Relative to what, you ask? Relative to the directory in which the file which defines the view configuration lives. In this case, this is the directory containing the file that defines the `my_view` function.

Although a renderer path is usually just a simple relative pathname, a path named as a renderer can be absolute, starting with a slash on UNIX or a drive letter prefix on Windows. The path can alternately be a *resource specification* in the form `some.dotted.package_name:relative/path`, making it possible to address template resources which live in another package.

When a template *renderer* is used to render the result of a view callable, several names are passed into the template as top-level names by default, including `context` and `request`. Similar renderer configuration can be done imperatively and via *ZCML*. See *Writing View Callables Which Use a Renderer* (pp. 109). See also *Built-In Renderers* (pp. 110).

Not just any template from any arbitrary templating system may be used as a renderer. Bindings must exist specifically for `repoze.bfg` to use a templating language template as a renderer. Currently, `repoze.bfg` has built-in support for two Chameleon templating languages: ZPT and text. See *Built-In Renderers* (pp. 110) for a discussion of their details. `repoze.bfg` also supports the use of *Jinja2* templates as renderers. See *Available Add-On Template System Bindings* (pp. 160).

Why Use A Renderer

Using a renderer is usually a better way to render templates than using any templating API directly from within a *view callable* because it makes the view callable more unit-testable. Views which use templating APIs directly must return a *Response* object. Making testing assertions about response objects is typically an indirect process, because it means that your test code often needs to somehow needs to parse information out of the response body (often HTML). View callables which use renderers typically return a dictionary, and making assertions about the information is almost always more direct than needing to parse HTML. Specifying a renderer from within *ZCML* (as opposed to imperatively or via a `bfg_view` decorator, or using a template directly from within a view callable) also makes it possible for someone to modify the template used to render a view without needing to fork your code to do so. See *Extending An Existing repoze.bfg Application* (pp. 207) for more information.

By default, views rendered via a template renderer return a *Response* object which has a *status code* of `200 OK` and a *content-type* of `text/html`. To vary attributes of the response of a view that uses a renderer, such as the content-type, headers, or status attributes, you must set attributes on the *request* object within the view before returning the dictionary. See *Varying Attributes of Rendered Responses* (pp. 113) for more information.

13.3 *Chameleon* ZPT Templates

Like *Zope*, `repoze.bfg` uses *ZPT* (Zope Page Templates) as its default templating language. However, `repoze.bfg` uses a different implementation of the *ZPT* specification than Zope does: the *Chameleon* templating engine. The Chameleon engine complies largely with the Zope Page Template (http://wiki.zope.org/ZPT/FrontPage) template specification. However, it is significantly faster.

The language definition documentation for Chameleon ZPT-style templates is available from the Chameleon website (http://chameleon.repoze.org/).

⚠️ *Chameleon* only works on *CPython* platforms and *Google App Engine*. On *Jython* and other non-CPython platforms, you should use `jinja2` instead. See *Available Add-On Template System Bindings* (pp. 160).

Given that there is a *Chameleon* ZPT template named `foo.pt` in a directory in your application named `templates`, you can render the template as a *renderer* like so:

```
1  from repoze.bfg.view import bfg_view
2
3  @bfg_view(renderer='templates/foo.pt')
4  def my_view(request):
5      return {'foo':1, 'bar':2}
```

If you'd rather use templates directly within a view callable (without the indirection of using a renderer), see *repoze.bfg.chameleon_zpt* (pp. 365) for the API description.

See also *Built-In Renderers* (pp. 110) for more general information about renderers, including Chameleon ZPT renderers.

13.3.1 A Sample ZPT Template

Here's what a simple *Chameleon* ZPT template used under `repoze.bfg` might look like:

```
1  <!DOCTYPE html PUBLIC "-//W3C//DTD XHTML 1.0 Strict//EN"
2     "http://www.w3.org/TR/xhtml1/DTD/xhtml1-strict.dtd">
3  <html xmlns="http://www.w3.org/1999/xhtml"
4        xmlns:tal="http://xml.zope.org/namespaces/tal">
5  <head>
6     <meta http-equiv="content-type" content="text/html; charset=utf-8" />
7     <title>${project} Application</title>
8  </head>
9    <body>
10     <h1 class="title">Welcome to <code>${project}</code>, an
11     application generated by the <a
12     href="http://static.repoze.org/bfgdocs">repoze.bfg</a> web
13     application framework.</h1>
14    </body>
15  </html>
```

Note the use of *Genshi* -style `${replacements}` above. This is one of the ways that *Chameleon* ZPT differs from standard ZPT. The above template expects to find a `project` key in the set of keywords passed in to it via `chameleon_zpt.render_template()` (pp. 365) or `render_template_to_response()`. Typical ZPT attribute-based syntax (e.g. `tal:content` and `tal:replace`) also works in these templates.

13.3.2 Using ZPT Macros in `repoze.bfg`

When a *renderer* is used to render a template, `repoze.bfg` makes at least two top-level names available to the template by default: `context` and `request`. One of the common needs in ZPT-based template is to one template's "macros" from within a different template. In Zope, this is typically handled by retrieving the template from the `context`. But having a hold of the context in `repoze.bfg` is not helpful: templates cannot usually be retrieved from models. To use macros in `repoze.bfg`, you need to make the macro template itself available to the rendered template by passing template in which the macro is defined (or even the macro itself) *into* the rendered template. To make a macro available to the rendered template, you can retrieve a different template using the `chameleon_zpt.get_template()` (pp. 365) API, and pass it in to the template being rendered. For example, using a *view configuration* via a `view.bfg_view` (pp. 428) decorator that uses a *renderer*:

```
from repoze.bfg.chameleon_zpt import get_template
from repoze.bfg.view import bfg_view

@bfg_view(renderer='templates/mytemplate.pt')
def my_view(request):
    main = get_template('templates/master.pt')
    return {'main':main}
```

Where `templates/master.pt` might look like so:

```
<html xmlns="http://www.w3.org/1999/xhtml"
      xmlns:tal="http://xml.zope.org/namespaces/tal"
      xmlns:metal="http://xml.zope.org/namespaces/metal">
   <span metal:define-macro="hello">
    <h1>
      Hello <span metal:define-slot="name">Fred</span>!
    </h1>
   </span>
</html>
```

And `templates/mytemplate.pt` might look like so:

```
<html xmlns="http://www.w3.org/1999/xhtml"
      xmlns:tal="http://xml.zope.org/namespaces/tal"
      xmlns:metal="http://xml.zope.org/namespaces/metal">
   <span metal:use-macro="main.macros['hello']">
```

```
5      <span metal:fill-slot="name">Chris</span>
6    </span>
7  </html>
```

13.4 Templating with *Chameleon* Text Templates

`repoze.bfg` also allows for the use of templates which are composed entirely of non-XML text via *Chameleon*. To do so, you can create templates that are entirely composed of text except for `${name}` -style substitution points.

Here's an example usage of a Chameleon text template. Create a file on disk named `mytemplate.txt` in your project's `templates` directory with the following contents:

```
Hello, ${name}!
```

Then in your project's `views.py` module, you can create a view which renders this template:

```
1  from repoze.bfg.chameleon_zpt import get_template
2  from repoze.bfg.view import bfg_view
3
4  @bfg_view(renderer='templates/mytemplate.txt')
5  def my_view(request):
6      return {'name':'world'}
```

When the template is rendered, it will show:

```
Hello, world!
```

If you'd rather use templates directly within a view callable (without the indirection of using a renderer), see *repoze.bfg.chameleon_text* (pp. 363) for the API description.

See also *Built-In Renderers* (pp. 110) for more general information about renderers, including Chameleon text renderers.

13.5 Side Effects of Rendering a Chameleon Template

When a Chameleon template is rendered from a file, the templating engine writes a file in the same directory as the template file itself as a kind of cache, in order to do less work the next time the template needs to be read from disk. If you see "strange" `.py` files showing up in your `templates` directory (or otherwise directly "next" to your templates), it is due to this feature.

If you're using a version control system such as Subversion, you should cause it to ignore these files. Here's the contents of the author's `svn propedit svn:ignore .` in each of my `templates` directories.

```
1  *.pt.py
2  *.txt.py
```

Note that I always name my Chameleon ZPT template files with a `.pt` extension and my Chameleon text template files with a `.txt` extension so that these `svn:ignore` patterns work.

13.6 Automatically Reloading Templates

It's often convenient to see changes you make to a template file appear immediately without needing to restart the application process. `repoze.bfg` allows you configure your application development environment so that a change to a template will be automatically detected, and the template will be reloaded on the next rendering.

> ⚠ auto-template-reload behavior is not recommended for production sites as it slows rendering slightly; it's usually only desirable during development.

In order to turn on automatic reloading of templates, you can use an environment variable setting or a configuration file setting.

To use an environment variable, start your application under a shell using the `BFG_RELOAD_TEMPLATES` operating system environment variable set to 1, For example:

```
$ BFG_RELOAD_TEMPLATES=1 bin/paster serve myproject.ini
```

To use a setting in the application `.ini` file for the same purpose, set the `reload_templates` key to `true` within the application's configuration section, e.g.:

```
[app:main]
use = egg:MyProject#app
reload_templates = true
```

13.7 *Chameleon* Template Internationalization

See the internationalization chapter (http://chameleon.repoze.org/docs/latest/i18n.html) of the Chameleon documentation for information about supporting internationalized units of text within *Chameleon* templates.

13.8 Available Add-On Template System Bindings

Jinja2 template bindings are available for `repoze.bfg` in the `jinja2` package. It lives in the Repoze Subversion repository at http://svn.repoze.org/repoze.bfg.jinja2 (http://svn.repoze.org/repoze.bfg.jinja2); it is also available from *PyPI*.

MODELS

A *model* class is typically a simple Python class defined in a module. References to these classes and instances of such classes are omnipresent in `repoze.bfg`:

- Model instances make up the graph that `repoze.bfg` is willing to walk over when *traversal* is used.

- The `context` and `containment` arguments to `configuration.Configurator.add_view()` (pp. 374) often reference a model class.

- A *root factory* returns a model instance.

- A model instance is generated as a result of *url dispatch* (see the `factory` argument to `configuration.Configurator.add_route()` (pp. 369)).

- A model instance is exposed to *view* code as the *context* of a view.

Model objects typically store data and offer methods related to mutating that data.

A terminology overlap confuses people who write applications that always use ORM packages such as SQLAlchemy, which has a very different notion of the definition of a "model". When using the API of common ORM packages, its conception of "model" is almost certainly not the same conception of "model" used by `repoze.bfg`. In particular, it can be unnatural to think of `repoze.bfg` model objects as "models" if you develop your application using *traversal* and a relational database. When you develop such applications, the object graph *might* be composed completely of "model" objects (as defined by the ORM) but it also might not be. The things that `repoze.bfg` refers to as "models" in such an application may instead just be stand-ins that perform a query and generate some wrapper *for* an ORM "model" or set of ORM models. This naming overlap is slightly unfortunate. However, many `repoze.bfg` applications (especially ones which use *ZODB*) do indeed traverse a graph full of literal model nodes. Each node in the graph is a separate persistent object that is stored within a database. This was the use case considered when coming up with the "model" terminology. However, if we had it to do all over again, we'd probably call these objects something different to avoid confusion.

14.1 Defining a Model Constructor

An example of a model constructor, `BlogEntry` is presented below. It is implemented as a class which, when instantiated, becomes a model instance.

```
import datetime

class BlogEntry(object):
    def __init__(self, title, body, author):
        self.title = title
        self.body =  body
        self.author = author
        self.created = datetime.datetime.now()
```

A model constructor may be essentially any Python object which is callable, and which returns a model instance. In the above example, the `BlogEntry` class can be "called", returning a model instance.

14.2 Model Instances Which Implement Interfaces

Model instances can optionally be made to implement an *interface*. An interface is used to tag a model object with a "type" that can later be referred to within *view configuration*.

Specifying an interface instead of a class as the `context` or `containment` arguments within *view configuration* statements effectively makes it possible to use a single view callable for more than one class of object. If your application is simple enough that you see no reason to want to do this, you can skip reading this section of the chapter.

For example, here's some code which describes a blog entry which also declares that the blog entry implements an *interface*.

```
import datetime
from zope.interface import implements
from zope.interface import Interface

class IBlogEntry(Interface):
    pass

class BlogEntry(object):
```

```
 9        implements(IBlogEntry)
10        def __init__(self, title, body, author):
11            self.title = title
12            self.body =  body
13            self.author = author
14            self.created = datetime.datetime.now()
```

This model consists of two things: the class which defines the model constructor (above as the class `BlogEntry`), and an *interface* attached to the class (via an `implements` statement at class scope using the `IBlogEntry` interface as its sole argument).

The interface object used must be an instance of a class that inherits from `zope.interface.Interface`.

A model class may *implement* zero or more interfaces. You specify that a model implements an interface by using the `zope.interface.implements()` function at class scope. The above `BlogEntry` model implements the `IBlogEntry` interface.

You can also specify that a *particular* model instance provides an interface (as opposed to its class). To do so, use the `zope.interface.directlyProvides()` function:

```
 1  from zope.interface import directlyProvides
 2  from zope.interface import Interface
 3
 4  class IBlogEntry(Interface):
 5      pass
 6
 7  class BlogEntry(object):
 8      def __init__(self, title, body, author):
 9          self.title = title
10          self.body =  body
11          self.author = author
12          self.created = datetime.datetime.now()
13
14  entry = BlogEntry('title', 'body', 'author')
15  directlyProvides(entry, IBlogEntry)
```

`zope.interface.directlyProvides()` will replace any existing interface that was previously provided by an instance. If a model object already has instance-level interface declarations that you don't want to replace, use the `zope.interface.alsoProvides()` function:

```
1  from zope.interface import alsoProvides
2  from zope.interface import directlyProvides
3  from zope.interface import Interface
4
5  class IBlogEntry1(Interface):
6      pass
7
8  class IBlogEntry2(Interface):
9      pass
10
11 class BlogEntry(object):
12     def __init__(self, title, body, author):
13         self.title = title
14         self.body =  body
15         self.author = author
16         self.created = datetime.datetime.now()
17
18 entry = BlogEntry('title', 'body', 'author')
19 directlyProvides(entry, IBlogEntry1)
20 alsoProvides(entry, IBlogEntry2)
```

`zope.interface.alsoProvides()` will augment the set of interfaces directly provided by an instance instead of overwriting them like `zope.interface.directlyProvides()` does.

For more information about how model interfaces can be used by view configuration, see *Using Model Interfaces In View Configuration* (pp. 133).

14.3 Defining a Graph of Model Instances for Traversal

When *traversal* is used (as opposed to a purely *url dispatch* based application), `repoze.bfg` expects to be able to traverse a graph composed of model instances. Traversal begins at a root model, and descends into the graph recursively via each found model's __getitem__ method. `repoze.bfg` imposes the following policy on model instance nodes in the graph:

- Nodes which contain other nodes (aka "container" nodes) must supply a __getitem__ method which is willing to resolve a unicode name to a subobject. If a subobject by that name does not exist in the container, __getitem__ must raise a `KeyError`. If a subobject by that name *does* exist, the container should return the subobject (another model instance).

- Nodes which do not contain other nodes (aka "leaf" nodes) must not implement a __getitem__, or if they do, their __getitem__ method must raise a `KeyError`.

See *Traversal* (pp. 61) for more information about how traversal works against model instances.

14.4 Location-Aware Model Instances

Using `repoze.bfg.traversalwrapper`

If you'd rather not manage the __name__ and __parent__ attributes of your models "by hand", an add on package named `traversalwrapper` can help.

In order to use this helper feature, you must first install the `traversalwrapper` package (available via SVN (http://svn.repoze.org/repoze.bfg.traversalwrapper)), then register its `ModelGraphTraverser` as the traversal policy, rather than the default `repoze.bfg` traverser. The package contains instructions.

Once `repoze.bfg` is configured with this feature, you will no longer need to manage the __parent__ and __name__ attributes on graph objects "by hand". Instead, as necessary, during traversal `repoze.bfg` will wrap each object (even the root object) in a `LocationProxy` which will dynamically assign a __name__ and a __parent__ to the traversed object (based on the last traversed object and the name supplied to __getitem__). The root object will have a __name__ attribute of `None` and a __parent__ attribute of `None`.

Applications which use *traversal* to locate the *context* of a view must ensure that the model instances that make up the model graph are "location aware".

In order for `repoze.bfg` location, security, URL-generation, and traversal functions (such as the functions exposed in *repoze.bfg.location* (pp. 387), *repoze.bfg.traversal* (pp. 413), and *repoze.bfg.url* (pp. 421) as well as certain functions in *repoze.bfg.security* (pp. 395)) to work properly against a instances in an object graph, all nodes in the graph must be *location* -aware. This means they must have two attributes: __parent__ and __name__.

The __parent__ attribute should be a reference to the node's parent model instance in the graph. The __name__ attribute should be the name that a node's parent refers to the node via __getitem__.

The __parent__ of the root object should be `None` and its __name__ should be the empty string. For instance:

```
class MyRootObject(object):
    __name__ = ''
    __parent__ = None
```

A node returned from the root item's __getitem__ method should have a __parent__ attribute that is a reference to the root object, and its __name__ attribute should match the name by which it is are reachable via the root object's __getitem__. *That* object's __getitem__ should return objects that have a __parent__ attribute that points at that object, and __getitem__-returned objects should have a __name__ attribute that matches the name by which they are retrieved via __getitem__, and so on.

> ⚠ If your root model object has a __name__ argument that is not None or the empty string, URLs returned by the url.model_url() (pp. 421) function and paths generated by the traversal.model_path() (pp. 414) and traversal.model_path_tuple() (pp. 415) APIs will be generated improperly. The value of __name__ will be prepended to every path and URL generated (as opposed to a single leading slash or empty tuple element).

14.5 repoze.bfg API Functions That Act Against Models

A model instance is used as the *context* argument provided to a view. See *Traversal* (pp. 61) and *URL Dispatch* (pp. 73) for more information about how a model instance becomes the context.

The APIs provided by *repoze.bfg.traversal* (pp. 413) are used against model instances. These functions can be used to find the "path" of a model, the root model in an object graph, or generate a URL to a model.

The APIs provided by *repoze.bfg.location* (pp. 387) are used against model instances. These can be used to walk down an object graph, or conveniently locate one object "inside" another.

Some APIs in *repoze.bfg.security* (pp. 395) accept a model object as a parameter. For example, the security.has_permission() (pp. 396) API accepts a "context" (a model object) as one of its arguments; the ACL is obtained from this model or one of its ancestors. Other APIs in the security (pp. 395) module also accept *context* as an argument, and a context is always a model.

SECURITY

`repoze.bfg` provides an optional declarative authorization system that prevents a *view* from being invoked when the user represented by credentials in the *request* does not have an appropriate level of access within a particular *context*. Here's how it works at a high level:

- A *request* is generated when a user visits our application.

- Based on the request, a *context* is located through *context finding*. A context is located differently depending on whether the application uses *traversal* or *URL dispatch*, but a context is ultimately found in either case. See *Context Finding and View Lookup* (pp. 57) for more information about context finding.

- A *view callable* is located by *view lookup* using the context as well as other attributes of the request.

- If an *authentication policy* is in effect, it is passed the request; it returns some number of *principal* identifiers.

- If an *authorization policy* is in effect and the *view configuration* associated with the view callable that was found has a *permission* associated with it, the authorization policy is passed the *context*, some number of *principal* identifiers returned by the authentication policy, and the *permission* associated with the view; it will allow or deny access.

- If the authorization policy allows access, the view callable is invoked.

- If the authorization policy denies access, the view callable is not invoked; instead the *forbidden view* is invoked.

Authorization is enabled by modifying your application to include a *authentication policy* and *authorization policy*. repoze.bfg comes with a variety of implementations of these policies. To provide maximal flexibility, repoze.bfg also allows you to create custom authentication policies and authorization policies.

⚠ Various systems exist for adding authentication and authorization to arbitrary web frameworks. Two of these, repoze.who and repoze.what are even written under the same Repoze "flag" as repoze.bfg! However, neither repoze.who nor repoze.what is required to add authorization or authentication to a repoze.bfg application. In fact, unless you have very specific requirements that include some sort of "single sign on" or you need to integrate authorization across multiple non-repoze.bfg Python applications, you can probably safely ignore the existence of both repoze.who and repoze.what. Those packages are useful when adding authentication and authorization to a web framework such as Pylons which has no built-in authentication or authorization machinery. Because repoze.bfg already has facilities for authentication and authorization built in, the use of repoze.who or repoze.what is not required within repoze.bfg applications.

15.1 Enabling an Authorization Policy

By default, repoze.bfg enables no authorization policy. All views are accessible by completely anonymous users. In order to begin protecting views from execution based on security settings, you need to enable an authorization policy.

You can enable an authorization policy imperatively, or declaratively via ZCML.

15.1.1 Enabling an Authorization Policy Imperatively

Passing an authorization_policy argument to the constructor of the configuration.Configurator (pp. 367) class enables an authorization policy.

You must also enable an *authentication policy* in order to enable the an authorization policy. This is because authorization, in general, depends upon authentication. Use the authorization_policy argument to the configuration.Configurator (pp. 367) class during application setup to specify an authentication policy.

For example:

```
1  from repoze.bfg.configuration import Configurator
2  from repoze.bfg.authentication import AuthTktAuthenticationPolicy
3  from repoze.bfg.authorization import ACLAuthorizationPolicy
4  authentication_policy = AuthTktAuthenticationPolicy('seekrit')
5  authorization_policy = ACLAuthorizationPolicy()
6  config = Configurator(authentication_policy=authentication_policy,
7                        authorization_policy=authorization_policy)
```

The above configuration enables a policy which compares the value of an "auth ticket" cookie passed in the request's environment which contains a reference to a single *principal* against the principals present in any *ACL* found in model data when attempting to call some *view*.

While it is possible to mix and match different authentication and authorization policies, it is an error to pass an authentication policy without the an authorization policy or vice versa to a *Configurator* constructor.

See also the authorization (pp. 357) and authentication (pp. 359) modules for alternate implementations of authorization and authentication policies.

15.1.2 Enabling an Authorization Policy Via ZCML

If you'd rather use *ZCML* to specify an authorization policy than imperative configuration, modify the ZCML file loaded by your application (usually named configure.zcml) to enable an authorization policy.

For example, to enable a policy which compares the value of an "auth ticket" cookie passed in the request's environment which contains a reference to a single *principal* against the principals present in any *ACL* found in model data when attempting to call some *view*, modify your configure.zcml to look something like this:

```
1   <configure xmlns="http://namespaces.repoze.org/bfg">
2
3     <!-- views and other directives before this... -->
4
5     <authtktauthenticationpolicy
6         secret="iamsosecret"/>
7
8     <aclauthorizationpolicy/>
9
10  </configure>
```

169

"Under the hood", these statements cause an instance of the class `authentication.AuthTktAuthenticationPolicy` (pp. 359) to be injected as the *authentication policy* used by this application and an instance of the class `authorization.ACLAuthorizationPolicy` (pp. 357) to be injected as the *authorization policy* used by this application.

`repoze.bfg` ships with a number of authorization and authentication policy ZCML directives that should prove useful. See *Built-In Authentication Policy ZCML Directives* (pp. 177) and *Built-In Authorization Policy ZCML Directives* (pp. 178) for more information.

15.2 Protecting Views with Permissions

To protect a *view callable* from invocation based on a user's security settings in a *context*, you must pass a *permission* to *view configuration*. Permissions are usually just strings, and they have no required composition: you can name permissions whatever you like.

For example, the following declaration protects the view named `add_entry.html` when invoked against a `Blog` context with the `add` permission:

```
<view
    context=".models.Blog"
    view=".views.blog_entry_add_view"
    name="add_entry.html"
    permission="add"
    />
```

The equivalent view registration including the `add` permission name may be performed via the `@bfg_view` decorator:

```
from repoze.bfg.view import bfg_view
from models import Blog

@bfg_view(context=Blog, name='add_entry.html', permission='add')
def blog_entry_add_view(request):
    """ Add blog entry code goes here """
    pass
```

Or an the same thing can be done using the `configuration.Configurator.add_view()` (pp. 374) method:

170

```
1  config.add_view(blog_entry_add_view,
2                  context=Blog, name='add_entry.html', permission='add')
```

As a result of any of these various view configuration statements, if an authorization policy is in place when the view callable is found during normal application operations, the requesting user will need to possess the add permission against the *context* to be able to invoke the blog_entry_add_view view. If he does not, the *Forbidden view* will be invoked.

15.3 Assigning ACLs to your Model Objects

When the default repoze.bfg *authorization policy* determines whether a user possesses a particular permission in a *context*, it examines the *ACL* associated with the context. An ACL is associated with a context by virtue of the __acl__ attribute of the model object representing the *context*. This attribute can be defined on the model *instance* if you need instance-level security, or it can be defined on the model *class* if you just need type-level security.

For example, an ACL might be attached to model for a blog via its class:

```
1  from repoze.bfg.security import Everyone
2  from repoze.bfg.security import Allow
3
4  class Blog(object):
5      __acl__ = [
6          (Allow, Everyone, 'view'),
7          (Allow, 'group:editors', 'add'),
8          (Allow, 'group:editors', 'edit'),
9          ]
```

Or, if your models are persistent, an ACL might be specified via the __acl__ attribute of an *instance* of a model:

```
1  from repoze.bfg.security import Everyone
2  from repoze.bfg.security import Allow
3
4  class Blog(object):
5      pass
```

171

```
6
7  blog = Blog()
8
9  blog.__acl__ = [
10         (Allow, Everyone, 'view'),
11         (Allow, 'group:editors', 'add'),
12         (Allow, 'group:editors', 'edit'),
13         ]
```

Whether an ACL is attached to a model's class or an instance of the model itself, the effect is the same. It is useful to decorate individual model instances with an ACL (as opposed to just decorating their class) in applications such as "CMS" systems where fine-grained access is required on an object-by-object basis.

15.4 Elements of an ACL

Here's an example ACL:

```
1  from repoze.bfg.security import Everyone
2  from repoze.bfg.security import Allow
3
4  __acl__ = [
5         (Allow, Everyone, 'view'),
6         (Allow, 'group:editors', 'add'),
7         (Allow, 'group:editors', 'edit'),
8         ]
```

The example ACL indicates that the security.Everyone (pp. 397) principal – a special system-defined principal indicating, literally, everyone – is allowed to view the blog, the group:editors principal is allowed to add to and edit the blog.

Each elements of an ACL is an *ACE* or access control entry. For example, in the above code block, there are three ACEs: (Allow, Everyone, 'view'), (Allow, 'group:editors', 'add'), and (Allow, 'group:editors', 'edit').

The first element of any ACE is either security.Allow (pp. 397), or security.Deny (pp. 397), representing the action to take when the ACE matches. The second element is a *principal*. The third argument is a permission or sequence of permission names.

A principal is usually a user id, however it also may be a group id if your authentication system provides group information and the effective *authentication policy* policy is written to respect group information. For example, the `authentication.RepozeWhoAuthenicationPolicy` enabled by the `repozewhoauthenticationpolicy` ZCML directive respects group information if you configure it with a `callback`. See *Built-In Authentication Policy ZCML Directives* (pp. 177) for more information about the `callback` attribute.

Each ACE in an ACL is processed by an authorization policy *in the order dictated by the ACL*. So if you have an ACL like this:

```
1  from repoze.bfg.security import Everyone
2  from repoze.bfg.security import Allow
3  from repoze.bfg.security import Deny
4
5  __acl__ = [
6      (Allow, Everyone, 'view'),
7      (Deny, Everyone, 'view'),
8      ]
```

The default authorization policy will *allow* everyone the view permission, even though later in the ACL you have an ACE that denies everyone the view permission. On the other hand, if you have an ACL like this:

```
1  from repoze.bfg.security import Everyone
2  from repoze.bfg.security import Allow
3  from repoze.bfg.security import Deny
4
5  __acl__ = [
6      (Deny, Everyone, 'view'),
7      (Allow, Everyone, 'view'),
8      ]
```

The authorization policy will deny everyone the view permission, even though later in the ACL is an ACE that allows everyone.

The third argument in an ACE can also be a sequence of permission names instead of a single permission name. So instead of creating multiple ACEs representing a number of different permission grants to a single `group:editors` group, we can collapse this into a single ACE, as below.

```
1  from repoze.bfg.security import Everyone
2  from repoze.bfg.security import Allow
3
4  __acl__ = [
5      (Allow, Everyone, 'view'),
6      (Allow, 'group:editors', ('add', 'edit')),
7      ]
```

15.5 Special Principal Names

Special principal names exist in the `security` (pp. 395) module. They can be imported for use in your own code to populate ACLs, e.g. `security.Everyone` (pp. 397).

`security.Everyone` (pp. 397)

>   Literally, everyone, no matter what. This object is actually a string "under the hood" (`system.Everyone`). Every user "is" the principal named Everyone during every request, even if a security policy is not in use.

`security.Authenticated` (pp. 397)

>   Any user with credentials as determined by the current security policy. You might think of it as any user that is "logged in". This object is actually a string "under the hood" (`system.Authenticated`).

15.6 Special Permissions

Special permission names exist in the `security` (pp. 395) module. These can be imported for use in ACLs.

`security.ALL_PERMISSIONS` (pp. 397)

>   An object representing, literally, *all* permissions. Useful in an ACL like so: `(Allow, 'fred', ALL_PERMISSIONS)`. The `ALL_PERMISSIONS` object is actually a stand-in object that has a `__contains__` method that always returns `True`, which, for all known authorization policies, has the effect of indicating that a given principal "has" any permission asked for by the system.

15.7 Special ACEs

A convenience *ACE* is defined representing a deny to everyone of all permissions in `security.DENY_ALL` (pp. 397). This ACE is often used as the *last* ACE of an ACL to explicitly cause inheriting authorization policies to "stop looking up the traversal tree" (effectively breaking any inheritance). For example, an ACL which allows *only* `fred` the view permission in a particular traversal context despite what inherited ACLs may say when the default authorization policy is in effect might look like so:

```
from repoze.bfg.security import Allow
from repoze.bfg.security import DENY_ALL

__acl__ = [ (Allow, 'fred', 'view'), DENY_ALL ]
```

"Under the hood", the `security.DENY_ALL` (pp. 397) ACE equals the following:

```
from repoze.bfg.security import ALL_PERMISSIONS
(Deny, Everyone, ALL_PERMISSIONS)
```

15.8 ACL Inheritance and Location-Awareness

While the default *authorization policy* is in place, if a model object does not have an ACL when it is the context, its *parent* is consulted for an ACL. If that object does not have an ACL, *its* parent is consulted for an ACL, ad infinitum, until we've reached the root and there are no more parents left.

In order to allow the security machinery to perform ACL inheritance, model objects must provide *location*-awareness. Providing *location-awareness* means two things: the root object in the graph must have a _name__ attribute and a __parent__ attribute.

```
class Blog(object):
    __name__ = ''
    __parent__ = None
```

An object with a __parent__ attribute and a __name__ attribute is said to be *location-aware*. Location-aware objects define an __parent__ attribute which points at their parent object. The root object's __parent__ is None.

See *repoze.bfg.location* (pp. 387) for documentations of functions which use location-awareness. See also *Location-Aware Model Instances* (pp. 165).

15.9 Changing the Forbidden View

When `repoze.bfg` denies a view invocation due to an authorization denial, the special `forbidden` view is invoked. "Out of the box", this forbidden view is very plain. See *Changing the Forbidden View* (pp. 202) within *Using Hooks* (pp. 201) for instructions on how to create a custom forbidden view and arrange for it to be called when view authorization is denied.

15.10 Debugging View Authorization Failures

If your application in your judgment is allowing or denying view access inappropriately, start your application under a shell using the `BFG_DEBUG_AUTHORIZATION` environment variable set to 1. For example:

```
$ BFG_DEBUG_AUTHORIZATION=1 bin/paster serve myproject.ini
```

When any authorization takes place during a top-level view rendering, a message will be logged to the console (to stderr) about what ACE in which ACL permitted or denied the authorization based on authentication information.

This behavior can also be turned on in the application `.ini` file by setting the `debug_authorization` key to `true` within the application's configuration section, e.g.:

```
[app:main]
use = egg:MyProject#app
debug_authorization = true
```

With this debug flag turned on, the response sent to the browser will also contain security debugging information in its body.

15.11 Debugging Imperative Authorization Failures

The `security.has_permission()` (pp. 396) API is used to check security within view functions imperatively. It returns instances of objects that are effectively booleans. But these objects are not raw `True` or `False` objects, and have information attached to them about why the permission was allowed or denied. The object will be one of `security.ACLAllowed` (pp. 398), `security.ACLDenied` (pp. 397), `security.Allowed` (pp. 398), or `security.Denied` (pp. 398), as documented in *repoze.bfg.security* (pp. 395). At very minimum these objects will have a `msg` attribute, which is a string indicating why permission was denied or allowed. Introspecting this information in the debugger or via print statements when a call to `security.has_permission()` (pp. 396) fails is often useful.

15.12 Built-In Authentication Policy ZCML Directives

Instead of configuring an authentication policy and authorization policy imperatively, `repoze.bfg` ships with a few "pre-chewed" authentication policy ZCML directives that you can make use of within your application.

15.12.1 `authtktauthenticationpolicy`

When this directive is used, authentication information is obtained from an "auth ticket" cookie value, assumed to be set by a custom login form.

An example of its usage, with all attributes fully expanded:

```
 1  <authtktauthenticationpolicy
 2   secret="goshiamsosecret"
 3   callback=".somemodule.somefunc"
 4   cookie_name="mycookiename"
 5   secure="false"
 6   include_ip="false"
 7   timeout="86400"
 8   reissue_time="600"
 9   max_age="31536000"
10   path="/"
11   http_only="False"
12   />
```

See *authtktauthenticationpolicy* (pp. 443) for details about this directive.

15.12.2 `remoteuserauthenticationpolicy`

When this directive is used, authentication information is obtained from a REMOTE_USER key in the WSGI environment, assumed to be set by a WSGI server or an upstream middleware component.

An example of its usage, with all attributes fully expanded:

```
 1  <remoteuserauthenticationpolicy
 2   environ_key="REMOTE_USER"
 3   callback=".somemodule.somefunc"
 4   />
```

See *remoteuserauthenticationpolicy* (pp. 457) for detailed information.

15.12.3 `repozewho1authenticationpolicy`

When this directive is used, authentication information is obtained from a `repoze.who.identity` key in the WSGI environment, assumed to be set by *repoze.who* middleware.

An example of its usage, with all attributes fully expanded:

```
<repozewho1authenticationpolicy
  identifier_name="auth_tkt"
  callback=".somemodule.somefunc"
/>
```

See *repozewho1authenticationpolicy* (pp. 461) for detailed information.

15.13 Built-In Authorization Policy ZCML Directives

`aclauthorizationpolicy`

When this directive is used, authorization information is obtained from *ACL* objects attached to model instances.

An example of its usage, with all attributes fully expanded:

```
<aclauthorizationpolicy/>
```

In other words, it has no configuration attributes; its existence in a `configure.zcml` file enables it.

See *aclauthorizationpolicy* (pp. 439) for detailed information.

15.14 Creating Your Own Authentication Policy

`repoze.bfg` ships with a number of useful out-of-the-box security policies (see `authentication` (pp. 359)). However, creating your own authentication policy is often necessary when you want to control the "horizontal and vertical" of how your users authenticate. Doing so is matter of creating an instance of something that implements the following interface:

```
class AuthenticationPolicy(object):
    """ An object representing a BFG authentication policy. """
    def authenticated_userid(self, request):
        """ Return the authenticated userid or ''None'' if no
        authenticated userid can be found. """

    def effective_principals(self, request):
        """ Return a sequence representing the effective principals
        including the userid and any groups belonged to by the current
        user, including 'system' groups such as Everyone and
        Authenticated. """

    def remember(self, request, principal, **kw):
        """ Return a set of headers suitable for 'remembering' the
        principal named ''principal'' when set in a response.  An
        individual authentication policy and its consumers can decide
        on the composition and meaning of **kw. """

    def forget(self, request):
        """ Return a set of headers suitable for 'forgetting' the
        current user on subsequent requests. """
```

After you do so, you can pass an instance of such a class into the `configuration.Configurator` (pp. 367) class at configuration time as `authentication_policy` to use it.

15.15 Creating Your Own Authorization Policy

An authentication policy the policy that allows or denies access after a user has been authenticated. By default, `repoze.bfg` will use the `authorization.ACLAuthorizationPolicy` (pp. 357) if an authentication policy is activated and an authorization policy isn't otherwise specified.

In some cases, it's useful to be able to use a different authentication policy than the `authorization.ACLAuthorizationPolicy` (pp. 357). For example, it might be desirable to construct an alternate authorization policy which allows the application to use an authorization mechanism that does not involve *ACL* objects.

`repoze.bfg` ships with only a single default authorization policy, so you'll need to create your own if you'd like to use a different one. Creating and using your own authorization policy is a matter of creating an instance of an object that implements the following interface:

179

```
class IAuthorizationPolicy(object):
    """ An object representing a BFG authorization policy. """
    def permits(self, context, principals, permission):
        """ Return True if any of the principals is allowed the
        permission in the current context, else return False """

    def principals_allowed_by_permission(self, context, permission):
        """ Return a set of principal identifiers allowed by the
            permission """
```

After you do so, you can pass an instance of such a class into the `configuration.Configurator` (pp. 367) class at configuration time as `authorization_policy` to use it.

VIRTUAL HOSTING

"Virtual hosting" is, loosely, the act of serving a `repoze.bfg` application or a portion of a `repoze.bfg` application under a URL space that it does not "naturally" inhabit.

`repoze.bfg` provides facilities for serving an application under a URL "prefix", as well as serving a *portion* of a *traversal* based application under a root URL.

16.1 Hosting an Application Under a URL Prefix

`repoze.bfg` supports a common form of virtual hosting whereby you can host a `repoze.bfg` application as a "subset" of some other site (e.g. under `http://example.com/mybfgapplication/` as opposed to under `http://example.com/`).

If you use a "pure Python" environment, this functionality is provided by Paste's urlmap (http://pythonpaste.org/modules/urlmap.html) "composite" WSGI application. Alternately, you can use *mod_wsgi* to serve your application, which handles this virtual hosting translation for you "under the hood".

If you use the `urlmap` composite application "in front" of a `repoze.bfg` application or if you use *mod_wsgi* to serve up a `repoze.bfg` application, nothing special needs to be done within the application for URLs to be generated that contain a prefix. `paste.urlmap` and *mod_wsgi* and manipulate the *WSGI* environment in such a way that the PATH_INFO and SCRIPT_NAME variables are correct for some given prefix.

Here's an example of a PasteDeploy configuration snippet that includes a `urlmap` composite.

```
[app:mybfgapp]
use = egg:mybfgapp#app

[composite:main]
use = egg:Paste#urlmap
/bfgapp =  bfgapp
```

This "roots" the `repoze.bfg` application at the prefix `/bfgapp` and serves up the composite as the "main" application in the file.

> ⓘ If you're using an Apache server to proxy to a Paste `urlmap` composite, you may have to use the ProxyPreserveHost (http://httpd.apache.org/docs/2.2/mod/mod_proxy.html#proxypreservehost) directive to pass the original `HTTP_HOST` header along to the application, so URLs get generated properly. As of this writing the `urlmap` composite does not seem to respect the `HTTP_X_FORWARDED_HOST` parameter, which will contain the original host header even if `HTTP_HOST` is incorrect.

If you use *mod_wsgi*, you do not need to use a `composite` application in your `.ini` file. The `WSGIScriptAlias` configuration setting in a *mod_wsgi* configuration does the work for you:

```
WSGIScriptAlias /bfgapp /Users/chrism/projects/modwsgi/env/bfg.wsgi
```

In the above configuration, we root a `repoze.bfg` application at `/bfgapp` within the Apache configuration.

16.2 Virtual Root Support

`repoze.bfg` also supports "virtual roots", which can be used in *traversal* -based (but not *URL dispatch* -based) applications.

Virtual root support is useful when you'd like to host some model in a `repoze.bfg` object graph as an application under a URL pathname that does not include the model path itself. For example, you might want to serve the object at the traversal path `/cms` as an application reachable via `http://example.com/` (as opposed to `http://example.com/cms`).

To specify a virtual root, cause an environment variable to be inserted into the WSGI environ named HTTP_X_VHM_ROOT with a value that is the absolute pathname to the model object in the traversal graph that should behave as the "root" model. As a result, the traversal machinery will respect this value during traversal (prepending it to the PATH_INFO before traversal starts), and the url.model_url() (pp. 421) API will generate the "correct" virtually-rooted URLs.

An example of an Apache mod_proxy configuration that will host the /cms subobject as http://www.example.com/ using this facility is below:

```
1  NameVirtualHost *:80
2
3  <VirtualHost *:80>
4    ServerName www.example.com
5    RewriteEngine On
6    RewriteRule ^/(.*) http://127.0.0.1:6543/$1 [L,P]
7    ProxyPreserveHost on
8    RequestHeader add X-Vhm-Root /cms
9  </VirtualHost>
```

> ℹ️ Use of the RequestHeader directive requires that the Apache mod_headers (http://httpd.apache.org/docs/2.2/mod/mod_headers.html) module be available in the Apache environment you're using.

For a repoze.bfg application running under *mod_wsgi*, the same can be achieved using SetEnv:

```
1  <Location />
2    SetEnv HTTP_X_VHM_ROOT /cms
3  </Location>
```

Setting a virtual root has no effect when using an application based on *URL dispatch*.

16.3 Further Documentation and Examples

The API documentation in *repoze.bfg.traversal* (pp. 413) documents a traversal.virtual_root() (pp. 416) API. When called, it returns the virtual root object (or the physical root object if no virtual root has been specified).

Running a repoze.bfg Application under mod_wsgi (pp. 337) has detailed information about using *mod_wsgi* to serve repoze.bfg applications.

USING EVENTS

An *event* is an object broadcast by the `repoze.bfg` framework at interesting points during the lifetime of an application. You don't need to use events in order to create most `repoze.bfg` applications, but they can be useful when you want to perform slightly advanced operations. For example, subscribing to an event can allow you to run some code as the result of every new request.

Events in `repoze.bfg` are always broadcast by the framework. However, they only become useful when you register a *subscriber*. A subscriber is a function that accepts a single argument named *event*:

```
def mysubscriber(event):
    print event
```

The above is a subscriber that simply prints the event to the console when it's called.

The mere existence of a subscriber function, however, is not sufficient to arrange for it to be called. To arrange for the subscriber to be called, you'll need to use the `configurator.Configurator.add_subscriber()` method to register the subscriber imperatively, or you'll need to use ZCML for the same purpose:

Configuring an Event Listener Imperatively

You can imperatively configure a subscriber function to be called for some event type via the `configuration.Configurator.add_subscriber()` (pp. 374) method (see also *Configurator*):

```
from repoze.bfg.interfaces import INewRequest

from subscribers import mysubscriber

# "config" below is assumed to be an instance of a
# repoze.bfg.configuration.Configurator object

config.add_subscriber(mysubscriber, INewRequest)
```

The first argument to `configuration.Configurator.add_subscriber()` (pp. 374) is the subscriber function; the second argument is the event type.

Configuring an Event Listener Through ZCML

You can configure an event listener by modifying your application's `configure.zcml`. Here's an example of a bit of XML you can add to the `configure.zcml` file which registers the above `mysubscriber` function, which we assume lives in a `subscribers.py` module within your application:

```
<subscriber
    for="repoze.bfg.interfaces.INewRequest"
    handler=".subscribers.mysubscriber"
/>
```

See also *subscriber* (pp. 475).

Either of the above registration examples implies that every time the `repoze.bfg` framework emits an event object that supplies an `interfaces.INewRequest` (pp. 385) interface, the `mysubscriber` function will be called with an *event* object.

As you can see, a subscription is made in terms of an *interface*. The event object sent to a subscriber will always be an object that possesses an interface. The interface itself provides documentation of what attributes of the event are available.

The return value of a subscriber function is ignored. Subscribers to the same event type are not guaranteed to be called in any particular order relative to each other.

All the concrete `repoze.bfg` event types are documented in the *repoze.bfg.events* (pp. 381) API documentation.

17.1 An Example

If you create event listener functions in a `subscribers.py` file in your application like so:

```
def handle_new_request(event):
    print 'request', event.request

def handle_new_response(event):
    print 'response', event.response
```

You may configure these functions to be called at the appropriate times by adding the following ZCML to your application's `configure.zcml` file:

```
<subscriber
   for="repoze.bfg.interfaces.INewRequest"
   handler=".subscribers.handle_new_request"
 />

<subscriber
   for="repoze.bfg.interfaces.INewResponse"
   handler=".subscribers.handle_new_response"
 />
```

If you're not using ZCML, the `configuration.Configurator.add_subscriber()` (pp. 374) method can alternately be used to perform the same job:

```
from repoze.bfg.interfaces import INewRequest
from repoze.bfg.interfaces import INewResponse

from subscribers import handle_new_request
from subscribers import handle_new_response

# "config" below is assumed to be an instance of a
# repoze.bfg.configuration.Configurator object

config.add_subscriber(handle_new_request, INewRequest)
config.add_subscriber(handle_new_response, INewResponse)
```

Either mechanism causes the functions in `subscribers.py` to be registered as event subscribers. Under this configuration, when the application is run, each time a new request or response is detected, a message will be printed to the console.

Each of our subscriber functions accepts an `event` object and prints an attribute of the event object. This begs the question: how can we know which attributes a particular event has?

We know that `interfaces.INewRequest` (pp. 385) event objects have a `request` attribute, which is a *request* object, because the interface defined at `interfaces.INewRequest` (pp. 385) says it must. Likewise, we know that `interfaces.INewResponse` (pp. 385) events have a `response` attribute, which is a response object constructed by your application, because the interface defined at `interfaces.INewResponse` (pp. 385) says it must.

ENVIRONMENT VARIABLES AND .INI FILE SETTINGS

`repoze.bfg` behavior can be configured through a combination of operating system environment variables and `.ini` configuration file application section settings. The meaning of the environment variables and the configuration file settings overlap.

> Where a configuration file setting exists with the same meaning as an environment variable, and both are present at application startup time, the environment variable setting takes precedence.

The term "configuration file setting name" refers to a key in the `.ini` configuration for your application. The configuration file setting names documented in this chapter are reserved for `repoze.bfg` use. You should not use them to indicate application-specific configuration settings.

18.1 Reloading Templates

When this value is true, reload templates without a restart.

Environment Variable Name	Config File Setting Name
`BFG_RELOAD_TEMPLATES`	`reload_templates`

18.2 Reloading Resources

Don't cache any resource file data when this value is true. See also *Overriding Resources* (pp. 214).

Environment Variable Name	Config File Setting Name
BFG_RELOAD_RESOURCES	reload_resources

18.3 Debugging Authorization

Print view authorization failure and success information to stderr when this value is true. See also *Debugging View Authorization Failures* (pp. 176).

Environment Variable Name	Config File Setting Name
BFG_DEBUG_AUTHORIZATION	debug_authorization

18.4 Debugging Not Found Errors

Print view-related NotFound debug messages to stderr when this value is true. See also *NotFound Errors* (pp. 136).

Environment Variable Name	Config File Setting Name
BFG_DEBUG_NOTFOUND	debug_notfound

18.5 Debugging All

Turns on all debug* settings.

Environment Variable Name	Config File Setting Name
BFG_DEBUG_ALL	debug_all

18.6 Reloading All

Turns on all reload* settings.

Environment Variable Name	Config File Setting Name
BFG_RELOAD_ALL	reload_all

18.7 Examples

Let's presume your configuration file is named `MyProject.ini`, and there is a section representing your application named `[app:main]` within the file that represents your `repoze.bfg` application. The configuration file settings documented in the above "Config File Setting Name" column would go in the `[app:main]` section. Here's an example of such a section:

```
[app:main]
use = egg:MyProject#app
reload_templates = true
debug_authorization = true
```

You can also use environment variables to accomplish the same purpose for settings documented as such. For example, you might start your `repoze.bfg` application using the following command line:

```
$ BFG_DEBUG_AUTHORIZATION=1 BFG_RELOAD_TEMPLATES=1 bin/paster serve \
        MyProject.ini
```

If you started your application this way, your `repoze.bfg` application would behave in the same manner as if you had placed the respective settings in the `[app:main]` section of your application's `.ini` file.

If you want to turn all `debug` settings (every setting that starts with `debug_`). on in one fell swoop, you can use `BFG_DEBUG_ALL=1` as an environment variable setting or you may use `debug_all=true` in the config file. Note that this does not effect settings that do not start with `debug_*` such as `reload_templates`.

If you want to turn all `reload` settings (every setting that starts with `reload_`). on in one fell swoop, you can use `BFG_RELOAD_ALL=1` as an environment variable setting or you may use `reload_all=true` in the config file. Note that this does not effect settings that do not start with `reload_*` such as `debug_notfound`.

18.8 Understanding the Distinction Between `reload_templates` and `reload_resources`

The difference between `reload_resources` and `reload_templates` is a bit subtle. Templates are themselves also treated by `repoze.bfg` as *pkg_resources* resource files (along with static files and

191

other resources), so the distinction can be confusing. It's helpful to read *Overriding Resources* (pp. 214) for some context about resources in general.

When `reload_templates` is true, `repoze.bfg` ` takes advantage of the underlying templating systems' ability to check for file modifications to an individual template file. When `reload_templates` is true but `reload_resources` is *not* true, the template filename returned by pkg_resources is cached by `repoze.bfg` on the first request. Subsequent requests for the same template file will return a cached template filename. The underlying templating system checks for modifications to this particular file for every request. Setting `reload_templates` to `True` doesn't effect performance dramatically (although it should still not be used in production because it has some effect).

However, when `reload_resources` is true, `repoze.bfg` will not cache the template filename, meaning you can see the effect of changing the content of an overridden resource directory for templates without restarting the server after every change. Subsequent requests for the same template file may return different filenames based on the current state of overridden resource directories. Setting `reload_resources` to `True` effects performance *dramatically*, slowing things down by an order of magnitude for each template rendering. However, it's convenient to enable when moving files around in overridden resource directories. `reload_resources` makes the system *very slow* when templates are in use. Never set `reload_resources` to `True` on a production system.

UNIT AND INTEGRATION TESTING

Unit testing is, not surprisingly, the act of testing a "unit" in your application. In this context, a "unit" is often a function or a method of a class instance. The unit is also referred to as a "unit under test".

The goal of a single unit test is to test **only** some permutation of the "unit under test". If you write a unit test that aims to verify the result of a particular codepath through a Python function, you need only be concerned about testing the code that *lives in the function body itself*. If the function accepts a parameter that represents a complex application "domain object" (such as a model, a database connection, or an SMTP server), the argument provided to this function during a unit test *need not be* and likely *should not be* a "real" implementation object. For example, although a particular function implementation may accept an argument that represents an SMTP server object, and the function may call a method of this object when the system is operating normally that would result in an email being sent, a unit test of this codepath of the function does *not* need to test that an email is actually sent. It just needs to make sure that the function calls the method of the object provided as an argument that *would* send an email if the argument happened to be the "real" implementation of an SMTP server object.

An *integration test*, on the other hand, is a different form of testing in which the interaction between two or more "units" is explicitly tested. Integration tests verify that the components of your application work together. You *might* make sure that an email was actually sent in an integration test.

It is often considered best practice to write both types of tests for any given codebase. Unit testing often provides the opportunity to obtain better "coverage": it's usually possible to supply a unit under test with arguments and/or an environment which causes *all* of its potential codepaths to be executed. This is usually not as easy to do with a set of integration tests, but integration testing provides a measure of assurance that your "units" work together, as they will be expected to when your application is run in production.

The suggested mechanism for unit and integration testing of a `repoze.bfg` application is the Python `unittest` module. Although this module is named `unittest`, it is actually capable of driving both unit and integration tests. A good `unittest` tutorial is available within Dive Into Python (http://diveintopython.org/unit_testing/index.html) by Mark Pilgrim.

`repoze.bfg` provides a number of facilities that make unit and integration tests easier to write. The facilities become particularly useful when your code calls into `repoze.bfg`-related framework functions.

19.1 Test Set Up and Tear Down

`repoze.bfg` uses a "global" (actually *thread local*) data structure to hold on to two items: the current *request* and the current *application registry*. These data structures are available via the `threadlocal.get_current_request()` (pp. 411) and `threadlocal.get_current_registry()` (pp. 411) functions, respectively. See *Thread Locals* (pp. 227) for information about these functions and the data structures they return.

If your code uses these `get_current_*` functions or calls `repoze.bfg` code which uses `get_current_*` functions, you will need to construct at *Configurator* and call its `begin` method within the `setUp` method of your unit test and call the same configurator's `end` method within the `tearDown` method of your unit test.

The use of a Configurator and its `begin` and `end` methods allows you to supply each unit test method in a test case with an environment that has a isolated registry and an isolated request for the duration of a single test. Here's an example of using this feature:

```
import unittest
from repoze.bfg.configuration import Configurator

class MyTest(unittest.TestCase):
    def setUp(self):
        self.config = Configurator()
        self.config.begin()

    def tearDown(self):
        self.config.end()
```

The above will make sure that `threadlocal.get_current_registry()` (pp. 411) will return the *application registry* associated with the `config` Configurator instance when `threadlocal.get_current_registry()` (pp. 411) is called in a test case method attached to `MyTest`. Each test case method attached to `MyTest` will use an isolated registry.

194

The `configuration.Configurator.begin()` (pp. 368) method accepts various arguments that influence the code run during the test. See the *repoze.bfg.configuration* (pp. 367) chapter for information about the API of a *Configurator*, including its `begin` and `end` methods.

If you also want to make `get_current_registry()` return something other than `None` during the course of a single test, you can pass a *request* object into the `configuration.Configurator.begin()` (pp. 368) method of the Configurator within the `setUp` method of your test:

```
import unittest
from repoze.bfg.configuration import Configurator
from repoze.bfg import testing

class MyTest(unittest.TestCase):
    def setUp(self):
        self.config = Configurator()
        request = testing.DummyRequest()
        self.config.begin(request=request)

    def tearDown(self):
        self.config.end()
```

If you pass a *request* object into the `begin` method of the configurator within your test case's `setUp`, any test method attached to the `MyTest` test case that directly or indirectly calls `threadlocal.get_current_request()` (pp. 411) will receive the request you passed into the `begin` method. Otherwise, during testing, `threadlocal.get_current_request()` (pp. 411) will return `None`. We use a "dummy" request implementation supplied by `testing.DummyRequest` (pp. 408) because it's easier to construct than a "real" `repoze.bfg` request object.

19.1.1 What?

Thread local data structures are always a bit confusing, especially when they're used by frameworks. Sorry. So here's a rule of thumb: if you don't *know* whether you're calling code that uses the `threadlocal.get_current_registry()` (pp. 411) or `threadlocal.get_current_request()` (pp. 411) functions, or you don't care about any of this, but you still want to write test code, just always create a Configurator instance and call its `begin` method within the `setUp` of a unit test, then subsequently call its `end` method in the test's `tearDown`. This won't really hurt anything if the application you're testing does not call any `get_current*` function.

19.2 Using the `Configurator` and `repoze.bfg.testing` APIs in Unit Tests

The `Configurator` API and the `testing` module provide a number of functions which can be used during unit testing. These functions make *configuration declaration* calls to the current *application registry*, but typically register a "stub" or "dummy" feature in place of the "real" feature that the code would call if it was being run normally.

For example, let's imagine you want to unit test a `repoze.bfg` view function.

```
def view_fn(request):
    from repoze.bfg.chameleon_zpt import render_template_to_response
    if 'say' in request.params:
        return render_template_to_response('templates/submitted.pt',
                                           say=request.params['say'])
    return render_template_to_response('templates/show.pt', say='Hello')
```

Without invoking any startup code or using the testing API, an attempt to run this view function in a unit test will result in an error. When a `repoze.bfg` application starts normally, it will populate a *application registry* using *configuration declaration* calls made against a *Configurator* (sometimes deferring to the application's `configure.zcml` *ZCML* file via `load_zcml`). But if this application registry is not created and populated (e.g. with an `configuration.Configurator.add_view()` (pp. 374) *configuration declaration* or `view` declarations in *ZCML*), like when you invoke application code via a unit test, `repoze.bfg` API functions will tend to fail.

The testing API provided by `repoze.bfg` allows you to simulate various application registry registrations for use under a unit testing framework without needing to invoke the actual application configuration implied by its `run.py`. For example, if you wanted to test the above `view_fn` (assuming it lived in the package named `my.package`), you could write a `unittest.TestCase` that used the testing API.

```
import unittest
from repoze.bfg.configuration import Configurator
from repoze.bfg import testing

class MyTest(unittest.TestCase):
    def setUp(self):
        self.config = Configurator()
        self.config.begin()

    def tearDown(self):
```

```
11          self.config.end()
12
13      def test_view_fn_not_submitted(self):
14          from my.package import view_fn
15          renderer = self.config.testing_add_template('templates/show.pt')
16          request = testing.DummyRequest()
17          response = view_fn(request)
18          renderer.assert_(say='Hello')
19
20      def test_view_fn_submitted(self):
21          from my.package import view_fn
22          renderer = self.config.testing_add_template(
23                              'templates/submitted.pt')
24          request = testing.DummyRequest()
25          request.params['say'] = 'Yo'
26          response = view_fn(request)
27          renderer.assert_(say='Yo')
```

In the above example, we create a `MyTest` test case that inherits from `unittest.TestCase`. If it's in our `repoze.bfg` application, it will be found when `setup.py test` is run. It has two test methods.

The first test method, `test_view_fn_not_submitted` tests the `view_fn` function in the case that no "form" values (represented by request.params) have been submitted. Its first line registers a "dummy template renderer" named `templates/show.pt` via the `configuration.Configurator.testing_add_template()` (pp. 380) method; this method returns a `testing.DummyTemplateRenderer` (pp. 409) instance which we hang on to for later.

We then create a `testing.DummyRequest` (pp. 408) object which simulates a WebOb request object API. A `testing.DummyRequest` (pp. 408) is a request object that requires less setup than a "real" `repoze.bfg` request. We call the function being tested with the manufactured request. When the function is called, `chameleon_zpt.render_template_to_response()` (pp. 365) will call the "dummy" template renderer object instead of the real template renderer object. When the dummy renderer is called, it will set attributes on itself corresponding to the non-path keyword arguments provided to the `chameleon_zpt.render_template_to_response()` (pp. 365) function. We check that the `say` parameter sent into the template rendering function was `Hello` in this specific example. The `assert_` method of the renderer we've created will raise an `AssertionError` if the value passed to the renderer as `say` does not equal `Hello` (any number of keyword arguments are supported).

The second test method, named `test_view_fn_submitted` tests the alternate case, where the `say` form value has already been set in the request and performs a similar template registration and assertion. We assert at the end of this that the renderer's `say` attribute is `Yo`, as this is what is expected of the view function in the branch it's testing.

Note that the test calls the `configuration.Configurator.begin()` (pp. 368) method in its `setUp` method and the `end` method of the same in its `tearDown` method. If you use any of the `configuration.Configurator` (pp. 367) APIs during testing, be sure to use this pattern in your test case's `setUp` and `tearDown`; these methods make sure you're using a "fresh" *application registry* per test run.

See the *repoze.bfg.testing* (pp. 401) chapter for the entire `repoze.bfg` -specific testing API. This chapter describes APIs for registering a security policy, registering models at paths, registering event listeners, registering views and view permissions, and classes representing "dummy" implementations of a request and a model.

See also the various methods of the *Configurator* documented in *repoze.bfg.configuration* (pp. 367) that begin with the `testing_` prefix.

19.3 Creating Integration Tests

In `repoze.bfg`, a *unit test* typically relies on "mock" or "dummy" implementations to give the code under test only enough context to run.

"Integration testing" implies another sort of testing. In the context of a `repoze.bfg`, integration test, the test logic tests the functionality of some code *and* its integration with the rest of the `repoze.bfg` framework.

In `repoze.bfg` applications that use *ZCML*, you can create an integration test by *loading its ZCML* in the test's setup code. This causes the entire `repoze.bfg` environment to be set up and torn down as if your application was running "for real". This is a heavy-hammer way of making sure that your tests have enough context to run properly, and it tests your code's integration with the rest of `repoze.bfg`.

Let's demonstrate this by showing an integration test for a view. The below test assumes that your application's package name is `myapp`, and that there is a `views` module in the app with a function with the name `my_view` in it that returns the response 'Welcome to this application' after accessing some values that require a fully set up environment.

```
import unittest

from repoze.bfg.configuration import Configurator
from repoze.bfg import testing

class ViewIntegrationTests(unittest.TestCase):
    def setUp(self):
```

```
8      """ This sets up the application registry with the
9      registrations your application declares in its configure.zcml
10     (including dependent registrations for repoze.bfg itself).
11     """
12     import myapp
13     self.config = Configurator(package=myapp)
14     self.config.begin()
15     self.config.load_zcml('myapp:configure.zcml')
16
17  def tearDown(self):
18     """ Clear out the application registry """
19     self.config.end()
20
21  def test_my_view(self):
22     from myapp.views import my_view
23     request = testing.DummyRequest()
24     result = my_view(request)
25     self.assertEqual(result.status, '200 OK')
26     body = result.app_iter[0]
27     self.failUnless('Welcome to' in body)
28     self.assertEqual(len(result.headerlist), 2)
29     self.assertEqual(result.headerlist[0],
30                 ('Content-Type', 'text/html; charset=UTF-8'))
31     self.assertEqual(result.headerlist[1], ('Content-Length',
32                                   str(len(body))))
```

Unless you cannot avoid it, you should prefer writing unit tests that use the configuration, Configurator API to set up the right "mock" registrations rather than creating an integration test. Unit tests will run faster (because they do less for each test) and the result of a unit test is usually easier to make assertions about.

USING HOOKS

"Hooks" can be used to influence the behavior of the `repoze.bfg` framework in various ways.

20.1 Changing the Not Found View

When `repoze.bfg` can't map a URL to view code, it invokes a *not found view*, which is a *view callable*. The view it invokes can be customized through application configuration. This view can be configured in via *imperative configuration* or *ZCML*.

Using Imperative Configuration

If your application uses *imperative configuration*, you can replace the Not Found view by using the `configuration.Configurator.set_notfound_view()` (pp. 379) method:

```
1  import helloworld.views
2  config.set_notfound_view(helloworld.views.notfound_view)
```

Replace `helloworld.views.notfound_view` with a reference to the Python *view callable* you want to use to represent the Not Found view.

Using ZCML

If your application uses *ZCML*, you can replace the Not Found view by placing something like the following ZCML in your `configure.zcml` file.

```
<notfound
    view="helloworld.views.notfound_view"/>
```

Replace `helloworld.views.notfound_view` with the Python dotted name to the notfound view you want to use.

Other attributes of the `notfound` directive are documented at *notfound* (pp. 455).

Here's some sample code that implements a minimal NotFound view:

```
from webob.exc import HTTPNotFound

def notfound_view(request):
    return HTTPNotFound()
```

When a NotFound view is invoked, it is passed a *request*. The `environ` attribute of the request is the WSGI environment. Within the WSGI environ will be a key named `message` that has a value explaining why the not found error was raised. This error will be different when the `debug_notfound` environment setting is true than it is when it is false.

20.2 Changing the Forbidden View

When `repoze.bfg` can't authorize execution of a view based on the *authorization policy* in use, it invokes a *forbidden view*. The default forbidden response has a 401 status code and is very plain, but it can be overridden as necessary using either *imperative configuration* or *ZCML*:

Using Imperative Configuration

If your application uses *imperative configuration*, you can replace the Forbidden view by using the `configuration.Configurator.set_forbidden_view()` (pp. 379) method:

```
import helloworld.views
config.set_forbiddden_view(helloworld.views.forbidden_view)
```

Replace `helloworld.views.forbidden_view` with a reference to the Python *view callable* you want to use to represent the Forbidden view.

Using ZCML

If your application uses *ZCML*, you can replace the Forbidden view by placing something like the following ZCML in your `configure.zcml` file.

```
<forbidden
    view="helloworld.views.forbidden_view"/>
```

Replace `helloworld.views.forbidden_view` with the Python dotted name to the forbidden view you want to use.
Other attributes of the `forbidden` directive are documented at *forbidden* (pp. 451).

Like any other view, the forbidden view must accept at least a `request` parameter, or both `context` and `request`. The `context` (available as `request.context` if you're using the request-only view argument pattern) is the context found by the router when the view invocation was denied. The `request` is the current *request* representing the denied action.

Here's some sample code that implements a minimal forbidden view:

```
from repoze.bfg.chameleon_zpt import render_template_to_response

def forbidden_view(request):
    return render_template_to_response('templates/login_form.pt')
```

> When a forbidden view is invoked, it is passed the *request* as the second argument. An attribute of the request is `environ`, which is the WSGI environment. Within the WSGI environ will be a key named `message` that has a value explaining why the current view invocation was forbidden. This error will be different when the `debug_authorization` environment setting is true than it is when it is false.

> ⚠ the default forbidden view sends a response with a `401 Unauthorized` status code for backwards compatibility reasons. You can influence the status code of Forbidden responses by using an alternate forbidden view. For example, it would make sense to return a response with a `403 Forbidden` status code.

20.3 Changing the Traverser

The default *traversal* algorithm that BFG uses is explained in *The Traversal Algorithm* (pp. 66). Though it is rarely necessary, this default algorithm can be swapped out selectively for a different traversal pattern via configuration.

Use an `adapter` stanza in your application's `configure.zcml` to change the default traverser:

```
1  <adapter
2    factory="myapp.traversal.Traverser"
3    provides="repoze.bfg.interfaces.ITraverser"
4    for="*"
5    />
```

In the example above, `myapp.traversal.Traverser` is assumed to be a class that implements the following interface:

```
1  class Traverser(object):
2      def __init__(self, root):
3          """ Accept the root object returned from the root factory """
4
5      def __call__(self, request):
6          """ Return a dictionary with (at least) the keys ''root'',
7          ''context'', ''view_name'', ''subpath'', ''traversed'',
8          ''virtual_root'', and ''virtual_root_path''.  These values are
9          typically the result of an object graph traversal.  ''root''
10         is the physical root object, ''context'' will be a model
11         object, ''view_name'' will be the view name used (a Unicode
12         name), ''subpath'' will be a sequence of Unicode names that
13         followed the view name but were not traversed, ''traversed''
14         will be a sequence of Unicode names that were traversed
15         (including the virtual root path, if any) ''virtual_root''
```

```
16          will be a model object representing the virtual root (or the
17          physical root if traversal was not performed), and
18          ''virtual_root_path'' will be a sequence representing the
19          virtual root path (a sequence of Unicode names) or None if
20          traversal was not performed.
21
22          Extra keys for special purpose functionality can be added as
23          necessary.
24
25          All values returned in the dictionary will be made available
26          as attributes of the ''request'' object.
27          """
```

> ⚠ In 1.0 and previous versions, the traverser __call__ method accepted a WSGI *environment* dictionary rather than a *request* object. The request object passed to the traverser implements a dictionary-like API which mutates and queries the environment, as a backwards compatibility shim, in order to allow older code to work. However, for maximum forward compatibility, traverser code targeting repoze.bfg 1.1 and higher should expect a request object directly.

More than one traversal algorithm can be active at the same time. For instance, if your *root factory* returns more than one type of object conditionally, you could claim that an alternate traverser adapter is for only one particular class or interface. When the root factory returned an object that implemented that class or interface, a custom traverser would be used. Otherwise, the default traverser would be used. For example:

```
1    <adapter
2      factory="myapp.traversal.Traverser"
3      provides="repoze.bfg.interfaces.ITraverser"
4      for="myapp.models.MyRoot"
5      />
```

If the above stanza was added to a configure.zcml file, repoze.bfg would use the myapp.traversal.Traverser only when the application *root factory* returned an instance of the myapp.models.MyRoot object. Otherwise it would use the default repoze.bfg traverser to do traversal.

Example implementations of alternate traversers can be found "in the wild" within repoze.bfg.traversalwrapper (http://pypi.python.org/pypi/repoze.bfg.traversalwrapper) and repoze.bfg.metatg (http://svn.repoze.org/repoze.bfg.metatg/trunk/).

20.4 Changing How `repoze.bfg.url.model_url` Generates a URL

When you add a traverser as described in *Changing the Traverser* (pp. 204), it's often convenient to continue to use the `url.model_url()` (pp. 421) API. However, since the way traversal is done will have been modified, the URLs it generates by default may be incorrect.

If you've added a traverser, you can change how `url.model_url()` (pp. 421) generates a URL for a specific type of *context* by adding an adapter stanza for `interfaces.IContextURL` to your application's `configure.zcml`:

```
<adapter
  factory="myapp.traversal.URLGenerator"
  provides="repoze.bfg.interfaces.IContextURL"
  for="myapp.models.MyRoot *"
  />
```

In the above example, the `myapp.traversal.URLGenerator` class will be used to provide services to `url.model_url()` (pp. 421) any time the *context* passed to `model_url` is of class `myapp.models.MyRoot`. The asterisk following represents the type of interface that must be possessed by the *request* (in this case, any interface, represented by asterisk).

The API that must be implemented by a class that provides `interfaces.IContextURL` is as follows:

```
from zope.interface import Interface

class IContextURL(Interface):
    """ An adapter which deals with URLs related to a context.
    """
    def __init__(self, context, request):
        """ Accept the context and request """

    def virtual_root(self):
        """ Return the virtual root object related to a request and the
        current context"""

    def __call__(self):
        """ Return a URL that points to the context """
```

The default context URL generator is available for perusal as the class `traversal.TraversalContextURL` in the traversal module (http://svn.repoze.org/repoze.bfg/trunk/repoze/bfg/traversal.py) of the *Repoze* Subversion repository.

EXTENDING AN EXISTING
REPOZE.BFG APPLICATION

If the developer of a `repoze.bfg` application has obeyed certain constraints while building that application, a third party should be able to change its behavior without needing to modify its source code. The behavior of a `repoze.bfg` application that obeys certain constraints can be *overridden* or *extended* without modification.

21.1 Rules for Building An Extensible Application

There's only one rule you need to obey if you want to build a maximally extensible `repoze.bfg` application: you should not use any *configuration decoration* or *imperative configuration*. This means the application developer should avoid relying on *configuration decoration* meant to be detected via the a *scan*, and you mustn't configure your `repoze.bfg` application *imperatively* by using any code which configures the application through methods of the *Configurator* (except for the `configuration.Configurator.load_zcml()` (pp. 378) method).

Instead, must always use *ZCML* for the equivalent purposes. *ZCML* declarations that belong to an application can be "overridden" by integrators as necessary, but decorators and imperative code which perform the same tasks cannot. Use only *ZCML* to configure your application if you'd like it to be extensible.

21.1.1 Fundamental Plugpoints

The fundamental "plug points" of an application developed using `repoze.bfg` are *routes*, *views*, and *resources*. Routes are declarations made using the ZCML `<route>` directive. Views are declarations made using the ZCML `<view>` directive (or the `@bfg_view` decorator). Resources are files that are accessed by repoze bfg using the *pkg_resources* API such as static files and templates.

207

21.1.2 ZCML Granularity

It's extremely helpful to third party application "extenders" (aka "integrators") if the *ZCML* that composes the configuration for an application is broken up into separate files which do very specific things. These more specific ZCML files can be reintegrated within the application's main `configure.zcml` via `<include file="otherfile.zcml"/>` declarations. When ZCML files contain sets of specific declarations, an integrator can avoid including any ZCML he does not want by including only ZCML files which contain the declarations he needs. He is not forced to "accept everything" or "use nothing".

For example, it's often useful to put all `<route>` declarations in a separate ZCML file, as `<route>` statements have a relative ordering that is extremely important to the application: if an extender wants to add a route to the "middle" of the routing table, he will always need to disuse all the routes and cut and paste the routing configuration into his own application. It's useful for the extender to be able to disuse just a *single* ZCML file in this case, accepting the remainder of the configuration from other *ZCML* files in the original application.

Granularizing ZCML is not strictly required. An extender can always disuse *all* your ZCML, choosing instead to copy and paste it into his own package, if necessary. However, doing so is considerate, and allows for the best reusability.

21.2 Extending an Existing Application

The steps for extending an existing application depend largely on whether the application does or does not use configuration decorators and/or imperative code.

21.2.1 Extending an Application Which Possesses Configuration Decorators Or Which Does Configuration Imperatively

If you've inherited a `repoze.bfg` application which uses `view.bfg_view` (pp. 428) decorators or which performs configuration imperatively, one of two things may be true:

- If you just want to *extend* the application, you can write additional ZCML that registers more views or routes, loading any existing ZCML and continuing to use any existing imperative configuration done by the original application.

- If you want to *override* configuration in the application, you *may* need to change the source code of the original application.

  If the only source of trouble is the existence of `view.bfg_view` (pp. 428) decorators, you can just prevent a *scan* from happening (by omitting the `<scan>` declaration from ZCML or omitting any call to the `configuration.Configurator.scan()` (pp. 378) method). This will cause the decorators to do nothing. At this point, you will need to convert all the configuration done in decorators into equivalent *ZCML* and add that ZCML to an a separate Python package as described in *Extending an Application Which Does Not Possess Configuration Decorators or Imperative Configuration* (pp. 209).

  If the source of trouble is configuration done imperatively in a function called during application startup, you'll need to change the code: convert imperative configuration statements into equivalent *ZCML* declarations.

Once this is done, you should be able to extend or override the application like any other (see *Extending an Application Which Does Not Possess Configuration Decorators or Imperative Configuration* (pp. 209)).

21.2.2 Extending an Application Which Does Not Possess Configuration Decorators or Imperative Configuration

To extend or override the behavior of an existing application, you will need to write some *ZCML*, and perhaps some implementations of the types of things you'd like to override (such as views), which are referred to within that ZCML.

The general pattern for extending an existing application looks something like this:

- Create a new Python package. The easiest way to do this is to create a new `repoze.bfg` application using the "paster" template mechanism. See *Creating the Project* (pp. 38) for more information.

- Install the new package into the same Python environment as the original application (e.g. `python setup.py develop` or `python setup.py install`).

- Change the `configure.zcml` in the new package to include the original `repoze.bfg` application's `configure.zcml` via an include statement, e.g. `<include package="theoriginalapp"/>`. Alternately, if the original application writer anticipated overriding some things and not others, instead of including the "main" `configure.zcml` of the original application, include only specific ZCML files from the original application using the `file` attribute of the `<include>` statement, e.g. `<include package="theoriginalapp" file="views.zcml"/>`.

- On a line in the new package's `configure.zcml` file that falls after (XML-ordering-wise) the all `include` statements of original package ZCML, put an `includeOverrides` statement which identifies *another* ZCML file within the new package (for example `<includeOverrides file="overrides.zcml"/>`.

- Create an `overrides.zcml` file within the new package. The statements in the `overrides.zcml` file will override any ZCML statements made within the original application (such as view declarations).

- Create Python files containing views and other overridden elements, such as templates and static resources as necessary, and wire these up using ZCML registrations within the `overrides.zcml` file. These registrations may extend or override the original view registrations. See *Overriding Views* (pp. 210), *Overriding Routes* (pp. 210) and *Overriding Resources* (pp. 211).

- Change the Paste `.ini` file that starts up the original application. Add a `configure_zcml` key within the application's section in the file which points at your *new* package's `configure.zcml` file. See *Environment Variables and .ini File Settings* (pp. 189) for more information about this setting.

21.2.3 Overriding Views

The ZCML `<view>` declarations you make which *override* application behavior will usually have the same `context` and `name` (and *predicate* attributes, if used) as the original. These `<view>` declarations will point at "new" view code. The new view code itself will usually be cut-n-paste copies of view callables from the original application with slight tweaks. For example:

```
<view context="theoriginalapplication.models.SomeModel"
      name="theview"
      view=".views.a_view_that_does_something_slightly_different"
/>
```

A similar pattern can be used to *extend* the application with `<view>` declarations. Just register a new view against some existing model type and make sure the URLs it implies are available on some other page rendering.

21.2.4 Overriding Routes

Route setup is currently typically performed in a sequence of ordered ZCML `<route>` declarations. Because these declarations are ordered relative to each other, and because this ordering is typically important, you should retain the relative ordering of these declarations when performing an override. Typically, this means *copying* all the `<route>` declarations into an external ZCML file and changing them as necessary. Then disinclude any ZCML from the original application which contains the original declarations.

21.2.5 Overriding Resources

"Resource" files are static files on the filesystem that are accessible within a Python *package*. An entire chapter is devoted to resources: *Resources* (pp. 213). Within this chapter is a section named *Overriding Resources* (pp. 214). This section of that chapter describes in detail how to override package resources with other resources by using *ZCML* `<resource>` declarations. Add such `<resource>` declarations to your override package's `configure.zcml` to perform overrides.

21.3 Dealing With ZCML Inclusions

Sometimes it's possible to include only certain ZCML files from an application that contain only the registrations you really need, omitting others. But sometimes it's not. For brute force purposes, when you're getting `view` or `route` registrations that you don't actually want in your overridden application, it's always appropriate to just *not include* any ZCML file from the overridden application. Instead, just cut and paste the entire contents of the `configure.zcml` (and any ZCML file included by the overridden application's `configure.zcml`) into your own package and omit the `<include package=""/>` ZCML declaration in the overriding package's `configure.zcml`.

RESOURCES

A *resource* is any file contained within a Python *package* which is *not* a Python source code file. For example, each of the following is a resource:

- a *Chameleon* template file contained within a Python package.

- a GIF image file contained within a Python package.

- a CSS file contained within a Python package.

- a JavaScript source file contained within a Python package.

- A directory within a package that does not have an __init__.py in it (if it possessed an __init__.py it would *be* a package).

The use of resources is quite common in most web development projects. For example, when you create a repoze.bfg application using one of the available "paster" templates, as described in *Creating the Project* (pp. 38), the directory representing the application contains a Python *package*. Within that Python package, there are directories full of files which are resources. For example, there is a templates directory which contains .pt files, and a static directory which contains .css, .js, and .gif files.

22.1 Understanding Resources

Let's imagine you've created a repoze.bfg application that uses a *Chameleon* ZPT template via the chameleon_zpt.render_template_to_response() (pp. 365) API. For example, the application might address the resource named templates/some_template.pt using that API within a views.py file inside a myapp package:

```
from repoze.bfg.chameleon_zpt import render_template_to_response
render_template_to_response('templates/some_template.pt')
```

"Under the hood", when this API is called, repoze.bfg attempts to make sense out of the string templates/some_template.pt provided by the developer. To do so, it first finds the "current" package. The "current" package is the Python package in which the views.py module which contains this code lives. This would be the myapp package, according to our example so far. By resolving the current package, repoze.bfg has enough information to locate the actual template file. These are the elements it needs:

- The *package name* (myapp)

- The *resource name* (templates/some_template.pt)

repoze.bfg uses the *pkg_resources* API to resolve the package name and resource name to an absolute (operating-system-specific) file name. It eventually passes this resolved absolute filesystem path to the Chameleon templating engine, which then uses it to load, parse, and execute the template file.

Package names often contain dots. For example, repoze.bfg is a package. Resource names usually look a lot like relative UNIX file paths.

22.2 Overriding Resources

It can often be useful to override specific resources "from outside" a given repoze.bfg application. For example, you may wish to reuse an existing repoze.bfg application more or less unchanged. However, some specific template file owned by the application might have inappropriate HTML, or some static resource (such as a logo file or some CSS file) might not appropriate. You *could* just fork the application entirely, but it's often more convenient to just override the resources that are inappropriate and reuse the application "as is". This is particularly true when you reuse some "core" application over and over again for some set of customers (such as a CMS application, or some bug tracking application), and you want to make arbitrary visual modifications to a particular application deployment without forking the underlying code.

To this end, repoze.bfg contains a feature that makes it possible to "override" one resource with one or more other resources. In support of this feature, a *ZCML* directive exists named resource. The resource directive allows you to *override* the following kinds of resources defined in any Python package:

214

- Individual *Chameleon* templates.

- A directory containing multiple Chameleon templates.

- Individual static files served up by an instance of the `view.static` helper class.

- A directory of static files served up by an instance of the `view.static` helper class.

- Any other resource (or set of resources) addressed by code that uses the setuptools *pkg_resources* API.

Usually, overriding a resource in an existing application means performing the following steps:

- Create a new Python package. The easiest way to do this is to create a new `repoze.bfg` application using the "paster" template mechanism. See *Creating the Project* (pp. 38) for more information.

- Install the new package into the same Python environment as the original application (e.g. `python setup.py develop` or `python setup.py install`).

- Change the `configure.zcml` in the new package to include one or more `resource` ZCML directives (see *resource* (pp. 463) below). The new package's `configure.zcml` should then include the original `repoze.bfg` application's `configure.zcml` via an include statement, e.g. `<include package="theoriginalpackage"/>`.

- Add override resources to the package as necessary.

- Change the Paste `.ini` file that starts up the original application. Add a `configure_zcml` statement within the application's section in the file which points at your *new* package's `configure.zcml` file. See *Environment Variables and .ini File Settings* (pp. 189) for more information about this setting.

Note that overriding resources is not the only way to extend or modify the behavior of an existing `repoze.bfg` application. A "heavier hammer" way to do the same thing is explained in *Extending An Existing repoze.bfg Application* (pp. 207). The heavier hammer way allows you to replace a *view* wholesale rather than resources that might be used by a view.

22.2.1 The `override_resource` API

An individual call to `configuration.Configurator.override_resource()` (pp. 378) can override a single resource. For example:

215

```
1  config.override_resource(
2          to_override='some.package:templates/mytemplate.pt',
3          override_with='another.package:othertemplates/anothertemplate.pt')
```

The string value passed to both `to_override` and `override_with` attached to a resource directive is called a "specification". The colon separator in a specification separates the *package name* from the *resource name*. The colon and the following resource name are optional. If they are not specified, the override attempts to resolve every lookup into a package from the directory of another package. For example:

```
1  config.override_resource(to_override='some.package',
2                           override_with='another.package')
```

Individual subdirectories within a package can also be overridden:

```
1  config.override_resource(to_override='some.package:templates/',
2                           override_with='another.package:othertemplates/')
```

If you wish to override a directory with another directory, you *must* make sure to attach the slash to the end of both the `to_override` specification and the `override_with` specification. If you fail to attach a slash to the end of a specification that points a directory, you will get unexpected results.

You cannot override a directory specification with a file specification, and vice versa: a startup error will occur if you try. You cannot override a resource with itself: a startup error will occur if you try.

Only individual *package* resources may be overridden. Overrides will not traverse through subpackages within an overridden package. This means that if you want to override resources for both `some.package:templates`, and `some.package.views:templates`, you will need to register two overrides.

The package name in a specification may start with a dot, meaning that the package is relative to the package in which the configuration construction file resides (or the `package` argument to the `configuration.Configurator` (pp. 367) class construction). For example:

```
1  config.override_resource(to_override='.subpackage:templates/',
2                           override_with='another.package:templates/')
```

Multiple `override_resource` statements which name a shared `to_override` but a different `override_with` specification can be "stacked" to form a search path. The first resource that exists in the search path will be used; if no resource exists in the override path, the original resource is used.

Resource overrides can actually override resources other than templates and static files. Any software which uses the `pkg_resources.get_resource_filename()`, `pkg_resources.get_resource_stream()` or `pkg_resources.get_resource_string()` APIs will obtain an overridden file when an override is used.

22.2.2 The `resource` ZCML Directive

Instead of using `configuration.Configurator.override_resource()` (pp. 378) during *imperative configuration*, an equivalent can be used to perform all the tasks described above within *ZCML*. The ZCML `resource` tag is a frontend to using `override_resource`.

An individual `repoze.bfg` resource ZCML statement can override a single resource. For example:

```
<resource
  to_override="some.package:templates/mytemplate.pt"
  override_with="another.package:othertemplates/anothertemplate.pt"
/>
```

The string value passed to both `to_override` and `override_with` attached to a resource directive is called a "specification". The colon separator in a specification separates the *package name* from the *resource name*. The colon and the following resource name are optional. If they are not specified, the override attempts to resolve every lookup into a package from the directory of another package. For example:

```
<resource
  to_override="some.package"
  override_with="another.package"
/>
```

Individual subdirectories within a package can also be overridden:

```
<resource
  to_override="some.package:templates/"
  override_with="another.package:othertemplates/"
/>
```

If you wish to override a directory with another directory, you *must* make sure to attach the slash to the end of both the `to_override` specification and the `override_with` specification. If you fail to attach a slash to the end of a specification that points a directory, you will get unexpected results.

The package name in a specification may start with a dot, meaning that the package is relative to the package in which the ZCML file resides. For example:

```
<resource
  to_override=".subpackage:templates/"
  override_with="another.package:templates/"
/>
```

See also *resource* (pp. 463).

REQUEST PROCESSING

Once a `repoze.bfg` application is up and running, it is ready to accept requests and return responses.

What happens from the time a *WSGI* request enters a `repoze.bfg` application through to the point that `repoze.bfg` hands off a response back to WSGI for upstream processing?

1. A user initiates a request from his browser to the hostname and port number of the WSGI server used by the `repoze.bfg` application.

2. The WSGI server used by the `repoze.bfg` application passes the WSGI environment to the `__call__` method of the `repoze.bfg` *router* object.

3. A *request* object is created based on the WSGI environment.

4. A `interfaces.INewRequest` (pp. 385) *event* is sent to any subscribers.

5. If any *route* has been defined within application configuration, the `repoze.bfg` *router* calls a *URL dispatch* "route mapper." The job of the mapper is to examine the `PATH_INFO` implied by the request to determine whether any user-defined *route* matches the current WSGI environment. The *router* passes the request as an argument to the mapper.

6. If any route matches, the WSGI environment is mutated; a `bfg.routes.route` key and a `bfg.routes.matchdict` are added to the WSGI environment, and an attribute named `matchdict` is added to the request. A root object associated with the route found is also generated. If a the *route configuration* which matched has an associated a `factory` argument, this factory is used to generate the root object, otherwise a default *root factory* is used.

7. If a route match was *not* found, and a `root_factory` argument was passed to the *Configurator* constructor, that callable is used to generate the root object. If the `root_factory` argument passed to the Configurator constructor is `None`, a default root factory is used to generate a root object.

8. The `repoze.bfg` router calls a "traverser" function with the root object and the request. The traverser function attempts to traverse the root object (using any existing `__getitem__` on the root object and subobjects) to find a *context*. If the root object has no `__getitem__` method, the root itself is assumed to be the context. The exact traversal algorithm is described in *Traversal* (pp. 61). The traverser function returns a dictionary, which contains a *context* and a *view name* as well as other ancillary information.

9. The request is decorated with various names returned from the traverser (such as `context`, `view_name`, and so forth), so they can be accessed via e.g. `request.context` within *view* code.

10. A `interfaces.IAfterTraversal` (pp. 385) *event* is sent to any subscribers.

11. `repoze.bfg` looks up a *view* callable using the context, the request, and the view name. If a view callable doesn't exist for this combination of objects (based on the type of the context, the type of the request, and the value of the view name, and any *predicate* attributes applied to the view configuration), `repoze.bfg` uses a "not found" view callable to generate a response, and returns that response.

12. If a view callable was found, `repoze.bfg` calls the view function.

13. If an *authorization policy* is in use, and the view was protected by a *permission*, `repoze.bfg` passes the context, the request, and the view_name to a function which determines whether the view being asked for can be executed by the requesting user, based on credential information in the request and security information attached to the context. If it returns `True`, `repoze.bfg` calls the view callable to obtain a response. If it returns `False`, it uses a *forbidden view* callable to generate a response.

14. A `interfaces.INewResponse` (pp. 385) *event* is sent to any subscribers.

15. The response object's `app_iter`, `status`, and `headerlist` attributes are used to generate a WSGI response. The response is sent back to the upstream WSGI server.

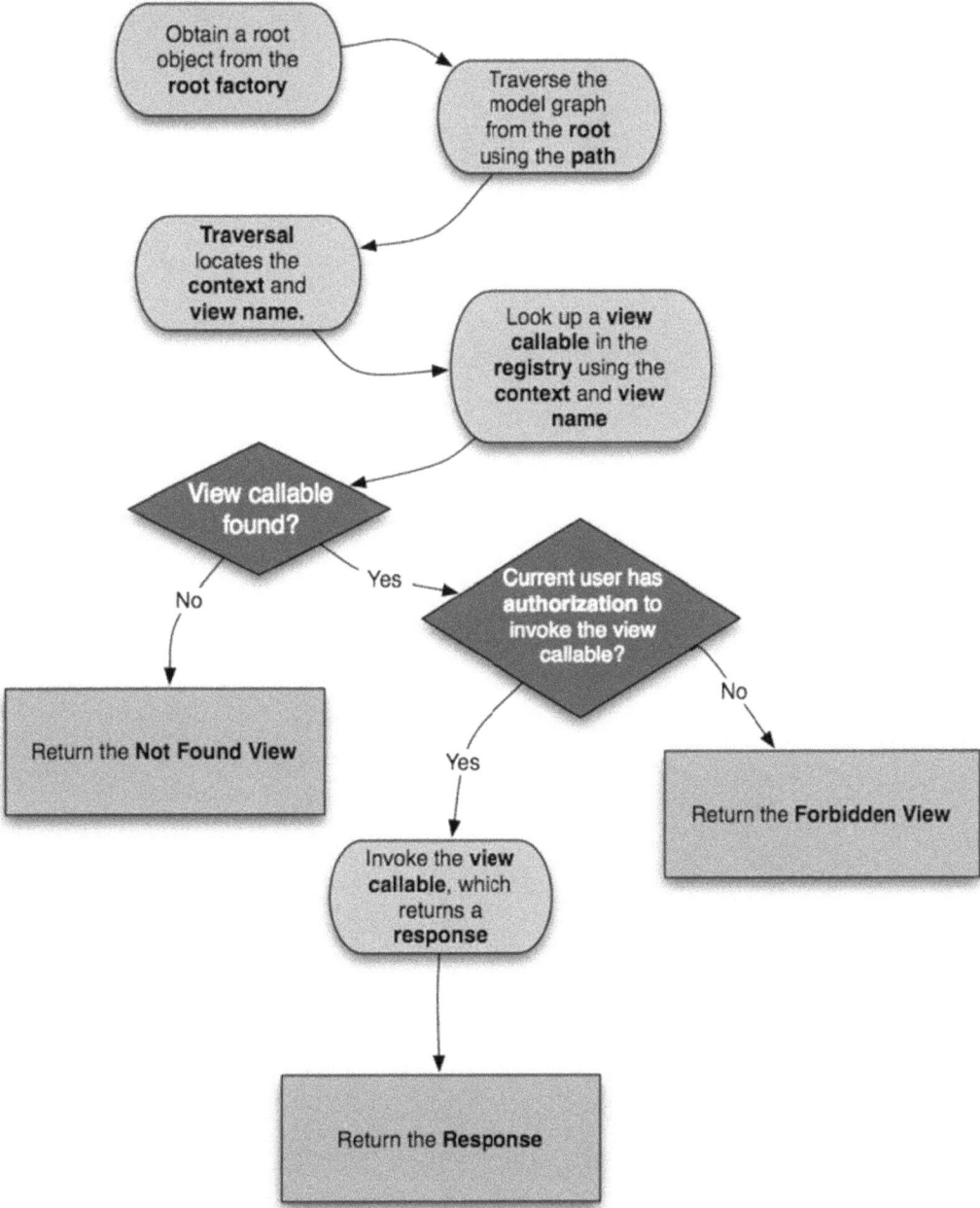

This is a very high-level overview that leaves out various details. For more detail about subsystems invoked by the BFG router such as traversal, URL dispatch, views, and event processing, see *Context Finding and View Lookup* (pp. 57), *Views* (pp. 105), and *Using Events* (pp. 185).

STARTUP

When you cause `repoze.bfg` to start up in a console window, you'll see something much like this show up on the console:

```
$ paster serve myproject/MyProject.ini
Starting server in PID 16601.
serving on 0.0.0.0:6543 view at http://127.0.0.1:6543
```

This chapter explains what happens between the time you press the "Return" key on your keyboard after typing `paster serve myproject/MyProject.ini` and the time the line `serving on 0.0.0.0:6543 ...` is output to your console.

24.1 The Startup Process

The easiest and best-documented way to start and serve a `repoze.bfg` application is to use the `paster serve` command against a *PasteDeploy* `.ini` file. This uses the `.ini` file to infer settings and starts a server listening on a port. For the purposes of this discussion, we'll assume that you are using this command to run your `repoze.bfg` application.

Here's a high-level time-ordered overview of what happens when you press `return` after running `paster serve MyProject.ini`.

1. The *PasteDeploy* `paster` command is invoked under your shell with the arguments `serve` and `MyProject.ini`. As a result, the *PasteDeploy* framework recognizes that it is meant to begin to run and serve an application using the information contained within the `MyProject.ini` file.

2. The PasteDeploy framework finds a section named either `[app:main]`, `[pipeline:main]`, or `[composite::main]` in the `.ini` file. This section represents the configuration of a *WSGI* application that will be served. If you're using a simple application (e.g. an `[app:main]` section of a default-generated `repoze.bfg` project), the application *entry point* or *dotted Python name* will be named on the `use=` line within the section's configuration. If, instead of a simple application, you're using a WSGI *pipeline* (e.g. a `[pipeline:main]` section), the application named on the "last" element will refer to your `repoze.bfg` application. If instead of a simple application or a pipeline, you're using a Paste "composite" (e.g. `[composite:main]`), refer to the documentation for that particular composite to understand how to make it refer to your `repoze.bfg` application.

3. The application's *constructor* (named by the entry point reference or dotted Python name on the `use=` line) is passed the key/value parameters mentioned within the section in which it's defined. The constructor is meant to return a *router* instance, which is a *WSGI* application.

   For `repoze.bfg` applications, the constructor will be a function named `app` in the `run.py` file within the *package* in which your application lives. If this function succeeds, it will return a `repoze.bfg` *router* instance. Here's the contents of an example `run.py` module:

```python
from repoze.bfg.configuration import Configurator
from myproject.models import get_root

def app(global_config, **settings):
    """ This function returns a WSGI application.

    It is usually called by the PasteDeploy framework during
    ''paster serve''.
    """
    config = Configurator(root_factory=get_root, settings=settings)
    config.begin()
    zcml_file = settings.get('configure_zcml', 'configure.zcml')
    config.load_zcml(zcml_file)
    config.end()
    return config.make_wsgi_app()
```

Note that the constructor function accepts a `global_config` argument (which is a dictionary of key/value pairs mentioned in the `[DEFAULT]` section of the configuration file). It also accepts a `**settings` argument, which collects another set of arbitrary key/value pairs. The arbitrary key/value pairs received by this function in `**settings` will be composed of all the key/value pairs that are present in the `[app:main]` section (except for the `use=` setting) when this function is called by the *PasteDeploy* framework when you run `paster serve`.

Our generated `MyProject.ini` file looks like so:

```
[DEFAULT]
debug = true

[app:main]
use = egg:MyProject#app
reload_templates = true
debug_authorization = false
debug_notfound = false

[server:main]
use = egg:Paste#http
host = 0.0.0.0
port = 6543
```

In this case, the `myproject.run:app` function referred to by the entry point URI `egg:MyProject#app` (see *MyProject.ini* (pp. 45) for more information about entry point URIs, and how they relate to callables), will receive the key/value pairs `{'reload_templates':'true', 'debug_authorization':'false', 'debug_notfound':'false'}`.

4. The PasteDeploy application constructor itself is invoked. It is represented by the `app` function in `run.py`. A typical `repoze.bfg` app function will look like the below.

```
1  from repoze.bfg.configuration import Configurator
2  from myproject.models import get_root
3
4  def app(global_config, **settings):
5      """ This function returns a WSGI application.
6
7      It is usually called by the PasteDeploy framework during
8      ''paster serve''.
9      """
10     config = Configurator(root_factory=get_root, settings=settings)
11     config.begin()
12     zcml_file = settings.get('configure_zcml', 'configure.zcml')
13     config.load_zcml(zcml_file)
14     config.end()
15     return config.make_wsgi_app()
```

Note that the `app` function imports the `get_root` *root factory* function from the `myproject.models` Python module.

225

5. The `app` function first constructs a `configuration.Configurator` (pp. 367) instance, passing `get_root` to it as its `root_factory` argument, and `settings` dictionary captured via the `**settings` kwarg as its `settings` argument.

   `get_root` is a root factory callable that is invoked on every request to retrieve the application root. It is not called during startup, only when a request is handled.

   `settings` dictionary contains all the options in the `[app:main]` section of our .ini file except the "use" option (which is internal to paste). In this case, `**settings` will be something like `{'reload_templates':'true', 'debug_authorization':'false', 'debug_notfound':'false'}`.

6. The `app` function then calls the `configuration.Configurator.load_zcml()` (pp. 378) method, passing in a `zcml_file` value. `zcml_file` is the value of the `configure_zcml` setting or a default of `configure.zcml`. This filename is relative to the run.py file that the `app` function lives in. The `load_zcml` function processes each *ZCML declaration* in the ZCML file implied by the `zcml_file` argument. If `load_zcml` fails to parse the ZCML file (or any file which is included by the ZCML file), a `XMLConfigurationError` is raised and processing ends. If it succeeds, an *application registry* is populated using all the *ZCML declaration* statements present in the file.

7. The `configuration.Configurator.make_wsgi_app()` (pp. 378) method is called. The result is a *router* instance. The router is associated with the *application registry* implied by the configurator previously populated by ZCML. The router is a WSGI application.

8. A `interfaces.WSGIApplicationCreatedEvent` event is emitted (see *Using Events* (pp. 185) for more information about events).

9. Assuming there were no errors, the `app` function in `myproject` returns the router instance created by `make_wsgi_app` back to PasteDeploy. As far as PasteDeploy is concerned, it is "just another WSGI application".

10. PasteDeploy starts the WSGI *server* defined within the `[server:main]` section. In our case, this is the `Paste#http` server (`use = egg:Paste#http`), and it will listen on all interfaces (`host = 0.0.0.0`), on port number 6543 (`port = 6543`). The server code itself is what prints `serving on 0.0.0.0:6543 view at http://127.0.0.1:6543`. The server serves the application, and the application is running, waiting to receive requests.

THREAD LOCALS

A *thread local* variable is a variable that appears to be a "global" variable to an application which uses it. However, unlike a true global variable, one thread or process serving the application may receive a different value than another thread or process when that variable is "thread local".

When a request is processed, `repoze.bfg` makes two *thread local* variables available to the application: a "registry" and a "request".

25.1 Why and How `repoze.bfg` Uses Thread Local Variables

How are thread locals beneficial to `repoze.bfg` and application developers who use `repoze.bfg`? Well, usually they're decidedly **not**. Using a global or a thread local variable in any application usually makes it a lot harder to understand for a casual reader. Use of a thread local or a global is usually just a way to avoid passing some value around between functions, which is itself usually a very bad idea, at least if code readability counts as an important concern.

For historical reasons, however, thread local variables are indeed consulted by various `repoze.bfg` API functions. For example, the implementation of the `security` (pp. 395) function named `security.authenticated_userid()` (pp. 395) retrieves the thread local *application registry* as a matter of course to find a *authentication policy*. It uses the `threadlocal.get_current_registry()` (pp. 411) function to retrieve the application registry, from which it looks up the authentication policy; it then uses the authentication policy to retrieve the authenticated user id. This is how `repoze.bfg` allows arbitrary authentication policies to be "plugged in".

When they need to do so, `repoze.bfg` internals use two API functions to retrieve the *request* and *application registry*: `threadlocal.get_current_request()` (pp. 411) and `threadlocal.get_current_registry()` (pp. 411). The former returns the "current" request; the latter returns the "current" registry. Both `get_current_*` functions retrieve an object from a thread-local data structure. These API functions are documented in *repoze.bfg.threadlocal* (pp. 411).

These values are thread locals rather than true globals because one Python process may be handling multiple simultaneous requests or even multiple `repoze.bfg` applications. If they were true globals, `repoze.bfg` could not handle multiple simultaneous requests or allow more than one `repoze.bfg` application instance to exist in a single Python process.

Because one `repoze.bfg` application is permitted to call *another* `repoze.bfg` application from its own *view* code (perhaps as a *WSGI* app with help from the `wsgi.wsgiapp2()` (pp. 436) decorator), these variables are managed in a *stack* during normal system operations. The stack instance itself is a threading.local (http://docs.python.org/library/threading.html#threading.local).

During normal operations, the thread locals stack is managed by a *Router* object. At the beginning of a request, the Router pushes the application's registry and the request on to the stack. At the end of a request, the stack is popped. The topmost request and registry on the stack are considered "current". Therefore, when the system is operating normally, the very definition of "current" is defined entirely by the behavior of a repoze.bfg *Router*.

However, during unit testing, no Router code is ever invoked, and the definition of "current" is defined by the boundary between calls to the `configuration.Configurator.begin()` (pp. 368) and `configuration.Configurator.end()` (pp. 368) methods (or between calls to the `testing.setUp()` (pp. 406) and `testing.tearDown()` (pp. 407) functions). These functions push and pop the threadlocal stack when the system is under test. See *Test Set Up and Tear Down* (pp. 194) for the definitions of these functions.

Scripts which use `repoze.bfg` machinery but never actually start a WSGI server or receive requests via HTTP such as scripts which use the `scripting`‘ API will never cause any Router code to be executed. However, the `scripting` (pp. 393) APIs also push some values on to the thread locals stack as a matter of course. Such scripts should expect the `threadlocal.get_current_request()` (pp. 411) function to always return `None`, and should expect the `threadlocal.get_current_registry()` (pp. 411) function to return exactly the same *application registry* for every request.

25.2 Why You Shouldn't Abuse Thread Locals

You probably should almost never use the `threadlocal.get_current_request()` (pp. 411) or `threadlocal.get_current_registry()` (pp. 411) functions, except perhaps in tests. In particular, it's almost always a mistake to use `get_current_request` or `get_current_registry` in application code because its usage makes it possible to write code that can be neither easily tested nor scripted. Inappropriate usage is defined as follows:

- `get_current_request` should never be called within the body of a *view callable*, or within code called by a view callable. View callables already have access to the request (it's passed in to each as `request`).

- `get_current_request` should never be called in *model* code. Model code should never require any access to the request; if your model code requires access to a request object, you've almost certainly factored something wrong, and you should change your code rather than using this function.

- `get_current_request` function should never be called because it's "easier" or "more elegant" to think about calling it than to pass a request through a series of function calls when creating some API design. Your application should instead almost certainly pass data derived from the request around rather than relying on being able to call this function to obtain the request in places that actually have no business knowing about it. Parameters are *meant* to be passed around as function arguments, this is why they exist. Don't try to "save typing" or create "nicer APIs" by using this function in the place where a request is required; this will only lead to sadness later.

- Neither `get_current_request` nor `get_current_registry` should ever be called within application-specific forks of third-party library code. The library you've forked almost certainly has nothing to do with `repoze.bfg`, and making it dependent on `repoze.bfg` (rather than making your `repoze.bfg` application depend upon it) means you're forming a dependency in the wrong direction.

Use of the `threadlocal.get_current_request()` (pp. 411) function in application code *is* still useful in very limited circumstances. As a rule of thumb, usage of `get_current_request` is useful **within code which is meant to eventually be removed**. For instance, you may find yourself wanting to deprecate some API that expects to be passed a request object in favor of one that does not expect to be passed a request object. But you need to keep implementations of the old API working for some period of time while you deprecate the older API. So you write a "facade" implementation of the new API which calls into the code which implements the older API. Since the new API does not require the request, your facade implementation doesn't have local access to the request when it needs to pass it into the older API implementation. After some period of time, the older implementation code is disused and the hack that uses `get_current_request` is removed. This would be an appropriate place to use the `get_current_request`.

Use of the `threadlocal.get_current_registry()` (pp. 411) function should be limited to testing scenarios. The registry made current by use of the `configuration.Configurator.begin()` (pp. 368) method during a test (or via `testing.setUp()` (pp. 406)) when you do not pass one in is available to you via this API.

USING THE ZOPE COMPONENT ARCHITECTURE IN REPOZE.BFG

Under the hood, `repoze.bfg` uses a *Zope Component Architecture* component registry as its *application registry*. The Zope Component Architecture is referred to colloquially as the "ZCA."

The `zope.component` API used to access data in a traditional Zope application can be opaque. For example, here is a typical "unnamed utility" lookup using the `zope.component.getUtility()` global API as it might appear in a traditional Zope application:

```
1  from repoze.bfg.interfaces import ISettings
2  from zope.component import getUtility
3  settings = getUtility(ISettings)
```

After this code runs, `settings` will be a Python dictionary. But it's unlikely that any "civilian" will be able to figure this out just by reading the code casually. When the `zope.component.getUtility` API is used by a developer, the conceptual load on a casual reader of code is high.

While the ZCA is an excellent tool with which to build a *framework* such as `repoze.bfg`, it is not always the best tool with which to build an *application* due to the opacity of the `zope.component` APIs. Accordingly, `repoze.bfg` tends to hide the the presence of the ZCA from application developers. You needn't understand the ZCA to create a `repoze.bfg` application; its use is effectively only a framework implementation detail.

However, developers whom are already used to writing *Zope* applications often still wish to use the ZCA while building a `repoze.bfg` application; `repoze.bfg` makes this possible.

26.1 Using the ZCA Global API in a `repoze.bfg` Application

Zope uses a single ZCA registry – the "global" ZCA registry – for all Zope applications run in the same Python process, effectively making it impossible to run more than one Zope application in a single process.

However, for ease of deployment, it's often useful to be able to run more than a single application per process. For example, use of a *Paste* "composite" allows you to run separate individual WSGI applications in the same process, each answering requests for some URL prefix. This makes it possible to run, for example, a TurboGears application at `/turbogears` and a BFG application at `/bfg`, both served up using the same *WSGI* server within a single Python process.

Most production Zope applications are relatively large, making it impractical due to memory constraints to run more than one Zope application per Python process. However, a `repoze.bfg` application may be very small and consume very little memory, so it's a reasonable goal to be able to want to run more than one BFG application per process.

In order to make it possible to run more than one `repoze.bfg` application in a single process, `repoze.bfg` defaults to using a separate ZCA registry *per application*.

While this services a reasonable goal, it causes some issues when trying to use patterns which you might use to build a typical *Zope* application to build a `repoze.bfg` application. Without special help, ZCA "global" APIs such as `zope.component.getUtility` and `zope.component.getSiteManager` will use the ZCA "global" registry. Therefore, these APIs application will appear to fail when used in a `repoze.bfg` application, because they'll be consulting the ZCA global registry rather than the component registry associated with your `repoze.bfg` application.

There are three ways to fix this: by disusing the ZCA global API entirely, by using `configuration.Configurator.hook_zca()` (pp. 368) or by passing the ZCA global registry to the *Configurator* constructor at startup time. We'll describe all three methods in this section.

26.1.1 Disusing the Global ZCA API

ZCA "global" API functions such as `zope.component.getSiteManager`, `zope.component.getUtility`, `zope.component.getAdapter`, and `zope.component.getMultiAdapter` aren't strictly necessary. Every component registry has a method API that offers the same functionality; it can be used instead. For example, presuming the `registry` value below is a Zope Component Architecture component registry, the following bit of code is equivalent to `zope.component.getUtility(IFoo)`:

```
registry.getUtility(IFoo)
```

The full method API is documented in the `zope.component` package, but it largely mirrors the "global" API almost exactly.

If you are willing to disuse the "global" ZCA APIs and use the method interface of a registry instead, you need only know how to obtain the `repoze.bfg` component registry.

There are two ways of doing so:

- use the `threadlocal.get_current_registry()` (pp.   411) function within `repoze.bfg` view or model code.   This will always return the "current" `repoze.bfg` application registry.

- use the attribute of the *request* object named `registry` in your `repoze.bfg` view code, eg. `request.registry`. This is the ZCA component registry related to the running `repoze.bfg` application.

See   *Thread   Locals*   (pp.   227)   for   more   information   about `threadlocal.get_current_registry()` (pp. 411).

26.1.2 Enabling the ZCA Global API by Using `hook_zca`

Consider the following bit of idiomatic `repoze.bfg` startup code:

```python
from zope.component import getGlobalSiteManager
from repoze.bfg.configuration import Configurator

def app(global_settings, **settings):
    config = Configurator(settings=settings)
    config.begin()
    config.load_zcml('configure.zcml')
    config.end()
    return config.make_wsgi_app()
```

When the `app` function above is run, a *Configurator* is constructed. When the configurator is created, it creates a *new application registry* (a ZCA component registry). A new registry is constructed whenever the `registry` argument is omitted when a *Configurator* constructor is called, or when a `registry` argument with a value of `None` is passed to a *Configurator* constructor.

During a request, the application registry created by the Configurator is "made current". This means calls to `threadlocal.get_current_registry()` (pp. 411) in the thread handling the request will return the component registry associated with the application.

As a result, application developers can use `get_current_registry` to get the registry and thus get access to utilities and such, as per *Disusing the Global ZCA API* (pp. 232). But they still cannot use the global ZCA API. Without special treatment, the ZCA global APIs will always return the global ZCA registry (the one in `zope.component.globalregistry.base`).

To "fix" this and make the ZCA global APIs use the "current" BFG registry, you need to call `configuration.Configurator.hook_zca()` (pp. 368) within your setup code. For example:

```
from zope.component import getGlobalSiteManager
from repoze.bfg.configuration import Configurator

def app(global_settings, **settings):
    config = Configurator(settings=settings)
    config.hook_zca()
    config.begin()
    config.load_zcml('configure.zcml')
    config.end()
    return config.make_wsgi_app()
```

We've added a line to our original startup code, line number 6, which calls `config.hook_zca()`. The effect of this line under the hood is that an analogue of the following code is executed:

```
from zope.component import getSiteManager
from repoze.bfg.threadlocal import get_current_registry
getSiteManager.sethook(get_current_registry)
```

This causes the ZCA global API to start using the `repoze.bfg` application registry in threads which are running a `repoze.bfg` request.

Calling `hook_zca` is usually sufficient to "fix" the problem of being able to use the global ZCA API within a `repoze.bfg` application. However, it also means that a Zope application that is running in the same process may start using the `repoze.bfg` global registry instead of the Zope global registry, effectively inverting the original problem. In such a case, follow the steps in the next section, *Enabling the ZCA Global API by Using The ZCA Global Registry* (pp. 235).

26.1.3 Enabling the ZCA Global API by Using The ZCA Global Registry

You can tell your `repoze.bfg` application to use the ZCA global registry at startup time instead of constructing a new one:

```
1  from zope.component import getGlobalSiteManager
2  from repoze.bfg.configuration import Configurator
3
4  def app(global_settings, **settings):
5      globalreg = getGlobalSiteManager()
6      config = Configurator(registry=globalreg)
7      config.setup_registry(settings=settings)
8      config.hook_zca()
9      config.begin()
10     config.load_zcml('configure.zcml')
11     config.end()
12     return config.make_wsgi_app()
```

Lines 5, 6, and 7 above are the interesting ones. Line 5 retrieves the global ZCA component registry. Line 6 creates a *Configurator*, passing the global ZCA registry into its constructor as the `registry` argument. Line 7 "sets up" the global registry with BFG-specific registrations; this is code that is normally executed when a registry is constructed rather than created, but we must call it "by hand" when we pass an explicit registry.

At this point, `repoze.bfg` will use the ZCA global registry rather than creating a new application-specific registry; since by default the ZCA global API will use this registry, things will work as you might expect a Zope app to when you use the global ZCA API.

26.2 Using Broken ZCML Directives

Some *Zope* and third-party *ZCML* directives use the `zope.component.getGlobalSiteManager` API to get "the registry" when they should actually be calling `zope.component.getSiteManager`.

`zope.component.getSiteManager` can be overridden by `repoze.bfg` via `configuration.Configurator.hook_zca()` (pp. 368), while `zope.component.getGlobalSiteManager` cannot. Directives that use `zope.component.getGlobalSiteManager` are effectively broken; no ZCML directive should be using this function to find a registry to populate.

You cannot use ZCML directives which use `zope.component.getGlobalSiteManager` within a `repoze.bfg` application without passing the ZCA global registry to the *Configurator* constructor at application startup, as per *Enabling the ZCA Global API by Using The ZCA Global Registry* (pp. 235).

One alternative exists: fix the ZCML directive to use `getSiteManager` rather than `getGlobalSiteManager`. If a directive disuses `getGlobalSiteManager`, the `hook_zca` method of using a component registry as documented in *Enabling the ZCA Global API by Using hook_zca* (pp. 233) will begin to work, allowing you to make use of the ZCML directive without also using the ZCA global registry.

Part II

Tutorials

ZODB + TRAVERSAL WIKI TUTORIAL

This tutorial introduces a *traversal* -based `repoze.bfg` application to a developer familiar with Python. When we're done with the tutorial, the developer will have created a basic Wiki application with authentication.

For cut and paste purposes, the source code for all stages of this tutorial can be browsed at docs.repoze.org (http://docs.repoze.org/bfgwiki-1.2).

27.1 Background

This version of the `repoze.bfg` wiki tutorial presents a `repoze.bfg` application that uses technologies which will be familiar to someone with *Zope* experience. It uses *ZODB* as a persistence mechanism and *traversal* to map URLs to code. It can also be followed by people without any prior Python web framework experience.

To code along with this tutorial, the developer will need a UNIX machine with development tools (Mac OS X with XCode, any Linux or BSD variant, etc) *or* he will need a Windows system of any kind.

This tutorial targets `repoze.bfg` version 1.2.

Have fun!

27.2 Installation

For the most part, the installation process for this tutorial duplicates the steps described in *Installing repoze.bfg* (pp. 7) and *Creating a repoze.bfg Project* (pp. 37), however it also explains how to install additional libraries for tutorial purposes.

27.2.1 Preparation

Please take the following steps to prepare for the tutorial. The steps to prepare for the tutorial are slightly different depending on whether you're using UNIX or Windows.

Preparation, UNIX

1. If you don't already have a Python 2.5 interpreter installed on your system, obtain, install, or find Python 2.5 (http://python.org/download/releases/2.5.4/) for your system.

2. Install the latest *setuptools* into the Python you obtained/installed/found in the step above: download ez_setup.py (http://peak.telecommunity.com/dist/ez_setup.py) and run it using the `python` interpreter of your Python 2.5 installation:

```
$ /path/to/my/Python-2.5/bin/python ez_setup.py
```

3. Use that Python's *bin/easy_install* to install *virtualenv*:

```
$ /path/to/my/Python-2.5/bin/easy_install virtualenv
```

4. Use that Python's virtualenv to make a workspace:

```
$ path/to/my/Python-25/bin/virtualenv --no-site-packages bigfntut
```

5. Switch to the `bigfntut` directory:

```
$ cd bigfntut
```

6. (Optional) Consider using `source bin/activate` to make your shell environment wired to use the virtualenv.

7. Use `easy_install` and point to the `repoze.bfg` "current" index to get `repoze.bfg` and its direct dependencies installed:

```
$ bin/easy_install -i http://dist.repoze.org/bfg/current/simple \
            repoze.bfg
```

8. Use `easy_install` to install `docutils`, `repoze.tm`, `repoze.zodbconn`, `repoze.who`, `nose` and `coverage` from a different custom index (the "bfgsite" index).

```
$ bin/easy_install -i http://dist.repoze.org/bfgsite/simple \
    docutils repoze.tm repoze.zodbconn repoze.who nose coverage
```

Preparation, Windows

1. Install, or find Python 2.5 (http://python.org/download/releases/2.5.4/) for your system.

2. Install the latest *setuptools* into the Python you obtained/installed/found in the step above: download ez_setup.py (http://peak.telecommunity.com/dist/ez_setup.py) and run it using the `python` interpreter of your Python 2.5 installation using a command prompt:

```
c:\> c:\Python25\python ez_setup.py
```

3. Use that Python's *bin/easy_install* to install *virtualenv*:

```
c:\> c:\Python25\Scripts\easy_install virtualenv
```

4. Use that Python's virtualenv to make a workspace:

241

```
c:\> c:\Python25\Scripts\virtualenv --no-site-packages bigfntut
```

5. Switch to the `bigfntut` directory:

```
c:\> cd bigfntut
```

6. (Optional) Consider using `bin\activate.bat` to make your shell environment wired to use the virtualenv.

7. Use `easy_install` and point to the `repoze.bfg` "current" index to get `repoze.bfg` and its direct dependencies installed:

```
c:\bigfntut> Scripts\easy_install -i \
        http://dist.repoze.org/bfg/current/simple repoze.bfg
```

8. Use `easy_install` to install `docutils`, `repoze.tm`, `repoze.zodbconn`, `repoze.who`, `nose` and `coverage` from a *different* index (the "bfgsite" index).

```
c:\bigfntut> Scripts\easy_install -i \
        http://dist.repoze.org/bfgsite/simple docutils repoze.tm \
        repoze.zodbconn repoze.who nose coverage
```

27.2.2 Making a Project

Your next step is to create a project. `repoze.bfg` supplies a variety of templates to generate sample projects. For this tutorial, we will use the *ZODB* -oriented template named `bfg_zodb`.

The below instructions assume your current working directory is the "virtualenv" named "bigfntut".

On UNIX:

```
$ bin/paster create -t bfg_zodb tutorial
```

On Windows:

```
c:\bigfntut> Scripts\paster create -t bfg_zodb tutorial
```

ⓘ If you are using Windows, the bfg_zodb Paster template doesn't currently deal gracefully with installation into a location that contains spaces in the path. If you experience startup problems, try putting both the virtualenv and the project into directories that do not contain spaces in their paths.

27.2.3 Installing the Project in "Development Mode"

In order to do development on the project easily, you must "register" the project as a development egg in your workspace using the setup.py develop command. In order to do so, cd to the "tutorial" directory you created in *Making a Project* (pp. 242), and run the "setup.py develop" command using virtualenv Python interpreter.

On UNIX:

```
$ cd tutorial
$ ../bin/python setup.py develop
```

On Windows:

```
C:\bigfntut> cd tutorial
C:\bigfntut\tutorial> ..\Scripts\python setup.py develop
```

27.2.4 Running the Tests

After you've installed the project in development mode, you may run the tests for the project.

On UNIX:

```
$ ../bin/python setup.py test -q
```

On Windows:

```
c:\bigfntut\tutorial> ..\Scripts\python setup.py test -q
```

27.2.5 Starting the Application

Start the application.

On UNIX:

```
$ ../bin/paster serve tutorial.ini --reload
```

On Windows:

```
c:\bifgfntut\tutorial> ..\Scripts\paster serve tutorial.ini --reload
```

27.2.6 Exposing Test Coverage Information

You can run the nosetests command to see test coverage information. This runs the tests in the same way that setup.py test does but provides additional "coverage" information, exposing which lines of your project are "covered" (or not covered) by the tests.

On UNIX:

```
$ ../bin/nosetests --cover-package=tutorial --cover-erase --with-coverage
```

On Windows:

```
c:\bigfntut\tutorial> ..\Scripts\nosetests --cover-package=tutorial \
      --cover-erase --with-coverage
```

Looks like the code in the bfg_zodb template for ZODB projects is missing some test coverage, particularly in the file named models.py.

244

27.2.7 Visit the Application in a Browser

In a browser, visit http://localhost:6543/ (http://localhost:6543). You will see the generated application's default page.

27.2.8 Decisions the `bfg_zodb` Template Has Made For You

Creating a project using the `bfg_zodb` template makes the assumption that you are willing to use *ZODB* as persistent storage and *traversal* to map URLs to code. `repoze.bfg` supports any persistent storage mechanism (e.g. a SQL database or filesystem files, etc). It also supports an additional mechanism to map URLs to code (*URL dispatch*). However, for the purposes of this tutorial, we'll only be using traversal and ZODB.

27.3 Basic Layout

The starter files generated by the `bfg_zodb` template are basic, but they provide a good orientation for the high-level patterns common to most *traversal* -based `repoze.bfg` (and *ZODB* based) projects.

The source code for this tutorial stage can be browsed at docs.repoze.org (http://docs.repoze.org/bfgwiki-1.2/basiclayout).

27.3.1 `__init__.py`

A directory on disk can be turned into a Python *package* by containing an `__init__.py` file. Even if empty, this marks a directory as a Python package.

27.3.2 Configuration With `configure.zcml`

The `bfg_zodb` template uses *ZCML* to perform system configuration. The ZCML file generated by the template looks like the following:

```
1   <configure xmlns="http://namespaces.repoze.org/bfg">
2
3     <!-- this must be included for the view declarations to work -->
4     <include package="repoze.bfg.includes" />
5
6     <view
7         context=".models.MyModel"
8         view=".views.my_view"
9         renderer="templates/mytemplate.pt"
10        />
11
12    <static
13        name="static"
14        path="templates/static"
15        />
16
17  </configure>
```

1. *Line 1.* The root <configure> element, in a bfg namespace.

2. *Line 4.* Boilerplate, the comment explains.

3. *Lines 6-10.* Register a <view> that names a context type that is a class. .views.my_view is a *function* we write (generated by the bfg_zodb template) that is given a context object and a request and which returns a dictionary. The renderer tag indicates that the templates/mytemplate.pt template should be used to turn the dictionary returned by the view into a response. templates/mytemplate.pt is a *relative* path: it names the mytemplate.pt file which lives in the templates subdirectory of the directory in which this configure.zcml lives in. In this case, it means it lives in the tutorial package's templates directory as mytemplate.pt

   Since this <view> doesn't have a name attribute, it is the "default" view for that class.

4. *Lines 12-15.* Register a static view which answers requests which start with /static. This is a view that will serve up static resources for us, in this case, at http://localhost:6543/static/ and below. The path element of this tag is a relative directory name, so it finds the resources it should serve within the templates/static directory inside the tutorial package.

27.3.3 Content Models with `models.py`

`repoze.bfg` often uses the word *model* when talking about content resources arranged in the hierarchical *object graph* consulted by *traversal*. The `models.py` file is where the `bfg_zodb` Paster template put the classes that implement our model objects.

Here is the source for `models.py`:

```
1  from persistent.mapping import PersistentMapping
2
3  class MyModel(PersistentMapping):
4      __parent__ = __name__ = None
5
6  def appmaker(zodb_root):
7      if not 'app_root' in zodb_root:
8          app_root = MyModel()
9          zodb_root['app_root'] = app_root
10         import transaction
11         transaction.commit()
12     return zodb_root['app_root']
```

1. *Lines 3-4.* The `MyModel` class we referred to in the ZCML file named `configure.zcml` is implemented here. Instances of this class will be capable of being persisted in *ZODB* because the class inherits from the `persistint.mapping.PersistentMapping` class. The `__parent__` and `__name__` are important parts of the *traversal* protocol. By default, have these as `None` indicating that this is the *root* object.

2. *Lines 6-12.* `appmaker` is used to return the *application root* object. It is called on *every request* to the `repoze.bfg` application. It also performs bootstrapping by *creating* an application root (inside the ZODB root object) if one does not already exist.

   We do so by first seeing if the database has the persistent application root. If not, we make an instance, store it, and commit the transaction. We then return the application root object.

27.3.4 App Startup with `run.py`

When you run the application using the `paster` command using the `tutorial.ini` generated config file, the application configuration points at an Setuptools *entry point* described as `egg:tutorial#app`. In our application, because the application's `setup.py` file says so, this entry point happens to be the `app` function within the file named `run.py`:

```
1   from repoze.bfg.configuration import Configurator
2   from repoze.zodbconn.finder import PersistentApplicationFinder
3
4   from tutorial.models import appmaker
5
6   def app(global_config, **settings):
7       """ This function returns a WSGI application.
8
9       It is usually called by the PasteDeploy framework during
10      ``paster serve``.
11      """
12      zodb_uri = settings.get('zodb_uri')
13      if zodb_uri is None:
14          raise ValueError("No 'zodb_uri' in application configuration.")
15      finder = PersistentApplicationFinder(zodb_uri, appmaker)
16      def get_root(request):
17          return finder(request.environ)
18      config = Configurator(root_factory=get_root, settings=settings)
19      config.begin()
20      config.load_zcml('configure.zcml')
21      config.end()
22      return config.make_wsgi_app()
```

1. *Lines 1-2.* Perform some dependency imports.

2. *Line 12.* Get the ZODB configuration from the `tutorial.ini` file's `[app:main]` section represented by the `settings` dictionary passed to our `app` function. This will be a URI (something like `file:///path/to/Data.fs`).

3. *Line 15.* We create a "finder" object using the `PersistentApplicationFinder` helper class, passing it the ZODB URI and the "appmaker" we've imported from `models.py`.

4. *Lines 16 - 17.* We create a *root factory* which uses the finder to return a ZODB root object.

5. *Line 18.* We construct a *Configurator* with a *root factory* and the settings keywords parsed by PasteDeploy. The root factory is named `get_root`.

6. *Lines 19-21.* Begin configuration using the `begin` method of the `configuration.Configurator()` (pp. 367) class, load the `configure.zcml` file from our package using the `configuration.Configurator.load_zcml()` (pp. 378) method, and end configuration using the `configuration.Configurator.end()` (pp. 368) method.

7. *Line 22.* Use the `configuration.Configurator.make_wsgi_app()` (pp. 378) method to return a *WSGI* application.

27.4 Defining Models

The first change we'll make to our bone-stock `paster`-generated application will be to define a number of *model* constructors. For this application, which will be a Wiki, we will need two kinds of model constructors: a "Wiki" model constructor, and a "Page" model constructor. Both our Page and Wiki constructors will be class objects. A single instance of the "Wiki" class will serve as a container for "Page" objects, which will be instances of the "Page" class.

The source code for this tutorial stage can be browsed at docs.repoze.org (http://docs.repoze.org/bfgwiki-1.2/models).

27.4.1 Deleting the Database

We're going to remove the `MyModel` Python model class from our `models.py` file. Since this class is referred to within our persistent storage (represented on disk as a file named `Data.fs`), we'll have strange things happen the next time we want to visit the application in a browser. Remove the `Data.fs` from the `tutorial` directory before proceeding any further. It's always fine to do this as long as you don't care about the content of the database; the database itself will be recreated as necessary.

27.4.2 Adding Model Classes

The next thing we want to do is remove the `MyModel` class from the generated `models.py` file. The `MyModel` class is only a sample and we're not going to use it.

> ⓘ There is nothing automagically special about the filename `models.py`. A project may have many models throughout its codebase in arbitrarily-named files. Files implementing models often have `model` in their filenames (or they may live in a Python subpackage of your application package named `models`), but this is only by convention.

Then, we'll add a `Wiki` class. Because this is a ZODB application, this class should inherit from `persistent.mapping.PersistentMapping`. We want it to inherit from the `persistent.mapping.PersistentMapping` class because our Wiki class will be a mapping of wiki page names to `Page` objects. The `persistent.mapping.PersistentMapping` class provides our class with mapping behavior, and makes sure that our Wiki page is stored as a "first-class" persistent object in our ZODB database.

Our `Wiki` class should also have a __name__ attribute set to `None` at class scope, and should have a __parent__ attribute set to `None` at class scope as well. If a model has a __parent__ attribute of `None` in a traversal-based `repoze.bfg` application, it means that it's the *root* model. The __name__ of the root model is also always `None`.

Then we'll add a `Page` class. This class should inherit from the `persistent.Persistent` class. We'll also give it an __init__ method that accepts a single parameter named `data`. This parameter will contain the *ReStructuredText* body representing the wiki page content. Note that `Page` objects don't have an initial __name__ or __parent__ attribute. All objects in a traversal graph must have a __name__ and a __parent__ attribute. We don't specify these here because both __name__ and __parent__ will be set by by a *view* function when a Page is added to our Wiki mapping.

27.4.3 Add an Appmaker

We're using a mini-framework callable named `PersistentApplicationFinder` in our application (see `run.py`). A `PersistentApplicationFinder` accepts a ZODB URL as well as an "appmaker" callback. This callback typically lives in the `models.py` file.

We want to change the appmaker function in our `models.py` file so that our application root is a Wiki instance, and we'll also slot a single page object (the front page) into the wiki.

27.4.4 Looking at the Result of Our Edits to `models.py`

The result of all of our edits to `models.py` will end up looking something like this:

```
1  from persistent import Persistent
2  from persistent.mapping import PersistentMapping
3
4  class Wiki(PersistentMapping):
5      __name__ = None
6      __parent__ = None
7
8  class Page(Persistent):
9      def __init__(self, data):
10         self.data = data
11
12 def appmaker(zodb_root):
13     if not 'app_root' in zodb_root:
14         app_root = Wiki()
15         frontpage = Page('This is the front page')
```

```
16        app_root['FrontPage'] = frontpage
17        frontpage.__name__ = 'FrontPage'
18        frontpage.__parent__ = app_root
19        zodb_root['app_root'] = app_root
20        import transaction
21        transaction.commit()
22    return zodb_root['app_root']
```

27.4.5 Testing the Models

To make sure the code we just wrote works, we write tests for the model classes and the appmaker. Changing tests.py, we'll write a separate test class for each model class, and we'll write a test class for the appmaker.

To do so, we'll retain the tutorial.tests.ViewTests class provided as a result of the bfg_zodb project generator. We'll add three test classes: one for the Page model named PageModelTests, one for the Wiki model named WikiModelTests, and one for the appmaker named AppmakerTests.

When we're done changing tests.py, it will look something like so:

```
1  import unittest
2
3  from repoze.bfg.configuration import Configurator
4  from repoze.bfg import testing
5
6  class PageModelTests(unittest.TestCase):
7
8      def _getTargetClass(self):
9          from tutorial.models import Page
10         return Page
11
12     def _makeOne(self, data=u'some data'):
13         return self._getTargetClass()(data=data)
14
15     def test_constructor(self):
16         instance = self._makeOne()
17         self.assertEqual(instance.data, u'some data')
18
19  class WikiModelTests(unittest.TestCase):
20
21      def _getTargetClass(self):
```

251

```
22          from tutorial.models import Wiki
23          return Wiki
24
25      def _makeOne(self):
26          return self._getTargetClass()()
27
28      def test_it(self):
29          wiki = self._makeOne()
30          self.assertEqual(wiki.__parent__, None)
31          self.assertEqual(wiki.__name__, None)
32
33  class AppmakerTests(unittest.TestCase):
34
35      def _callFUT(self, zodb_root):
36          from tutorial.models import appmaker
37          return appmaker(zodb_root)
38
39      def test_no_app_root(self):
40          root = {}
41          self._callFUT(root)
42          self.assertEqual(root['app_root']['FrontPage'].data,
43                          'This is the front page')
44
45      def test_w_app_root(self):
46          app_root = object()
47          root = {'app_root': app_root}
48          self._callFUT(root)
49          self.failUnless(root['app_root'] is app_root)
50
51  class ViewTests(unittest.TestCase):
52      def setUp(self):
53          self.config = Configurator()
54          self.config.begin()
55
56      def tearDown(self):
57          self.config.end()
58
59      def test_my_view(self):
60          from tutorial.views import my_view
61          context = testing.DummyModel()
62          request = testing.DummyRequest()
63          info = my_view(context, request)
64          self.assertEqual(info['project'], 'tutorial')
```

27.4.6 Running the Tests

We can run these tests by using `setup.py test` in the same way we did in *Running the Tests* (pp. 243). Assuming our shell's current working directory is the "tutorial" distribution directory:

On UNIX:

```
$ ../bin/python setup.py test -q
```

On Windows:

```
c:\bigfntut\tutorial> ..\Scripts\python setup.py test -q
```

The expected output is something like this:

```
.....
----------------------------------------------------------------------
Ran 5 tests in 0.008s

OK
```

27.4.7 Declaring Dependencies in Our `setup.py` File

Our application depends on packages which are not dependencies of the original "tutorial" application as it was generated by the `paster create` command. We'll add these dependencies to our `tutorial` package's `setup.py` file by assigning these dependencies to both the `install_requires` and the `tests_require` parameters to the `setup` function. In particular, we require the `docutils` package.

Our resulting `setup.py` should look like so:

```
1  import os
2
3  from setuptools import setup, find_packages
4
5  here = os.path.abspath(os.path.dirname(__file__))
```

253

```
 6  README = open(os.path.join(here, 'README.txt')).read()
 7  CHANGES = open(os.path.join(here, 'CHANGES.txt')).read()
 8
 9  requires = [
10      'repoze.bfg',
11      'docutils',
12      'ZODB3',
13      'repoze.zodbconn',
14      'repoze.tm',
15      ]
16
17  setup(name='tutorial',
18        version='0.0',
19        description='tutorial',
20        long_description=README + '\n\n' +  CHANGES,
21        classifiers=[
22          "Intended Audience :: Developers",
23          "Framework :: BFG",
24          "Programming Language :: Python",
25          "Topic :: Internet :: WWW/HTTP",
26          "Topic :: Internet :: WWW/HTTP :: WSGI :: Application",
27          ],
28        author='',
29        author_email='',
30        url='',
31        keywords='web wsgi bfg',
32        packages=find_packages(),
33        include_package_data=True,
34        zip_safe=False,
35        install_requires=requires,
36        tests_require=requires,
37        test_suite="tutorial",
38        entry_points = """\
39        [paste.app_factory]
40        app = tutorial.run:app
41        """
42        )
```

27.5 Defining Views

A *view callable* in a traversal-based `repoze.bfg` applications is typically a simple Python function that accepts two parameters: *context*, and *request*. A view callable is assumed to return a *response* object.

A `repoze.bfg` view can also be defined as callable which accepts *one* arguments: a *request*. You'll see this one-argument pattern used in other `repoze.bfg` tutorials and applications. Either calling convention will work in any `repoze.bfg` application; the calling conventions can be used interchangeably as necessary. In *traversal* based applications, such as this tutorial, the context is used frequently within the body of a view method, so it makes sense to use the two-argument syntax in this application. However, in *url dispatch* based applications, however, the context object is rarely used in the view body itself, so within code that uses URL-dispatch-only, it's common to define views as callables that accept only a request to avoid the visual "noise".

We're going to define several *view callable* functions then wire them into `repoze.bfg` using some *view configuration* via *ZCML*.

The source code for this tutorial stage can be browsed at docs.repoze.org (http://docs.repoze.org/bfgwiki-1.2/views).

27.5.1 Adding View Functions

We're going to add four *view callable* functions to our `views.py` module. One view (named `view_wiki`) will display the wiki itself (it will answer on the root URL), another named `view_page` will display an individual page, another named `add_page` will allow a page to be added, and a final view named `edit_page` will allow a page to be edited.

There is nothing automagically special about the filename `views.py`. A project may have many views throughout its codebase in arbitrarily-named files. Files implementing views often have `view` in their filenames (or may live in a Python subpackage of your application package named `views`), but this is only by convention.

The `view_wiki` view function

The `view_wiki` function will be configured to respond as the default view of a `Wiki` model object. It always redirects to the `Page` object named "FrontPage". It returns an instance of the `webob.exc.HTTPFound` class (instances of which implement the WebOb *response* interface), and the `url.model_url()` (pp. 421) API. `url.model_url()` (pp. 421) constructs a URL to the `FrontPage` page (e.g. `http://localhost:6543/FrontPage`), and uses it as the "location" of the HTTPFound response, forming an HTTP redirect.

The `view_page` view function

The `view_page` function will be configured to respond as the default view of a `Page` object. The `view_page` function renders the *ReStructuredText* body of a page (stored as the `data` attribute of the context passed to the view; the context will be a Page object) as HTML. Then it substitutes an HTML anchor for each *WikiWord* reference in the rendered HTML using a compiled regular expression.

The curried function named `check` is used as the first argument to `wikiwords.sub`, indicating that it should be called to provide a value for each WikiWord match found in the content. If the wiki (our page's `__parent__`) already contains a page with the matched WikiWord name, the `check` function generates a view link to be used as the substitution value and returns it. If the wiki does not already contain a page with with the matched WikiWord name, the function generates an "add" link as the substitution value and returns it.

As a result, the `content` variable is now a fully formed bit of HTML containing various view and add links for WikiWords based on the content of our current page object.

We then generate an edit URL (because it's easier to do here than in the template), and we wrap up a number of arguments in a dictionary and return it.

The arguments we wrap into a dictionary include `page`, `content`, and `edit_url`. As a result, the *template* associated with this view callable will be able to use these names to perform various rendering tasks. The template associated with this view callable will be a template which lives in `templates/view.pt`, which we'll associate with this view via the *view configuration* which lives in the `configure.zcml` file.

Note the contrast between this view callable and the `view_wiki` view callable. In the `view_wiki` view callable, we return a *response* object. In the `view_page` view callable, we return a *dictionary*. It is *always* fine to return a *response* object from a `repoze.bfg` view. Returning a dictionary is allowed only when there is a *renderer* associated with the view callable in the view configuration.

The `add_page` view function

The `add_page` function will be invoked when a user clicks on a WikiWord which isn't yet represented as a page in the system. The `check` function within the `view_page` view generates URLs to this view. It also acts as a handler for the form that is generated when we want to add a page object. The `context` of the `add_page` view is always a Wiki object (*not* a Page object).

The request *subpath* in `repoze.bfg` is the sequence of names that are found *after* the view name in the URL segments given in the `PATH_INFO` of the WSGI request as the result of *traversal*. If our add view is invoked via, e.g. `http://localhost:6543/add_page/SomeName`, the *subpath* will be a tuple: (`'SomeName',`).

The add view takes the zeroth element of the subpath (the wiki page name), and aliases it to the name attribute in order to know the name of the page we're trying to add.

If the view rendering is *not* a result of a form submission (if the expression `'form.submitted'` in `request.params` is `False`), the view renders a template. To do so, it generates a "save url" which the template use as the form post URL during rendering. We're lazy here, so we're trying to use the same template (`templates/edit.pt`) for the add view as well as the page edit view. To do so, we create a dummy Page object in order to satisfy the edit form's desire to have *some* page object exposed as `page`, and we'll render the template to a response.

If the view rendering *is* a result of a form submission (if the expression `'form.submitted'` in `request.params` is `True`), we scrape the page body from the form data, create a Page object using the name in the subpath and the page body, and save it into "our context" (the wiki) using the `__setitem__` method of the context. We then redirect back to the `view_page` view (the default view for a page) for the newly created page.

The `edit_page` view function

The `edit_page` function will be invoked when a user clicks the "Edit this Page" button on the view form. It renders an edit form but it also acts as the handler for the form it renders. The `context` of the `edit_page` view will *always* be a Page object (never a Wiki object).

If the view execution is *not* a result of a form submission (if the expression `'form.submitted'` in `request.params` is `False`), the view simply renders the edit form, passing the request, the page object, and a save_url which will be used as the action of the generated form.

If the view execution *is* a result of a form submission (if the expression `'form.submitted'` in `request.params` is `True`), the view grabs the `body` element of the request parameter and sets it as the `data` attribute of the page context. It then redirects to the default view of the context (the page), which will always be the `view_page` view.

27.5.2 Viewing the Result of Our Edits to `views.py`

The result of all of our edits to `views.py` will leave it looking like this:

```
1  from docutils.core import publish_parts
2  import re
3
4  from webob.exc import HTTPFound
5  from repoze.bfg.url import model_url
6
7  from tutorial.models import Page
8
9  # regular expression used to find WikiWords
10 wikiwords = re.compile(r"\b([A-Z]\w+[A-Z]+\w+)")
11
12 def view_wiki(context, request):
13     return HTTPFound(location = model_url(context, request, 'FrontPage'))
14
15 def view_page(context, request):
16     wiki = context.__parent__
17
18     def check(match):
19         word = match.group(1)
20         if word in wiki:
21             page = wiki[word]
22             view_url = model_url(page, request)
23             return '<a href="%s">%s</a>' % (view_url, word)
24         else:
25             add_url = request.application_url + '/add_page/' + word
26             return '<a href="%s">%s</a>' % (add_url, word)
27
28     content = publish_parts(context.data, writer_name='html')['html_body']
29     content = wikiwords.sub(check, content)
30     edit_url = model_url(context, request, 'edit_page')
31     return dict(page = context, content = content, edit_url = edit_url)
32
33 def add_page(context, request):
34     name = request.subpath[0]
35     if 'form.submitted' in request.params:
36         body = request.params['body']
37         page = Page(body)
38         page.__name__ = name
39         page.__parent__ = context
40         context[name] = page
41         return HTTPFound(location = model_url(page, request))
42     save_url = model_url(context, request, 'add_page', name)
43     page = Page('')
44     page.__name__ = name
45     page.__parent__ = context
46     return dict(page = page, save_url = save_url)
```

```
47
48  def edit_page(context, request):
49      if 'form.submitted' in request.params:
50          context.data = request.params['body']
51          return HTTPFound(location = model_url(context, request))
52
53      return dict(page = context,
54                  save_url = model_url(context, request, 'edit_page'))
```

27.5.3 Adding Templates

Most view callables we've added expected to be rendered via a *template*. Each template is a *Chameleon* template. The default templating system in `repoze.bfg` is a variant of *ZPT* provided by Chameleon. These templates will live in the `templates` directory of our tutorial package.

The `view.pt` Template

The `view.pt` template is used for viewing a single wiki page. It is used by the `view_page` view function. It should have a div that is "structure replaced" with the `content` value provided by the view. It should also have a link on the rendered page that points at the "edit" URL (the URL which invokes the `edit_page` view for the page being viewed).

Once we're done with the `view.pt` template, it will look a lot like the below:

```
1  <!DOCTYPE html PUBLIC "-//W3C//DTD XHTML 1.0 Transitional//EN"
2    "http://www.w3.org/TR/xhtml1/DTD/xhtml1-transitional.dtd">
3  <html
4      xmlns="http://www.w3.org/1999/xhtml"
5        xmlns:tal="http://xml.zope.org/namespaces/tal">
6
7  <head>
8      <meta content="text/html; charset=utf-8" http-equiv="Content-Type"/>
9      <title>${page.__name__} - bfg tutorial wiki
10             (based on TurboGears 20-Minute Wiki)
11     </title>
12         <link rel="stylesheet" type="text/css"
13           href="${request.application_url}/static/style.css" />
14 </head>
15
```

```
16  <body>
17
18  <div class="main_content">
19  <div style="float:right; width: 10em;"> Viewing
20  <span tal:replace="page.__name__">Page Name Goes Here</span> <br/>
21  You can return to the
22  <a href="${request.application_url}">FrontPage</a>.
23  </div>
24
25  <div tal:replace="structure content">Page text goes here.</div>
26  <p><a tal:attributes="href edit_url" href="">Edit this page</a></p>
27  </div>
28
29  </body></html>
```

> ⓘ   The names available for our use in a template are always those that are present in the dictionary returned by the view callable. But our templates make use of a request object that none of our tutorial views return in their dictionary. This value appears as if "by magic". However, request is one of several names that are available "by default" in a template when a template renderer is used. See *.pt or *.txt: Chameleon Template Renderers* (pp. 112) for more information about other names that are available by default in a template when a Chameleon template is used as a renderer.

The edit.pt Template

The edit.pt template is used for adding and editing a wiki page. It is used by the add_page and edit_page view functions. It should display a page containing a form that POSTs back to the "save_url" argument supplied by the view. The form should have a "body" textarea field (the page data), and a submit button that has the name "form.submitted". The textarea in the form should be filled with any existing page data when it is rendered.

Once we're done with the edit.pt template, it will look a lot like the below:

```
1  <!DOCTYPE html PUBLIC "-//W3C//DTD XHTML 1.0 Transitional//EN"
2    "http://www.w3.org/TR/xhtml1/DTD/xhtml1-transitional.dtd">
3  <html
4      xmlns="http://www.w3.org/1999/xhtml"
5        xmlns:tal="http://xml.zope.org/namespaces/tal">
6
7  <head>
```

```
8      <meta content="text/html; charset=utf-8" http-equiv="Content-Type"/>
9      <title>bfg tutorial wiki (based on TurboGears 20-Minute Wiki)
10          Editing: ${page.__name__}</title>
11        <link rel="stylesheet" type="text/css"
12          href="${request.application_url}/static/style.css" />
13   </head>
14
15   <body>
16
17   <div class="main_content">
18     <div style="float:right; width: 10em;"> Viewing
19       <span tal:replace="page.__name__">Page Name Goes Here</span> <br/>
20       You can return to the <a href="${request.application_url}"
21          >FrontPage</a>.
22     </div>
23
24     <div>
25       <form action="${save_url}" method="post">
26         <textarea name="body" tal:content="page.data" rows="10" cols="60"/>
27         <input type="submit" name="form.submitted" value="Save"/>
28       </form>
29     </div>
30   </div>
31   </body>
32   </html>
```

Static Resources

Our templates name a single static resource named `style.css`. We need to create this and place it in a file named `style.css` within our package's `templates/static` directory. This file is a little too long to replicate within the body of this guide, however it is available online (http://docs.repoze.org/bfgwiki-1.2/views/tutorial/templates/static/style.css).

This CSS file will be accessed via e.g. `http://localhost:6543/static/style.css` by virtue of the `static` directive we've defined in the `configure.zcml` file. Any number and type of static resources can be placed in this directory (or subdirectories) and are just referred to by URL within templates.

27.5.4 Testing the Views

We'll modify our `tests.py` file, adding tests for each view function we added above. As a result, we'll *delete* the `ViewTests` test in the file, and add four other test classes: `ViewWikiTests`,

261

ViewPageTests, AddPageTests, and EditPageTests. These test the view_wiki,
view_page, add_page, and edit_page views respectively.

Once we're done with the tests.py module, it will look a lot like the below:

```
import unittest

from repoze.bfg import testing

class PageModelTests(unittest.TestCase):

    def _getTargetClass(self):
        from tutorial.models import Page
        return Page

    def _makeOne(self, data=u'some data'):
        return self._getTargetClass()(data=data)

    def test_constructor(self):
        instance = self._makeOne()
        self.assertEqual(instance.data, u'some data')

class WikiModelTests(unittest.TestCase):

    def _getTargetClass(self):
        from tutorial.models import Wiki
        return Wiki

    def _makeOne(self):
        return self._getTargetClass()()

    def test_it(self):
        wiki = self._makeOne()
        self.assertEqual(wiki.__parent__, None)
        self.assertEqual(wiki.__name__, None)

class AppmakerTests(unittest.TestCase):
    def _callFUT(self, zodb_root):
        from tutorial.models import appmaker
        return appmaker(zodb_root)

    def test_it(self):
        root = {}
        self._callFUT(root)
        self.assertEqual(root['app_root']['FrontPage'].data,
                         'This is the front page')
```

```python
class ViewWikiTests(unittest.TestCase):
    def test_it(self):
        from tutorial.views import view_wiki
        context = testing.DummyModel()
        request = testing.DummyRequest()
        response = view_wiki(context, request)
        self.assertEqual(response.location, 'http://example.com/FrontPage')


class ViewPageTests(unittest.TestCase):
    def _callFUT(self, context, request):
        from tutorial.views import view_page
        return view_page(context, request)

    def test_it(self):
        wiki = testing.DummyModel()
        wiki['IDoExist'] = testing.DummyModel()
        context = testing.DummyModel(data='Hello CruelWorld IDoExist')
        context.__parent__ = wiki
        context.__name__ = 'thepage'
        request = testing.DummyRequest()
        info = self._callFUT(context, request)
        self.assertEqual(info['page'], context)
        self.assertEqual(
            info['content'],
            '<div class="document">\n'
            '<p>Hello <a href="http://example.com/add_page/CruelWorld">'
            'CruelWorld</a> '
            '<a href="http://example.com/IDoExist/">'
            'IDoExist</a>'
            '</p>\n</div>\n')
        self.assertEqual(info['edit_url'],
                         'http://example.com/thepage/edit_page')


class AddPageTests(unittest.TestCase):
    def _callFUT(self, context, request):
        from tutorial.views import add_page
        return add_page(context, request)

    def test_it_notsubmitted(self):
        from repoze.bfg.url import model_url
        context = testing.DummyModel()
        request = testing.DummyRequest()
        request.subpath = ['AnotherPage']
        info = self._callFUT(context, request)
```

```
88          self.assertEqual(info['page'].data,'')
89          self.assertEqual(
90              info['save_url'],
91              model_url(context, request, 'add_page', 'AnotherPage'))
92
93      def test_it_submitted(self):
94          context = testing.DummyModel()
95          request = testing.DummyRequest({'form.submitted':True,
96                                          'body':'Hello yo!'})
97          request.subpath = ['AnotherPage']
98          self._callFUT(context, request)
99          page = context['AnotherPage']
100         self.assertEqual(page.data, 'Hello yo!')
101         self.assertEqual(page.__name__, 'AnotherPage')
102         self.assertEqual(page.__parent__, context)
103
104 class EditPageTests(unittest.TestCase):
105     def _callFUT(self, context, request):
106         from tutorial.views import edit_page
107         return edit_page(context, request)
108
109     def test_it_notsubmitted(self):
110         from repoze.bfg.url import model_url
111         context = testing.DummyModel()
112         request = testing.DummyRequest()
113         info = self._callFUT(context, request)
114         self.assertEqual(info['page'], context)
115         self.assertEqual(info['save_url'],
116                          model_url(context, request, 'edit_page'))
117
118     def test_it_submitted(self):
119         context = testing.DummyModel()
120         request = testing.DummyRequest({'form.submitted':True,
121                                         'body':'Hello yo!'})
122         response = self._callFUT(context, request)
123         self.assertEqual(response.location, 'http://example.com/')
124         self.assertEqual(context.data, 'Hello yo!')
```

27.5.5 Running the Tests

We can run these tests by using `setup.py test` in the same way we did in *Running the Tests* (pp. 243). Assuming our shell's current working directory is the "tutorial" distribution directory:

On UNIX:

```
$ ../bin/python setup.py test -q
```

On Windows:

```
c:\bigfntut\tutorial> ..\Scripts\python setup.py test -q
```

The expected result looks something like:

```
.........
----------------------------------------------------------------
Ran 9 tests in 0.203s

OK
```

27.5.6 Mapping Views to URLs in `configure.zcml`

The `configure.zcml` file contains `view` declarations which serve to map URLs (via *traversal*) to view functions. This is also known as *view configuration*. You'll need to add four `view` declarations to `configure.zcml`.

1. Add a declaration which maps the "Wiki" class in our `models.py` file to the view named `view_wiki` in our `views.py` file with no view name. This is the default view for a Wiki. It does not use a `renderer` because the `view_wiki` view callable always returns a *response* object rather than a dictionary.

2. Add a declaration which maps the "Wiki" class in our `models.py` file to the view named `add_page` in our `views.py` file with the view name `add_page`. Associate this view with the `templates/edit.pt` template file via the `renderer` attribute. This view will use the *Chameleon* ZPT renderer configured with the `templates/edit.pt` template to render non-*response* return values from the `add_page` view. This is the add view for a new Page.

3. Add a declaration which maps the "Page" class in our `models.py` file to the view named `view_page` in our `views.py` file with no view name. Associate this view with the `templates/view.pt` template file via the `renderer` attribute. This view will use the *Chameleon* ZPT renderer configured with the `templates/view.pt` template to render non-*response* return values from the `view_page` view. This is the default view for a Page.

4. Add a declaration which maps the "Page" class in our `models.py` file to the view named `edit_page` in our `views.py` file with the view name `edit_page`. Associate this view with the `templates/edit.pt` template file via the `renderer` attribute. This view will use the *Chameleon* ZPT renderer configured with the `templates/edit.pt` template to render *non-response* return values from the `edit_page` view. This is the edit view for a page.

As a result of our edits, the `configure.zcml` file should look something like so:

```
1  <configure xmlns="http://namespaces.repoze.org/bfg">
2
3    <!-- this must be included for the view declarations to work -->
4    <include package="repoze.bfg.includes" />
5
6    <static
7      name="static"
8      path="templates/static"
9      />
10
11   <view
12     context=".models.Wiki"
13     view=".views.view_wiki"
14     />
15
16   <view
17     context=".models.Wiki"
18     name="add_page"
19     view=".views.add_page"
20     renderer="templates/edit.pt"
21     />
22
23   <view
24     context=".models.Page"
25     view=".views.view_page"
26     renderer="templates/view.pt"
27     />
28
29   <view
30     context=".models.Page"
31     name="edit_page"
32     view=".views.edit_page"
33     renderer="templates/edit.pt"
34     />
35
36 </configure>
```

27.5.7 Examining `tutorial.ini`

Let's take a look at our `tutorial.ini` file. The contents of the file are as follows:

```
[DEFAULT]
debug = true

[app:zodb]
use = egg:tutorial#app
reload_templates = true
debug_authorization = false
debug_notfound = false
zodb_uri = file://%(here)s/Data.fs?connection_cache_size=20000

[pipeline:main]
pipeline =
    egg:repoze.zodbconn#closer
    egg:repoze.tm#tm
    zodb

[server:main]
use = egg:Paste#http
host = 0.0.0.0
port = 6543
```

The WSGI Pipeline

Within `tutorial.ini`, note the existence of a `[pipeline:main]` section which specifies our WSGI pipeline. This "pipeline" will be served up as our WSGI application. As far as the WSGI server is concerned the pipeline *is* our application. Simpler configurations don't use a pipeline: instead they expose a single WSGI application as "main". Our setup is more complicated, so we use a pipeline.

`egg:repoze.zodbconn#closer` is at the "top" of the pipeline. This is a piece of middleware which closes the ZODB connection opened by the PersistentApplicationFinder at the end of the request.

`egg:repoze.tm#tm` is the second piece of middleware in the pipeline. This commits a transaction near the end of the request unless there's an exception raised.

267

Adding an Element to the Pipeline

Let's add a piece of middleware to the WSGI pipeline: `egg:Paste#evalerror` middleware which displays debuggable errors in the browser while you're developing (not recommended for deployment). Let's insert evalerror into the pipeline right below "egg:repoze.zodbconn#closer", making our resulting `tutorial.ini` file look like so:

```
[DEFAULT]
debug = true

[app:zodb]
use = egg:tutorial#app
reload_templates = true
debug_authorization = false
debug_notfound = false
zodb_uri = file://%(here)s/Data.fs?connection_cache_size=20000

[pipeline:main]
pipeline =
    egg:repoze.zodbconn#closer
    egg:Paste#evalerror
    egg:repoze.tm#tm
    zodb

[server:main]
use = egg:Paste#http
host = 0.0.0.0
port = 6543
```

27.5.8 Viewing the Application in a Browser

Once we've set up the WSGI pipeline properly, we can finally examine our application in a browser. The views we'll try are as follows:

- Visiting `http://localhost:6543/` in a browser invokes the `view_wiki` view. This always redirects to the `view_page` view of the FrontPage page object.

- Visiting `http://localhost:6543/FrontPage/` in a browser invokes the `view_page` view of the front page page object. This is because it's the *default view* (a view without a `name`) for Page objects.

- Visiting `http://localhost:6543/FrontPage/edit_page` in a browser invokes the edit view for the front page object.

- Visiting `http://localhost:6543/add_page/SomePageName` in a browser invokes the add view for a page.

- To generate an error, visit `http://localhost:6543/add_page` which will generate an `IndexError` for the expression `request.subpath[0]`. You'll see an interactive traceback facility provided by evalerror.

27.6 Using View Decorators Rather than ZCML `view` directives

So far we've been using *ZCML* to map model types to views. It's often easier to use the `bfg_view` view decorator to do this mapping. Using view decorators provides better locality of reference for the mapping, because you can see which model types and view names the view will serve right next to the view function itself. In this mode, however, you lose the ability for some views to be overridden "from the outside" (by someone using your application as a framework, as explained in the *Extending An Existing repoze.bfg Application* (pp. 207)). Since this application is not meant to be a framework, it makes sense for us to switch over to using view decorators.

27.6.1 Adding View Decorators

We're going to import the `view.bfg_view` (pp. 428) callable. This callable can be used as a function, class, or method decorator. We'll use it to decorate our `view_wiki`, `view_page`, `add_page` and `edit_page` view functions.

The `view.bfg_view` (pp. 428) callable accepts a number of arguments:

`context`

> The model type which the *context* of our view will be, in our case a class.

`name`

> The name of the view.

`renderer`

> The renderer (usually a *template name*) that will be used when the view returns a non-*response* object.

There are other arguments which this callable accepts, but these are the ones we're going to use.

The `view_wiki` view function

The decorator above the `view_wiki` function will be:

```
@bfg_view(context=Wiki)
```

This indicates that the view is for the Wiki class and has the *empty* view_name (indicating the *default view* for the Wiki class). After injecting this decorator, we can now *remove* the following from our `configure.zcml` file:

```
1  <view
2      context=".models.Wiki"
3      view=".views.view_wiki"
4      />
```

Our new decorator takes its place.

The `view_page` view function

The decorator above the `view_page` function will be:

```
@bfg_view(context=Page, renderer='templates/view.pt')
```

This indicates that the view is for the Page class and has the *empty* view_name (indicating the *default view* for the Page class). After injecting this decorator, we can now *remove* the following from our `configure.zcml` file:

```
1  <view
2      context=".models.Page"
3      view=".views.view_page"
4      renderer="templates/view.pt"
5      />
```

Our new decorator takes its place.

The `add_page` view function

The decorator above the `add_page` function will be:

```
@bfg_view(context=Wiki, name='add_page', renderer='templates/edit.pt')
```

This indicates that the view is for the Wiki class and has the `add_page` view_name. After injecting this decorator, we can now *remove* the following from our `configure.zcml` file:

```
1  <view
2     context=".models.Wiki"
3     name="add_page"
4     view=".views.add_page"
5     renderer="templates/edit.pt"
6     />
```

Our new decorator takes its place.

The `edit_page` view function

The decorator above the `edit_page` function will be:

```
@bfg_view(context=Page, name='edit_page', renderer='templates/edit.pt')
```

This indicates that the view is for the Page class and has the `edit_page` view_name. After injecting this decorator, we can now *remove* the following from our `configure.zcml` file:

```
1  <view
2     context=".models.Page"
3     name="edit_page"
4     view=".views.edit_page"
5     renderer="templates/edit.pt"
6     />
```

Our new decorator takes its place.

27.6.2 Adding a Scan Directive

In order for our decorators to be recognized, we must add a bit of boilerplate to our `configure.zcml` file which tells `repoze.bfg` to kick off a *scan* at startup time. Add the following tag anywhere beneath the `<include package="includes">` tag but before the ending `</configure>` tag within `configure.zcml`:

```
<scan package="."/>
```

27.6.3 Viewing the Result of Our Edits to `views.py`

The result of all of our edits to `views.py` will leave it looking like this:

```
from docutils.core import publish_parts
import re

from webob.exc import HTTPFound
from repoze.bfg.url import model_url
from repoze.bfg.view import bfg_view

from tutorial.models import Page
from tutorial.models import Wiki

# regular expression used to find WikiWords
wikiwords = re.compile(r"\b([A-Z]\w+[A-Z]+\w+)")

@bfg_view(context=Wiki)
def view_wiki(context, request):
    return HTTPFound(location = model_url(context, request, 'FrontPage'))

@bfg_view(context=Page, renderer='templates/view.pt')
def view_page(context, request):
    wiki = context.__parent__

    def check(match):
        word = match.group(1)
        if word in wiki:
            page = wiki[word]
            view_url = model_url(page, request)
            return '<a href="%s">%s</a>' % (view_url, word)
```

```
28      else:
29          add_url = request.application_url + '/add_page/' + word
30          return '<a href="%s">%s</a>' % (add_url, word)
31
32      content = publish_parts(context.data, writer_name='html')['html_body']
33      content = wikiwords.sub(check, content)
34      edit_url = model_url(context, request, 'edit_page')
35      return dict(page = context, content = content, edit_url = edit_url)
36
37  @bfg_view(context=Wiki, name='add_page', renderer='templates/edit.pt')
38  def add_page(context, request):
39      name = request.subpath[0]
40      if 'form.submitted' in request.params:
41          body = request.params['body']
42          page = Page(body)
43          page.__name__ = name
44          page.__parent__ = context
45          context[name] = page
46          return HTTPFound(location = model_url(page, request))
47      save_url = model_url(context, request, 'add_page', name)
48      page = Page('')
49      page.__name__ = name
50      page.__parent__ = context
51      return dict(page = page, save_url = save_url)
52
53  @bfg_view(context=Page, name='edit_page', renderer='templates/edit.pt')
54  def edit_page(context, request):
55      if 'form.submitted' in request.params:
56          context.data = request.params['body']
57          return HTTPFound(location = model_url(context, request))
58
59      return dict(page = context,
60                  save_url = model_url(context, request, 'edit_page'))
```

27.6.4 Viewing the Results of Our Edits to `configure.zcml`

The result of all of our edits to `configure.zcml` will leave it looking like this:

```
1  <configure xmlns="http://namespaces.repoze.org/bfg">
2
3      <!-- this must be included for the view declarations to work -->
4      <include package="repoze.bfg.includes" />
```

```
5
6    <scan package="."/>
7
8    <static
9      name="static"
10     path="templates/static"
11     />
12
13  </configure>
```

27.6.5 Running the Tests

We can run these tests by using `setup.py test` in the same way we did in *Running the Tests* (pp. 243). Assuming our shell's current working directory is the "tutorial" distribution directory:

On UNIX:

```
$ ../bin/python setup.py test -q
```

On Windows:

```
c:\bigfntut\tutorial> ..\Scripts\python setup.py test -q
```

Hopefully nothing will have changed. The expected result looks something like:

```
.........
----------------------------------------------------------------------
Ran 9 tests in 0.203s

OK
```

27.6.6 Viewing the Application in a Browser

Once we've set up the WSGI pipeline properly, we can finally examine our application in a browser. We'll make sure that we didn't break any views by trying each of them.

- Visiting `http://localhost:6543/` in a browser invokes the `view_wiki` view. This always redirects to the `view_page` view of the FrontPage page object.

- Visiting `http://localhost:6543/FrontPage/` in a browser invokes the `view_page` view of the front page page object. This is because it's the *default view* (a view without a `name`) for Page objects.

- Visiting `http://localhost:6543/FrontPage/edit_page` in a browser invokes the edit view for the front page object.

- Visiting `http://localhost:6543/add_page/SomePageName` in a browser invokes the add view for a page.

27.7 Adding Authorization

Our application currently allows anyone with access to the server to view, edit, and add pages to our wiki. For purposes of demonstration we'll change our application to allow people whom possess a specific username (*editor*) to add and edit wiki pages but we'll continue allowing anyone with access to the server to view pages. `repoze.bfg` provides facilities for *authorization* and *authentication*. We'll make use of both features to provide security to our application.

The source code for this tutorial stage can be browsed at docs.repoze.org (http://docs.repoze.org/bfgwiki-1.2/authorization).

27.7.1 Configuring a `repoze.bfg` Authentication Policy

For any `repoze.bfg` application to perform authorization, we need to add a `security.py` module and we'll need to change our *application registry* to add an *authentication policy* and a *authorization policy*.

Changing `configure.zcml`

We'll change our `configure.zcml` file to enable an `AuthTktAuthenticationPolicy` and an `ACLAuthorizationPolicy` to enable declarative security checking. We'll also add a `forbidden` stanza, which species a *forbidden view*. This configures our login view to show up when `repoze.bfg` detects that a view invocation can not be authorized. When you're done, your `configure.zcml` will look like so:

```
1  <configure xmlns="http://namespaces.repoze.org/bfg">
2
3    <!-- this must be included for the view declarations to work -->
4    <include package="repoze.bfg.includes" />
5
6    <scan package="."/>
7
8    <forbidden
9      view=".login.login"
10     renderer="templates/login.pt"/>
11
12   <authtktauthenticationpolicy
13     secret="sosecret"
14     />
15
16   <aclauthorizationpolicy/>
17
18   <static
19     name="static"
20     path="templates/static"
21     />
22
23 </configure>
```

Adding `security.py`

Add a `security.py` module within your package (in the same directory as `run.py`, `views.py`, etc) with the following content:

```
1  USERS = {'editor':'editor',
2           'viewer':'viewer'}
3  GROUPS = {'editor':['group.editors']}
4
5  def groupfinder(userid, request):
6      if userid in USERS:
7          return GROUPS.get(userid, [])
```

The `groupfinder` function defined here is an authorization policy "callback"; it is a callable that accepts a userid and a request. If the userid exists in the set of users known by the system, the callback will return a sequence of group identifiers (or an empty sequence if the user isn't a member of any groups). If the userid *does not* exist in the system, the callback will return None. We'll use "dummy" data to represent user and groups sources.

Adding Login and Logout Views

We'll add a login view which renders a login form and processes the post from the login form, checking credentials.

We'll also add a logout view to our application and provide a link to it. This view will clear the credentials of the logged in user and redirect back to the front page.

We'll add a different file (for presentation convenience) to add login and logout views. Add a file named login.py to your application (in the same directory as views.py) with the following content:

```
1  from webob.exc import HTTPFound
2
3  from repoze.bfg.view import bfg_view
4  from repoze.bfg.url import model_url
5
6  from repoze.bfg.security import remember
7  from repoze.bfg.security import forget
8
9  from tutorial.models import Wiki
10 from tutorial.security import USERS
11
12 @bfg_view(context=Wiki, name='login', renderer='templates/login.pt')
13 def login(context, request):
14     login_url = model_url(context, request, 'login')
15     referrer = request.url
16     if referrer == login_url:
17         referrer = '/' # never use the login form itself as came_from
18     came_from = request.params.get('came_from', referrer)
19     message = ''
20     login = ''
21     password = ''
22     if 'form.submitted' in request.params:
23         login = request.params['login']
24         password = request.params['password']
25         if USERS.get(login) == password:
26             headers = remember(request, login)
27             return HTTPFound(location = came_from,
28                              headers = headers)
```

```
29          message = 'Failed login'
30
31      return dict(
32          message = message,
33          url = request.application_url + '/login',
34          came_from = came_from,
35          login = login,
36          password = password,
37          )
38
39  @bfg_view(context=Wiki, name='logout')
40  def logout(context, request):
41      headers = forget(request)
42      return HTTPFound(location = model_url(context, request),
43                       headers = headers)
```

Changing Existing Views

Then we need to change each of our view_page, edit_page and add_page views in views.py to pass a "logged in" parameter into its template. We'll add something like this to each view body:

```
1  from repoze.bfg.security import authenticated_userid
2  logged_in = authenticated_userid(request)
```

We'll then change the return value of each view that has an associated renderer to pass the *resulting* *'logged_in'* value to the template. For example:

```
1  return dict(page = context,
2              content = content,
3              logged_in = logged_in,
4              edit_url = edit_url)
```

Adding the login.pt Template

Add a login.pt template to your templates directory. It's referred to within the login view we just added to login.py.

```
1  <!DOCTYPE html PUBLIC "-//W3C//DTD XHTML 1.0 Transitional//EN"
2    "http://www.w3.org/TR/xhtml1/DTD/xhtml1-transitional.dtd">
3  <html
4      xmlns="http://www.w3.org/1999/xhtml"
5      xmlns:tal="http://xml.zope.org/namespaces/tal">
6
7  <head>
8    <meta content="text/html; charset=utf-8" http-equiv="Content-Type"/>
9    <title>bfg tutorial wiki (based on TurboGears 20-Minute Wiki)</title>
10   <link rel="stylesheet" type="text/css"
11         href="${request.application_url}/static/style.css" />
12  </head>
13
14  <body>
15
16  <h1>Log In</h1>
17
18  <div tal:replace="message"/>
19
20  <div class="main_content">
21    <form action="${url}" method="post">
22      <input type="hidden" name="came_from" value="${came_from}"/>
23      <input type="text" name="login" value="${login}"/>
24      <br/>
25      <input type="password" name="password" value="${password}"/>
26      <br/>
27      <input type="submit" name="form.submitted" value="Log In"/>
28    </form>
29  </div>
30
31  </body>
32  </html>
```

Change `view.pt` and `edit.pt`

We'll also need to change our `edit.pt` and `view.pt` templates to display a "Logout" link if someone is logged in. This link will invoke the logout view.

To do so we'll add this to both templates within the `<div class="main_content">` div:

```
1  <span tal:condition="logged_in">
2      <a href="${request.application_url}/logout">Logout</a>
3  </span>
```

27.7.2 Giving Our Root Model Object an ACL

We need to give our root model object an *ACL*. This ACL will be sufficient to provide enough information to the repoze.bfg security machinery to challenge a user who doesn't have appropriate credentials when he attempts to invoke the add_page or edit_page views.

We need to perform some imports at module scope in our models.py file:

```
1  from repoze.bfg.security import Allow
2  from repoze.bfg.security import Everyone
```

Our root model is a Wiki object. We'll add the following line at class scope to our Wiki class:

```
1  __acl__ = [ (Allow, Everyone, 'view'), (Allow, 'editor', 'edit') ]
```

It's only happenstance that we're assigning this ACL at class scope. An ACL can be attached to an object *instance* too; this is how "row level security" can be achieved in repoze.bfg applications. We actually only need *one* ACL for the entire system, however, because our security requirements are simple, so this feature is not demonstrated.

Our resulting models.py file will now look like so:

```
1  from persistent import Persistent
2  from persistent.mapping import PersistentMapping
3
4  from repoze.bfg.security import Allow
5  from repoze.bfg.security import Everyone
6
7  class Wiki(PersistentMapping):
8      __name__ = None
9      __parent__ = None
10     __acl__ = [ (Allow, Everyone, 'view'), (Allow, 'editor', 'edit') ]
```

```
11
12  class Page(Persistent):
13      def __init__(self, data):
14          self.data = data
15
16  def appmaker(zodb_root):
17      if not 'app_root' in zodb_root:
18          app_root = Wiki()
19          frontpage = Page('This is the front page')
20          app_root['FrontPage'] = frontpage
21          frontpage.__name__ = 'FrontPage'
22          frontpage.__parent__ = app_root
23          zodb_root['app_root'] = app_root
24          import transaction
25          transaction.commit()
26      return zodb_root['app_root']
```

27.7.3 Adding `permission` Declarations to our `bfg_view` Decorators

To protect each of our views with a particular permission, we need to pass a `permission` argument to each of our `view.bfg_view` (pp. 428) decorators. To do so, within `views.py`:

- We add `permission='view'` to the decorator attached to the `view_wiki` view function. This makes the assertion that only users who possess the effective `view` permission at the time of the request may invoke this view. We've granted `security.Everyone` (pp. 397) the view permission at the root model via its ACL, so everyone will be able to invoke the `view_wiki` view.

- We add `permission='view'` to the decorator attached to the `view_page` view function. This makes the assertion that only users who possess the effective `view` permission at the time of the request may invoke this view. We've granted `security.Everyone` (pp. 397) the view permission at the root model via its ACL, so everyone will be able to invoke the `view_page` view.

- We add `permission='edit'` to the decorator attached to the `add_page` view function. This makes the assertion that only users who possess the effective `view` permission at the time of the request may invoke this view. We've granted the "editor" principal the view permission at the root model via its ACL, so only the user named `editor` will able to invoke the `add_page` view.

- We add `permission='edit'` to the `bfg_view` decorator attached to the `edit_page` view function. This makes the assertion that only users who possess the effective `view` permission at the time of the request may invoke this view. We've granted `editor` the view permission at the root model via its ACL, so only the user named `editor` will able to invoke the `edit_page` view.

281

27.7.4 Viewing the Application in a Browser

We can finally examine our application in a browser. The views we'll try are as follows:

- Visiting `http://localhost:6543/` in a browser invokes the `view_wiki` view. This always redirects to the `view_page` view of the FrontPage page object. It is executable by any user.

- Visiting `http://localhost:6543/FrontPage/` in a browser invokes the `view_page` view of the front page page object. This is because it's the *default view* (a view without a `name`) for `Page` objects. It is executable by any user.

- Visiting `http://localhost:6543/FrontPage/edit_page` in a browser invokes the edit view for the front page object. It is executable by only the `editor` user. If a different user (or the anonymous user) invokes it, a login form will be displayed. Supplying the credentials with the username `editor`, password `editor` will show the edit page form being displayed.

- Visiting `http://localhost:6543/add_page/SomePageName` in a browser invokes the add view for a page. It is executable by only the `editor` user. If a different user (or the anonymous user) invokes it, a login form will be displayed. Supplying the credentials with the username `editor`, password `editor` will show the edit page form being displayed.

27.7.5 Seeing Our Changes To `views.py` and our Templates

Our `views.py` module will look something like this when we're done:

```
 1  from docutils.core import publish_parts
 2  import re
 3
 4  from webob.exc import HTTPFound
 5  from repoze.bfg.url import model_url
 6
 7  from repoze.bfg.security import authenticated_userid
 8
 9  from repoze.bfg.view import bfg_view
10
11  from tutorial.models import Page
12  from tutorial.models import Wiki
13
14  # regular expression used to find WikiWords
15  wikiwords = re.compile(r"\b([A-Z]\w+[A-Z]+\w+)")
16
```

```
17  @bfg_view(context=Wiki, permission='view')
18  def view_wiki(context, request):
19      return HTTPFound(location = model_url(context, request, 'FrontPage'))
20
21  @bfg_view(context=Page, renderer='templates/view.pt', permission='view')
22  def view_page(context, request):
23      wiki = context.__parent__
24
25      def check(match):
26          word = match.group(1)
27          if word in wiki:
28              page = wiki[word]
29              view_url = model_url(page, request)
30              return '<a href="%s">%s</a>' % (view_url, word)
31          else:
32              add_url = request.application_url + '/add_page/' + word
33              return '<a href="%s">%s</a>' % (add_url, word)
34
35      content = publish_parts(context.data, writer_name='html')['html_body']
36      content = wikiwords.sub(check, content)
37      edit_url = model_url(context, request, 'edit_page')
38
39      logged_in = authenticated_userid(request)
40
41      return dict(page = context, content = content, edit_url = edit_url,
42                  logged_in = logged_in)
43
44  @bfg_view(context=Wiki, name='add_page', renderer='templates/edit.pt',
45            permission='edit')
46  def add_page(context, request):
47      name = request.subpath[0]
48      if 'form.submitted' in request.params:
49          body = request.params['body']
50          page = Page(body)
51          page.__name__ = name
52          page.__parent__ = context
53          context[name] = page
54          return HTTPFound(location = model_url(page, request))
55      save_url = model_url(context, request, 'add_page', name)
56      page = Page('')
57      page.__name__ = name
58      page.__parent__ = context
59
60      logged_in = authenticated_userid(request)
61
62      return dict(page = page, save_url = save_url, logged_in = logged_in)
```

```
63
64  @bfg_view(context=Page, name='edit_page', renderer='templates/edit.pt',
65          permission='edit')
66  def edit_page(context, request):
67      if 'form.submitted' in request.params:
68          context.data = request.params['body']
69          return HTTPFound(location = model_url(context, request))
70
71      logged_in = authenticated_userid(request)
72
73      return dict(page = context,
74                  save_url = model_url(context, request, 'edit_page'),
75                  logged_in = logged_in)
```

Our edit.pt template will look something like this when we're done:

```
1   <!DOCTYPE html PUBLIC "-//W3C//DTD XHTML 1.0 Transitional//EN"
2     "http://www.w3.org/TR/xhtml1/DTD/xhtml1-transitional.dtd">
3   <html
4       xmlns="http://www.w3.org/1999/xhtml"
5         xmlns:tal="http://xml.zope.org/namespaces/tal">
6
7   <head>
8       <meta content="text/html; charset=utf-8" http-equiv="Content-Type"/>
9       <title>bfg tutorial wiki (based on TurboGears 20-Minute Wiki)
10              Editing: ${page.__name__}</title>
11          <link rel="stylesheet" type="text/css"
12            href="${request.application_url}/static/style.css" />
13  </head>
14
15  <body>
16
17  <div class="main_content">
18    <div style="float:right; width: 10em;"> Viewing
19      <span tal:replace="page.__name__">Page Name Goes Here</span> <br/>
20      You can return to the <a href="${request.application_url}"
21            >FrontPage</a>.
22     <span tal:condition="logged_in"><a
23          href="${request.application_url}/logout">Logout</a></span>
24    </div>
25
26    <div>
27      <form action="${save_url}" method="post">
28        <textarea name="body" tal:content="page.data" rows="10" cols="60"/>
```

```
29        <input type="submit" name="form.submitted" value="Save"/>
30      </form>
31    </div>
32  </div>
33  </body>
34  </html>
```

Our `view.pt` template will look something like this when we're done:

```
1  <!DOCTYPE html PUBLIC "-//W3C//DTD XHTML 1.0 Transitional//EN"
2    "http://www.w3.org/TR/xhtml1/DTD/xhtml1-transitional.dtd">
3  <html
4      xmlns="http://www.w3.org/1999/xhtml"
5        xmlns:tal="http://xml.zope.org/namespaces/tal">
6
7  <head>
8      <meta content="text/html; charset=utf-8" http-equiv="Content-Type"/>
9      <title>${page.__name__} - bfg tutorial wiki
10             (based on TurboGears 20-Minute Wiki)
11      </title>
12          <link rel="stylesheet" type="text/css"
13            href="${request.application_url}/static/style.css" />
14  </head>
15
16  <body>
17
18  <div class="main_content">
19  <div style="float:right; width: 10em;"> Viewing
20  <span tal:replace="page.__name__">Page Name Goes Here</span> <br/>
21  You can return to the <a href="${request.application_url}">FrontPage</a>.
22  <span tal:condition="logged_in">
23    <a href="${request.application_url}/logout">Logout</a>
24  </span>
25  </div>
26
27  <div tal:replace="structure content">Page text goes here.</div>
28  <p><a tal:attributes="href edit_url" href="">Edit this page</a></p>
29  </div>
30
31  </body></html>
```

27.7.6 Revisiting the Application

When we revisit the application in a browser, and log in (as a result of hitting an edit or add page and submitting the login form with the editor credentials), we'll see a Logout link in the upper right hand corner. When we click it, we're logged out, and redirected back to the front page.

27.8 Distributing Your Application

Once your application works properly, you can create a "tarball" from it by using the setup.py sdist command. The following commands assume your current working directory is the tutorial package we've created and that the parent directory of the tutorial package is a virtualenv representing a repoze.bfg environment.

On UNIX:

```
$ ../bin/python setup.py sdist
```

On Windows:

```
c:\bigfntut> ..\Scripts\python setup.py sdist
```

> If your project files are not checked in to a version control repository (such as Subversion), the dist tarball will *not* contain all the files it needs to. In particular, it will not contain non-Python-source files (such as templates and static files). To ensure that these are included, check your files into a version control repository before running setup.py sdist.

The output of such a command will be something like:

```
running sdist
# .. more output ..
creating dist
tar -cf dist/tutorial-0.1.tar tutorial-0.1
gzip -f9 dist/tutorial-0.1.tar
removing 'tutorial-0.1' (and everything under it)
```

Note that this command creates a tarball in the "dist" subdirectory named `tutorial-0.1.tar.gz`. You can send this file to your friends to show them your cool new application. They should be able to install it by pointing the `easy_install` command directly at it. Or you can upload it to PyPI (http://pypi.python.org) and share it with the rest of the world, where it can be downloaded via `easy_install` remotely like any other package people download from PyPI.

SQLALCHEMY + URL DISPATCH WIKI TUTORIAL

This tutorial introduces a *SQLAlchemy* and *url dispatch* -based `repoze.bfg` application to a developer familiar with Python. When the tutorial is finished, the developer will have created a basic Wiki application with authentication.

For cut and paste purposes, the source code for all stages of this tutorial can be browsed at docs.repoze.org (http://docs.repoze.org/bfgwiki2-1.2).

28.1 Background

This tutorial presents a `repoze.bfg` application that uses technologies which will be familiar to someone with *Pylons* experience. It uses *SQLAlchemy* as a persistence mechanism and *url dispatch* to map URLs to code. It can also be followed by people without any prior Python web framework experience.

To code along with this tutorial, the developer will need a UNIX machine with development tools (Mac OS X with XCode, any Linux or BSD variant, etc) *or* he will need a Windows system of any kind.

This tutorial is targeted at `repoze.bfg` version 1.2.

Have fun!

28.2 Installation

For the most part, the installation process for this tutorial duplicates the steps described in *Installing repoze.bfg* (pp. 7) and *Creating a repoze.bfg Project* (pp. 37), however it also explains how to install additional libraries for tutorial purposes.

28.2.1 Preparation

Please take the following steps to prepare for the tutorial. The steps are slightly different depending on whether you're using UNIX or Windows.

Preparation, UNIX

1. Install SQLite3 and its development packages if you don't already have them installed. Usually this is via your system's package manager. For example, on a Debian Linux system, do `sudo apt-get install libsqlite3-dev`.

2. If you don't already have a Python 2.5 interpreter installed on your system, obtain, install, or find Python 2.5 (http://python.org/download/releases/2.5.4/) for your system.

3. Install the latest *setuptools* into the Python you obtained/installed/found in the step above: download ez_setup.py (http://peak.telecommunity.com/dist/ez_setup.py) and run it using the `python` interpreter of your Python 2.5 installation:

```
$ /path/to/my/Python-2.5/bin/python ez_setup.py
```

4. Use that Python's *bin/easy_install* to install *virtualenv*:

```
$ /path/to/my/Python-2.5/bin/easy_install virtualenv
```

5. Use that Python's virtualenv to make a workspace:

```
$ path/to/my/Python-25/bin/virtualenv --no-site-packages bigfntut
```

6. Switch to the `bigfntut` directory:

```
$ cd bigfntut
```

7. (Optional) Consider using `source bin/activate` to make your shell environment wired to use the virtualenv.

8. Use `easy_install` and point to the BFG "current" index to get `repoze.bfg` and its direct dependencies installed:

```
$ bin/easy_install -i http://dist.repoze.org/bfg/current/simple \
        repoze.bfg
```

9. Use `easy_install` to install various packages from PyPI.

```
$ bin/easy_install docutils nose coverage zope.sqlalchemy SQLAlchemy \
        repoze.tm2
```

Preparation, Windows

1. Install, or find Python 2.5 (http://python.org/download/releases/2.5.4/) for your system.

2. Install the latest *setuptools* into the Python you obtained/installed/found in the step above: download ez_setup.py (http://peak.telecommunity.com/dist/ez_setup.py) and run it using the `python` interpreter of your Python 2.5 installation using a command prompt:

```
c:\> c:\Python25\python ez_setup.py
```

3. Use that Python's *bin/easy_install* to install *virtualenv*:

```
c:\> c:\Python25\Scripts\easy_install virtualenv
```

4. Use that Python's virtualenv to make a workspace:

```
c:\> c:\Python25\Scripts\virtualenv --no-site-packages bigfntut
```

5. Switch to the `bigfntut` directory:

```
c:\> cd bigfntut
```

6. (Optional) Consider using `bin\activate.bat` to make your shell environment wired to use the virtualenv.

7. Use `easy_install` and point to the BFG "current" index to get `repoze.bfg` and its direct dependencies installed:

```
c:\bigfntut> Scripts\easy_install -i \
        http://dist.repoze.org/bfg/current/simple repoze.bfg
```

8. Use `easy_install` to install various packages from PyPI.

```
c:\bigfntut> Scripts\easy_install -i \
        http://dist.repoze.org/bfg/current/simple docutils \
        nose coverage zope.sqlalchemy SQLAlchemy repoze.tm2
```

28.2.2 Making a Project

Your next step is to create a project. `repoze.bfg` supplies a variety of templates to generate sample projects. We will use the `bfg_routesalchemy` template, which generates an application that uses *SQLAlchemy* and *URL dispatch*.

The below instructions assume your current working directory is the "virtualenv" named "bigfntut".

On UNIX:

```
$ bin/paster create -t bfg_routesalchemy tutorial
```

On Windows:

```
c:\bigfntut> Scripts\paster create -t bfg_routesalchemy tutorial
```

> ⓘ If you are using Windows, the `bfg_routesalchemy` Paster template may not deal gracefully with installation into a location that contains spaces in the path. If you experience startup problems, try putting both the virtualenv and the project into directories that do not contain spaces in their paths.

28.2.3 Installing the Project in "Development Mode"

In order to do development on the project easily, you must "register" the project as a development egg in your workspace using the `setup.py develop` command. In order to do so, cd to the "tutorial" directory you created in *Making a Project* (pp. 292), and run the "setup.py develop" command using virtualenv Python interpreter.

On UNIX:

```
$ cd tutorial
$ ../bin/python setup.py develop
```

On Windows:

```
c:\bigfntut> cd tutorial
c:\bigfntut\tutorial> ..\Scripts\python setup.py develop
```

28.2.4 Running the Tests

After you've installed the project in development mode, you may run the tests for the project.

On UNIX:

```
$ ../bin/python setup.py test -q
```

On Windows:

```
c:\bigfntut\tutorial> ..\Scripts\python setup.py test -q
```

28.2.5 Starting the Application

Start the application.

On UNIX:

```
$ ../bin/paster serve tutorial.ini --reload
```

On Windows:

```
c:\bifgfntut\tutorial> ..\Scripts\paster serve tutorial.ini --reload
```

28.2.6 Exposing Test Coverage Information

You can run the `nosetests` command to see test coverage information. This runs the tests in the same way that `setup.py test` does but provides additional "coverage" information, exposing which lines of your project are "covered" (or not covered) by the tests.

To get this functionality working, we'll need to install a couple of other packages into our `virtualenv`: `nose` and `coverage`:

On UNIX:

```
$ ../bin/easy_install nose coverage
```

On Windows:

```
c:\bfgfntut\tutorial> ..\Scripts\easy_install nose coverage
```

Once `nose` and `coverage` are installed, we can actually run the coverage tests.

On UNIX:

```
$ ../bin/nosetests --cover-package=tutorial --cover-erase --with-coverage
```

On Windows:

```
c:\bigfntut\tutorial> ..\Scripts\nosetests --cover-package=tutorial \
        --cover-erase --with-coverage
```

Looks like our package's `models` module doesn't quite have 100% test coverage.

28.2.7 Visit the Application in a Browser

In a browser, visit `http://localhost:6543/`. You will see the generated application's default page.

28.2.8 Decisions the `bfg_routesalchemy` Template Has Made For You

Creating a project using the `bfg_routesalchemy` template makes the assumption that you are willing to use *SQLAlchemy* as a database access tool and *url dispatch* to map URLs to code. `repoze.bfg` supports any persistent storage mechanism (e.g. object database or filesystem files, etc). It also supports an additional mechanism to map URLs to code (*traversal*). However, for the purposes of this tutorial, we'll only be using url dispatch and SQLAlchemy.

28.3 Basic Layout

The starter files generated by the `bfg_routesalchemy` template are basic, but they provide a good orientation for the high-level patterns common to most *url dispatch* -based `repoze.bfg` projects.

The source code for this tutorial stage can be browsed at docs.repoze.org (http://docs.repoze.org/bfgwiki2-1.2/basiclayout).

28.3.1 __init__.py

A directory on disk can be turned into a Python *package* by containing an __init__.py file. Even if empty, this marks a directory as a Python package.

28.3.2 Configuration With `configure.zcml`

`repoze.bfg` uses a configuration markup language syntactically the same as Zope's implementation of *ZCML*, but using a different default XML namespace. Our sample ZCML file looks like the following:

```
 1  <configure xmlns="http://namespaces.repoze.org/bfg">
 2
 3    <!-- this must be included for the view declarations to work -->
 4    <include package="repoze.bfg.includes" />
 5
 6    <subscriber for="repoze.bfg.interfaces.INewRequest"
 7      handler=".run.handle_teardown"/>
 8
 9    <route path=""
10      name="home"
11      view=".views.my_view"
12      view_renderer="templates/mytemplate.pt"
13      />
14
15    <static
16      name="static"
17      path="templates/static"
18      />
19
20  </configure>
```

1. *Line 1.* The root `<configure>` element, using the `http://namespaces.repoze.org/bfg` namespace.

2. *Line 4.* Boilerplate, the comment explains.

3. *Lines 6-7.* Register a *subscriber* that tears down the SQLAlchemy connection after a request is finished.

4. *Lines 9-13.* Register a `<route>` *route configuration* that will be used when the URL is /. Since this `<route>` has an empty `path` attribute, it is the "default" route. The attribute named `view` with the value `.views.my_view` is the dotted name to a *function* we write (generated by the `bfg_routesalchemy` template) that is given a `request` object and which returns a response or a dictionary. You will use mostly `<route>` statements in a *URL dispatch* based application to map URLs to code. This `route` also names a `view_renderer`, which is a template which lives in the `templates` subdirectory of the package. When the `.views.my_view` view returns a dictionary, a *renderer* will use this template to create a response.

5. *Lines 15-18*. Register a <static> directive that will match any URL that starts with /static/. This will serve up static resources for us, in this case, at http://localhost:6543/static/ and below. With this declaration, we're saying that any URL that starts with /static should go to the static view; any remainder of its path (e.g. the /foo in /static/foo) will be used to compose a path to a static file resource, such as a CSS file.

28.3.3 Content Models with models.py

In a SQLAlchemy-based application, a *model* object is an object composed by querying the SQL database which backs an application. SQLAlchemy is an "object relational mapper" (an ORM). The models.py file is where the bfg_routesalchemy Paster template put the classes that implement our models.

Here is the source for models.py:

```
 1  import transaction
 2
 3  from sqlalchemy import create_engine
 4  from sqlalchemy import Column
 5  from sqlalchemy import Integer
 6  from sqlalchemy import MetaData
 7  from sqlalchemy import Table
 8  from sqlalchemy import Unicode
 9
10  from sqlalchemy.exc import IntegrityError
11
12  from sqlalchemy.orm import scoped_session
13  from sqlalchemy.orm import sessionmaker
14  from sqlalchemy.orm import mapper
15
16  from zope.sqlalchemy import ZopeTransactionExtension
17
18  DBSession = scoped_session(
19      sessionmaker(extension=ZopeTransactionExtension()))
20
21  metadata = MetaData()
22
23  class Model(object):
24      def __init__(self, name=''):
25          self.name = name
26
27  models_table = Table(
28      'models',
29      metadata,
```

```
30        Column('id', Integer, primary_key=True),
31        Column('name', Unicode(255), unique=True),
32        )
33
34  models_mapper = mapper(Model, models_table)
35
36  def populate():
37        session = DBSession()
38        model = Model(name=u'root')
39        session.add(model)
40        session.flush()
41        transaction.commit()
42
43  def initialize_sql(db_string, echo=False):
44        engine = create_engine(db_string, echo=echo)
45        DBSession.configure(bind=engine)
46        metadata.bind = engine
47        metadata.create_all(engine)
48        try:
49            populate()
50        except IntegrityError:
51            pass
```

1. *Lines 1-16.* Imports to support later code.

2. *Line 18.* We set up a SQLAlchemy "DBSession" object here. We specify that we'd like to use the "ZopeTransactionExtension". This extension is an extension which allows us to use a *transaction manager* instead of controlling commits and aborts to database operations by hand.

3. *Line 21.* Set up a SQLAlchemy metadata object.

4. *Lines 23-25.* A model class named Model. It has an __init__ that takes a single argument (name). It stores a single attribute named name.

5. *Lines 27-32.* A SQLAlchemy Table declaration named models_table which we'll use later to map onto our Model class.

6. *Line 34.* We map our models_table table to our Models class here. This makes an association between the Model class and the models table in the database, as far as SQLAlchemy is concerned.

7. *Lines 36-41.* A function named populate which adds a single model instance into our SQL storage and commits a transaction.

8. *Lines 43-51.* A function named initialize_sql which sets up an actual SQL database and binds it to our SQLAlchemy DBSession object. It also calls the populate function, to do initial database population.

28.3.4 App Startup with `run.py`

When you run the application using the `paster` command using the `tutorial.ini` generated config file, the application configuration points at an Setuptools *entry point* described as `egg:tutorial#app`. In our application, because the application's `setup.py` file says so, this entry point happens to be the `app` function within the file named `run.py`:

```
import transaction

from repoze.bfg.configuration import Configurator
from repoze.tm import after_end
from repoze.tm import isActive

from tutorial.models import DBSession
from tutorial.models import initialize_sql

def handle_teardown(event):
    environ = event.request.environ
    if isActive(environ):
        t = transaction.get()
        after_end.register(DBSession.remove, t)

def app(global_config, **settings):
    """ This function returns a WSGI application.

    It is usually called by the PasteDeploy framework during
    ``paster serve``.
    """
    db_string = settings.get('db_string')
    if db_string is None:
        raise ValueError("No 'db_string' value in application "
                         "configuration.")
    initialize_sql(db_string)
    config = Configurator(settings=settings)
    config.begin()
    config.load_zcml('configure.zcml')
    config.end()
    return config.make_wsgi_app()
```

1. *Lines 1-8.* Imports to support later code.

2. *Lines 10-14.* An event *subscriber* which performs cleanup at transaction boundaries. As a result of registering this event subscriber, after the current transaction is committed or aborted, our database connection will be removed.

3. *Lines 22-25*. Get the database configuration string from the `tutorial.ini` file's `[app:sql]` section. This will be a URI (something like `sqlite://`).

4. Line *26*. We initialize our SQL database using SQLAlchemy, passing it the db string.

5. *Line 27*. We construct a *Configurator*. The first argument provided to the configurator is the *root factory*, which is used by the `repoze.bfg` *traversal* mechanism. Since this is a URL dispatch application, the root factory is `None`. The second argument `settings` is passed as a keyword argument. It contains a dictionary of settings parsed by PasteDeploy.

6. *Lines 28-31*. We then load a ZCML file to do application configuration, and use the `configuration.Configurator.make_wsgi_app()` (pp. 378) method to return a *WSGI* application.

28.4 Defining Models

The first change we'll make to our stock paster-generated application will be to define a *model* constructor representing a wiki page. We'll do this inside our `models.py` file.

The source code for this tutorial stage can be browsed at docs.repoze.org (http://docs.repoze.org/bfgwiki2-1.2/models).

28.4.1 Making Edits to `models.py`

> ⓘ   There is nothing automagically special about the filename `models.py`. A project may have many models throughout its codebase in arbitrarily-named files. Files implementing models often have `model` in their filenames (or they may live in a Python subpackage of your application package named `models`), but this is only by convention.

The first thing we want to do is remove the stock `Model` class from the generated `models.py` file. The `Model` class is only a sample and we're not going to use it.

Then, we'll add a `Page` class. Because this is a SQLAlchemy application, this class should inherit from an instance of `sqlalchemy.ext.declarative.declarative_base`. Declarative SQLAlchemy models are easier to use than directly-mapped ones. The code generated by our `routesalchemy` paster template does not use declarative SQLAlchemy syntax, so we'll need to change various things to begin to use declarative syntax.

Our `Page` class will have a class level attribute `__tablename__` which equals the string `pages`. This means that SQLAlchemy will store our wiki data in a SQL table named `pages`. Our Page class will also have class-level attributes named `id`, `pagename` and `data` (all instances of `sqlalchemy.Column`). These will map to columns in the `pages` table. The `id` attribute will be the primary key in the table. The `name` attribute will be a text attribute, each value of which needs to be unique within the column. The `data` attribute is a text attribute that will hold the body of each page.

We'll also remove our `populate` function. We'll inline the populate step into `initialize_sql`, changing our `initialize_sql` function to add a FrontPage object to our database at startup time. We're also going to use slightly different binding syntax. It will will otherwise largely be the same as the `initialize_sql` in the paster-generated `models.py`.

Our DBSession assignment stays the same as the original generated `models.py`.

28.4.2 Looking at the Result of Our Edits to `models.py`

The result of all of our edits to `models.py` will end up looking something like this:

```
 1  import transaction
 2
 3  from sqlalchemy import create_engine
 4  from sqlalchemy import Column
 5  from sqlalchemy import Integer
 6  from sqlalchemy import Text
 7
 8  from sqlalchemy.exc import IntegrityError
 9
10  from sqlalchemy.orm import scoped_session
11  from sqlalchemy.orm import sessionmaker
12
13  from sqlalchemy.ext.declarative import declarative_base
14
15  from zope.sqlalchemy import ZopeTransactionExtension
16
17  DBSession = scoped_session(
18      sessionmaker(extension=ZopeTransactionExtension()))
19  Base = declarative_base()
20
21  class Page(Base):
22      """ The SQLAlchemy declarative model class for a Page object. """
23      __tablename__ = 'pages'
24      id = Column(Integer, primary_key=True)
```

```
25      name = Column(Text, unique=True)
26      data = Column(Text)
27
28      def __init__(self, name, data):
29          self.name = name
30          self.data = data
31
32  def initialize_sql(db, echo=False):
33      engine = create_engine(db, echo=echo)
34      DBSession.configure(bind=engine)
35      Base.metadata.bind = engine
36      Base.metadata.create_all(engine)
37      try:
38          session = DBSession()
39          page = Page('FrontPage', 'initial data')
40          session.add(page)
41          transaction.commit()
42      except IntegrityError:
43          # already created
44          pass
```

28.4.3 Viewing the Application in a Browser

We can't. At this point, our system is in a "non-runnable" state; we'll need to change view-related files in the next chapter to be able to start the application successfully. If you try to start the application, you'll wind up with a Python traceback on your console that ends with this exception:

```
ImportError: cannot import name Model
```

28.5 Defining Views

A *view callable* in a *url dispatch* -based `repoze.bfg` application is typically a simple Python function that accepts a single parameter named *request*. A view callable is assumed to return a *response* object.

> ⓘ A repoze.bfg view can also be defined as callable which accepts *two* arguments: a *context* and a *request*. You'll see this two-argument pattern used in other repoze.bfg tutorials and applications. Either calling convention will work in any repoze.bfg application; the calling conventions can be used interchangeably as necessary. In *url dispatch* based applications, however, the context object is rarely used in the view body itself, so within this tutorial we define views as callables that accept only a request to avoid the visual "noise". If you do need the context within a view function that only takes the request as a single argument, you can obtain it via request.context.

The request passed to every view that is called as the result of a route match has an attribute named matchdict that contains the elements placed into the URL by the path of a route statement. For instance, if a route statement in configure.zcml had the path :one/:two, and the URL at http://example.com/foo/bar was invoked, matching this path, the matchdict dictionary attached to the request passed to the view would have a one key with the value foo and a two key with the value bar.

The source code for this tutorial stage can be browsed at docs.repoze.org (http://docs.repoze.org/bfgwiki2-1.2/views).

28.5.1 Declaring Dependencies in Our setup.py File

The view code in our application will depend on a package which is not a dependency of the original "tutorial" application. The original "tutorial" application was generated by the paster create command; it doesn't know about our custom application requirements. We need to add a dependency on the docutils package to our tutorial package's setup.py file by assigning this dependency to the install_requires parameter in the setup function.

Our resulting setup.py should look like so:

```
import os
import sys

from setuptools import setup, find_packages

here = os.path.abspath(os.path.dirname(__file__))
README = open(os.path.join(here, 'README.txt')).read()
CHANGES = open(os.path.join(here, 'CHANGES.txt')).read()

requires = [
    'repoze.bfg',
```

```
12      'SQLAlchemy',
13      'transaction',
14      'repoze.tm2',
15      'zope.sqlalchemy',
16      'docutils'
17      ]
18
19   if sys.version_info[:3] < (2,5,0):
20       requires.append('pysqlite')
21
22   setup(name='tutorial',
23         version='0.0',
24         description='tutorial',
25         long_description=README + '\n\n' + CHANGES,
26         classifiers=[
27           "Programming Language :: Python",
28           "Framework :: BFG",
29           "Topic :: Internet :: WWW/HTTP",
30           "Topic :: Internet :: WWW/HTTP :: WSGI :: Application",
31           ],
32         author='',
33         author_email='',
34         url='',
35         keywords='web wsgi bfg',
36         packages=find_packages(),
37         include_package_data=True,
38         zip_safe=False,
39         test_suite='tutorial',
40         install_requires = requires,
41         entry_points = """\
42         [paste.app_factory]
43         app = tutorial.run:app
44         """
45         )
```

> ℹ️ After these new dependencies are added, you will need to rerun `python setup.py develop` inside the root of the `tutorial` package to obtain and register the newly added dependency package.

28.5.2 Adding View Functions

We'll get rid of our `my_view` view function in our `views.py` file. It's only an example and isn't relevant to our application.

Then we're going to add four *view callable* functions to our `views.py` module. One view callable (named `view_wiki`) will display the wiki itself (it will answer on the root URL), another named `view_page` will display an individual page, another named `add_page` will allow a page to be added, and a final view callable named `edit_page` will allow a page to be edited. We'll describe each one briefly and show the resulting `views.py` file afterward.

> There is nothing special about the filename `views.py`. A project may have many view callables throughout its codebase in arbitrarily-named files. Files implementing view callables often have `view` in their filenames (or may live in a Python subpackage of your application package named `views`), but this is only by convention.

The `view_wiki` view function

The `view_wiki` function will respond as the *default view* of a `Wiki` model object. It always redirects to a URL which represents the path to our "FrontPage". It returns an instance of the `webob.exc.HTTPFound` class (instances of which implement the WebOb *response* interface), It will use the `url.route_url()` (pp. 423) API to construct a URL to the `FrontPage` page (e.g. `http://localhost:6543/FrontPage`), and will use it as the "location" of the HTTPFound response, forming an HTTP redirect.

The `view_page` view function

The `view_page` function will respond as the *default view* of a `Page` object. The `view_page` function renders the *ReStructuredText* body of a page (stored as the `data` attribute of a Page object) as HTML. Then it substitutes an HTML anchor for each *WikiWord* reference in the rendered HTML using a compiled regular expression.

The curried function named `check` is used as the first argument to `wikiwords.sub`, indicating that it should be called to provide a value for each WikiWord match found in the content. If the wiki already contains a page with the matched WikiWord name, the `check` function generates a view link to be used as the substitution value and returns it. If the wiki does not already contain a page with with the matched WikiWord name, the function generates an "add" link as the substitution value and returns it.

As a result, the `content` variable is now a fully formed bit of HTML containing various view and add links for WikiWords based on the content of our current page object.

We then generate an edit URL (because it's easier to do here than in the template), and we return a dictionary with a number of arguments. The fact that this view returns a dictionary (as opposed to a *response* object) is a cue to `repoze.bfg` that it should try to use a *renderer* associated with the view configuration to render a template. In our case, the template which will be rendered will be the `templates/view.pt` template, as per the configuration put into effect in `configure.zcml`.

The `add_page` view function

The `add_page` function will be invoked when a user clicks on a *WikiWord* which isn't yet represented as a page in the system. The `check` function within the `view_page` view generates URLs to this view. It also acts as a handler for the form that is generated when we want to add a page object. The `matchdict` attribute of the request passed to the `add_page` view will have the values we need to construct URLs and find model objects.

The matchdict will have a `pagename` key that matches the name of the page we'd like to add. If our add view is invoked via, e.g. `http://localhost:6543/add_page/SomeName`, the `pagename` value in the matchdict will be `SomeName`.

If the view execution is *not* a result of a form submission (if the expression `'form.submitted'` in `request.params` is `False`), the view callable renders a template. To do so, it generates a "save url" which the template use as the form post URL during rendering. We're lazy here, so we're trying to use the same template (`templates/edit.pt`) for the add view as well as the page edit view, so we create a dummy Page object in order to satisfy the edit form's desire to have *some* page object exposed as `page`, and `repoze.bfg` will render the template associated with this view to a response.

If the view execution *is* a result of a form submission (if the expression `'form.submitted'` in `request.params` is `True`), we scrape the page body from the form data, create a Page object using the name in the matchdict `pagename`, and obtain the page body from the request, and save it into the database using `session.add`. We then redirect back to the `view_page` view (the *default view* for a Page) for the newly created page.

The `edit_page` view function

The `edit_page` function will be invoked when a user clicks the "Edit this Page" button on the view form. It renders an edit form but it also acts as the handler for the form it renders. The `matchdict` attribute of the request passed to the `add_page` view will have a `pagename` key matching the name of the page the user wants to edit.

If the view execution is *not* a result of a form submission (if the expression `'form.submitted'` in `request.params` is `False`), the view simply renders the edit form, passing the request, the page object, and a save_url which will be used as the action of the generated form.

If the view execution *is* a result of a form submission (if the expression `'form.submitted'` in `request.params` is `True`), the view grabs the `body` element of the request parameter and sets it as the `data` key in the matchdict. It then redirects to the default view of the wiki page, which will always be the `view_page` view.

28.5.3 Viewing the Result of Our Edits to `views.py`

The result of all of our edits to `views.py` will leave it looking like this:

```python
import re

from docutils.core import publish_parts

from webob.exc import HTTPFound

from repoze.bfg.url import route_url

from tutorial.models import DBSession
from tutorial.models import Page

# regular expression used to find WikiWords
wikiwords = re.compile(r"\b([A-Z]\w+[A-Z]+\w+)")

def view_wiki(request):
    return HTTPFound(location = route_url('view_page', request,
                                          pagename='FrontPage'))

def view_page(request):
    matchdict = request.matchdict
    session = DBSession()
    page = session.query(Page).filter_by(name=matchdict['pagename']).one()

    def check(match):
        word = match.group(1)
        exists = session.query(Page).filter_by(name=word).all()
        if exists:
            view_url = route_url('view_page', request, pagename=word)
            return '<a href="%s">%s</a>' % (view_url, word)
        else:
            add_url = route_url('add_page', request, pagename=word)
            return '<a href="%s">%s</a>' % (add_url, word)

    content = publish_parts(page.data, writer_name='html')['html_body']
    content = wikiwords.sub(check, content)
    edit_url = route_url('edit_page', request,
                         pagename=matchdict['pagename'])
    return dict(page=page, content=content, edit_url=edit_url)

def add_page(request):
    name = request.matchdict['pagename']
```

```
42    if 'form.submitted' in request.params:
43        session = DBSession()
44        body = request.params['body']
45        page = Page(name, body)
46        session.add(page)
47        return HTTPFound(location = route_url('view_page', request,
48                                              pagename=name))
49    save_url = route_url('add_page', request, pagename=name)
50    page = Page('', '')
51    return dict(page=page, save_url=save_url)
52
53 def edit_page(request):
54    name = request.matchdict['pagename']
55    session = DBSession()
56    page = session.query(Page).filter_by(name=name).one()
57    if 'form.submitted' in request.params:
58        page.data = request.params['body']
59        session.add(page)
60        return HTTPFound(location = route_url('view_page', request,
61                                              pagename=name))
62    return dict(
63        page=page,
64        save_url = route_url('edit_page', request, pagename=name),
65        )
```

28.5.4 Adding Templates

The views we've added all reference a *template*. Each template is a *Chameleon* template. The default templating system in `repoze.bfg` is a variant of *ZPT* provided by *Chameleon*. These templates will live in the `templates` directory of our tutorial package.

The `view.pt` Template

The `view.pt` template is used for viewing a single wiki page. It is used by the `view_page` view function. It should have a div that is "structure replaced" with the `content` value provided by the view. It should also have a link on the rendered page that points at the "edit" URL (the URL which invokes the `edit_page` view for the page being viewed).

Once we're done with the `view.pt` template, it will look a lot like the below:

```
1  <!DOCTYPE html PUBLIC "-//W3C//DTD XHTML 1.0 Transitional//EN"
2    "http://www.w3.org/TR/xhtml1/DTD/xhtml1-transitional.dtd">
3  <html
4      xmlns="http://www.w3.org/1999/xhtml"
5        xmlns:tal="http://xml.zope.org/namespaces/tal">
6
7  <head>
8      <meta content="text/html; charset=utf-8" http-equiv="Content-Type"/>
9      <title>${page.name} - bfg tutorial wiki
10              (based on TurboGears 20-Minute Wiki)</title>
11          <link rel="stylesheet" type="text/css"
12            href="${request.application_url}/static/style.css" />
13  </head>
14
15  <body>
16
17  <div class="main_content">
18  <div style="float:right; width: 10em;"> Viewing
19  <span tal:replace="page.name">Page Name Goes Here</span> <br/>
20  You can return to the <a href="${request.application_url}">FrontPage</a>.
21  </div>
22
23  <div tal:replace="structure content">Page text goes here.</div>
24  <p><a tal:attributes="href edit_url" href="">Edit this page</a></p>
25  </div>
26
27  </body>
28  </html>
```

> ⓘ The names available for our use in a template are always those that are present in the dictionary returned by the view callable. But our templates make use of a `request` object that none of our tutorial views return in their dictionary. This value appears as if "by magic". However, `request` is one of several names that are available "by default" in a template when a template renderer is used. See **.pt or *.txt: Chameleon Template Renderers* (pp. 112) for more information about other names that are available by default in a template when a Chameleon template is used as a renderer.

The `edit.pt` Template

The `edit.pt` template is used for adding and editing a wiki page. It is used by the `add_page` and `edit_page` view functions. It should display a page containing a form that POSTs back to the "save_url" argument supplied by the view. The form should have a "body" textarea field (the page data), and a submit button that has the name "form.submitted". The textarea in the form should be filled with any existing page data when it is rendered.

Once we're done with the edit.pt template, it will look a lot like the below:

```
1   <!DOCTYPE html PUBLIC "-//W3C//DTD XHTML 1.0 Transitional//EN"
2     "http://www.w3.org/TR/xhtml1/DTD/xhtml1-transitional.dtd">
3   <html
4       xmlns="http://www.w3.org/1999/xhtml"
5         xmlns:tal="http://xml.zope.org/namespaces/tal">
6
7   <head>
8       <meta content="text/html; charset=utf-8" http-equiv="Content-Type"/>
9       <title>bfg tutorial wiki (based on TurboGears 20-Minute Wiki)
10              Editing: ${page.name}</title>
11          <link rel="stylesheet" type="text/css"
12            href="${request.application_url}/static/style.css" />
13  </head>
14
15  <body>
16
17  <div class="main_content">
18    <div style="float:right; width: 10em;"> Viewing
19      <span tal:replace="page.name">Page Name Goes Here</span> <br/>
20      You can return to the <a href="${request.application_url}"
21         >FrontPage</a>.
22    </div>
23
24    <div>
25      <form action="${save_url}" method="post">
26        <textarea name="body" tal:content="page.data" rows="10" cols="60"/>
27        <input type="submit" name="form.submitted" value="Save"/>
28      </form>
29    </div>
30  </div>
31  </body>
32  </html>
```

Static Resources

Our templates name a single static resource named style.css. We need to create this and place it in a file named style.css within our package's templates/static directory. This file is a little too long to replicate within the body of this guide, however it is available online (http://docs.repoze.org/bfgwiki2-1.2/views/tutorial/templates/static/style.css).

This CSS file will be accessed via e.g. `http://localhost:6543/static/style.css` by virtue of the `<static>` directive we've defined in the `configure.zcml` file. Any number and type of static resources can be placed in this directory (or subdirectories) and are just referred to by URL within templates.

28.5.5 Mapping Views to URLs in `configure.zcml`

The `configure.zcml` file contains `route` declarations (and a lone `view` declaration) which serve to map URLs via *url dispatch* to view functions. First, we'll get rid of the existing `route` created by the template using the name `home`. It's only an example and isn't relevant to our application.

We then need to add four `route` declarations to `configure.zcml`. Note that the *ordering* of these declarations is very important. `route` declarations are matched in the order they're found in the `configure.zcml` file.

1. Add a declaration which maps the empty path (signifying the root URL) to the view named `view_wiki` in our `views.py` file with the name `view_wiki`. This is the *default view* for the wiki.

2. Add a declaration which maps the path pattern `:pagename` to the view named `view_page` in our `views.py` file with the view name `view_page`. This is the regular view for a page.

3. Add a declaration which maps the path pattern `:pagename/edit_page` to the view named `edit_page` in our `views.py` file with the name `edit_page`. This is the edit view for a page.

4. Add a declaration which maps the path pattern `add_page/:pagename` to the view named `add_page` in our `views.py` file with the name `add_page`. This is the add view for a new page.

As a result of our edits, the `configure.zcml` file should look something like so:

```
1  <configure xmlns="http://namespaces.repoze.org/bfg">
2
3    <!-- this must be included for the view declarations to work -->
4    <include package="repoze.bfg.includes" />
5
6    <subscriber for="repoze.bfg.interfaces.INewRequest"
7      handler=".run.handle_teardown"/>
```

```
 8
 9    <static
10      name="static"
11      path="templates/static"
12      />
13
14    <route
15      path=""
16      name="view_wiki"
17      view=".views.view_wiki"
18      />
19
20    <route
21      path=":pagename"
22      name="view_page"
23      view=".views.view_page"
24      view_renderer="templates/view.pt"
25      />
26
27    <route
28      path="add_page/:pagename"
29      name="add_page"
30      view=".views.add_page"
31      view_renderer="templates/edit.pt"
32      />
33
34    <route
35      path=":pagename/edit_page"
36      name="edit_page"
37      view=".views.edit_page"
38      view_renderer="templates/edit.pt"
39      />
40
41  </configure>
```

The WSGI Pipeline

Within `tutorial.ini`, note the existence of a `[pipeline:main]` section which specifies our WSGI pipeline. This "pipeline" will be served up as our WSGI application. As far as the WSGI server is concerned the pipeline *is* our application. Simpler configurations don't use a pipeline: instead they expose a single WSGI application as "main". Our setup is more complicated, so we use a pipeline.

`egg:repoze.tm2#tm` is at the "top" of the pipeline. This is a piece of middleware which commits a transaction if no exception occurs; if an exception occurs, the transaction will be aborted. This is the piece of software that allows us to forget about needing to do manual commits and aborts of our database connection in view code.

Adding an Element to the Pipeline

Let's add a piece of middleware to the WSGI pipeline. We'll add `egg:Paste#evalerror` middleware which displays debuggable errors in the browser while you're developing (this is *not* recommended for deployment as it is a security risk). Let's insert evalerror into the pipeline right above `egg:repoze.tm2#tm`, making our resulting `tutorial.ini` file look like so:

```
[DEFAULT]
debug = true

[app:sql]
use = egg:tutorial#app
reload_templates = true
debug_authorization = false
debug_notfound = false
db_string = sqlite:///%(here)s/tutorial.db

[pipeline:main]
pipeline =
    egg:Paste#evalerror
    egg:repoze.tm2#tm
    sql

[server:main]
use = egg:Paste#http
host = 0.0.0.0
port = 6543
```

28.5.6 Viewing the Application in a Browser

Once we've set up the WSGI pipeline properly, we can finally examine our application in a browser. The views we'll try are as follows:

- Visiting `http://localhost:6543` in a browser invokes the `view_wiki` view. This always redirects to the `view_page` view of the FrontPage page object.

- Visiting `http://localhost:6543/FrontPage` in a browser invokes the `view_page` view of the front page page object.

- Visiting `http://localhost:6543/FrontPage/edit_page` in a browser invokes the edit view for the front page object.

- Visiting `http://localhost:6543/add_page/SomePageName` in a browser invokes the add view for a page.

Try generating an error within the body of a view by adding code to the top of it that generates an exception (e.g. `raise Exception('Forced Exception')`). Then visit the error-raising view in a browser. You should see an interactive exception handler in the browser which allows you to examine values in a post-mortem mode.

28.5.7 Adding Tests

Since we've added a good bit of imperative code here, it's useful to define tests for the views we've created. We'll change our tests.py module to look like this:

```
import unittest

from repoze.bfg.configuration import Configurator
from repoze.bfg import testing

def _initTestingDB():
    from tutorial.models import DBSession
    from tutorial.models import Base
    from sqlalchemy import create_engine
    engine = create_engine('sqlite://')
    DBSession.configure(bind=engine)
    Base.metadata.bind = engine
    Base.metadata.create_all(engine)
    return DBSession

def _registerRoutes(config):
    config.add_route('view_page', ':pagename')
    config.add_route('edit_page', ':pagename/edit_page')
    config.add_route('add_page', 'add_page/:pagename')

class ViewWikiTests(unittest.TestCase):
    def setUp(self):
        self.config = Configurator()
```

```
24          self.config.begin()
25
26      def tearDown(self):
27          self.config.end()
28
29      def test_it(self):
30          from tutorial.views import view_wiki
31          self.config.add_route('view_page', ':pagename')
32          request = testing.DummyRequest()
33          response = view_wiki(request)
34          self.assertEqual(response.location, 'http://example.com/FrontPage')
35
36  class ViewPageTests(unittest.TestCase):
37      def setUp(self):
38          self.session = _initTestingDB()
39          self.config = Configurator()
40          self.config.begin()
41
42      def tearDown(self):
43          self.session.remove()
44          self.config.end()
45
46      def _callFUT(self, request):
47          from tutorial.views import view_page
48          return view_page(request)
49
50      def test_it(self):
51          from tutorial.models import Page
52          request = testing.DummyRequest()
53          request.matchdict['pagename'] = 'IDoExist'
54          page = Page('IDoExist', 'Hello CruelWorld IDoExist')
55          self.session.add(page)
56          _registerRoutes(self.config)
57          info = self._callFUT(request)
58          self.assertEqual(info['page'], page)
59          self.assertEqual(
60              info['content'],
61              '<div class="document">\n'
62              '<p>Hello <a href="http://example.com/add_page/CruelWorld">'
63              'CruelWorld</a> '
64              '<a href="http://example.com/IDoExist">'
65              'IDoExist</a>'
66              '</p>\n</div>\n')
67          self.assertEqual(info['edit_url'],
68                          'http://example.com/IDoExist/edit_page')
69
```

315

```
70
71  class AddPageTests(unittest.TestCase):
72      def setUp(self):
73          self.session = _initTestingDB()
74          self.config = Configurator()
75          self.config.begin()
76
77      def tearDown(self):
78          self.session.remove()
79          self.config.end()
80
81      def _callFUT(self, request):
82          from tutorial.views import add_page
83          return add_page(request)
84
85      def test_it_notsubmitted(self):
86          _registerRoutes(self.config)
87          request = testing.DummyRequest()
88          request.matchdict = {'pagename':'AnotherPage'}
89          info = self._callFUT(request)
90          self.assertEqual(info['page'].data,'')
91          self.assertEqual(info['save_url'],
92                           'http://example.com/add_page/AnotherPage')
93
94      def test_it_submitted(self):
95          from tutorial.models import Page
96          _registerRoutes(self.config)
97          request = testing.DummyRequest({'form.submitted':True,
98                                          'body':'Hello yo!'})
99          request.matchdict = {'pagename':'AnotherPage'}
100         self._callFUT(request)
101         page = self.session.query(Page).filter_by(name='AnotherPage').one()
102         self.assertEqual(page.data, 'Hello yo!')
103
104 class EditPageTests(unittest.TestCase):
105     def setUp(self):
106         self.session = _initTestingDB()
107         self.config = Configurator()
108         self.config.begin()
109
110     def tearDown(self):
111         self.session.remove()
112         self.config.end()
113
114     def _callFUT(self, request):
115         from tutorial.views import edit_page
```

```
116        return edit_page(request)
117
118    def test_it_notsubmitted(self):
119        from tutorial.models import Page
120        _registerRoutes(self.config)
121        request = testing.DummyRequest()
122        request.matchdict = {'pagename':'abc'}
123        page = Page('abc', 'hello')
124        self.session.add(page)
125        info = self._callFUT(request)
126        self.assertEqual(info['page'], page)
127        self.assertEqual(info['save_url'],
128                         'http://example.com/abc/edit_page')
129
130    def test_it_submitted(self):
131        from tutorial.models import Page
132        _registerRoutes(self.config)
133        request = testing.DummyRequest({'form.submitted':True,
134                                        'body':'Hello yo!'})
135        request.matchdict = {'pagename':'abc'}
136        page = Page('abc', 'hello')
137        self.session.add(page)
138        response = self._callFUT(request)
139        self.assertEqual(response.location, 'http://example.com/abc')
140        self.assertEqual(page.data, 'Hello yo!')
```

We can then run the tests using something like:

```
$ python setup.py test -q
```

The expected output is something like:

```
running test
running egg_info
writing requirements to tutorial.egg-info/requires.txt
writing tutorial.egg-info/PKG-INFO
writing top-level names to tutorial.egg-info/top_level.txt
writing dependency_links to tutorial.egg-info/dependency_links.txt
writing entry points to tutorial.egg-info/entry_points.txt
unrecognized .svn/entries format in
reading manifest file 'tutorial.egg-info/SOURCES.txt'
writing manifest file 'tutorial.egg-info/SOURCES.txt'
```

317

```
11  running build_ext
12  ......
13  ---------------------------------------------------------------
14  Ran 6 tests in 0.181s
15
16  OK
```

28.6 Adding Authorization

Our application currently allows anyone with access to the server to view, edit, and add pages to our wiki. For purposes of demonstration we'll change our application to allow only people whom possess a specific username (*editor*) to add and edit wiki pages but we'll continue allowing anyone with access to the server to view pages. `repoze.bfg` provides facilities for *authorization* and *authentication*. We'll make use of both features to provide security to our application.

The source code for this tutorial stage can be browsed at docs.repoze.org (http://docs.repoze.org/bfgwiki2-1.2/authorization).

28.6.1 Adding A Root Factory

We're going to start to use a custom *root factory* within our `run.py` file. The objects generated by the root factory will be used as the *context* of each request to our application. In order for `repoze.bfg` declarative security to work properly, the context object generated during a request must be decorated with security declarations; when we begin to use a custom root factory to generate our contexts, we can begin to make use of the declarative security features of `repoze.bfg`.

Let's modify our `run.py`, passing in a *root factory* to our *Configurator* constructor. We'll point it at a new class we create inside our `models.py` file. Add the following statements to your `models.py` file:

```python
from repoze.bfg.security import Allow
from repoze.bfg.security import Everyone

class RootFactory(object):
    __acl__ = [ (Allow, Everyone, 'view'), (Allow, 'editor', 'edit') ]
    def __init__(self, request):
        self.__dict__.update(request.matchdict)
```

The `RootFactory` class we've just added will be used by `repoze.bfg` to construct a `context` object. The context is attached to the request object passed to our view callables as the `context` attribute.

All of our context objects will possess an `__acl__` attribute that allows `security.Everyone` (pp. 397) (a special principal) to view all pages, while allowing only a user named `editor` to edit and add pages. The `__acl__` attribute attached to a context is interpreted specially by `repoze.bfg` as an access control list during view callable execution. See *Assigning ACLs to your Model Objects* (pp. 171) for more information about what an *ACL* represents.

We'll pass the `RootFactory` we created in the step above in as the `root_factory` argument to a *Configurator*. When we're done, your application's `run.py` will look like this.

```
import transaction

from repoze.bfg.configuration import Configurator
from repoze.tm import after_end
from repoze.tm import isActive

from tutorial.models import DBSession
from tutorial.models import initialize_sql
from tutorial.models import RootFactory

def handle_teardown(event):
    environ = event.request.environ
    if isActive(environ):
        t = transaction.get()
        after_end.register(DBSession.remove, t)

def app(global_config, **settings):
    """ This function returns a WSGI application.

    It is usually called by the PasteDeploy framework during
    ``paster serve``.
    """
    db_string = settings.get('db_string')
    if db_string is None:
        raise ValueError("No 'db_string' value in application "
                         "configuration.")
    initialize_sql(db_string)
    config = Configurator(settings=settings, root_factory=RootFactory)
    config.begin()
    config.load_zcml('configure.zcml')
    config.end()
    return config.make_wsgi_app()
```

28.6.2 Configuring a `repoze.bfg` Authorization Policy

For any `repoze.bfg` application to perform authorization, we need to add a `security.py` module and we'll need to change our `configure.zcml` file to add an *authentication policy* and an *authorization policy*.

Changing `configure.zcml`

We'll change our `configure.zcml` file to enable an `AuthTktAuthenticationPolicy` and an `ACLAuthorizationPolicy` to enable declarative security checking. We'll also change `configure.zcml` to add a `forbidden` stanza which points at our `login` *view callable*, also known as a *forbidden view*. This configures our newly created login view to show up when `repoze.bfg` detects that a view invocation can not be authorized. Also, we'll add `view_permission` attributes with the value `edit` to the `edit_page` and `add_page` route declarations. This indicates that the view callables which these routes reference cannot be invoked without the authenticated user possessing the `edit` permission with respect to the current context. When you're done, your `configure.zcml` will look like so

```
1   <configure xmlns="http://namespaces.repoze.org/bfg">
2
3     <!-- this must be included for the view declarations to work -->
4     <include package="repoze.bfg.includes" />
5
6     <subscriber for="repoze.bfg.interfaces.INewRequest"
7       handler=".run.handle_teardown"/>
8
9     <static
10      name="static"
11      path="templates/static"
12      />
13
14    <route
15       path="login"
16       name="login"
17       view=".login.login"
18       view_renderer="templates/login.pt"
19       />
20
21    <route
22       path="logout"
23       name="logout"
24       view=".login.logout"
```

```
25        />
26
27    <route
28        path=""
29        name="view_wiki"
30        view=".views.view_wiki"
31        />
32
33    <route
34        path=":pagename"
35        name="view_page"
36        view=".views.view_page"
37        view_renderer="templates/view.pt"
38        />
39
40    <route
41        path="add_page/:pagename"
42        name="add_page"
43        view=".views.add_page"
44        view_renderer="templates/edit.pt"
45        view_permission="edit"
46        />
47
48    <route
49        path=":pagename/edit_page"
50        name="edit_page"
51        view=".views.edit_page"
52        view_renderer="templates/edit.pt"
53        view_permission="edit"
54        />
55
56    <forbidden
57        view=".login.login"
58        renderer="templates/login.pt"/>
59
60    <authtktauthenticationpolicy
61        secret="sosecret"
62        />
63
64    <aclauthorizationpolicy/>
65
66 </configure>
```

Adding `security.py`

Add a `security.py` module within your package (in the same directory as "run.py", "views.py", etc) with the following content: The groupfinder defined here is an *authentication policy* "callback"; it is a callable that accepts a userid and a request. If the userid exists in the system, the callback will return a sequence of group identifiers (or an empty sequence if the user isn't a member of any groups). If the userid *does not* exist in the system, the callback will return `None`. We'll use "dummy" data to represent user and groups sources. When we're done, your application's `security.py` will look like this.

```
1  USERS = {'editor':'editor',
2           'viewer':'viewer'}
3  GROUPS = {'editor':['group.editors']}
4
5  def groupfinder(userid, request):
6      if userid in USERS:
7          return GROUPS.get(userid, [])
```

Adding Login and Logout Views

We'll add a `login` view callable which renders a login form and processes the post from the login form, checking credentials.

We'll also add a `logout` view callable to our application and provide a link to it. This view will clear the credentials of the logged in user and redirect back to the front page.

We'll add a different file (for presentation convenience) to add login and logout view callables. Add a file named `login.py` to your application (in the same directory as `views.py`) with the following content:

```
1   from webob.exc import HTTPFound
2
3   from repoze.bfg.security import remember
4   from repoze.bfg.security import forget
5   from repoze.bfg.url import route_url
6
7   from tutorial.security import USERS
8
9   def login(request):
10      login_url = route_url('login', request)
11      referrer = request.url
12      if referrer == login_url:
```

```
13          referrer = '/' # never use the login form itself as came_from
14      came_from = request.params.get('came_from', referrer)
15      message = ''
16      login = ''
17      password = ''
18      if 'form.submitted' in request.params:
19          login = request.params['login']
20          password = request.params['password']
21          if USERS.get(login) == password:
22              headers = remember(request, login)
23              return HTTPFound(location = came_from,
24                              headers = headers)
25          message = 'Failed login'
26
27      return dict(
28          message = message,
29          url = request.application_url + '/login',
30          came_from = came_from,
31          login = login,
32          password = password,
33          )
34
35  def logout(request):
36      headers = forget(request)
37      return HTTPFound(location = route_url('view_wiki', request),
38                      headers = headers)
```

Changing Existing Views

Then we need to change each of our `view_page`, `edit_page` and `add_page` views in `views.py` to pass a "logged in" parameter to its template. We'll add something like this to each view body:

```
1  from repoze.bfg.security import authenticated_userid
2  logged_in = authenticated_userid(request)
```

We'll then change the return value of these views to pass the *resulting 'logged_in'* value to the template, e.g.:

```
1  return dict(page = context,
2              content = content,
```

323

```
3          logged_in = logged_in,
4          edit_url = edit_url)
```

Adding the `login.pt` Template

Add a `login.pt` template to your templates directory. It's referred to within the login view we just added to `login.py`.

```
1  <!DOCTYPE html PUBLIC "-//W3C//DTD XHTML 1.0 Transitional//EN"
2    "http://www.w3.org/TR/xhtml1/DTD/xhtml1-transitional.dtd">
3  <html
4      xmlns="http://www.w3.org/1999/xhtml"
5      xmlns:tal="http://xml.zope.org/namespaces/tal">
6
7  <head>
8    <meta content="text/html; charset=utf-8" http-equiv="Content-Type"/>
9    <title>bfg tutorial wiki (based on TurboGears 20-Minute Wiki)</title>
10   <link rel="stylesheet" type="text/css"
11         href="${request.application_url}/static/style.css" />
12  </head>
13
14  <body>
15
16  <h1>Log In</h1>
17
18  <div tal:replace="message"/>
19
20  <div class="main_content">
21    <form action="${url}" method="post">
22      <input type="hidden" name="came_from" value="${came_from}"/>
23      <input type="text" name="login" value="${login}"/>
24      <br/>
25      <input type="password" name="password" value="${password}"/>
26      <br/>
27      <input type="submit" name="form.submitted" value="Log In"/>
28    </form>
29  </div>
30
31  </body>
32  </html>
```

Change `view.pt` and `edit.pt`

We'll also need to change our `edit.pt` and `view.pt` templates to display a "Logout" link if someone is logged in. This link will invoke the logout view.

To do so we'll add this to both templates within the `<div class="main_content">` div:

```
<span tal:condition="logged_in">
  <a href="${request.application_url}/logout">Logout</a>
</span>
```

28.6.3 Viewing the Application in a Browser

We can finally examine our application in a browser. The views we'll try are as follows:

- Visiting `http://localhost:6543/` in a browser invokes the `view_wiki` view. This always redirects to the `view_page` view of the FrontPage page object. It is executable by any user.

- Visiting `http://localhost:6543/FrontPage` in a browser invokes the `view_page` view of the FrontPage page object.

- Visiting `http://localhost:6543/FrontPage/edit_page` in a browser invokes the edit view for the FrontPage object. It is executable by only the `editor` user. If a different user (or the anonymous user) invokes it, a login form will be displayed. Supplying the credentials with the username `editor`, password `editor` will display the edit page form.

- Visiting `http://localhost:6543/add_page/SomePageName` in a browser invokes the add view for a page. It is executable by only the `editor` user. If a different user (or the anonymous user) invokes it, a login form will be displayed. Supplying the credentials with the username `editor`, password `editor` will display the edit page form.

28.6.4 Seeing Our Changes To `views.py` and our Templates

Our `views.py` module will look something like this when we're done:

```
1   import re
2
3   from docutils.core import publish_parts
4
5   from webob.exc import HTTPFound
6
7   from repoze.bfg.security import authenticated_userid
8   from repoze.bfg.url import route_url
9
10  from tutorial.models import DBSession
11  from tutorial.models import Page
12
13  # regular expression used to find WikiWords
14  wikiwords = re.compile(r"\b([A-Z]\w+[A-Z]+\w+)")
15
16  def view_wiki(request):
17      return HTTPFound(location = route_url('view_page', request,
18                                            pagename='FrontPage'))
19
20  def view_page(request):
21      pagename = request.matchdict['pagename']
22      session = DBSession()
23      page = session.query(Page).filter_by(name=pagename).one()
24
25      def check(match):
26          word = match.group(1)
27          exists = session.query(Page).filter_by(name=word).all()
28          if exists:
29              view_url = route_url('view_page', request, pagename=word)
30              return '<a href="%s">%s</a>' % (view_url, word)
31          else:
32              add_url = route_url('add_page', request, pagename=word)
33              return '<a href="%s">%s</a>' % (add_url, word)
34
35      content = publish_parts(page.data, writer_name='html')['html_body']
36      content = wikiwords.sub(check, content)
37      edit_url = route_url('edit_page', request, pagename=pagename)
38      logged_in = authenticated_userid(request)
39      return dict(page=page, content=content, edit_url=edit_url,
40                  logged_in=logged_in)
41
42  def add_page(request):
43      name = request.matchdict['pagename']
44      if 'form.submitted' in request.params:
45          session = DBSession()
46          body = request.params['body']
```

```
47        page = Page(name, body)
48        session.add(page)
49        return HTTPFound(location = route_url('view_page', request,
50                                            pagename=name))
51    save_url = route_url('add_page', request, pagename=name)
52    page = Page('', '')
53    logged_in = authenticated_userid(request)
54    return dict(page=page, save_url=save_url, logged_in=logged_in)
55
56 def edit_page(request):
57    name = request.matchdict['pagename']
58    session = DBSession()
59    page = session.query(Page).filter_by(name=name).one()
60    if 'form.submitted' in request.params:
61        page.data = request.params['body']
62        session.add(page)
63        return HTTPFound(location = route_url('view_page', request,
64                                            pagename=name))
65
66    logged_in = authenticated_userid(request)
67    return dict(
68        page=page,
69        save_url = route_url('edit_page', request, pagename=name),
70        logged_in = logged_in,
71        )
```

Our `edit.pt` template will look something like this when we're done:

```
1  <!DOCTYPE html PUBLIC "-//W3C//DTD XHTML 1.0 Transitional//EN"
2    "http://www.w3.org/TR/xhtml1/DTD/xhtml1-transitional.dtd">
3  <html
4     xmlns="http://www.w3.org/1999/xhtml"
5       xmlns:tal="http://xml.zope.org/namespaces/tal">
6
7  <head>
8     <meta content="text/html; charset=utf-8" http-equiv="Content-Type"/>
9     <title>bfg tutorial wiki (based on TurboGears 20-Minute Wiki)
10            Editing: ${page.name}</title>
11        <link rel="stylesheet" type="text/css"
12          href="${request.application_url}/static/style.css" />
13  </head>
14
15  <body>
16
```

```
17  <div class="main_content">
18    <div style="float:right; width: 10em;"> Viewing
19      <span tal:replace="page.name">Page Name Goes Here</span> <br/>
20      You can return to the <a href="${request.application_url}"
21              >FrontPage</a>.
22    <span tal:condition="logged_in">
23        <a href="${request.application_url}/logout">Logout</a>
24    </span>
25    </div>
26
27    <div>
28      <form action="${save_url}" method="post">
29        <textarea name="body" tal:content="page.data" rows="10" cols="60"/>
30        <input type="submit" name="form.submitted" value="Save"/>
31      </form>
32    </div>
33  </div>
34  </body>
35  </html>
```

Our `view.pt` template will look something like this when we're done:

```
1   <!DOCTYPE html PUBLIC "-//W3C//DTD XHTML 1.0 Transitional//EN"
2     "http://www.w3.org/TR/xhtml1/DTD/xhtml1-transitional.dtd">
3   <html
4       xmlns="http://www.w3.org/1999/xhtml"
5         xmlns:tal="http://xml.zope.org/namespaces/tal">
6
7   <head>
8       <meta content="text/html; charset=utf-8" http-equiv="Content-Type"/>
9       <title>${page.name} - bfg tutorial wiki
10            (based on TurboGears 20-Minute Wiki)</title>
11          <link rel="stylesheet" type="text/css"
12            href="${request.application_url}/static/style.css" />
13  </head>
14
15  <body>
16
17  <div class="main_content">
18  <div style="float:right; width: 10em;"> Viewing
19  <span tal:replace="page.name">Page Name Goes Here</span> <br/>
20  You can return to the <a href="${request.application_url}">FrontPage</a>.
21  <span tal:condition="logged_in">
22    <a href="${request.application_url}/logout">Logout</a>
```

```
23  </span>
24  </div>
25
26  <div tal:replace="structure content ">Page text goes here.</div>
27  <p><a tal:attributes="href edit_url" href="">Edit this page</a></p>
28  </div>
29
30  </body>
31  </html>
```

28.6.5 Revisiting the Application

When we revisit the application in a browser, and log in (as a result of hitting an edit or add page and submitting the login form with the editor credentials), we'll see a Logout link in the upper right hand corner. When we click it, we're logged out, and redirected back to the front page.

28.7 Distributing Your Application

Once your application works properly, you can create a "tarball" from it by using the setup.py sdist command. The following commands assume your current working directory is the tutorial package we've created and that the parent directory of the tutorial package is a virtualenv representing a repoze.bfg environment.

On UNIX:

```
$ ../bin/python setup.py sdist
```

On Windows:

```
c:\bigfntut> ..\Scripts\python setup.py sdist
```

> ⚠ If your project files are not checked in to a version control repository (such as Subversion), the dist tarball will *not* contain all the files it needs to. In particular, it will not contain non-Python-source files (such as templates and static files). To ensure that these are included, check your files into a version control repository before running `setup.py sdist`.

The output of such a command will be something like:

```
running sdist
# ... more output ...
creating dist
tar -cf dist/tutorial-0.1.tar tutorial-0.1
gzip -f9 dist/tutorial-0.1.tar
removing 'tutorial-0.1' (and everything under it)
```

Note that this command creates a tarball in the "dist" subdirectory named `tutorial-0.1.tar.gz`. You can send this file to your friends to show them your cool new application. They should be able to install it by pointing the `easy_install` command directly at it. Or you can upload it to PyPI (http://pypi.python.org) and share it with the rest of the world, where it can be downloaded via `easy_install` remotely like any other package people download from PyPI.

RUNNING REPOZE.BFG ON GOOGLE'S APP ENGINE

As of `repoze.bfg` version 0.8, it is possible to run a `repoze.bfg` application on Google's App Engine (http://code.google.com/appengine/). Content from this tutorial was contributed by YoungKing, based on the "appengine-monkey" tutorial for Pylons (http://code.google.com/p/appengine-monkey/wiki/Pylons). This tutorial is written in terms of using the command line on a UNIX system; it should be possible to perform similar actions on a Windows system.

1. Download Google's App Engine SDK (http://code.google.com/appengine/downloads.html) and install it on your system.

2. Use Subversion to check out the source code for `appengine-monkey`.

   ```
   $ svn co http://appengine-monkey.googlecode.com/svn/trunk/ \
       appengine-monkey
   ```

3. Use `appengine_homedir.py` script in `appengine-monkey` to create a *virtualenv* for your application.

   ```
   $ export GAE_PATH=/usr/local/google_appengine
   $ python2.5 /path/to/appengine-monkey/appengine-homedir.py --gae \
     $GAE_PATH bfgapp
   ```

Note that $GAE_PATH should be the path where you have unpacked the App Engine SDK. (On Mac OS X at least, /usr/local/google_appengine is indeed where the installer puts it).

This will set up an environment in bfgapp/, with some tools installed in bfgapp/bin. There will also be a directory bfgapp/app/ which is the directory you will upload to appengine.

4. Install repoze.bfg into the virtualenv

```
$ cd bfgapp/
$ bin/easy_install -i http://dist.repoze.org/bfg/current/simple/ \
      repoze.bfg
```

This will install repoze.bfg in the environment.

5. Create your application

We'll use the standard way to create a repoze.bfg application, but we'll have to move some files around when we are done. The below commands assume your current working directory is the bfgapp virtualenv directory you created in the third step above:

```
$ cd app
$ rm -rf bfgapp
$ bin/paster create -t bfg_starter bfgapp
$ mv bfgapp aside
$ mv aside/bfgapp .
$ rm -rf aside
```

6. Edit config.py

Edit the APP_NAME and APP_ARGS settings within config.py. The APP_NAME must be bfgapp.run:app, and the APP_ARGS must be ({},). Any other settings in config.py should remain the same.

```
APP_NAME = 'bfgapp.run:app'
APP_ARGS = ({},)
```

7. Edit runner.py

To prevent errors for import site, add this code stanza before import site in app/runner.py:

332

```
import sys
sys.path = [path for path in sys.path if 'site-packages' not in path]
import site
```

You will also need to comment out the line that starts with `assert sys.path` in the file.

```
# comment the sys.path assertion out
# assert sys.path[:len(cur_sys_path)] == cur_sys_path, (
#   "addsitedir() caused entries to be prepended to sys.path")
```

For GAE development environment 1.3.0 or better, you will also need the following somewhere near the top of the `runner.py` file to fix a compatibility issue with `appengine-monkey`:

```
import os
os.mkdir = None
```

8. Run the application. `dev_appserver.py` is typically installed by the SDK in the global path but you need to be sure to run it with Python 2.5 (or whatever version of Python your GAE SDK expects).

```
1 $ cd ../..
2 $ python2.5 /usr/local/bin/dev_appserver.py bfgapp/app/
```

Startup success looks something like this:

```
[chrism@vitaminf bfg_gae]$ python2.5 /usr/local/bin/dev_appserver.py \
        bfgapp/app/
INFO      2009-05-03 22:23:13,887 appengine_rpc.py:157] # ... more...
Running application bfgapp on port 8080: http://localhost:8080
```

You may need to run "Make Symlinks" from the Google App Engine Launcher GUI application if your system doesn't already have the `dev_appserver.py` script sitting around somewhere.

9. Hack on your bfg application, using a normal run, debug, restart process. For tips on how to use the pdb module within Google App Engine, see this blog post (http://jjinux.blogspot.com/2008/05/python-debugging-google-app-engine-apps.html). In particular, you can create a function like so and call it to drop your console into a pdb trace:

```
1  def set_trace():
2      import pdb, sys
3      debugger = pdb.Pdb(stdin=sys.__stdin__,
4          stdout=sys.__stdout__)
5      debugger.set_trace(sys._getframe().f_back)
```

10. Sign up for a GAE account (http://code.google.com/appengine/) and create an application. You'll need a mobile phone to accept an SMS in order to receive authorization.

11. Edit the application's ID in app.yaml to match the application name you created during GAE account setup.

```
application: mycoolbfgapp
```

12. Upload the application

```
$ python2.5 /usr/local/bin/appcfg.py update bfgapp/app
```

You almost certainly won't hit the 3000-file GAE file number limit when invoking this command. If you do, however, it will look like so:

```
HTTPError: HTTP Error 400: Bad Request
Rolling back the update.
Error 400: --- begin server output ---
Max number of files and blobs is 3000.
--- end server output ---
```

If you do experience this error, you will be able to get around this by zipping libraries. You can use pip to create zipfiles from packages. See *Zipping Files Via Pip* (pp. 335) for more information about this.

A successful upload looks like so:

```
[chrism@vitaminf bfgapp]$ python2.5 /usr/local/bin/appcfg.py update \
        ../bfgapp/app/
Scanning files on local disk.
Scanned 500 files.
# ... more output ...
Will check again in 16 seconds.
Checking if new version is ready to serve.
Closing update: new version is ready to start serving.
Uploading index definitions.
```

13. Visit http://<yourapp>.appspot.com in a browser.

29.1 Zipping Files Via Pip

If you hit the Google App Engine 3000-file limit, you may need to create zipfile archives out of some distributions installed in your application's virtualenv.

First, see which packages are available for zipping:

```
$ bin/pip zip -l
```

This shows your zipped packages (by default, none) and your unzipped packages. You can zip a package like so:

```
$ bin/pip zip pytz-2009g-py2.5.egg
```

Note that it requires the whole egg file name. For a BFG app, the following packages are good candidates to be zipped.

- pytz
- chameleon.core
- chameleon.zpt
- zope.i18n
- zope.testing

Once the zipping procedure is finished you can try uploading again.

335

RUNNING A REPOZE.BFG APPLICATION UNDER MOD_WSGI

mod_wsgi is an Apache module developed by Graham Dumpleton. It allows *WSGI* programs to be served using the Apache web server.

This guide will outline broad steps that can be used to get a `repoze.bfg` application running under Apache via `mod_wsgi`. This particular tutorial was developed under Apple's Mac OS X platform (Snow Leopard, on a 32-bit Mac), but the instructions should be largely the same for all systems, delta specific path information for commands and files.

> ⓘ Unfortunately these instructions almost certainly won't work for deploying a `repoze.bfg` application on a Windows system using `mod_wsgi`. If you have experience with `repoze.bfg` and and `mod_wsgi` on Windows systems, please help us document this experience by submitting documentation to the mailing list (http://lists.repoze.org/listinfo/repoze-dev).

1. The tutorial assumes you have Apache already installed on your system. If you do not, install Apache 2.X for your platform in whatever manner makes sense.

2. Once you have Apache installed, install `mod_wsgi`. Use the (excellent) installation instructions (http://code.google.com/p/modwsgi/wiki/InstallationInstructions) for your platform into your system's Apache installation.

3. Install *virtualenv* into the Python which mod_wsgi will run using the `easy_install` program.

```
$ sudo /usr/bin/easy_install-2.6 virtualenv
```

This command may need to be performed as the root user.

4. Create a *virtualenv* which we'll use to install our application.

```
$ cd ~
$ mkdir modwsgi
$ cd modwsgi
$ /usr/local/bin/virtualenv --no-site-packages env
```

5. Install repoze.bfg into the newly created virtualenv:

```
$ cd ~/modwsgi/env
$ bin/easy_install -i http://dist.repoze.org/bfg/current/simple \
      repoze.bfg
```

6. Create and install your repoze.bfg application. For the purposes of this tutorial, we'll just be using the bfg_starter application as a baseline application. Substitute your existing repoze.bfg application as necessary if you already have one.

```
$ cd ~/modwsgi/env
$ bin/paster create -t bfg_starter myapp
$ cd myapp
$ ../bin/python setup.py install
```

7. Within the virtualenv directory (~/modwsgi/env), create a script named bfg.wsgi. Give it these contents:

```
from repoze.bfg.paster import get_app
application = get_app(
  '/Users/chrism/modwsgi/env/myapp/myapp.ini', 'main')
```

The first argument to `get_app` is the project Paste configuration file name. The second is the name of the section within the .ini file that should be loaded by `mod_wsgi`. The assignment to the name `application` is important: mod_wsgi requires finding such an assignment when it opens the file.

8. Make the `bfg.wsgi` script executable.

```
$ cd ~/modwsgi/env
$ chmod 755 bfg.wsgi
```

9. Edit your Apache configuration and add some stuff. I happened to create a file named `/etc/apache2/other/modwsgi.conf` on my own system while installing Apache, so this stuff went in there.

```
# Use only 1 Python sub-interpreter.  Multiple sub-interpreters
# play badly with C extensions.
WSGIApplicationGroup %{GLOBAL}
WSGIPassAuthorization On
WSGIDaemonProcess bfg user=chrism group=staff processes=1 threads=4 \
   python-path=/Users/chrism/modwsgi/env/lib/python2.6/site-packages
WSGIScriptAlias /myapp /Users/chrism/modwsgi/env/bfg.wsgi

<Directory /Users/chrism/modwsgi/env>
  WSGIProcessGroup bfg
  Order allow, deny
  Allow from all
</Directory>
```

10. Restart Apache

```
$ sudo /usr/sbin/apachectl restart
```

11. Visit `http://localhost/myapp` in a browser. You should see the sample application rendered in your browser.

mod_wsgi has many knobs and a great variety of deployment modes. This is just one representation of how you might use it to serve up a `repoze.bfg` application. See the mod_wsgi configuration documentation (http://code.google.com/p/modwsgi/wiki/ConfigurationGuidelines) for more in-depth configuration information.

USING ZODB WITH ZEO

ZODB is a Python object persistence mechanism. *ZODB* works well as a storage mechanism for `repoze.bfg` applications, especially in applications that use *traversal*.

ZEO is an extension to ZODB which allows more than one process to simultaneously communicate with a ZODB storage. Making a ZODB database accessible to more than one process means that you can debug your application objects at the same time that a `repoze.bfg` server that accesses the database is running, and will also allow your application to run under multiprocess configurations, such as those exposed by *mod_wsgi*.

The easiest way to get started with ZODB in a `repoze.bfg` application is to use the ZODB `bfg_zodb` paster template. See *Paster Templates Included with repoze.bfg* (pp. 37) for more information about using this template. However, the Paster template does not set up a ZEO-capable application. This chapter shows you how to do that "from scratch".

31.1 Installing Dependencies

1. Edit your `repoze.bfg` application's `setup.py` file, adding the following packages to the `install_requires` of the application:

   - `repoze.folder`

   - `repoze.retry`

   - `repoze.tm2`

   - `repoze.zodbconn`

   For example, the relevant portion of your application's `setup.py` file might look like so when you're finished adding the dependencies.

```
1  setup(
2      # ... other elements left out for brevity
3      install_requires=[
4              'repoze.bfg',
5              'repoze.folder',
6              'repoze.retry',
7              'repoze.tm2',
8              'repoze.zodbconn',
9              ],
10     # ... other elements left out for brevity
11       )
```

2. Rerun your application's `setup.py` file (e.g. using `python setup.py develop`) to get these packages installed. A number of packages will be installed, including ZODB. For the purposes of this tutorial, we'll assume that your "application" is actually just the result of the `bfg_starter` Paster template.

31.2 Configuration

1. Edit your application's Paste `.ini` file.

   If you already have an `app` section in the `.ini` file named `main`, rename this section to `myapp` (e.g. `app:main` -> `app:myapp`). Add a key to it named `zodb_uri`, e.g.

   ```
   [app:myapp]
   use = egg:myapp#app
   zodb_uri = zeo://%(here)s/zeo.sock
   reload_templates = true
   debug_authorization = false
   debug_notfound = false
   ```

   If a `pipeline` named `main` does not already exist in the paste `.ini` file , add a `pipeline` section named `main`. Put the names `connector`, `egg:repoze.retry#retry`, and `egg:repoze.tm2#tm` to the top of the pipeline.

```
[pipeline:main]
pipeline =
        egg:repoze.retry#retry
        egg:repoze.tm2#tm
        myapp
```

When you're finished, your `.ini` file might look like so:

```
[DEFAULT]
debug = true

[app:myapp]
use = egg:myapp#app
zodb_uri = zeo://%(here)s/zeo.sock
reload_templates = true
debug_authorization = false
debug_notfound = false

[pipeline:main]
pipeline =
        egg:repoze.retry#retry
        egg:repoze.tm2#tm
        myapp

[server:main]
use = egg:Paste#http
host = 0.0.0.0
port = 6543
```

See *MyProject.ini* (pp. 45) for more information about project Paste `.ini` files.

2. Add a `zeo.conf` file to your package with the following contents:

```
%define INSTANCE .

<zeo>
  address $INSTANCE/zeo.sock
  read-only false
  invalidation-queue-size 100
  pid-filename $INSTANCE/zeo.pid
</zeo>
```

```
<blobstorage 1>
  <filestorage>
    path $INSTANCE/myapp.db
  </filestorage>
  blob-dir $INSTANCE/blobs
</blobstorage>
```

3. For the purposes of this tutorial we'll assume that you want your `repoze.bfg` application's *root* object to be a "folderish" object. To achieve this, change your application's `models.py` file to look like the below:

```python
from repoze.folder import Folder

class MyModel(Folder):
    pass

def appmaker(root):
    if not 'myapp' in root:
        root['myapp'] = MyModel()
        transaction.commit()
    return root['myapp']
```

4. Change your application's `run.py` to look something like the below:

```python
from repoze.bfg.configuration import Configurator
from repoze.zodbconn.finder import PersistentApplicationFinder
from myapp.models import appmaker
import transaction

def app(global_config, **settings):
    """ This function returns a ``repoze.bfg`` WSGI
    application.

    It is usually called by the PasteDeploy framework during
    ``paster serve``"""
    # paster app config callback
    zodb_uri = settings['zodb_uri']
    finder = PersistentApplicationFinder(zodb_uri, appmaker)
    def get_root(request):
        return finder(request.environ)
```

```
config = Configurator(root_factory=get_root, settings=settings)
return config.make_wsgi_app()
```

31.3 Running

1. Start the ZEO server in a terminal with the current directory set to the package directory:

```
../bin/runzeo -C zeo.conf
```

You should see something like this, as a result:

```
1 [chrism@snowpro myapp]$ ../bin/runzeo -C zeo.conf
2 ------
3 2009-09-19T13:48:41 INFO ZEO.runzeo (9910) created PID file './zeo.pid'
4 # ... more output ...
5 2009-09-19T13:48:41 INFO ZEO.zrpc (9910) listening on ./zeo.sock
```

2. While the ZEO server is running, start the application server:

```
1 [chrism@snowpro myapp]$ ../bin/paster serve myapp.ini
2 Starting server in PID 10177.
3 serving on 0.0.0.0:6543 view at http://127.0.0.1:6543
```

3. The root object is now a "folderish" ZODB object. Nothing else about the application has changed.

4. You can manipulate the database directly (even when the application's HTTP server is running) by using the bfgshell command in a third terminal window:

```
1 [chrism@snowpro sess]$ ../bin/paster --plugin=repoze.bfg bfgshell \
2        myapp.ini myapp
3 Python 2.5.4 (r254:67916, Sep  4 2009, 02:12:16)
4 [GCC 4.2.1 (Apple Inc. build 5646)] on darwin
5 Type "help" for more information. "root" is the BFG app root object.
```

345

```
6  >>> root
7  <sess.models.MyModel object None at 0x16438f0>
8  >>> root.foo = 'bar'
9  >>> import transaction
10 >>> transaction.commit()
```

USING ZODB-BASED SESSIONS

Sessions are server-side namespaces which are associated with a site user that expire automatically after some period of disuse.

If your application is ZODB-based (e.g. you've created an application from the `bfg_zodb` paster template, or you've followed the instructions in *Using ZODB with ZEO* (pp. 341)), you can make use of the `repoze.session` and `repoze.browserid` packages to add sessioning to your application.

> ⓘ You can use the `repoze.session` package even if your application is not ZODB-based, but its backing store requires ZODB, so it makes the most sense to use this package if your application already uses ZODB. This tutorial does not cover usage of `repoze.session`-based sessions in applications that don't already use ZODB. For this, see the standalone repoze.session usage documentation (http://docs.repoze.org/session/usage.html). If you don't want to use ZODB to do sessioning, you might choose to use a relational/filestorage sessioning system such as Beaker (http://pypi.python.org/pypi/Beaker). `repoze.bfg` is fully compatible with this system too.

32.1 Installing Dependencies

1. Edit your `repoze.bfg` application's `setup.py` file, adding the following packages to the `install_requires` of the application:

   - `repoze.session`

   - `repoze.browserid`

   For example, the relevant portion of your application's `setup.py` file might look like so when you're finished adding the dependencies.

```
1   setup(
2       # ... other elements left out for brevity
3       install_requires=[
4             'repoze.bfg',
5             'repoze.folder',
6             'repoze.retry',
7             'repoze.tm2',
8             'repoze.zodbconn',
9             'repoze.session'
10            'repoze.browserid',
11            ],
12      # ... other elements left out for brevity
13        )
```

2. Rerun your application's `setup.py` file (e.g. using `python setup.py develop`) to get these packages installed.

32.2 Configuration

1. Edit your application's Paste `.ini` file.

   If you already have an `app` section in the `.ini` file named `main`, rename this section to `myapp` (e.g. `app:main` -> `app:myapp`). Add a key to it named `zodb_uri`, e.g.

   ```
   [app:myapp]
   use = egg:myapp#app
   zodb_uri = zeo://%(here)s/zeo.sock
   reload_templates = true
   debug_authorization = false
   debug_notfound = false
   ```

   Add a `filter` section to the `.ini` file named "browserid":

   ```
   [filter:browserid]
   use = egg:repoze.browserid#browserid
   secret_key = my-secret-key
   ```

Replace `my-secret-key` with any random string. This string represents the value which the client-side "browser id" cookie is encrypted with, to prevent tampering.

If a `pipeline` named `main` does not already exist in the paste `.ini` file , add a `pipeline` section named `main`. Put the names `connector`, `egg:repoze.retry#retry`, and `egg:repoze.tm2#tm` to the top of the pipeline.

```
[pipeline:main]
pipeline =
      browserid
      egg:repoze.retry#retry
      egg:repoze.tm2#tm
      myapp
```

When you're finished, your `.ini` file might look like so:

```
[DEFAULT]
debug = true

[app:myapp]
use = egg:myapp#app
zodb_uri = zeo://%(here)s/zeo.sock
reload_templates = true
debug_authorization = false
debug_notfound = false

[filter:browserid]
use = egg:repoze.browserid#browserid
secret_key = my-secret-key

[pipeline:main]
pipeline =
      browserid
      egg:repoze.retry#retry
      egg:repoze.tm2#tm
      myapp

[server:main]
use = egg:Paste#http
host = 0.0.0.0
port = 6543
```

See *MyProject.ini* (pp. 45) for more information about project Paste `.ini` files.

2. Add a `get_session` API to your application. I've chosen to add it directly to my `views.py` file, although it can live anywhere.

```
from repoze.session.manager import SessionDataManager
from repoze.bfg.traversal import find_root

def get_session(context, request):
    root = find_root(context)
    if not hasattr(root, '_sessions'):
        root._sessions = SessionDataManager(3600, 5)
    session = root._sessions.get(request.environ['repoze.browserid'])
    return session
```

Note in the call to `SessionDataManager` that '3600' represents the disuse timeout (5 minutes == 3600 seconds), and '5' represents a write granularity time (the session will be marked as active at most every five seconds). Vary these values as necessary.

3. Whenever you want to use a session in your application, call this API:

```
from repoze.session.manager import SessionDataManager
from repoze.bfg.traversal import find_root
from repoze.bfg.chameleon_zpt import render_template_to_response

def my_view(context, request):
    session = get_session(context, request)
    session['abc'] = '123'
    return render_template_to_response('templates/mytemplate.pt',
                                       request = request,
                                       project = 'sess')

def get_session(context, request):
    root = find_root(context)
    if not hasattr(root, '_sessions'):
        root._sessions = SessionDataManager(3600, 5)
    session = root._sessions.get(request.environ['repoze.browserid'])
    return session
```

For more information, see the repoze.session documentation (http://docs.repoze.org/session/) and the repoze.browserid documentation (http://pypi.python.org/pypi/repoze.browserid).

USING REPOZE.CATALOG WITHIN REPOZE.BFG

repoze.catalog is a ZODB-based system that can be used to index Python objects. It also offers a query interface for retrieving previously indexed data. Those whom are used to Zope's "ZCatalog" implementation will feel at home using repoze.catalog.

This tutorial assumes that you want a Zope-like setup. For example, it assumes you want to use a persistent ZODB object as your *root* object, and that the repoze.catalog catalog will be an attribute of this root object. It is further assumed that you want the application to be based on *traversal*.

1. Follow the *Using ZODB with ZEO* (pp. 341) tutorial to get a system set up with ZODB and ZEO. When you are finished, come back here.

2. Install the repoze.catalog software within your application's environment:

```
$ easy_install repoze.catalog
```

3. Change your ZODB application's models.py file to look like the below:

```
1  from repoze.folder import Folder
2  from repoze.catalog.catalog import Catalog
3  from repoze.catalog.document import DocumentMap
4  from repoze.catalog.indexes.field import CatalogFieldIndex
5
```

```
 6  def get_title(object, default):
 7      title = getattr(object, 'title', '')
 8      if isinstance(title, basestring):
 9          # lowercase for alphabetic sorting
10          title = title.lower()
11      return title
12
13  class Document(Folder):
14      def __init__(self, title):
15          self.title = title
16          Folder.__init__(self)
17
18  class Site(Folder):
19      def __init__(self):
20          self.catalog = Catalog()
21          self.catalog.document_map = DocumentMap()
22          self.update_indexes()
23          Folder.__init__(self)
24
25      def update_indexes(self):
26          indexes = {
27              'title': CatalogFieldIndex(get_title),
28          }
29
30          catalog = self.catalog
31
32          # add indexes
33          for name, index in indexes.iteritems():
34              if name not in catalog:
35                  catalog[name] = index
36
37          # remove indexes
38          for name in catalog.keys():
39              if name not in indexes:
40                  del catalog[name]
41
42  def appmaker(root):
43      if not 'site' in root:
44          root['site'] = Site()
45          transaction.commit()
46      return root['site']
```

4. We'll demonstrate how you might interact with a catalog from code by manipulating the database directly using the `bfgshell` command in a terminal window:

```
[chrism@snowpro sess]$ ../bin/paster --plugin=repoze.bfg bfgshell \
       myapp.ini myapp
Python 2.5.4 (r254:67916, Sep  4 2009, 02:12:16)
[GCC 4.2.1 (Apple Inc. build 5646)] on darwin
Type "help" for more information. "root" is the BFG app root object.
>>> from repoze.bfg.traversal import model_path
>>> from myapp.models import Document
>>> root['name'] = Document('title')
>>> doc = root['name']
>>> docid = root.catalog.document_map.add(model_path(doc))
>>> root.catalog.index_doc(docid, doc)
>>> import transaction
>>> transaction.commit()
>>> root.catalog.search(title='title')
(1, IFSet([-787959756]))
```

As you need them, add other indexes required by your application to the catalog by modifying the `update_indexes` method of the `Site` object. Whenever an index is added or removed, invoke the `update_indexes` method of the site (the root object) from a script or from within a `bfgshell` session to update the set of indexes used by your application.

In *view* code, you should be able to get a hold of the root object via the `traversal.find_root()` (pp. 414) API. The `catalog` attribute of that root object will represent the catalog previously added.

Read the `repoze.catalog` documentation (http://docs.repoze.org/catalog) for further information about other types of indexes to add, using the document map, and how to issue queries using the catalog query API.

The `repoze.folder` implementation sends events that can be intercepted by a *subscriber* when objects are added and removed from a folder. It is often useful to hook these events for the purpose of mutating the catalog when a new documentlike object is added or removed. See the repoze.folder documentation (http://docs.repoze.org/folder) for more information about the events it sends.

Part III

API Reference

REPOZE.BFG.AUTHORIZATION

class **ACLAuthorizationPolicy**()

An *authorization policy* which consults an *ACL* object attached to a *context* to determine authorization information about a *principal* or multiple principals. If the context is part of a *lineage*, the context's parents are consulted for ACL information too. The following is true about this security policy.

- When checking whether the 'current' user is permitted (via the `permits` method), the security policy consults the `context` for an ACL first. If no ACL exists on the context, or one does exist but the ACL does not explicitly allow or deny access for any of the effective principals, consult the context's parent ACL, and so on, until the lineage is exhausted or we determine that the policy permits or denies.

  During this processing, if any `security.Deny` (pp. 397) ACE is found matching any principal in `principals`, stop processing by returning an `security.ACLDenied` (pp. 397) instance (equals `False`) immediately. If any `security.Allow` (pp. 397) ACE is found matching any principal, stop processing by returning an `security.ACLAllowed` (pp. 398) instance (equals `True`) immediately. If we exhaust the context's *lineage*, and no ACE has explicitly permitted or denied access, return an instance of `security.ACLDenied` (pp. 397) (equals `False`).

- When computing principals allowed by a permission via the `security.principals_allowed_by_permission()` (pp. 396) method, we compute the set of principals that are explicitly granted the `permission` in the provided `context`. We do this by walking 'up' the object graph *from the root* to the context. During this walking process, if we find an explicit `security.Allow` (pp. 397) ACE for a principal that matches the `permission`, the principal is included in the allow list. However, if later in the walking process that principal is mentioned in any `security.Deny` (pp. 397) ACE for the permission, the principal is removed from the allow list. If a `security.Deny` (pp. 397) to the principal `security.Everyone` (pp. 397) is encountered during the walking process that matches the `permission`, the allow list is cleared for all principals encountered in previous ACLs. The walking process ends after we've processed the any ACL directly attached to `context`; a set of principals is returned.

357

REPOZE.BFG.AUTHENTICATION

class AuthTktAuthenticationPolicy (*secret,* *callback=None,* *cookie_name='repoze.bfg.auth_tkt',* *secure=False,* *include_ip=False,* *timeout=None,* *reissue_time=None,* *max_age=None, path='/', http_only=False*)

A `repoze.bfg` *authentication policy* which obtains data from an `paste.auth.auth_tkt` cookie.

Constructor Arguments

`secret`

> The secret (a string) used for auth_tkt cookie encryption. Required.

`callback`

> Default: `None`. A callback passed the userid and the request, expected to return `None` if the userid doesn't exist or a sequence of group identifiers (possibly empty) if the user does exist. If `callback` is `None`, the userid will be assumed to exist with no groups. Optional.

`cookie_name`

> Default: `auth_tkt`. The cookie name used (string). Optional.

`secure`

> Default: `False`. Only send the cookie back over a secure conn. Optional.

include_ip

> Default: `False`. Make the requesting IP address part of the authentication data in the cookie. Optional.

timeout

> Default: `None`. Maximum number of seconds after which a newly issued ticket will be considered valid. After this amount of time, the ticket will expire (effectively logging the user out). If this value is `None`, the token never expires. Optional.

reissue_time

> Default: `None`. If this parameter is set, it represents the number of seconds that must pass before an authentication token cookie is reissued. The duration is measured as the number of seconds since the last auth_tkt cookie was issued and 'now'. If the `timeout` value is `None`, this parameter has no effect. If this parameter is provided, and the value of `timeout` is not `None`, the value of `reissue_time` must be smaller than value of `timeout`. A good rule of thumb: if you want auto-reissued cookies: set this to the `timeout` value divided by ten. If this value is `0`, a new ticket cookie will be reissued on every request which needs authentication. Optional.

max_age

> Default: `None`. The max age of the auth_tkt cookie, in seconds. This differs from `timeout` inasmuch as `timeout` represents the lifetime of the ticket contained in the cookie, while this value represents the lifetime of the cookie itself. When this value is set, the cookie's `Max-Age` and `Expires` settings will be set, allowing the auth_tkt cookie to last between browser sessions. It is typically nonsensical to set this to a value that is lower than `timeout` or `reissue_time`, although it is not explicitly prevented. Optional.

path

> Default: `/`. The path for which the auth_tkt cookie is valid. May be desirable if the application only serves part of a domain. Optional.

http_only

> Default: `False`. Hide cookie from JavaScript by setting the HttpOnly flag. Not honored by all browsers. Optional.

class RepozeWho1AuthenticationPolicy (*identifier_name='auth_tkt', callback=None*)

A `repoze.bfg` *authentication policy* which obtains data from the `repoze.who` 1.X WSGI 'API' (the `repoze.who.identity` key in the WSGI environment).

Constructor Arguments

`identifier_name`

> Default: `auth_tkt`. The `repoze.who` plugin name that performs remember/forget. Optional.

`callback`

> Default: `None`. A callback passed the `repoze.who` identity and the *request*, expected to return `None` if the user represented by the identity doesn't exist or a sequence of group identifiers (possibly empty) if the user does exist. If `callback` is None, the userid will be assumed to exist with no groups.

class RemoteUserAuthenticationPolicy (*environ_key='REMOTE_USER', callback=None*)

A `repoze.bfg` *authentication policy* which obtains data from the REMOTE_USER WSGI environment variable.

Constructor Arguments

`environ_key`

> Default: REMOTE_USER. The key in the WSGI environ which provides the userid.

`callback`

> Default: `None`. A callback passed the userid and the request, expected to return None if the userid doesn't exist or a sequence of group identifiers (possibly empty) if the user does exist. If `callback` is None, the userid will be assumed to exist with no groups.

REPOZE.BFG.CHAMELEON_TEXT

get_template(*path*)

> Return the underyling object representing a *Chameleon* text template using the template implied by the `path` argument. The `path` argument may be a package-relative path, an absolute path, or a *resource specification*.

render_template(*path, **kw*)

> Render a *Chameleon* text template using the template implied by the `path` argument. The `path` argument may be a package-relative path, an absolute path, or a *resource specification*. The arguments in `*kw` are passed as top-level names to the template, and so may be used within the template itself. Returns a string.

render_template_to_response(*path, **kw*)

> Render a *Chameleon* text template using the template implied by the `path` argument. The `path` argument may be a package-relative path, an absolute path, or a *resource specification*. The arguments in `*kw` are passed as top-level names to the template, and so may be used within the template itself. Returns a *Response* object with the body as the template result..

These APIs will will work against template files which contain simple `${Genshi}` - style replacement markers.

The API of `chameleon_text` (pp. 363) is identical to that of `chameleon_zpt` (pp. 365); only its import location is different. If you need to import an API functions from this module as well as the `chameleon_zpt` (pp. 365) module within the same view file, use the `as` feature of the Python import statement, e.g.:

```
from repoze.bfg.chameleon_zpt import render_template as zpt_render
from repoze.bfg.chameleon_text import render_template as text_render
```

REPOZE.BFG.CHAMELEON_ZPT

get_template(*path*)

Return the underlying object representing a *Chameleon* ZPT template using the template implied by the `path` argument. The `path` argument may be a package-relative path, an absolute path, or a *resource specification*.

render_template(*path, **kw*)

Render a *Chameleon* ZPT template using the template implied by the `path` argument. The `path` argument may be a package-relative path, an absolute path, or a *resource specification*. The arguments in `*kw` are passed as top-level names to the template, and so may be used within the template itself. Returns a string.

render_template_to_response(*path, **kw*)

Render a *Chameleon* ZPT template using the template implied by the `path` argument. The `path` argument may be a package-relative path, an absolute path, or a *resource specification*. The arguments in `*kw` are passed as top-level names to the template, and so may be used within the template itself. Returns a *Response* object with the body as the template result..

These APIs will work against files which supply template text which matches the *ZPT* specification.

The API of `chameleon_zpt` (pp. 365) is identical to that of `chameleon_text` (pp. 363); only its import location is different. If you need to import an API functions from this module as well as the `chameleon_text` (pp. 363) module within the same view file, use the `as` feature of the Python import statement, e.g.:

```
from repoze.bfg.chameleon_zpt import render_template as zpt_render
from repoze.bfg.chameleon_text import render_template as text_render
```

.

REPOZE.BFG.CONFIGURATION

class Configurator (*registry=None, package=None, settings=None, root_factory=None, authentication_policy=None, authorization_policy=None, renderers=DEFAULT_RENDERERS, debug_logger=None*)
A Configurator is used to configure a `repoze.bfg` *application registry*.

The Configurator accepts a number of arguments: `registry`, `package`, `settings`, `root_factory`, `zcml_file`, `authentication_policy`, `authorization_policy`, `renderers` and `debug_logger`.

If the `registry` argument is passed as a non-`None` value, it must be an instance of the `registry.Registry` class representing the registry to configure. If `registry` is `None`, the configurator will create a `registry.Registry` instance itself; it will also perform some default configuration that would not otherwise be done. After construction, the configurator may be used to add configuration to the registry. The overall state of a registry is called the 'configuration state'.

> ⚠ If a `registry` is passed to the Configurator constructor, all other constructor arguments except `package` are ignored.

If the `package` argument is passed, it must be a reference to a Python *package* (e.g. `sys.modules['thepackage']`). This value is used as a basis to convert relative paths passed to various configuration methods, such as methods which accept a `renderer` argument, into absolute paths. If `None` is passed (the default), the package is assumed to be the Python package in which the *caller* of the Configurator constructor lives.

If the `settings` argument is passed, it should be a Python dictionary representing the deployment settings for this application. These are later retrievable using the `settings.get_settings()` (pp. 399) API.

If the `root_factory` argument is passed, it should be an object representing the default *root factory* for your application. If it is `None`, a default root factory will be used.

If `authentication_policy` is passed, it should be an instance of an *authentication policy*.

If `authorization_policy` is passed, it should be an instance of an *authorization policy*.

> A `ConfigurationError` will be raised when an authorization policy is supplied without also supplying an authentication policy (authorization requires authentication).

If `renderers` is passed, it should be a list of tuples representing a set of *renderer* factories which should be configured into this application. If it is not passed, a default set of renderer factories is used.

If `debug_logger` is not passed, a default debug logger that logs to stderr will be used. If it is passed, it should be an instance of the `logging.Logger` (PEP 282) standard library class. The debug logger is used by `repoze.bfg` itself to log warnings and authorization debugging information.

registry

The *application registry* which holds the configuration associated with this configurator.

begin (*request=None*)

Indicate that application or test configuration has begun. This pushes a dictionary containing the *application registry* implied by `registry` attribute of this configurator and the *request* implied by the `request` argument on to the *thread local* stack consulted by various `threadlocal` (pp. 411) API functions.

end ()

Indicate that application or test configuration has ended. This pops the last value pushed on to the *thread local* stack (usually by the `begin` method) and returns that value.

hook_zca ()

Call `zope.component.getSiteManager.sethook()` with the argument `threadlocal.get_current_registry` (pp. 411), causing the *Zope Component Architecture* 'global' APIs such as `zope.component.getSiteManager()`, `zope.component.getAdapter()` and others to use the `repoze.bfg` *application registry* rather than the Zope 'global' registry. If `zope.component` cannot be imported, this method will raise an `ImportError`.

unhook_zca ()

> Call `zope.component.getSiteManager.reset()` to undo the action of `configuration.Configurator.hook_zca()` (pp. 368). If `zope.component` cannot be imported, this method will raise an `ImportError`.

setup_registry (*settings=None,   root_factory=None,   authentication_policy=None,   renderers=DEFAULT_RENDERERS, debug_logger=None*)

> When you pass a non-`None` `registry` argument to the *Configurator* constructor, no initial 'setup' is performed against the registry. This is because the registry you pass in may have already been initialized for use under `repoze.bfg` via a different configurator. However, in some circumstances, such as when you want to use the Zope 'global' registry instead of a registry created as a result of the Configurator constructor, or when you want to reset the initial setup of a registry, you *do* want to explicitly initialize the registry associated with a Configurator for use under `repoze.bfg`. Use `setup_registry` to do this initialization.
>
> `setup_registry` configures settings, a root factory, security policies, renderers, and a debug logger using the configurator's current registry, as per the descriptions in the Configurator constructor.

add_renderer (*name, factory*)

> Add a `repoze.bfg` *renderer* factory to the current configuration state.
>
> The `name` argument is the renderer name.
>
> The `factory` argument is Python reference to an implementation of a *renderer* factory.
>
> Note that this function must be called *before* any `add_view` invocation that names the renderer name as an argument. As a result, it's usually a better idea to pass globally used renderers into the `Configurator` constructor in the sequence of renderers passed as `renderer` than it is to use this method.

add_route (*name, path, view=None, view_for=None, permission=None, factory=None, for_=None, header=None, xhr=False, accept=None, path_info=None, request_method=None, request_param=None, custom_predicates=(), view_permission=None, renderer=None, view_renderer=None, view_context=None, view_attr=None, use_global_views=False, _info=u"*)

> Add a *route configuration* to the current configuration state, as well as possibly a *view configuration* to be used to specify a *view callable* that will be invoked when this route matches. The arguments to this method are divided into *predicate*, *non-predicate*, and *view-related* types. *Route predicate* arguments narrow the circumstances in which a route will be match a request; non-predicate arguments are informational.
>
> Non-Predicate Arguments
>
> name

The name of the route, e.g. `myroute`. This attribute is required. It must be unique among all defined routes in a given application.

factory

A reference to a Python object (often a function or a class) that will generate a `repoze.bfg` *context* object when this route matches. For example, `mypackage.models.MyFactoryClass`. If this argument is not specified, a default root factory will be used.

Predicate Arguments

path

The path of the route e.g. `ideas/:idea`. This argument is required. See *Route Path Pattern Syntax* (pp. 76) for information about the syntax of route paths. If the path doesn't match the current URL, route matching continues.

xhr

This value should be either `True` or `False`. If this value is specified and is `True`, the *request* must possess an `HTTP_X_REQUESTED_WITH` (aka `X-Requested-With`) header for this route to match. This is useful for detecting AJAX requests issued from jQuery, Prototype and other Javascript libraries. If this predicate returns `False`, route matching continues.

request_method

A string representing an HTTP method name, e.g. `GET`, `POST`, `HEAD`, `DELETE`, `PUT`. If this argument is not specified, this route will match if the request has *any* request method. If this predicate returns `False`, route matching continues.

path_info

This value represents a regular expression pattern that will be tested against the `PATH_INFO` WSGI environment variable. If the regex matches, this predicate will return `True`. If this predicate returns `False`, route matching continues.

request_param

This value can be any string. A view declaration with this argument ensures that the associated route will only match when the request has a key in the `request.params` dictionary (an HTTP `GET` or `POST` variable) that has a name which matches the supplied value. If the value supplied as the argument has a = sign in it, e.g. `request_params="foo=123"`, then the key (`foo`) must both exist in the `request.params` dictionary, and the value must match the right hand side of the expression (`123`) for the route to "match" the current request. If this predicate returns `False`, route matching continues.

header

This argument represents an HTTP header name or a header name/value pair. If the argument contains a : (colon), it will be considered a name/value pair (e.g. `User-Agent:Mozilla/.*` or `Host:localhost`). If the value contains a colon, the value portion should be a regular expression. If the value does not contain a colon, the entire value will be considered to be the header name (e.g. `If-Modified-Since`). If the value evaluates to a header name only without a value, the header specified by the name must be present in the request for this predicate to be true. If the value evaluates to a header name/value pair, the header specified by the name must be present in the request *and* the regular expression specified as the value must match the header value. Whether or not the value represents a header name or a header name/value pair, the case of the header name is not significant. If this predicate returns `False`, route matching continues.

accept

This value represents a match query for one or more mimetypes in the `Accept` HTTP request header. If this value is specified, it must be in one of the following forms: a mimetype match token in the form `text/plain`, a wildcard mimetype match token in the form `text/*` or a match-all wildcard mimetype match token in the form `*/*`. If any of the forms matches the `Accept` header of the request, this predicate will be true. If this predicate returns `False`, route matching continues.

custom_predicates

This value should be a sequence of references to custom predicate callables. Use custom predicates when no set of predefined predicates does what you need. Custom predicates can be combined with predefined predicates as necessary. Each custom predicate callable should accept two arguments: `context` and `request` and should return either `True` or `False` after doing arbitrary evaluation of the context and/or the request. If all callables return `True`, the associated route will be considered viable for a given request. If any custom predicate returns `False`, route matching continues. Note that the value `context` will always be `None` when passed to a custom route predicate.

> ⓘ This feature is new as of `repoze.bfg` 1.2.

View-Related Arguments

view

> A reference to a Python object that will be used as a view callable when this route matches. e.g. `mypackage.views.my_view`.

view_context

> A reference to a class or an *interface* that the *context* of the view should match for the view named by the route to be used. This argument is only useful if the `view` attribute is used. If this attribute is not specified, the default (`None`) will be used.

> If the `view` argument is not provided, this argument has no effect.

> This attribute can also be spelled as `for_` or `view_for`.

view_permission

> The permission name required to invoke the view associated with this route. e.g. `edit`. (see *Using repoze.bfg Security With URL Dispatch* (pp. 90) for more information about permissions).

> If the `view` attribute is not provided, this argument has no effect.

> This argument can also be spelled as `permission`.

view_renderer

> This is either a single string term (e.g. `json`) or a string implying a path or *resource specification* (e.g. `templates/views.pt`). If the renderer value is a single term (does not contain a dot `.`), the specified term will be used to look up a renderer implementation, and that renderer implementation will be used to construct a response from the view return value. If the renderer term contains a dot (`.`), the specified term will be treated as a path, and the filename extension of the last element in the path will be used to look up the renderer implementation, which will be passed the full path. The renderer implementation will be used to construct a response from the view return value. See *Writing View Callables Which Use a Renderer* (pp. 109) for more information.

> If the `view` argument is not provided, this argument has no effect.

> This argument can also be spelled as `renderer`.

372

view_attr

The view machinery defaults to using the `__call__` method of the view callable (or the function itself, if the view callable is a function) to obtain a response dictionary. The `attr` value allows you to vary the method attribute used to obtain the response. For example, if your view was a class, and the class has a method named `index` and you wanted to use this method instead of the class' `__call__` method to return the response, you'd say `attr="index"` in the view configuration for the view. This is most useful when the view definition is a class.

If the `view` argument is not provided, this argument has no effect.

use_global_views

When a request matches this route, and view lookup cannot find a view which has a `route_name` predicate argument that matches the route, try to fall back to using a view that otherwise matches the context, request, and view name (but which does not match the route_name predicate).

> ⓘ This feature is new as of `repoze.bfg` 1.2.

add_static_view (*name, path, cache_max_age=3600*)
Add a view used to render static resources to the current configuration state.

The `name` argument is a string representing *view name* of the view which is registered.

The `path` argument is the path on disk where the static files reside. This can be an absolute path, a package-relative path, or a *resource specification.*

See *Serving Static Resources Using a ZCML Directive* (pp. 137) for more information.

add_settings (*settings=None, **kw*)
Augment the `settings` argument passed in to the Configurator constructor with one or more 'setting' key/value pairs. A setting is a single key/value pair in the dictionary-ish object returned from the API `settings.get_settings()` (pp. 399).

You may pass a dictionary:

```
config.add_settings({'external_uri':'http://example.com'})
```

Or a set of key/value pairs:

```
config.add_settings(external_uri='http://example.com')
```

This function is useful when you need to test code that calls the `settings.get_settings()` (pp. 399) API and which uses return values from that API.

> ⓘ This method is new as of `repoze.bfg` 1.2.

add_subscriber (*subscriber, iface=None, info=u"*)

Add an event *subscriber* for the event stream implied by the supplied `iface` interface. The `subscriber` argument represents a callable object; it will be called with a single object `event` whenever `repoze.bfg` emits an *event* associated with the `iface`. Using the default `iface` value, `None` will cause the subscriber to be registered for all event types. See *Using Events* (pp. 185) for more information about events and subscribers.

add_view (*view=None,   name=",   for_=None,   permission=None,   request_type=None, route_name=None, request_method=None, request_param=None, containment=None, attr=None, renderer=None, wrapper=None, xhr=False, accept=None, header=None, path_info=None, custom_predicates=(), context=None, _info=u"*)

Add a *view configuration* to the current configuration state. Arguments to `add_view` are broken down below into *predicate* arguments and *non-predicate* arguments. Predicate arguments narrow the circumstances in which the view callable will be invoked when a request is presented to `repoze.bfg`; non-predicate arguments are informational.

Non-Predicate Arguments

view

> A reference to a *view callable*. This argument is required unless a `renderer` argument also exists. If a `renderer` argument is passed, and a `view` argument is not provided, the view callable defaults to a callable that returns an empty dictionary (see *Writing View Callables Which Use a Renderer* (pp. 109)).

permission

> The name of a *permission* that the user must possess in order to invoke the *view callable*. See *Configuring View Security* (pp. 135) for more information about view security and permissions.

attr

The view machinery defaults to using the __call__ method of the *view callable* (or the function itself, if the view callable is a function) to obtain a response. The attr value allows you to vary the method attribute used to obtain the response. For example, if your view was a class, and the class has a method named index and you wanted to use this method instead of the class' __call__ method to return the response, you'd say attr="index" in the view configuration for the view. This is most useful when the view definition is a class.

renderer

> This is either a single string term (e.g. json) or a string implying a path or *resource specification* (e.g. templates/views.pt) naming a *renderer* implementation. If the renderer value does not contain a dot ., the specified string will be used to look up a renderer implementation, and that renderer implementation will be used to construct a response from the view return value. If the renderer value contains a dot (.), the specified term will be treated as a path, and the filename extension of the last element in the path will be used to look up the renderer implementation, which will be passed the full path. The renderer implementation will be used to construct a *response* from the view return value.

> Note that if the view itself returns a *response* (see *View Callable Responses* (pp. 108)), the specified renderer implementation is never called.

> When the renderer is a path, although a path is usually just a simple relative path-name (e.g. templates/foo.pt, implying that a template named "foo.pt" is in the "templates" directory relative to the directory of the current *package* of the Configurator), a path can be absolute, starting with a slash on UNIX or a drive letter prefix on Windows. The path can alternately be a *resource specification* in the form some.dotted.package_name:relative/path, making it possible to address template resources which live in a separate package.

> The renderer attribute is optional. If it is not defined, the "null" renderer is assumed (no rendering is performed and the value is passed back to the upstream repoze.bfg machinery unmolested).

wrapper

> The *view name* of a different *view configuration* which will receive the response body of this view as the request.wrapped_body attribute of its own *request*, and the *response* returned by this view as the request.wrapped_response attribute of its own request. Using a wrapper makes it possible to "chain" views together to form a composite response. The response of the outermost wrapper view will be returned to the user. The wrapper view will be found as any view is found: see *View Lookup and Invocation* (pp. 135). The "best" wrapper view

will be found based on the lookup ordering: "under the hood" this wrapper view is looked up via `view.render_view_to_response(context, request, 'wrapper_viewname')`. The context and request of a wrapper view is the same context and request of the inner view. If this attribute is unspecified, no view wrapping is done.

Predicate Arguments

name

> The *view name*. Read *Traversal* (pp. 61) to understand the concept of a view name.

context

> An object representing Python class that the *context* must be an instance of, *or* the *interface* that the *context* must provide in order for this view to be found and called. This predicate is true when the *context* is an instance of the represented class or if the *context* provides the represented interface; it is otherwise false. This argument may also be provided to `add_view` as `for_` (an older, still-supported spelling).

route_name

> This value must match the `name` of a *route configuration* declaration (see *URL Dispatch* (pp. 73)) that must match before this view will be called. Note that the `route` configuration referred to by `route_name` usually has a `*traverse` token in the value of its `path`, representing a part of the path that will be used by *traversal* against the result of the route's *root factory*.

> ---
> ⚠ Using this argument services an advanced feature that isn't often used unless you want to perform traversal *after* a route has matched. See *Combining Traversal and URL Dispatch* (pp. 93) for more information on using this advanced feature.
> ---

request_type

> This value should be an *interface* that the *request* must provide in order for this view to be found and called. This value exists only for backwards compatibility purposes.

request_method

> This value can either be one of the strings `GET`, `POST`, `PUT`, `DELETE`, or `HEAD` representing an HTTP `REQUEST_METHOD`. A view declaration with this argument ensures that the view will only be called when the request's `method` attribute (aka the `REQUEST_METHOD` of the WSGI environment) string matches the supplied value.

request_param

> This value can be any string. A view declaration with this argument ensures that the view will only be called when the *request* has a key in the request.params dictionary (an HTTP GET or POST variable) that has a name which matches the supplied value. If the value supplied has a = sign in it, e.g. request_params="foo=123", then the key (foo) must both exist in the request.params dictionary, *and* the value must match the right hand side of the expression (123) for the view to "match" the current request.

containment

> This value should be a reference to a Python class or *interface* that a parent object in the *lineage* must provide in order for this view to be found and called. The nodes in your object graph must be "location-aware" to use this feature. See *Location-Aware Model Instances* (pp. 165) for more information about location-awareness.

xhr

> This value should be either True or False. If this value is specified and is True, the *request* must possess an HTTP_X_REQUESTED_WITH (aka X-Requested-With) header that has the value XMLHttpRequest for this view to be found and called. This is useful for detecting AJAX requests issued from jQuery, Prototype and other Javascript libraries.

accept

> The value of this argument represents a match query for one or more mimetypes in the Accept HTTP request header. If this value is specified, it must be in one of the following forms: a mimetype match token in the form text/plain, a wildcard mimetype match token in the form text/* or a match-all wildcard mimetype match token in the form */*. If any of the forms matches the Accept header of the request, this predicate will be true.

header

> This value represents an HTTP header name or a header name/value pair. If the value contains a : (colon), it will be considered a name/value pair (e.g. User-Agent:Mozilla/.* or Host:localhost). The value portion should be a regular expression. If the value does not contain a colon, the entire value will be considered to be the header name (e.g. If-Modified-Since). If the value evaluates to a header name only without a value, the header specified by the name must be present in the request for this predicate to be true. If the value evaluates to a header name/value pair, the header specified by the name must be present in the request *and* the regular expression specified as the value must match the header value. Whether or not the value represents a header name or a header name/value pair, the case of the header name is not significant.

path_info

This value represents a regular expression pattern that will be tested against the PATH_INFO WSGI environment variable. If the regex matches, this predicate will be True.

custom_predicates

This value should be a sequence of references to custom predicate callables. Use custom predicates when no set of predefined predicates do what you need. Custom predicates can be combined with predefined predicates as necessary. Each custom predicate callable should accept two arguments: context and request and should return either True or False after doing arbitrary evaluation of the context and/or the request. If all callables return True, the associated view callable will be considered viable for a given request.

> This feature is new as of repoze.bfg 1.2.

load_zcml (*spec*)

Load configuration from a *ZCML* file into the current configuration state. The spec argument is an absolute filename, a relative filename, or a *resource specification*, defaulting to configure.zcml (relative to the package of the configurator's caller).

make_wsgi_app ()

Returns a repoze.bfg WSGI application representing the current configuration state and sends a interfaces.IWSGIApplicationCreatedEvent (pp. 385) event to all listeners.

override_resource (*to_override, override_with*)

Add a repoze.bfg resource override to the current configuration state.

to_override is a *resource specification* to the resource being overridden.

override_with is a *resource specification* to the resource that is performing the override.

See *Resources* (pp. 213) for more information about resource overrides.

scan (*package*)

Scan a Python package and any of its subpackages for objects marked with *configuration decoration* such as view.bfg_view (pp. 428). Any decorated object found will influence the current configuration state.

The package argument should be a reference to a Python *package* or module object. If package is None, the package of the *caller* is used.

set_forbidden_view (*view=None, attr=None, renderer=None, wrapper=None*)
Add a default forbidden view to the current configuration state.

The `view` argument should be a *view callable*.

The `attr` argument should be the attribute of the view callable used to retrieve the response (see the `add_view` method's `attr` argument for a description).

The `renderer` argument should be the name of (or path to) a *renderer* used to generate a response for this view (see the `configuration.Configurator.add_view()` (pp. 374) method's `renderer` argument for information about how a configurator relates to a renderer).

The `wrapper` argument should be the name of another view which will wrap this view when rendered (see the `add_view` method's `wrapper` argument for a description).

See *Changing the Forbidden View* (pp. 202) for more information.

set_notfound_view (*view=None, attr=None, renderer=None, wrapper=None*)
Add a default not found view to the current configuration state.

The `view` argument should be a *view callable*.

The `attr` argument should be the attribute of the view callable used to retrieve the response (see the `add_view` method's `attr` argument for a description).

The `renderer` argument should be the name of (or path to) a *renderer* used to generate a response for this view (see the `configuration.Configurator.add_view()` (pp. 374) method's `renderer` argument for information about how a configurator relates to a renderer).

The `wrapper` argument should be the name of another view which will wrap this view when rendered (see the `add_view` method's `wrapper` argument for a description).

See *Changing the Not Found View* (pp. 201) for more information.

testing_securitypolicy (*userid=None, groupids=(), permissive=True*)
Unit/integration testing helper: Registers a pair of faux `repoze.bfg` security policies: a *authentication policy* and a *authorization policy*.

The behavior of the registered *authorization policy* depends on the `permissive` argument. If `permissive` is true, a permissive *authorization policy* is registered; this policy allows all access. If `permissive` is false, a nonpermissive *authorization policy* is registered; this policy denies all access.

The behavior of the registered *authentication policy* depends on the values provided for the `userid` and `groupids` argument. The authentication policy will return the userid identifier implied by the `userid` argument and the group ids implied by the `groupids` argument when the `security.authenticated_userid()` (pp. 395) or `security.effective_principals()` (pp. 395) APIs are used.

This function is most useful when testing code that uses the APIs named `security.has_permission()` (pp. 396), `security.authenticated_userid()` (pp. 395), `security.effective_principals()` (pp. 395), and `security.principals_allowed_by_permission()` (pp. 396).

`testing_models` (*models*)

Unit/integration testing helper: registers a dictionary of *model* objects that can be resolved via the `traversal.find_model()` (pp. 413) API.

The `traversal.find_model()` (pp. 413) API is called with a path as one of its arguments. If the dictionary you register when calling this method contains that path as a string key (e.g. `/foo/bar` or `foo/bar`), the corresponding value will be returned to `find_model` (and thus to your code) when `traversal.find_model()` (pp. 413) is called with an equivalent path string or tuple.

`testing_add_subscriber` (*event_iface=None*)

Unit/integration testing helper: Registers a *subscriber* which listens for events of the type `event_iface`. This method returns a list object which is appended to by the subscriber whenever an event is captured.

When an event is dispatched that matches the value implied by the `event_iface` argument, that event will be appended to the list. You can then compare the values in the list to expected event notifications. This method is useful when testing code that wants to call `registry.Registry.notify()`, `zope.component.event.dispatch()` or `zope.component.event.objectEventNotify()`.

The default value of `event_iface` (`None`) implies a subscriber registered for *any* kind of event.

`testing_add_template` (*path, renderer=None*)

Unit/integration testing helper: register a template renderer at `path` (usually a relative filename ala `templates/foo.pt`) and return the renderer object. If the `renderer` argument is None, a 'dummy' renderer will be used. This function is useful when testing code that calls the `chameleon_zpt.render_template_to_response()` (pp. 365) function or `chameleon_text.render_template_to_response()` (pp. 363) function or any other `render_template*` API of any built-in templating system (see `chameleon_zpt` (pp. 365) and `chameleon_text` (pp. 363)).

REPOZE.BFG.EVENTS

class NewRequest (*request*)

An instance of this class is emitted as an *event* whenever repoze.bfg begins to process a new request. The instance has an attribute, request, which is a *request* object. This class implements the interfaces.INewRequest (pp. 385) interface.

class NewResponse (*response*)

An instance of this class is emitted as an *event* whenever any repoze.bfg view returns a *response*. The instance has an attribute, response, which is the response object returned by the view. This class implements the interfaces.INewResponse (pp. 385) interface.

ⓘ Postprocessing a response is usually better handled in a WSGI *middleware* component than in subscriber code that is called by a interfaces.INewResponse (pp. 385) event. The interfaces.INewResponse (pp. 385) event exists almost purely for symmetry with the interfaces.INewRequest (pp. 385) event.

---

class WSGIApplicationCreatedEvent (*app*)

An instance of this class is emitted as an *event* when the configuration.Configurator.make_wsgi_app() (pp. 378) is called. The instance has an attribute, app, which is an instance of the *router* that will handle WSGI requests. This class implements the interfaces.IWSGIApplicationCreatedEvent (pp. 385) interface.

See *Using Events* (pp. 185) for more information about how to register code which subscribes to these events.

REPOZE.BFG.EXCEPTIONS

class Forbidden()

Raise this exception within *view* code to immediately return the *forbidden view* to the invoking user. Usually this is a basic 401 page, but the forbidden view can be customized as necessary. See *Changing the Forbidden View* (pp. 202).

This exception's constructor accepts a single positional argument, which should be a string. The value of this string will be placed into the WSGI environment under the message key, for availability to the Forbidden view.

class NotFound()

Raise this exception within *view* code to immediately return the *Not Found view* to the invoking user. Usually this is a basic 404 page, but the Not Found view can be customized as necessary. See *Changing the Not Found View* (pp. 201).

This exception's constructor accepts a single positional argument, which should be a string. The value of this string will be placed into the WSGI environment under the message key, for availability to the Not Found view.

class ConfigurationError()

Raised when inappropriate input values are supplied to an API method of a *Configurator*

REPOZE.BFG.INTERFACES

class IAfterTraversal (*name, bases=(), attrs=None, __doc__=None, __module__=None*)

An event type that is emitted after `repoze.bfg` completes traversal but before it calls any view code.

class INewRequest (*name, bases=(), attrs=None, __doc__=None, __module__=None*)

An event type that is emitted whenever `repoze.bfg` begins to process a new request

class INewResponse (*name, bases=(), attrs=None, __doc__=None, __module__=None*)

An event type that is emitted whenever any `repoze.bfg` view returns a response.

class IWSGIApplicationCreatedEvent (*name, bases=(), attrs=None, __doc__=None, __module__=None*)

Event issued when the `configuration.Configurator.make_wsgi_app()` (pp. 378) method is called.

REPOZE.BFG.LOCATION

lineage (*model*)

Return a generator representing the *lineage* of the *model* object implied by the model argument. The generator first returns model unconditionally. Then, if model supplies a __parent__ attribute, return the object represented by model.__parent__. If *that* object has a __parent__ attribute, return that object's parent, and so on, until the object being inspected either has no __parent__ attribute or which has a __parent__ attribute of None. For example, if the object tree is:

```
thing1 = Thing()
thing2 = Thing()
thing2.__parent__ = thing1
```

Calling lineage(thing2) will return a generator. When we turn it into a list, we will get:

```
list(lineage(thing2))
[ <Thing object at thing2>, <Thing object at thing1> ]
```

inside (*model1, model2*)

Is model1 'inside' model2? Return True if so, else False.

model1 is 'inside' model2 if model2 is a *lineage* ancestor of model1. It is a lineage ancestor if its parent (or one of its parent's parents, etc.) is an ancestor.

REPOZE.BFG.PASTER

get_app (*config_file, name*)

Return the WSGI application named `name` in the PasteDeploy config file `config_file`.

REPOZE.BFG.ROUTER

make_app (*root_factory, package=None, filename='configure.zcml', settings=None*)
Return a Router object, representing a fully configured `repoze.bfg` WSGI application.

> ⚠ Use of this function is deprecated as of `repoze.bfg` 1.2. You should instead use a `configuration.Configurator` (pp. 367) instance to perform startup configuration as shown in *Application Configuration* (pp. 15).

`root_factory` must be a callable that accepts a *request* object and which returns a traversal root object. The traversal root returned by the root factory is the *default* traversal root; it can be overridden on a per-view basis. `root_factory` may be `None`, in which case a 'default default' traversal root is used.

`package` is a Python *package* or module representing the application's package. It is optional, defaulting to `None`. `package` may be `None`. If `package` is `None`, the `filename` passed or the value in the `options` dictionary named `configure_zcml` must be a) absolute pathname to a *ZCML* file that represents the application's configuration *or* b) a *resource specification* to a *ZCML* file in the form `dotted.package.name:relative/file/path.zcml`.

`filename` is the filesystem path to a ZCML file (optionally relative to the package path) that should be parsed to create the application registry. It defaults to `configure.zcml`. It can also be a ;term:*resource specification* in the form `dotted_package_name:relative/file/path.zcml`. Note that if any value for `configure_zcml` is passed within the `settings` dictionary, the value passed as `filename` will be ignored, replaced with the `configure_zcml` value.

`settings`, if used, should be a dictionary containing runtime settings (e.g. the key/value pairs in an app section of a PasteDeploy file), with each key representing the option and the key's value representing the specific option value, e.g. `{'reload_templates':True}`. Note that the keyword parameter `options` is a backwards compatibility alias for the `settings` keyword parameter.

REPOZE.BFG.SCRIPTING

get_root (*app, request=None*)

Return a tuple composed of (root, closer) when provided a *router* instance as the app argument. The root returned is the application root object. The closer returned is a callable (accepting no arguments) that should be called when your scripting application is finished using the root. If request is not None, it is used as the request passed to the repoze.bfg application root factory. A request is constructed and passed to the root factory if request is None.

REPOZE.BFG.SECURITY

46.1 Authentication API Functions

authenticated_userid(*request*)

    Return the userid of the currently authenticated user or `None` if there is no *authentication policy* in effect or there is no currently authenticated user.

effective_principals(*request*)

    Return the list of 'effective' *principal* identifiers for the `request`. This will include the userid of the currently authenticated user if a user is currently authenticated. If no *authentication policy* is in effect, this will return an empty sequence.

forget(*request*)

    Return a sequence of header tuples (e.g. `[('Set-Cookie', 'foo=abc')]`) suitable for 'forgetting' the set of credentials possessed by the currently authenticated user. A common usage might look like so within the body of a view function (`response` is assumed to be an *WebOb*-style *response* object computed previously by the view code):

```
from repoze.bfg.security import forget
headers = forget(request)
response.headerlist.extend(headers)
return response
```

If no *authentication policy* is in use, this function will always return an empty sequence.

remember (*request, principal, **kw*)

Return a sequence of header tuples (e.g. [('Set-Cookie', 'foo=abc')]) suitable for 're-membering' a set of credentials implied by the data passed as principal and *kw using the current *authentication policy*. Common usage might look like so within the body of a view function (response is assumed to be an *WebOb* -style *response* object computed previously by the view code):

```
from repoze.bfg.security import remember
headers = remember(request, 'chrism', password='123', max_age='86400')
response.headerlist.extend(headers)
return response
```

If no *authentication policy* is in use, this function will always return an empty sequence. If used, the composition and meaning of **kw must be agreed upon by the calling code and the effective authentication policy.

46.2 Authorization API Functions

has_permission (*permission, context, request*)

Provided a permission (a string or unicode object), a context (a *model* instance) and a request object, return an instance of security.Allowed (pp. 398) if the permission is granted in this context to the user implied by the request. Return an instance of security.Denied if this permission is not granted in this context to this user. This function delegates to the current authentication and authorization policies. Return security.Allowed (pp. 398) unconditionally if no authentication policy has been configured in this application.

principals_allowed_by_permission (*context, permission*)

Provided a context (a model object), and a permission (a string or unicode object), if a *authorization policy* is in effect, return a sequence of *principal* ids that possess the permission in the context. If no authorization policy is in effect, this will return a sequence with the single value security.Everyone (the special principal identifier representing all principals).

> ⓘ   even if an *authorization policy* is in effect, some (exotic) authorization policies may not implement the required machinery for this function; those will cause a NotImplementedError exception to be raised when this function is invoked.

view_execution_permitted (*context, request, name=""*)

If the view specified by context and name is protected by a *permission*, check the permission associated with the view using the effective authentication/authorization policies and the request. Return a boolean result. If no *authorization policy* is in effect, or if the view is not protected by a permission, return True.

46.3 Constants

Everyone

The special principal id named 'Everyone'. This principal id is granted to all requests. Its actual value is the string 'system.Everyone'.

Authenticated

The special principal id named 'Authenticated'. This principal id is granted to all requests which contain any other non-Everyone principal id (according to the *authentication policy*). Its actual value is the string 'system.Authenticated'.

ALL_PERMISSIONS

An object that can be used as the `permission` member of an ACE which matches all permissions unconditionally. For example, an ACE that uses `ALL_PERMISSIONS` might be composed like so: (`'Deny'`, `'system.Everyone'`, `ALL_PERMISSIONS`).

DENY_ALL

A convenience shorthand ACE that defines (`'Deny'`, `'system.Everyone'`, `ALL_PERMISSIONS`). This is often used as the last ACE in an ACL in systems that use an "inheriting" security policy, representing the concept "don't inherit any other ACEs".

46.4 Return Values

Allow

The ACE "action" (the first element in an ACE e.g. (`Allow`, `Everyone`, `'read'`) that means allow access. A sequence of ACEs makes up an ACL. It is a string, and it's actual value is "Allow".

Deny

The ACE "action" (the first element in an ACE e.g. (`Deny`, `'george'`, `'read'`) that means deny access. A sequence of ACEs makes up an ACL. It is a string, and it's actual value is "Deny".

class ACLDenied()

An instance of `ACLDenied` represents that a security check made explicitly against ACL was denied. It evaluates equal to all boolean false types. It also has attributes which indicate which acl, ace, permission, principals, and context were involved in the request. Its __str__ method prints a summary of these attributes for debugging purposes. The same summary is available as the `msg` attribute.

class **ACLAllowed**()

An instance of ACLAllowed represents that a security check made explicitly against ACL was allowed. It evaluates equal to all boolean true types. It also has attributes which indicate which acl, ace, permission, principals, and context were involved in the request. Its __str__ method prints a summary of these attributes for debugging purposes. The same summary is available as the msg attribute.

class **Denied**()

An instance of Denied is returned when a security-related API or other repoze.bfg code denies an action unrelated to an ACL check. It evaluates equal to all boolean false types. It has an attribute named msg describing the circumstances for the deny.

class **Allowed**()

An instance of Allowed is returned when a security-related API or other repoze.bfg code allows an action unrelated to an ACL check. It evaluates equal to all boolean true types. It has an attribute named msg describing the circumstances for the allow.

REPOZE.BFG.SETTINGS

get_settings()

Return a 'settings' object for the current application. A 'settings' object is a dictionary-like object that contains key/value pairs based on the dictionary passed as the settings argument to the configuration.Configurator (pp. 367) constructor or the router.make_app() (pp. 391) API.

> For backwards compatibility, dictionary keys can also be looked up as attributes of the settings object.

REPOZE.BFG.TESTING

registerDummySecurityPolicy (*userid=None, groupids=(), permissive=True*)

Registers a pair of faux `repoze.bfg` security policies: a *authentication policy* and a *authorization policy*.

The behavior of the registered *authorization policy* depends on the `permissive` argument. If `permissive` is true, a permissive *authorization policy* is registered; this policy allows all access. If `permissive` is false, a nonpermissive *authorization policy* is registered; this policy denies all access.

The behavior of the registered *authentication policy* depends on the values provided for the `userid` and `groupids` argument. The authentication policy will return the userid identifier implied by the `userid` argument and the group ids implied by the `groupids` argument when the `security.authenticated_userid()` (pp. 395) or `security.effective_principals()` (pp. 395) APIs are used.

This function is most useful when testing code that uses the APIs named `security.has_permission()` (pp. 396), `security.authenticated_userid()` (pp. 395), `security.effective_principals()` (pp. 395), and `security.principals_allowed_by_permission()` (pp. 396).

⚠️   This API is deprecated as of `repoze.bfg` 1.2. Instead use the `configuration.Configurator.testing_securitypolicy()` (pp. 379) method in your unit and integration tests.

---

registerModels (*models*)

Registers a dictionary of *model* objects that can be resolved via the `traversal.find_model()` (pp. 413) API.

The `traversal.find_model()` (pp. 413) API is called with a path as one of its arguments. If the dictionary you register when calling this method contains that path as a string key (e.g. `/foo/bar` or `foo/bar`), the corresponding value will be returned to `find_model` (and thus to your code) when `traversal.find_model()` (pp. 413) is called with an equivalent path string or tuple.

> ⚠️   This API is deprecated as of `repoze.bfg` 1.2. Instead use the `configuration.Configurator.testing_models()` (pp. 380) method in your unit and integration tests.

registerEventListener (*event_iface=None*)

Registers an *event* listener (aka *subscriber*) listening for events of the type `event_iface`. This method returns a list object which is appended to by the subscriber whenever an event is captured.

When an event is dispatched that matches `event_iface`, that event will be appended to the list. You can then compare the values in the list to expected event notifications. This method is useful when testing code that wants to call `registry.Registry.notify()`, `zope.component.event.dispatch()` or `zope.component.event.objectEventNotify()`.

The default value of `event_iface` (`None`) implies a subscriber registered for *any* kind of event.

> ⚠️   This API is deprecated as of `repoze.bfg` 1.2. Instead use the `configuration.Configurator.testing_add_subscriber()` (pp. 380) method in your unit and integration tests.

registerTemplateRenderer (*path, renderer=None*)

Register a template renderer at `path` (usually a relative filename ala `templates/foo.pt`) and return the renderer object. If the `renderer` argument is None, a 'dummy' renderer will be used. This function is useful when testing code that calls the `chameleon_zpt.render_template_to_response()` (pp. 365) function or `chameleon_text.render_template_to_response()` (pp. 363) function or any other `render_template*` API of any built-in templating system (see `chameleon_zpt` (pp. 365) and `chameleon_text` (pp. 363)).

> ⚠️   This API is deprecated as of `repoze.bfg` 1.2. Instead use the `configuration.Configurator.testing_add_template`'() method in your unit and integration tests.

registerView (*name, result=", view=None, for_=(<InterfaceClass zope.interface.Interface>, <InterfaceClass zope.interface.Interface>), permission=None*)
Registers a `repoze.bfg` *view callable* under the name implied by the `name` argument. The view will return a *WebOb Response* object with the value implied by the `result` argument as its `body` attribute. To gain more control, if you pass in a non-`None` `view` argument, this value will be used as a view callable instead of an automatically generated view callable (and `result` is not used).

To protect the view using a *permission*, pass in a non-`None` value as `permission`. This permission will be checked by any active *authorization policy* when view execution is attempted.

This function is useful when testing code which calls `view.render_view_to_response()` (pp. 427).

> ⚠ This API is deprecated as of `repoze.bfg` 1.2. Instead use the `configuration.Configurator.add_view'()` method in your unit and integration tests.

registerViewPermission (*name,   result=True,   viewpermission=None, for_=(<InterfaceClass zope.interface.Interface>, <InterfaceClass zope.interface.Interface>))*)
Registers a `repoze.bfg` 'view permission' object under a name implied by the `name` argument.

> ⚠ This function was deprecated in repoze.bfg 1.1; it has no real effect in 1.2+.

registerUtility (*impl, iface=<InterfaceClass zope.interface.Interface>, name="*)
Register a ZCA utility component.

The `impl` argument specifies the implementation of the utility. The `iface` argument specifies the *interface* which will be later required to look up the utility (`zope.interface.Interface`, by default). The `name` argument implies the utility name; it is the empty string by default.

See The ZCA book (http://www.muthukadan.net/docs/zca.html) for more information about ZCA utilities.

> ⚠ This API is deprecated as of `repoze.bfg` 1.2. Instead use the `Registry.registerUtility()` method. The `registry` attribute of a *Configurator* in your unit and integration tests is an instance of the `Registry` class.

registerAdapter (*impl,   for_=<InterfaceClass   zope.interface.Interface>,   pro-vides=<InterfaceClass zope.interface.Interface>, name="*)
    Register a ZCA adapter component.

The `impl` argument specifies the implementation of the component (often a class). The `for_` argument implies the `for` interface type used for this registration; it is `zope.interface.Interface` by default. If `for` is not a tuple or list, it will be converted to a one-tuple before being passed to underlying `registry.registerAdapter()` API.

The `provides` argument specifies the ZCA 'provides' interface, `zope.interface.Interface` by default.

The `name` argument is the empty string by default; it implies the name under which the adapter is registered.

See The ZCA book (http://www.muthukadan.net/docs/zca.html) for more information about ZCA adapters.

> ⚠   This API is deprecated as of `repoze.bfg` 1.2.   Instead use the `Registry.registerAdapter()` method. The `registry` attribute of a *Configurator* in your unit and integration tests is an instance of the `Registry` class.

registerSubscriber (*subscriber, iface=<InterfaceClass zope.interface.Interface>*)
    Register a ZCA subscriber component.

The `subscriber` argument specifies the implementation of the subscriber component (often a function).

The `iface` argument is the interface type for which the subscriber will be registered (`zope.interface.Interface` by default). If `iface` is not a tuple or list, it will be converted to a one-tuple before being passed to the underlying ZCA `registry.registerHandler()` method.

See The ZCA book (http://www.muthukadan.net/docs/zca.html) for more information about ZCA subscribers.

> ⚠   This API is deprecated as of `repoze.bfg` 1.2.   Instead use the `configuration.Configurator.add_subscriber()` (pp.   374) method in your unit and integration tests.

registerRoute (*path, name, factory=None*)

Register a new *route* using a path (e.g. `:pagename`), a name (e.g. `home`), and an optional root factory.

The `path` argument implies the route path. The `name` argument implies the route name. The `factory` argument implies a *root factory* associated with the route.

This API is useful for testing code that calls e.g. `url.route_url()` (pp. 423).

> ⓘ This API was added in `repoze.bfg` version 1.1.

> ⚠ This API is deprecated as of `repoze.bfg` 1.2. Instead use the `configuration.Configurator.add_route()` (pp. 369) method in your unit and integration tests.

registerRoutesMapper (*root_factory=None*)

Register a routes 'mapper' object.

> ⓘ This API was added in `repoze.bfg` version 1.1.

> ⚠ This API is deprecated in `repoze.bfg` 1.2: a route mapper is no longer required to be present for successful system operation.

registerSettings (*dictarg=None, **kw*)

Register one or more 'setting' key/value pairs. A setting is a single key/value pair in the dictionary-ish object returned from the API `settings.get_settings()` (pp. 399).

You may pass a dictionary:

```
registerSettings({'external_uri':'http://example.com'})
```

Or a set of key/value pairs:

```
registerSettings(external_uri='http://example.com')
```

Use of this function is required when you need to test code that calls the `settings.get_settings()` (pp. 399) API and which uses return values from that API.

This API is new as of `repoze.bfg` 1.1.

This API is deprecated as of `repoze.bfg` 1.2. Instead use the `configuration.Configurator.add_settings()` (pp. 373) method in your unit and integration tests.

setUp (*registry=None, request=None, hook_zca=True*)
Set `repoze.bfg` registry and request thread locals for the duration of a single unit test.

The `setUp` function is new as of `repoze.bfg` 1.1.

Use this function in the `setUp` method of a unittest test case which directly or indirectly uses:

- any of the `register*` functions in `testing` (pp. 401) (such as `testing.registerModels()` (pp. 402))

- any method of the `configuration.Configurator` (pp. 367) object returned by this function.

- the `threadlocal.get_current_registry()` (pp. 411) or `threadlocal.get_current_request()` (pp. 411) functions.

If you use the `testing.register*` APIs, or the `get_current_*` functions (or call `repoze.bfg` code that uses these functions) without calling `setUp`, `threadlocal.get_current_registry()` (pp. 411) will return a *global application registry*, which may cause unit tests to not be isolated with respect to registrations they perform.

If the `registry` argument is `None`, a new empty *application registry* will be created (an instance of the `registry.Registry` class). If the `registry` argument is not `None`, the value passed in should be an instance of the `registry.Registry` class or a suitable testing analogue.

After setUp is finished, the registry returned by the `threadlocal.get_current_request()` (pp. 411) function will be the passed (or constructed) registry until `testing.tearDown()` (pp. 407) is called (or `testing.setUp()` (pp. 406) is called again).

ⓘ The `registry` argument is new as of `repoze.bfg` 1.2.

If the `hook_zca` argument is `True`, `setUp` will attempt to perform the operation `zope.component.getSiteManager.sethook(threadlocal.get_current_registry)`, which will cause the *Zope Component Architecture* global API (e.g. `zope.component.getSiteManager()`, `zope.component.getAdapter()`, and so on) to use the registry constructed by `setUp` as the value it returns from `zope.component.getSiteManager()`. If the `zope.component` package cannot be imported, or if `hook_zca` is `False`, the hook will not be set.

This function returns an instance of the `configuration.Configurator` (pp. 367) class, which can be used for further configuration to set up an environment suitable for a unit or integration test. The `registry` attribute attached to the Configurator instance represents the 'current' *application registry*; the same registry will be returned by `threadlocal.get_current_registry()` (pp. 411) during the execution of the test.

ⓘ The `hook_zca` argument is new as of `repoze.bfg` 1.2.

ⓘ The return value (a `Configurator` instance) is new as of `repoze.bfg` 1.2 (previous versions used to return `None`)

⚠ Although this method of setting up a test registry will never disappear, after `repoze.bfg` 1.2a6, using the `begin` and `end` methods of a `Configurator` are preferred to using `testing.setUp` and `testing.tearDown`. See *Unit and Integration Testing* (pp. 193) for more information.

---

tearDown (*unhook_zca=True*)

Undo the effects `testing.setUp()` (pp. 406). Use this function in the `tearDown` method of a unit test that uses `testing.setUp()` (pp. 406) in its `setUp` method.

ⓘ This function is new as of `repoze.bfg` 1.1.

If the unhook_zca argument is True (the default), call
zope.component.getSiteManager.reset(). This undoes the action of
testing.setUp() (pp. 406) called with the argument hook_zca=True. If
zope.component cannot be imported, ignore the argument.

> ⓘ The unhook_zca argument is new as of repoze.bfg 1.2.

> ⚠ Although this method of tearing a test setup down will never disappear, after
> repoze.bfg 1.2a6, using the begin and end methods of a Configurator are preferred
> to using testing.setUp and testing.tearDown. See *Unit and Integration Testing* (pp.
> 193) for more information.

cleanUp (*arg, **kw*)

testing.cleanUp() (pp. 408) is an alias for testing.setUp() (pp. 406). Although this
function is effectively deprecated as of repoze.bfg 1.1, due to its extensive production usage, it
will never be removed.

class DummyModel (*__name__=None, __parent__=None, __provides__=None, **kw*)

A dummy repoze.bfg *model* object.

clone (*__name__=<object object at 0x1a5508>, __parent__=<object object at 0x1a5508>, **kw*)

Create a clone of the model object. If ___name___ or ___parent___ arguments are passed,
use these values to override the existing ___name___ or ___parent___ of the model. If any
extra keyword args are passed in via the kw argument, use these keywords to add to or override
existing model keywords (attributes).

items ()

Return the items set by __setitem__

keys ()

Return the keys set by __setitem__

values ()

Return the values set by __setitem__

class DummyRequest (*params=None, environ=None, headers=None, path='/', cookies=None,
post=None, **kw*)

A dummy request object (imitates a *request* object).

The params, environ, headers, path, and cookies arguments correspond to their
:term'WebOb' equivalents.

The `post` argument, if passed, populates the request's `POST` attribute, but *not* `params`, in order to allow testing that the app accepts data for a given view only from POST requests. This argument also sets `self.method` to "POST".

Extra keyword arguments are assigned as attributes of the request itself.

class DummyTemplateRenderer (*string_response=""*)

An instance of this class is returned from `testing.registerTemplateRenderer()` (pp. 402). It has a helper function (`assert_`) that makes it possible to make an assertion which compares data passed to the renderer by the view function against expected key/value pairs.

assert_ (***kw*)

Accept an arbitrary set of assertion key/value pairs. For each assertion key/value pair assert that the renderer (eg. `chameleon_zpt.render_template_to_response()` (pp. 365)) received the key with a value that equals the asserted value. If the renderer did not receive the key at all, or the value received by the renderer doesn't match the assertion value, raise an `AssertionError`.

REPOZE.BFG.THREADLOCAL

get_current_request()
> Return the currently active request or None if no request is currently active.

> This function should be used *extremely sparingly*, usually only in unit testing code. it's almost always usually a mistake to use get_current_request outside a testing context because its usage makes it possible to write code that can be neither easily tested nor scripted.

get_current_registry()
> Return the currently active *application registry* or the global application registry if no request is currently active.

> This function should be used *extremely sparingly*, usually only in unit testing code. it's almost always usually a mistake to use get_current_registry outside a testing context because its usage makes it possible to write code that can be neither easily tested nor scripted.

REPOZE.BFG.TRAVERSAL

find_interface (*model, class_or_interface*)

Return the first object found in the parent chain of `model` which, a) if `class_or_interface` is a Python class object, is an instance of the class or any subclass of that class or b) if `class_or_interface` is a *interface*, provides the specified interface. Return `None` if no object providing `interface_or_class` can be found in the parent chain. The `model` passed in *must* be *location*-aware.

find_model (*model, path*)

Given a model object and a string or tuple representing a path (such as the return value of `traversal.model_path()` (pp. 414) or `traversal.model_path_tuple()` (pp. 415)), return a context in this application's model graph at the specified path. The model passed in *must* be *location*-aware. If the path cannot be resolved (if the respective node in the graph does not exist), a `KeyError` will be raised.

This function is the logical inverse of `traversal.model_path()` (pp. 414) and `traversal.model_path_tuple()` (pp. 415); it can resolve any path string or tuple generated by either of those functions.

Rules for passing a *string* as the `path` argument: if the first character in the path string is the with the / character, the path will considered absolute and the graph traversal will start at the root object. If the first character of the path string is *not* the / character, the path is considered relative and graph traversal will begin at the model object supplied to the function as the `model` argument. If an empty string is passed as `path`, the `model` passed in will be returned. Model path strings must be escaped in the following manner: each Unicode path segment must be encoded as UTF-8 and as each path segment must escaped via Python's `urllib.quote`. For example, `/path/to%20the/La%20Pe%C3%B1a` (absolute) or `to%20the/La%20Pe%C3%B1a` (relative). The `traversal.model_path()` (pp. 414) function generates strings which follow these rules (albeit only absolute ones).

Rules for passing a *tuple* as the `path` argument: if the first element in the path tuple is the empty string (for example (`''`, `'a'`, `'b'`, `'c'`), the path is considered absolute and the graph traversal will start at the graph root object. If the first element in the path tuple is not the empty string (for example (`'a'`, `'b'`, `'c'`)), the path is considered relative and graph traversal will begin at the model object supplied to the function as the `model` argument. If an empty sequence is passed as `path`, the `model` passed in itself will be returned. No URL-quoting or UTF-8-encoding of individual path segments within the tuple is required (each segment may be any string or unicode object representing a model name). Model path tuples generated by `traversal.model_path_tuple()` (pp. 415) can always be resolved by `find_model`.

find_root (*model*)

Find the root node in the graph to which `model` belongs. Note that `model` should be *location*-aware. Note that the root node is available in the request object by accessing the `request.root` attribute.

model_path (*model, *elements*)

Return a string object representing the absolute physical path of the model object based on its position in the model graph, e.g `/foo/bar`. Any positional arguments passed in as `elements` will be appended as path segments to the end of the model path. For instance, if the model's path is `/foo/bar` and `elements` equals (`'a'`, `'b'`), the returned string will be `/foo/bar/a/b`. The first character in the string will always be the `/` character (a leading `/` character in a path string represents that the path is absolute).

Model path strings returned will be escaped in the following manner: each unicode path segment will be encoded as UTF-8 and each path segment will be escaped via Python's `urllib.quote`. For example, `/path/to%20the/La%20Pe%C3%B1a`.

This function is a logical inverse of `traversal.find_model`: it can be used to generate path references that can later be resolved via that function.

The `model` passed in *must* be *location*-aware.

> ⓘ Each segment in the path string returned will use the __name__ attribute of the model it represents within the graph. Each of these segments *should* be a unicode or string object (as per the contract of *location*-awareness). However, no conversion or safety checking of model names is performed. For instance, if one of the models in your graph has a __name__ which (by error) is a dictionary, the `traversal.model_path()` (pp. 414) function will attempt to append it to a string and it will cause a `TypeError`.

> ⓘ The *root* model *must* have a __name__ attribute with a value of either `None` or the empty string for paths to be generated properly. If the root model has a non-null __name__ attribute, its name will be prepended to the generated path rather than a single leading '/' character.

model_path_tuple (*model, *elements*)

Return a tuple representing the absolute physical path of the `model` object based on its position in an object graph, e.g (", 'foo', 'bar'). Any positional arguments passed in as `elements` will be appended as elements in the tuple representing the model path. For instance, if the model's path is (", 'foo', 'bar') and elements equals ('a', 'b'), the returned tuple will be (", 'foo', 'bar', 'a', b'). The first element of this tuple will always be the empty string (a leading empty string element in a path tuple represents that the path is absolute).

This function is a logical inverse of `traversal.find_model()` (pp. 413): it can be used to generate path references that can later be resolved that function.

The `model` passed in *must* be *location*-aware.

Each segment in the path tuple returned will equal the ___name___ attribute of the model it represents within the graph. Each of these segments *should* be a unicode or string object (as per the contract of *location*-awareness). However, no conversion or safety checking of model names is performed. For instance, if one of the models in your graph has a ___name___ which (by error) is a dictionary, that dictionary will be placed in the path tuple; no warning or error will be given.

The *root* model *must* have a ___name___ attribute with a value of either `None` or the empty string for path tuples to be generated properly. If the root model has a non-null ___name___ attribute, its name will be the first element in the generated path tuple rather than the empty string.

---

quote_path_segment (*segment*)

Return a quoted representation of a 'path segment' (such as the string ___name___ attribute of a model) as a string. If the `segment` passed in is a unicode object, it is converted to a UTF-8 string, then it is URL-quoted using Python's `urllib.quote`. If the `segment` passed in is a string, it is URL-quoted using Python's `urllib.quote`. If the segment passed in is not a string or unicode object, an error will be raised. The return value of `quote_path_segment` is always a string, never Unicode.

The return value for each segment passed to this function is cached in a module-scope dictionary for speed: the cached version is returned when possible rather than recomputing the quoted version. No cache emptying is ever done for the lifetime of an application, however. If you pass arbitrary user-supplied strings to this function (as opposed to some bounded set of values from a 'working set' known to your application), it may become a memory leak.

virtual_root (*model, request*)

Provided any *model* and a *request* object, return the model object representing the *virtual root* of the current *request*. Using a virtual root in a *traversal* -based repoze.bfg application permits rooting, for example, the object at the traversal path /cms at http://example.com/ instead of rooting it at http://example.com/cms/.

If the model passed in is a context obtained via *traversal*, and if the HTTP_X_VHM_ROOT key is in the WSGI environment, the value of this key will be treated as a 'virtual root path': the traversal.find_model() (pp. 413) API will be used to find the virtual root object using this path; if the object is found, it will be returned. If the HTTP_X_VHM_ROOT key is is not present in the WSGI environment, the physical *root* of the graph will be returned instead.

Virtual roots are not useful at all in applications that use *URL dispatch*. Contexts obtained via URL dispatch don't really support being virtually rooted (each URL dispatch context is both its own physical and virtual root). However if this API is called with a model argument which is a context obtained via URL dispatch, the model passed in will be returned unconditionally.

traverse (*model, path*)

Given a model object as model and a string or tuple representing a path as path (such as the return value of traversal.model_path() (pp. 414) or traversal.model_path_tuple() (pp. 415) or the value of request.environ['PATH_INFO']), return a dictionary with the keys context, root, view_name, subpath, traversed, virtual_root, and virtual_root_path.

A definition of each value in the returned dictionary:

- context: The *context* (a *model* object) found via traversal or url dispatch. If the path passed in is the empty string, the value of the model argument passed to this function is returned.

- root: The model object at which *traversal* begins. If the model passed in was found via url dispatch or if the path passed in was relative (non-absolute), the value of the model argument passed to this function is returned.

- view_name: The *view name* found during *traversal* or *url dispatch*; if the model was found via traversal, this is usually a representation of the path segment which directly follows the path to the context in the path. The view_name will be a Unicode object or the empty string. The view_name will be the empty string if there is no element which follows the context path. An example: if the path passed is /foo/bar, and a context object is found at /foo (but not at /foo/bar), the 'view name' will be u'bar'. If the model was found via urldispatch, the view_name will be the name the route found was registered with.

- •subpath: For a `model` found via *traversal*, this is a sequence of path segments found in the `path` that follow the `view_name` (if any). Each of these items is a Unicode object. If no path segments follow the `view_name`, the subpath will be the empty sequence. An example: if the path passed is `/foo/bar/baz/buz`, and a context object is found at `/foo` (but not `/foo/bar`), the 'view name' will be `u'bar'` and the *subpath* will be `[u'baz', u'buz']`. For a `model` found via url dispatch, the subpath will be a sequence of values discerned from `*subpath` in the route pattern matched or the empty sequence.

- •traversed: The sequence of path elements traversed from the root to find the `context` object during *traversal*. Each of these items is a Unicode object. If no path segments were traversed to find the `context` object (e.g. if the `path` provided is the empty string), the `traversed` value will be the empty sequence. If the `model` is a model found via *url dispatch*, traversed will be None.

- •virtual_root: A model object representing the 'virtual' root of the object graph being traversed during *traversal*. See *Virtual Hosting* (pp. 181) for a definition of the virtual root object. If no virtual hosting is in effect, and the `path` passed in was absolute, the `virtual_root` will be the *physical* root object (the object at which *traversal* begins). If the `model` passed in was found via *URL dispatch* or if the `path` passed in was relative, the `virtual_root` will always equal the `root` object (the model passed in).

- •virtual_root_path – If *traversal* was used to find the `model`, this will be the sequence of path elements traversed to find the `virtual_root` object. Each of these items is a Unicode object. If no path segments were traversed to find the `virtual_root` object (e.g. if virtual hosting is not in effect), the `traversed` value will be the empty list. If url dispatch was used to find the `model`, this will be None.

If the path cannot be resolved, a `KeyError` will be raised.

Rules for passing a *string* as the `path` argument: if the first character in the path string is the with the `/` character, the path will considered absolute and the graph traversal will start at the root object. If the first character of the path string is *not* the `/` character, the path is considered relative and graph traversal will begin at the model object supplied to the function as the `model` argument. If an empty string is passed as `path`, the `model` passed in will be returned. Model path strings must be escaped in the following manner: each Unicode path segment must be encoded as UTF-8 and as each path segment must escaped via Python's `urllib.quote`. For example, `/path/to%20the/La%20Pe%C3%B1a` (absolute) or `to%20the/La%20Pe%C3%B1a` (relative). The `traversal.model_path()` (pp. 414) function generates strings which follow these rules (albeit only absolute ones).

Rules for passing a *tuple* as the `path` argument: if the first element in the path tuple is the empty string (for example `('', 'a', 'b', 'c')`, the path is considered absolute and the graph traversal will start at the graph root object. If the first element in the path tuple is not the empty string (for example `('a', 'b', 'c')`), the path is considered relative and graph traversal will begin at the model object supplied to the function as the `model` argument. If an empty sequence is passed as `path`, the `model` passed in itself will be returned. No URL-quoting or UTF-8-encoding of individual path segments within the tuple is required (each segment may be any string or unicode object representing a model name).

Explanation of the conversion of `path` segment values to Unicode during traversal: Each segment is URL-unquoted, and decoded into Unicode. Each segment is assumed to be encoded using the UTF-8 encoding (or a subset, such as ASCII); a `TypeError` is raised if a segment cannot be decoded. If a segment name is empty or if it is ., it is ignored. If a segment name is .., the previous segment is deleted, and the .. is ignored. As a result of this process, the return values `view_name`, each element in the `subpath`, each element in `traversed`, and each element in the `virtual_root_path` will be Unicode as opposed to a string, and will be URL-decoded.

traversal_path (*path*)

Given a `PATH_INFO` string (slash-separated path segments), return a tuple representing that path which can be used to traverse a graph. The `PATH_INFO` is split on slashes, creating a list of segments. Each segment is URL-unquoted, and decoded into Unicode. Each segment is assumed to be encoded using the UTF-8 encoding (or a subset, such as ASCII); a `TypeError` is raised if a segment cannot be decoded. If a segment name is empty or if it is ., it is ignored. If a segment name is .., the previous segment is deleted, and the .. is ignored. Examples:

```
/
```

```
    ()
```

```
/foo/bar/baz
```

```
    (u'foo', u'bar', u'baz')
```

```
foo/bar/baz
```

```
    (u'foo', u'bar', u'baz')
```

```
/foo/bar/baz/
```

```
    (u'foo', u'bar', u'baz')
```

```
/foo//bar//baz/
```

```
    (u'foo', u'bar', u'baz')
```

```
/foo/bar/baz/..
```

```
    (u'foo', u'bar')
```

```
/my%20archives/hello
```

(u'my archives', u'hello')

```
/archives/La%20Pe%C3%B1a
```

(u'archives', u'<unprintable unicode>')

ⓘ   This function does not generate the same type of tuples that `traversal.model_path_tuple()` (pp.   415) does.   In particular, the leading empty string is not present in the tuple it returns, unlike tuples returned by `traversal.model_path_tuple()` (pp.   415).   As a result, tuples generated by `traversal_path` are not resolveable by the `traversal.find_model()` (pp.   413) API. `traversal_path` is a function mostly used by the internals of `repoze.bfg` and by people writing their own traversal machinery, as opposed to users writing applications in `repoze.bfg`.

REPOZE.BFG.URL

Utility functions for dealing with URLs in repoze.bfg

model_url (*context, request, *elements, query=None, anchor=None*)
Generate a string representing the absolute URL of the `model` object based on the `wsgi.url_scheme`, `HTTP_HOST` or `SERVER_NAME` in the `request`, plus any `SCRIPT_NAME`. The overall result of this function is always a UTF-8 encoded string (never Unicode).

Examples:

```
model_url(context, request) =>

                    http://example.com/

model_url(context, request, 'a.html') =>

                    http://example.com/a.html

model_url(context, request, 'a.html', query={'q':'1'}) =>

                    http://example.com/a.html?q=1

model_url(context, request, 'a.html', anchor='abc') =>

                    http://example.com/a.html#abc
```

Any positional arguments passed in as elements must be strings or Unicode objects. These will be joined by slashes and appended to the generated model URL. Each of the elements passed in is URL-quoted before being appended; if any element is Unicode, it will converted to a UTF-8 bytestring before being URL-quoted.

⚠ if no elements arguments are specified, the model URL will end with a trailing slash. If any elements are used, the generated URL will *not* end in trailing a slash.

If a keyword argument query is present, it will used to compose a query string that will be tacked on to the end of the URL. The value of query must be a sequence of two-tuples *or* a data structure with an .items() method that returns a sequence of two-tuples (presumably a dictionary). This data structure will be turned into a query string per the documentation of repoze.url.urlencode function. After the query data is turned into a query string, a leading ? is prepended, and the resulting string is appended to the generated URL.

ⓘ Python data structures that are passed as query which are sequences or dictionaries are turned into a string under the same rules as when run through urllib.urlencode() with the doseq argument equal to True. This means that sequences can be passed as values, and a k=v pair will be placed into the query string for each value.

If a keyword argument anchor is present, its string representation will be used as a named anchor in the generated URL (e.g. if anchor is passed as foo and the model URL is http://example.com/model/url, the resulting generated URL will be http://example.com/model/url#foo).

ⓘ If anchor is passed as a string, it should be UTF-8 encoded. If anchor is passed as a Unicode object, it will be converted to UTF-8 before being appended to the URL. The anchor value is not quoted in any way before being appended to the generated URL.

If both anchor and query are specified, the anchor element will always follow the query element, e.g. http://example.com?foo=1#bar.

ⓘ If the model used is the result of a *traversal*, it must be *location*-aware. The model can also be the context of a *URL dispatch*; contexts found this way do not need to be location-aware.

422

> ℹ️ If a 'virtual root path' is present in the request environment (the value of the WSGI environ key HTTP_X_VHM_ROOT), and the model was obtained via *traversal*, the URL path will not include the virtual root prefix (it will be stripped off the left hand side of the generated URL).

route_url (*route_name, request, *elements, **kw*)
Generates a fully qualified URL for a named `repoze.bfg` *route configuration*.

Use the route's `name` as the first positional argument. Use a request object as the second positional argument. Additional positional arguments are appended to the URL as path segments after it is generated.

Use keyword arguments to supply values which match any dynamic path elements in the route definition. Raises a KeyError exception if the URL cannot be generated for any reason (not enough arguments, for example).

For example, if you've defined a route named "foobar" with the path :foo/:bar/*traverse:

```
route_url('foobar', request, foo='1')              => <KeyError exception>
route_url('foobar', request, foo='1', bar='2') => <KeyError exception>
route_url('foobar', request, foo='1', bar='2',
          'traverse=('a','b'))                     => http://e.com/1/2/a/b
route_url('foobar', request, foo='1', bar='2',
          'traverse=('/a/b'))                      => http://e.com/1/2/a/b
```

Values replacing :segment arguments can be passed as strings or Unicode objects. They will be encoded to UTF-8 and URL-quoted before being placed into the generated URL.

Values replacing *remainder arguments can be passed as strings *or* tuples of Unicode/string values. If a tuple is passed as a *remainder replacement value, its values are URL-quoted and encoded to UTF-8. The resulting strings are joined with slashes and rendered into the URL. If a string is passed as a *remainder replacement value, it is tacked on to the URL untouched.

If a keyword argument _query is present, it will used to compose a query string that will be tacked on to the end of the URL. The value of _query must be a sequence of two-tuples *or* a data structure with an .items() method that returns a sequence of two-tuples (presumably a dictionary). This data structure will be turned into a query string per the documentation of encode.urlencode() function. After the query data is turned into a query string, a leading ? is prepended, and the resulting string is appended to the generated URL.

> ℹ Python data structures that are passed as _query which are sequences or dictionaries are turned into a string under the same rules as when run through urllib.urlencode() with the doseq argument equal to True. This means that sequences can be passed as values, and a k=v pair will be placed into the query string for each value.

If a keyword argument _anchor is present, its string representation will be used as a named anchor in the generated URL (e.g. if _anchor is passed as foo and the model URL is http://example.com/model/url, the resulting generated URL will be http://example.com/model/url#foo).

> ℹ If _anchor is passed as a string, it should be UTF-8 encoded. If _anchor is passed as a Unicode object, it will be converted to UTF-8 before being appended to the URL. The anchor value is not quoted in any way before being appended to the generated URL.

If both _anchor and _query are specified, the anchor element will always follow the query element, e.g. http://example.com?foo=1#bar.

This function raises a KeyError if the URL cannot be generated due to missing replacement names. Extra replacement names are ignored.

static_url (*path, request, **kw*)

Generates a fully qualified URL for a static *resource*. The resource must live within a location defined via the configuration.Configurator.add_static_view() (pp. 373) *configuration declaration* or the <static> ZCML directive (see *Serving Static Resources Using a ZCML Directive* (pp. 137)).

Example:

```
static_url('mypackage:static/foo.css', request) =>

                    http://example.com/static/foo.css
```

The path argument points at a file or directory on disk which a URL should be generated for. The path may be either a relative path (e.g. static/foo.css) or a *resource specification* (e.g. mypackage:static/foo.css). A path may not be an absolute filesystem path (a ValueError will be raised if this function is supplied with an absolute path).

The request argument should be a *request* object.

The purpose of the `**kw` argument is the same as the purpose of the `url.route_url()` (pp. 423) `**kw` argument. See the documentation for that function to understand the arguments which you can provide to it. However, typically, you don't need to pass anything as `*kw` when generating a static resource URL.

This function raises a `ValueError` if a static view definition cannot be found which matches the path specification.

> ⓘ This feature is new in `repoze.bfg` 1.1.

urlencode (*query, doseq=True*)

An alternate implementation of Python's stdlib urllib.urlencode function (http://docs.python.org/library/urllib.html) which accepts unicode keys and values within the `query` dict/sequence; all Unicode keys and values are first converted to UTF-8 before being used to compose the query string.

The value of `query` must be a sequence of two-tuples representing key/value pairs *or* an object (often a dictionary) with an `.items()` method that returns a sequence of two-tuples representing key/value pairs.

For minimal calling convention backwards compatibility, this version of urlencode accepts *but ignores* a second argument conventionally named `doseq`. The Python stdlib version behaves differently when `doseq` is False and when a sequence is presented as one of the values. This version always behaves in the `doseq=True` mode, no matter what the value of the second argument.

See the Python stdlib documentation for `urllib.urlencode` for more information.

REPOZE.BFG.VIEW

render_view_to_response (*context, request, name=", secure=True*)

Call the *view callable* configured with a *view configuration* that matches the *view name* name registered against the specified `context` and `request` and return a *response* object. This function will return `None` if a corresponding *view callable* cannot be found (when no *view configuration* matches the combination of `name` / `context` / and `request`).

If *secure*' is `True`, and the *view callable* found is protected by a permission, the permission will be checked before calling the view function. If the permission check disallows view execution (based on the current *authorization policy*), a `exceptions.Forbidden` (pp. 383) exception will be raised. The exception's `args` attribute explains why the view access was disallowed.

If `secure` is `False`, no permission checking is done.

render_view_to_iterable (*context, request, name=", secure=True*)

Call the *view callable* configured with a *view configuration* that matches the *view name* name registered against the specified `context` and `request` and return an iterable object which represents the body of a response. This function will return `None` if a corresponding *view callable* cannot be found (when no *view configuration* matches the combination of `name` / `context` / and `request`). Additionally, this function will raise a `ValueError` if a view function is found and called but the view function's result does not have an `app_iter` attribute.

You can usually get the string representation of the return value of this function by calling `".join(iterable)`, or just use `view.render_view()` (pp. 428) instead.

If `secure` is `True`, and the view is protected by a permission, the permission will be checked before the view function is invoked. If the permission check disallows view execution (based on the current *authentication policy*), a `exceptions.Forbidden` (pp. 383) exception will be raised; its `args` attribute explains why the view access was disallowed.

If `secure` is `False`, no permission checking is done.

render_view (*context, request, name=", secure=True*)

Call the *view callable* configured with a *view configuration* that matches the *view name* name registered against the specified `context` and `request` and and unwind the view response's `app_iter` (see *View Callable Responses* (pp. 108)) into a single string. This function will return `None` if a corresponding *view callable* cannot be found (when no *view configuration* matches the combination of `name` / `context` / and `request`). Additionally, this function will raise a `ValueError` if a view function is found and called but the view function's result does not have an `app_iter` attribute. This function will return `None` if a corresponding view cannot be found.

If `secure` is `True`, and the view is protected by a permission, the permission will be checked before the view is invoked. If the permission check disallows view execution (based on the current *authorization policy*), a `exceptions.Forbidden` (pp. 383) exception will be raised; its `args` attribute explains why the view access was disallowed.

If `secure` is `False`, no permission checking is done.

is_response (*ob*)

Return `True` if `ob` implements the interface implied by *View Callable Responses* (pp. 108). `False` if not.

> ℹ️ this isn't a true interface check (in Zope terms), it's a duck-typing check, as response objects are not obligated to actually implement a Zope interface.

class bfg_view (*name=", request_type=None, for_=None, permission=None, route_name=None, request_method=None, request_param=None, containment=None, attr=None, renderer=None, wrapper=None, xhr=False, accept=None, header=None, path_info=None, custom_predicates=(), context=None*)

A function, class or method *decorator* which allows a developer to create view registrations nearer to a *view callable* definition than use of *ZCML* or *imperative configuration* to do the same.

For example, this code in a module `views.py`:

```python
from models import MyModel

@bfg_view(name='my_view', context=MyModel, permission='read',
          route_name='site1')
def my_view(context, request):
    return 'OK'
```

Might replace the following call to the `configuration.Configurator.add_view()` (pp. 374) method:

```
import views
import models
config.add_view(views.my_view, context=models.MyModel, name='my_view',
                permission='read', 'route_name='site1')
```

Or might replace the following ZCML `view` declaration:

```
<view
 for='.models.MyModel'
 view='.views.my_view'
 name='my_view'
 permission='read'
 route_name='site1'
 />
```

The following arguments are supported as arguments to `bfg_view`: `context`, `permission`, `name`, `request_type`, `route_name`, `request_method`, `request_param`, `containment`, `xhr`, `accept`, `header` and `path_info`.

If `context` is not supplied, the interface `zope.interface.Interface` (matching any context) is used. An alias for `context` is `for_`.

If `permission` is not supplied, no permission is registered for this view (it's accessible by any caller).

If `name` is not supplied, the empty string is used (implying the default view name).

If `attr` is not supplied, `None` is used (implying the function itself if the view is a function, or the `__call__` callable attribute if the view is a class).

If `renderer` is not supplied, `None` is used (meaning that no renderer is associated with this view).

If `wrapper` is not supplied, `None` is used (meaning that no view wrapper is associated with this view).

If `request_type` is not supplied, the interface `interfaces.IRequest` is used, implying the standard request interface type.

If `route_name` is not supplied, the view configuration is considered to be made against a URL that doesn't match any defined *route*. The use of a `route_name` is an advanced feature, useful only if you're also using *url dispatch*.

If `request_method` is not supplied, this view will match a request with any HTTP REQUEST_METHOD (GET/POST/PUT/HEAD/DELETE). If this parameter *is* supplied, it must be a string naming an HTTP REQUEST_METHOD, indicating that this view will only match when the current request has a REQUEST_METHOD that matches this value.

If `request_param` is not supplied, this view will be called when a request with any (or no) request GET or POST parameters is encountered. If the value is present, it must be a string. If the value supplied to the parameter has no = sign in it, it implies that the key must exist in the `request.params` dictionary for this view to 'match' the current request. If the value supplied to the parameter has a = sign in it, e.g. `request_params="foo=123"`, then the key (`foo`) must both exist in the `request.params` dictionary, and the value must match the right hand side of the expression (`123`) for the view to "match" the current request.

If `containment` is not supplied, this view will be called when the context of the request has any (or no) *lineage*. If `containment` *is* supplied, it must be a class or *interface*, denoting that the view 'matches' the current request only if any graph *lineage* node possesses this class or interface.

If `xhr` is specified, it must be a boolean value. If the value is `True`, the view will only be invoked if the request's X-Requested-With header has the value XMLHttpRequest.

If `accept` is specified, it must be a mimetype value. If `accept` is specified, the view will only be invoked if the Accept HTTP header matches the value requested. See the description of `accept` in *view* (pp. 479) for information about the allowable composition and matching behavior of this value.

If `header` is specified, it must be a header name or a `headername:headervalue` pair. If `header` is specified, and possesses a value the view will only be invoked if an HTTP header matches the value requested. If `header` is specified without a value (a bare header name only), the view will only be invoked if the HTTP header exists with any value in the request. See the description of `header` in *view* (pp. 479) for information about the allowable composition and matching behavior of this value.

If `path_info` is specified, it must be a regular expression. The view will only be invoked if the PATH_INFO WSGI environment variable matches the expression.

If `custom_predicates` is specified, it must be a sequence of *predicate* callables (a predicate callable accepts two arguments: `context` and `request` and returns `True` or `False`). The view will only be invoked if all custom predicates return `True`.

Any individual or all parameters can be omitted. The simplest `bfg_view` declaration is:

```
@bfg_view()
def my_view(...):
    ...
```

Such a registration implies that the view name will be my_view, registered for any *context* object, using no permission, registered against all non-URL-dispatch-based requests, with any REQUEST_METHOD, any set of request.params values, without respect to any object in the *lineage*.

The bfg_view decorator can also be used as a class decorator in Python 2.6 and better (Python 2.5 and below do not support class decorators):

```
from webob import Response
from repoze.bfg.view import bfg_view

@bfg_view()
class MyView(object):
    def __init__(self, context, request):
        self.context = context
        self.request = request
    def __call__(self):
        return Response('hello from %s!' % self.context)
```

In Python 2.5 and below, the bfg_view decorator can still be used against a class, although not in decorator form:

```
from webob import Response
from repoze.bfg.view import bfg_view

class MyView(object):
    def __init__(self, context, request):
        self.context = context
        self.request = request
    def __call__(self):
        return Response('hello from %s!' % self.context)

MyView = bfg_view()(MyView)
```

When a view is a class, the calling semantics are different than when it is a function or another non-class callable. See *Defining a View Callable as a Class* (pp. 106) for more information.

Using a class as a view is a new feature in 0.8.1+.

The bfg_view decorator can also be used against a class method:

```python
from webob import Response
from repoze.bfg.view import bfg_view

class MyView(object):
    def __init__(self, context, request):
        self.context = context
        self.request = request

    @bfg_view(name='hello')
    def amethod(self):
        return Response('hello from %s!' % self.context)
```

When the bfg_view decorator is used against a class method, a view is registered for the *class* (as described above), so the class constructor must accept either request or context, request. The method which is decorated must return a response (or rely on a *renderer* to generate one). Using the decorator against a particular method of a class is equivalent to using the attr parameter in a decorator attached to the class itself. For example, the above registration implied by the decorator being used against the amethod method could be spelled equivalently as:

```python
from webob import Response
from repoze.bfg.view import bfg_view

@bfg_view(attr='amethod', name='hello')
class MyView(object):
    def __init__(self, context, request):
        self.context = context
        self.request = request

    def amethod(self):
        return Response('hello from %s!' % self.context)
```

> ⚠ The ability to use the bfg_view decorator as a method decorator is new in repoze.bfg version 1.1.

To make use of any bfg_view declaration, you must perform a *scan*. To do so, either insert the following boilerplate into your application registry's ZCML:

```
<scan package="."/>
```

See *scan* (pp. 471) for more information about the ZCML `scan` directive.

Or, if you don't use ZCML, use the `configuration.Configurator.scan()` (pp. 378) method:

```
config.scan()
```

class static (*root_dir, cache_max_age=3600, package_name=None*)

An instance of this class is a callable which can act as a `repoze.bfg` *view callable*; this view will serve static files from a directory on disk based on the `root_dir` you provide to its constructor.

The directory may contain subdirectories (recursively); the static view implementation will descend into these directories as necessary based on the components of the URL in order to resolve a path into a response.

You may pass an absolute or relative filesystem path or a *resource specification* representing the directory containing static files as the `root_dir` argument to this class' constructor.

If the `root_dir` path is relative, and the `package_name` argument is None, `root_dir` will be considered relative to the directory in which the Python file which *calls* static resides. If the `package_name` name argument is provided, and a relative `root_dir` is provided, the `root_dir` will be considered relative to the Python *package* specified by `package_name` (a dotted path to a Python package).

`cache_max_age` influences the `Expires` and `Max-Age` response headers returned by the view (default is 3600 seconds or five minutes).

ⓘ If the `root_dir` is relative to a *package*, or is a *resource specification* the `repoze.bfg` `resource` ZCML directive or `configuration.Configurator` (pp. 367) method can be used to override resources within the named `root_dir` package-relative directory. However, if the `root_dir` is absolute, the `resource` directive will not be able to override the resources it contains.

`append_slash_notfound_view` *(context, request)*

For behavior like Django's `APPEND_SLASH=True`, use this view as the *Not Found view* in your application.

When this view is the Not Found view (indicating that no view was found), and any routes have been defined in the configuration of your application, if the value of the `PATH_INFO` WSGI environment variable does not already end in a slash, and if the value of `PATH_INFO` *plus* a slash matches any route's path, do an HTTP redirect to the slash-appended PATH_INFO. Note that this will *lose* `POST` data information (turning it into a GET), so you shouldn't rely on this to redirect POST requests.

If you use *ZCML*, add the following to your application's `configure.zcml` to use this view as the Not Found view:

```
<notfound
   view="repoze.bfg.view.append_slash_notfound_view"/>
```

Or use the `configuration.Configurator.set_notfound_view()` (pp. 379) method if you don't use ZCML:

```
from repoze.bfg.view import append_slash_notfound_view
config.set_notfound_view(append_slash_notfound_view)
```

See also *Changing the Not Found View* (pp. 201).

> This function is new as of `repoze.bfg` version 1.1.

REPOZE.BFG.WSGI

wsgiapp (*wrapped*)

Decorator to turn a WSGI application into a `repoze.bfg` *view callable*. This decorator differs from the `wsgi.wsgiapp2()` (pp. 436) decorator inasmuch as fixups of `PATH_INFO` and `SCRIPT_NAME` within the WSGI environment *are not* performed before the application is invoked.

E.g., the following in a `views.py` module:

```
@wsgiapp
def hello_world(environ, start_response):
    body = 'Hello world'
    start_response('200 OK', [ ('Content-Type', 'text/plain'),
                               ('Content-Length', len(body)) ] )
    return [body]
```

Allows the following ZCML view declaration to be made:

```
<view
   view=".views.hello_world"
   name="hello_world.txt"
 />
```

Or the following call to `configuration.Configurator.add_view()` (pp. 374):

```
from views import hello_world
config.add_view(hello_world, name='hello_world.txt')
```

The `wsgiapp` decorator will convert the result of the WSGI application to a *Response* and return it to `repoze.bfg` as if the WSGI app were a `repoze.bfg` view.

wsgiapp2 (*wrapped*)

Decorator to turn a WSGI application into a `repoze.bfg` view callable. This decorator differs from the `wsgi.wsgiapp()` (pp. 435) decorator inasmuch as fixups of `PATH_INFO` and `SCRIPT_NAME` within the WSGI environment *are* performed before the application is invoked.

E.g. the following in a `views.py` module:

```
@wsgiapp2
def hello_world(environ, start_response):
    body = 'Hello world'
    start_response('200 OK', [ ('Content-Type', 'text/plain'),
                               ('Content-Length', len(body)) ] )
    return [body]
```

Allows the following ZCML view declaration to be made:

```
<view
   view=".views.hello_world"
   name="hello_world.txt"
 />
```

Or the following call to `configuration.Configurator.add_view()` (pp. 374):

```
from views import hello_world
config.add_view(hello_world, name='hello_world.txt')
```

The `wsgiapp2` decorator will convert the result of the WSGI application to a Response and return it to `repoze.bfg` as if the WSGI app were a `repoze.bfg` view. The `SCRIPT_NAME` and `PATH_INFO` values present in the WSGI environment are fixed up before the application is invoked.

Part IV

ZCML Directive Reference

ACLAUTHORIZATIONPOLICY

When this directive is used, authorization information is obtained from *ACL* objects attached to model instances.

54.1 Attributes

None.

54.2 Example

```
<aclauthorizationpolicy/>
```

54.3 Alternatives

You may create an instance of the `authorization.ACLAuthorizationPolicy` (pp. 357) and pass it to the `configuration.Configurator` (pp. 367) constructor as the `authorization_policy` argument during initial application configuration.

54.4 See Also

See also *Built-In Authorization Policy ZCML Directives* (pp. 178) and *Security* (pp. 167).

ADAPTER

Register a *Zope Component Architecture* "adapter".

55.1 Attributes

factory The adapter factory (often a class).

provides The *interface* that an adapter instance resulting from a lookup will provide.

for Interfaces or classes to be adapted, separated by spaces, e.g. `interfaces.IFoo interfaces.IBar`.

name The adapter name.

55.2 Example

```
<adapter
  for=".foo.IFoo .bar.IBar"
  provides=".interfaces.IMyAdapter"
  factory=".adapters.MyAdapter"
  />
```

55.3 Alternatives

Use the `registerAdapter` method of the `registry` attribute of a *Configurator* instance during initial application setup.

55.4 See Also

None.

AUTHTKTAUTHENTICATIONPOLICY

When this directive is used, authentication information is obtained from an `paste.auth.auth_tkt` cookie value, assumed to be set by a custom login form.

56.1 Attributes

secret The `secret` is a string that will be used to encrypt the data stored by the cookie. It is required and has no default.

callback The `callback` is a Python dotted name to a function passed the string representing the userid stored in the cookie and the request as positional arguments. The callback is expected to return None if the user represented by the string doesn't exist or a sequence of group identifiers (possibly empty) if the user does exist. If `callback` is None, the userid will be assumed to exist with no groups. It defaults to `None`.

cookie_name The `cookie_name` is the name used for the cookie that contains the user information. It defaults to `auth_tkt`.

secure `secure` is a boolean value. If it's set to "true", the cookie will only be sent back by the browser over a secure (HTTPS) connection. It defaults to "false".

include_ip `include_ip` is a boolean value. If it's set to true, the requesting IP address is made part of the authentication data in the cookie; if the IP encoded in the cookie differs from the IP of the requesting user agent, the cookie is considered invalid. It defaults to "false".

timeout timeout is an integer value. It represents the maximum age in seconds which the auth_tkt ticket will be considered valid. If timeout is specified, and reissue_time is also specified, reissue_time must be a smaller value than timeout. It defaults to None, meaning that the ticket will be considered valid forever.

reissue_time reissue_time is an integer value. If reissue_time is specified, when we encounter a cookie that is older than the reissue time (in seconds), but younger that the timeout, a new cookie will be issued. It defaults to None, meaning that authentication cookies are never reissued. A value of 0 means reissue a cookie in the response to every request that requires authentication.

max_age max_age is the maximum age of the auth_tkt *cookie*, in seconds. This differs from timeout inasmuch as timeout represents the lifetime of the ticket contained in the cookie, while this value represents the lifetime of the cookie itself. When this value is set, the cookie's Max-Age and Expires settings will be set, allowing the auth_tkt cookie to last between browser sessions. It is typically nonsensical to set this to a value that is lower than timeout or reissue_time, although it is not explicitly prevented. It defaults to None, meaning (on all major browser platforms) that auth_tkt cookies will last for the lifetime of the user's browser session.

56.2 Example

```
1  <authtktauthenticationpolicy
2   secret="goshiamsosecret"
3   callback=".somemodule.somefunc"
4   cookie_name="mycookiename"
5   secure="false"
6   include_ip="false"
7   timeout="86400"
8   reissue_time="600"
9   max_age="31536000"
10  />
```

56.3 Alternatives

You may create an instance of the authentication.AuthTktAuthenticationPolicy (pp. 359) and pass it to the configuration.Configurator (pp. 367) constructor as the authentication_policy argument during initial application configuration.

56.4 See Also

See also *Built-In Authentication Policy ZCML Directives* (pp. 177) and `authentication.AuthTktAuthenticationPolicy` (pp. 359).

CONFIGURE

Because *ZCML* is XML, and because XML requires a single root tag for each document, every ZCML file used by `repoze.bfg` must contain a `configure` container directive, which acts as the root XML tag. It is a "container" directive because its only job is to contain other directives.

57.1 Attributes

xmlns The default XML namespace used for subdirectives.

57.2 Example

```
<configure xmlns="http://namespaces.repoze.org/bfg">

    <!-- other directives -->

</configure>
```

57.3 A Word On XML Namespaces

Usually, the start tag of the `<configure>` container tag has a default *XML namespace* associated with it. This is usually `http://namespaces.repoze.org/bfg`, named by the `xmlns` attribute of the `configure` start tag.

Using the `http://namespaces.repoze.org/bfg` namespace as the default XML namespace isn't strictly necessary; you can use a different default namespace as the default. However, if you do, the declaration tags which are defined by `repoze.bfg` such as the `view` declaration tag will need to be defined in such a way that the XML parser that `repoze.bfg` uses knows which namespace the `repoze.bfg` tags are associated with. For example, the following files are all completely equivalent:

Use of A Non-Default XML Namespace

```
1   <configure xmlns="http://namespaces.zope.org/zope"
2              xmlns:bfg="http://namespaces.repoze.org/bfg">
3
4     <include package="repoze.bfg.includes" />
5
6     <bfg:view
7        view="helloworld.hello_world"
8        />
9
10  </configure>
```

Use of A Per-Tag XML Namespace Without A Default XML Namespace

```
1   <configure>
2
3     <include package="repoze.bfg.includes" />
4
5     <view xmlns="http://namespaces.repoze.org/bfg"
6        view="helloworld.hello_world"
7        />
8
9   </configure>
```

For more information about XML namespaces, see this older, but simple XML.com article (http://www.xml.com/pub/a/1999/01/namespaces.html).

The conventions in this document assume that the default XML namespace is `http://namespaces.repoze.org/bfg`.

57.4 Alternatives

None.

57.5 See Also

See also *Hello World, Goodbye World (Declarative)* (pp. 29).

FORBIDDEN

When `repoze.bfg` can't authorize execution of a view based on the *authorization policy* in use, it invokes a *forbidden view*. The default forbidden response has a 401 status code and is very plain, but it can be overridden as necessary using the `forbidden` ZCML directive.

58.1 Attributes

view The *dotted Python name* to a *view callable*. This attribute is required unless a `renderer` attribute also exists. If a `renderer` attribute exists on the directive, this attribute defaults to a view that returns an empty dictionary (see *Writing View Callables Which Use a Renderer* (pp. 109)).

attr The attribute of the view callable to use if `__call__` is not correct (has the same meaning as in the context of *view* (pp. 479); see the description of `attr` there).

> This feature is new as of `repoze.bfg` 1.1.

renderer This is either a single string term (e.g. `json`) or a string implying a path or *resource specification* (e.g. `templates/views.pt`) used when the view returns a non-*response* object. This attribute has the same meaning as it would in the context of *view* (pp. 479); see the description of `renderer` there).

> This feature is new as of `repoze.bfg` 1.1.

wrapper The *view name* (*not* an object dotted name) of another view declared elsewhere in ZCML (or via the @bfg_view decorator) which will receive the response body of this view as the request.wrapped_body attribute of its own request, and the response returned by this view as the request.wrapped_response attribute of its own request. This attribute has the same meaning as it would in the context of *view* (pp. 479); see the description of wrapper there). Note that the wrapper view *should not* be protected by any permission; behavior is undefined if it does.

This feature is new as of repoze.bfg 1.1.

58.2 Example

```
<forbidden
    view="helloworld.views.forbidden_view"/>
```

58.3 Alternatives

The configuration.Configurator.set_forbidden_view() (pp. 379) method performs the same job as the forbidden ZCML directive.

58.4 See Also

See also *Changing the Forbidden View* (pp. 202).

INCLUDE

The `include` directive includes configuration from an external ZCML file. Use of the `include` tag allows a user to split configuration across multiple ZCML files, and allows package distributors to provide default ZCML configuration for specific purposes which can be included by the integrator of the package as necessary.

59.1 Attributes

package A *dotted Python name* which references a Python *package*.

filename An absolute or relative filename which references a ZCML file.

The `package` and `filename` attributes can be used together or separately as necessary.

59.2 Examples

Loading the File Named `configure.zcml` from a Package Implicitly

```
1  <include package="some.package" />
```

Loading the File Named `other.zcml` From the Current Package

```
<include filename="other.zcml" />
```

Loading a File From a Subdirectory of the Current Package

```
<include filename="subdir/other.zcml" />
```

Loading the File Named `/absolute/path/other.zcml`

```
<include filename="/absolute/path/other.zcml" />
```

Loading the File Named `other.zcml` From a Package Explicitly

```
<include package="some.package" filename="other.zcml" />
```

59.3 Alternatives

None.

59.4 See Also

See also *Hello World, Goodbye World (Declarative)* (pp. 29).

NOTFOUND

When `repoze.bfg` can't map a URL to view code, it invokes a *not found view*. The default not found view is very plain, but the view callable used can be configured via the `notfound` ZCML tag.

60.1 Attributes

view The *dotted Python name* to a *view callable*. This attribute is required unless a `renderer` attribute also exists. If a `renderer` attribute exists on the directive, this attribute defaults to a view that returns an empty dictionary (see *Writing View Callables Which Use a Renderer* (pp. 109)).

attr The attribute of the view callable to use if `__call__` is not correct (has the same meaning as in the context of *view* (pp. 479); see the description of `attr` there).

> ⓘ This feature is new as of `repoze.bfg` 1.1.

renderer This is either a single string term (e.g. `json`) or a string implying a path or *resource specification* (e.g. `templates/views.pt`) used when the view returns a non-*response* object. This attribute has the same meaning as it would in the context of *view* (pp. 479); see the description of `renderer` there).

> ⓘ This feature is new as of `repoze.bfg` 1.1.

wrapper The *view name* (*not* an object dotted name) of another view declared elsewhere in ZCML (or via the @bfg_view decorator) which will receive the response body of this view as the request.wrapped_body attribute of its own request, and the response returned by this view as the request.wrapped_response attribute of its own request. This attribute has the same meaning as it would in the context of *view* (pp. 479); see the description of wrapper there). Note that the wrapper view *should not* be protected by any permission; behavior is undefined if it does.

> ⓘ This feature is new as of repoze.bfg 1.1.

60.2 Example

```
<notfound
    view="helloworld.views.notfound_view"/>
```

60.3 Alternatives

The configuration.Configurator.set_notfound_view() (pp. 379) method performs the same job as the notfound ZCML directive.

60.4 See Also

See also *Changing the Not Found View* (pp. 201).

REMOTEUSERAUTHENTICATIONPOLICY

When this directive is used, authentication information is obtained from a REMOTE_USER key in the WSGI environment, assumed to be set by a WSGI server or an upstream middleware component.

61.1 Attributes

environ_key The environ_key is the name that will be used to obtain the remote user value from the WSGI environment. It defaults to REMOTE_USER.

callback The callback is a Python dotted name to a function passed the string representing the remote user and the request as positional arguments. The callback is expected to return None if the user represented by the string doesn't exist or a sequence of group identifiers (possibly empty) if the user does exist. If callback is None, the userid will be assumed to exist with no groups. It defaults to None.

61.2 Example

```
1  <remoteuserauthenticationpolicy
2    environ_key="REMOTE_USER"
3    callback=".somemodule.somefunc"
4    />
```

61.3 Alternatives

You may create an instance of the `authentication.RemoteUserAuthenticationPolicy` (pp. 361) and pass it to the `configuration.Configurator` (pp. 367) constructor as the `authentication_policy` argument during initial application configuration.

61.4 See Also

See also *Built-In Authentication Policy ZCML Directives* (pp. 177) and `authentication.RemoteUserAuthenticationPolicy` (pp. 361).

RENDERER

The `renderer` ZCML directive can be used to override an existing existing *renderer* or to add a new renderer.

62.1 Attributes

factory A *dotted Python name* referencing a callable object that accepts a renderer name and returns a *renderer* object.

name The renderer name, which is a string.

62.2 Examples

Registering a Non-Template Renderer

```
<renderer
  factory="some.renderer"
  name="mynewrenderer"
  />
```

Registering a Template Renderer

```
<renderer
    factory="some.jinja2.renderer"
    name=".jinja2"
    />
```

62.3 Alternatives

The `configuration.Configurator.add_renderer()` (pp. 369) method is equivalent to the `renderer` ZCML directive.

62.4 See Also

See also *Adding and Overriding Renderers* (pp. 114).

REPOZEWHO1AUTHENTICATIONPOLICY

When this directive is used, authentication information is obtained from a `repoze.who.identity` key in the WSGI environment, assumed to be set by *repoze.who* middleware.

63.1 Attributes

identifier_name The `identifier_name` controls the name used to look up the *repoze.who* "identifier" plugin within `request.environ['repoze.who.plugins']` which is used by this policy to "remember" and "forget" credentials. It defaults to `auth_tkt`.

callback The `callback` is a Python dotted name to a function passed the repoze.who identity and the request as positional arguments. The callback is expected to return None if the user represented by the identity doesn't exist or a sequence of group identifiers (possibly empty) if the user does exist. If `callback` is None, the userid will be assumed to exist with no groups. It defaults to None.

63.2 Example

```
1  <repozewho1authenticationpolicy
2    identifier_name="auth_tkt"
3    callback=".somemodule.somefunc"
4  />
```

63.3 Alternatives

You may create an instance of the `authentication.RepozeWho1AuthenticationPolicy` (pp. 361) and pass it to the `configuration.Configurator` (pp. 367) constructor as the `authentication_policy` argument during initial application configuration.

63.4 See Also

See also *Built-In Authentication Policy ZCML Directives* (pp. 177) and `authentication.RepozeWho1AuthenticationPolicy` (pp. 361).

RESOURCE

The `resource` directive adds a resource override for a single resource.

64.1 Attributes

to_override A *resource specification* specifying the resource to be overridden.

override_with A *resource specification* specifying the resource which is used as the override.

64.2 Examples

Overriding a Single Resource File

```
<resource
  to_override="some.package:templates/mytemplate.pt"
  override_with="another.package:othertemplates/anothertemplate.pt"
/>
```

Overriding all Resources in a Package

```
1  <resource
2    to_override="some.package"
3    override_with="another.package"
4  />
```

Overriding all Resources in a Subdirectory of a Package

```
1  <resource
2    to_override="some.package:templates/"
3    override_with="another.package:othertemplates/"
4  />
```

64.3 Alternatives

The `configuration.Configurator.override_resource()` (pp. 378) method can be used instead of the `resource` ZCML directive.

64.4 See Also

See also *The resource ZCML Directive* (pp. 217).

ROUTE

The route directive adds a single *route configuration* to the *application registry*.

65.1 Attributes

path The path of the route e.g. ideas/:idea. This attribute is required. See *Route Path Pattern Syntax* (pp. 76) for information about the syntax of route paths.

name The name of the route, e.g. myroute. This attribute is required. It must be unique among all defined routes in a given configuration.

factory The *dotted Python name* to a function that will generate a repoze.bfg context object when this route matches. e.g. mypackage.models.MyFactoryClass. If this argument is not specified, a default root factory will be used.

view The *dotted Python name* to a function that will be used as a view callable when this route matches. e.g. mypackage.views.my_view.

xhr This value should be either True or False. If this value is specified and is True, the *request* must possess an HTTP_X_REQUESTED_WITH (aka X-Requested-With) header for this route to match. This is useful for detecting AJAX requests issued from jQuery, Prototype and other Javascript libraries. If this predicate returns false, route matching continues.

This feature is new as of repoze.bfg 1.1.

465

request_method A string representing an HTTP method name, e.g. GET, POST, HEAD, DELETE, PUT. If this argument is not specified, this route will match if the request has *any* request method. If this predicate returns false, route matching continues.

> ⓘ This feature is new as of repoze.bfg 1.1.

path_info The value of this attribute represents a regular expression pattern that will be tested against the PATH_INFO WSGI environment variable. If the regex matches, this predicate will be true. If this predicate returns false, route matching continues.

> ⓘ This feature is new as of repoze.bfg 1.1.

request_param This value can be any string. A view declaration with this attribute ensures that the associated route will only match when the request has a key in the request.params dictionary (an HTTP GET or POST variable) that has a name which matches the supplied value. If the value supplied to the attribute has a = sign in it, e.g. request_params="foo=123", then the key (foo) must both exist in the request.params dictionary, and the value must match the right hand side of the expression (123) for the route to "match" the current request. If this predicate returns false, route matching continues.

> ⓘ This feature is new as of repoze.bfg 1.1.

header The value of this attribute represents an HTTP header name or a header name/value pair. If the value contains a : (colon), it will be considered a name/value pair (e.g. User-Agent:Mozilla/.* or Host:localhost). The *value* of an attribute that represent a name/value pair should be a regular expression. If the value does not contain a colon, the entire value will be considered to be the header name (e.g. If-Modified-Since). If the value evaluates to a header name only without a value, the header specified by the name must be present in the request for this predicate to be true. If the value evaluates to a header name/value pair, the header specified by the name must be present in the request *and* the regular expression specified as the value must match the header value. Whether or not the value represents a header name or a header name/value pair, the case of the header name is not significant. If this predicate returns false, route matching continues.

> ⓘ This feature is new as of repoze.bfg 1.1.

accept The value of this attribute represents a match query for one or more mimetypes in the `Accept` HTTP request header. If this value is specified, it must be in one of the following forms: a mimetype match token in the form `text/plain`, a wildcard mimetype match token in the form `text/*` or a match-all wildcard mimetype match token in the form `*/*`. If any of the forms matches the `Accept` header of the request, this predicate will be true. If this predicate returns false, route matching continues.

> This feature is new as of `repoze.bfg` 1.1.

custom_predicates This value should be a sequence of references to custom predicate callables. Use custom predicates when no set of predefined predicates does what you need. Custom predicates can be combined with predefined predicates as necessary. Each custom predicate callable should accept two arguments: `context` and `request` and should return either `True` or `False` after doing arbitrary evaluation of the context and/or the request. If all callables return `True`, the associated route will be considered viable for a given request. If any custom predicate returns `False`, route matching continues. Note that the value `context` will always be `None` when passed to a custom route predicate.

> This feature is new as of `repoze.bfg` 1.2.

view_context The *dotted Python name* to a class or an interface that the *context* of the view should match for the view named by the route to be used. This attribute is only useful if the `view` attribute is used. If this attribute is not specified, the default (`None`) will be used.

If the `view` attribute is not provided, this attribute has no effect.

This attribute can also be spelled as `view_for` or `for_`; these are valid older spellings.

view_permission The permission name required to invoke the view associated with this route. e.g. `edit`. (see *Using repoze.bfg Security With URL Dispatch* (pp. 90) for more information about permissions).

If the `view` attribute is not provided, this attribute has no effect.

This attribute can also be spelled as `permission`.

view_renderer This is either a single string term (e.g. json) or a string implying a path or *resource specification* (e.g. templates/views.pt). If the renderer value is a single term (does not contain a dot .), the specified term will be used to look up a renderer implementation, and that renderer implementation will be used to construct a response from the view return value. If the renderer term contains a dot (.), the specified term will be treated as a path, and the filename extension of the last element in the path will be used to look up the renderer implementation, which will be passed the full path. The renderer implementation will be used to construct a response from the view return value. See *Writing View Callables Which Use a Renderer* (pp. 109) for more information.

If the view attribute is not provided, this attribute has no effect.

This attribute can also be spelled as renderer.

> ⓘ This feature is new as of repoze.bfg 1.1.

view_attr The view machinery defaults to using the __call__ method of the view callable (or the function itself, if the view callable is a function) to obtain a response dictionary. The attr value allows you to vary the method attribute used to obtain the response. For example, if your view was a class, and the class has a method named index and you wanted to use this method instead of the class' __call__ method to return the response, you'd say attr="index" in the view configuration for the view. This is most useful when the view definition is a class.

If the view attribute is not provided, this attribute has no effect.

> ⓘ This feature is new as of repoze.bfg 1.1.

use_global_views When a request matches this route, and view lookup cannot find a view which has a 'route_name' predicate argument that matches the route, try to fall back to using a view that otherwise matches the context, request, and view name (but does not match the route name predicate).

> ⓘ This feature is new as of repoze.bfg 1.2.

65.2 Alternatives

You can also add a *route configuration* via:

- Using the configuration.Configurator.add_route() (pp. 369) method.

65.3 See Also

See also *URL Dispatch* (pp. 73).

SCAN

To make use of *configuration decoration* decorators, you must perform a *scan*. A scan finds these decorators in code. The scan ZCML directive tells repoze.bfg to begin such a scan.

66.1 Attributes

package The package to scan or the single dot (.), meaning the "current" package (the package in which the ZCML file lives).

66.2 Example

```
<scan package="."/>
```

66.3 Alternatives

The configuration.Configurator.scan() (pp. 378) method performs the same job as the scan ZCML directive.

66.4 See Also

See also *View Configuration Using the @bfg_view Decorator* (pp. 128).

STATIC

Use of the `static` ZCML directive or allows you to serve static resources (such as JavaScript and CSS files) within a `repoze.bfg` application. This mechanism makes static files available at a name relative to the application root URL.

67.1 Attributes

name The (application-root-relative) URL prefix of the static directory. For example, to serve static files from `/static` in most applications, you would provide a `name` of `static`.

path A path to a directory on disk where the static files live. This path may either be 1) absolute (e.g. `/foo/bar/baz`) 2) Python-package-relative (e.g. `(packagename:foo/bar/baz`) or 3) relative to the package directory in which the ZCML file which contains the directive (e.g. `foo/bar/baz`).

cache_max_age The number of seconds that the static resource can be cached, as represented in the returned response's `Expires` and/or `Cache-Control` headers, when any static file is served from this directive. This defaults to 3600 (5 minutes). Optional.

67.2 Examples

Serving Static Files from an Absolute Path

```
<static
    name="static"
    path="/var/www/static"
    />
```

Serving Static Files from a Package-Relative Path

```
<static
    name="static"
    path="some_package:a/b/c/static"
    />
```

Serving Static Files from a Current-Package-Relative Path

```
<static
    name="static"
    path="static_files"
    />
```

67.3 Alternatives

`configuration.configurator.add_static_view()` can also be used to add a static view.

67.4 See Also

See also *Serving Static Resources Using a ZCML Directive* (pp. 137) and *Generating Static Resource URLs* (pp. 138).

SUBSCRIBER

The `subscriber` ZCML directive configures an *subscriber* callable to listen for events broadcast by the `repoze.bfg` web framework.

68.1 Attributes

for The class or *interface* that you are subscribing the listener for, e.g. `interfaces.INewRequest` (pp. 385). Registering a subscriber for a specific class or interface limits the event types that the subscriber will receive to those specified by the interface or class. Default: `zope.interface.Interface` (implying *any* event type).

handler A *dotted Python name* which references an event handler callable. The callable should accept a single argument: `event`. The return value of the callable is ignored.

68.2 Examples

```
1  <subscriber
2    for="repoze.bfg.interfaces.INewRequest"
3    handler=".subscribers.handle_new_request"
4  />
```

68.3 Alternatives

You can also register an event listener by using the `configuration.Configurator.add_subscriber()` (pp. 374) method.

68.4 See Also

See also *Using Events* (pp. 185).

UTILITY

Register a *Zope Component Architecture* "utility".

69.1 Attributes

component The utility component (cannot be specified if `factory` is specified).

factory A factory that creates a component (cannot be specified if `component` is specified).

provides The *interface* that an utility instance resulting from a lookup will provide.

name The utility name.

69.2 Example

```
1  <utility
2    provides=".interfaces.IMyUtility"
3    component=".utilities.MyUtility"
4    />
```

69.3 Alternatives

Use the `registerUtility` method of the `registry` attribute of a *Configurator* instance during initial application setup.

69.4 See Also

None.

VIEW

A `view` declaration directs `repoze.bfg` to create a single *view configuration* registration in the current *application registry*.

The `view` ZCML directive has many possible attributes. Some of the attributes are descriptive or influence rendering. Other attributes are *predicate* attributes, meaning that they imply an evaluation to true or false when view lookup is performed.

All predicates named in a view configuration must evaluate to true in order for the view callable it names to be considered "invokable" for a given request. See *View Lookup and Invocation* (pp. 135) for a description of how a view configuration matches (or doesn't match) during a request.

The possible attributes of the `view` ZCML directive are described below. They are divided into predicate and non-predicate categories.

70.1 Attributes

70.1.1 Non-Predicate Attributes

view The *dotted Python name* to a *view callable*. This attribute is required unless a `renderer` attribute also exists. If a `renderer` attribute exists on the directive, this attribute defaults to a view that returns an empty dictionary (see *Writing View Callables Which Use a Renderer* (pp. 109)).

permission The name of a *permission* that the user must possess in order to call the view. See *Configuring View Security* (pp. 135) for more information about view security and permissions.

attr The view machinery defaults to using the __call__ method of the view callable (or the function itself, if the view callable is a function) to obtain a response dictionary. The attr value allows you to vary the method attribute used to obtain the response. For example, if your view was a class, and the class has a method named index and you wanted to use this method instead of the class' __call__ method to return the response, you'd say attr="index" in the view configuration for the view. This is most useful when the view definition is a class.

> ⓘ This feature is new as of repoze.bfg 1.1.

renderer This is either a single string term (e.g. json) or a string implying a path or *resource specification* (e.g. templates/views.pt). If the renderer value is a single term (does not contain a dot .), the specified term will be used to look up a renderer implementation, and that renderer implementation will be used to construct a response from the view return value. If the renderer term contains a dot (.), the specified term will be treated as a path, and the filename extension of the last element in the path will be used to look up the renderer implementation, which will be passed the full path. The renderer implementation will be used to construct a response from the view return value.

Note that if the view itself returns a response (see *View Callable Responses* (pp. 108)), the specified renderer implementation is never called.

When the renderer is a path, although a path is usually just a simple relative pathname (e.g. templates/foo.pt, implying that a template named "foo.pt" is in the "templates" directory relative to the directory in which the ZCML file is defined), a path can be absolute, starting with a slash on UNIX or a drive letter prefix on Windows. The path can alternately be a *resource specification* in the form some.dotted.package_name:relative/path, making it possible to address template resources which live in a separate package.

The renderer attribute is optional. If it is not defined, the "null" renderer is assumed (no rendering is performed and the value is passed back to the upstream BFG machinery unmolested).

> ⓘ This feature is new as of repoze.bfg 1.1.

wrapper The *view name* (*not* an object dotted name) of another view declared elsewhere in ZCML (or via the @bfg_view decorator) which will receive the response body of this view as the request.wrapped_body attribute of its own request, and the response returned by this view as the request.wrapped_response attribute of its own request. Using a wrapper makes it possible to "chain" views together to form a composite response. The response of the outermost wrapper view will be returned to the user. The wrapper view will be found as any view is found: see *View Lookup and Invocation* (pp. 135). The "best" wrapper view will be found based on the lookup ordering: "under the hood" this wrapper view is looked up via `view.render_view_to_response(context, request, 'wrapper_viewname')`. The context and request of a wrapper view is the same context and request of the inner view. If this attribute is unspecified, no view wrapping is done.

> This feature is new as of `repoze.bfg` 1.1.

70.1.2 Predicate Attributes

name The *view name*. Read the *Traversal* (pp. 61) to understand the concept of a view name.

context A *dotted Python name* representing the Python class that the *context* must be an instance of, *or* the *interface* that the *context* must provide in order for this view to be found and called. This predicate is true when the *context* is an instance of the represented class or if the *context* provides the represented interface; it is otherwise false. An alternate name for this attribute is `for` (this is an older spelling).

route_name *This attribute services an advanced feature that isn't often used unless you want to perform traversal after a route has matched.* This value must match the `name` of a `<route>` declaration (see *URL Dispatch* (pp. 73)) that must match before this view will be called. Note that the `route` configuration referred to by `route_name` usually has a `*traverse` token in the value of its `path`, representing a part of the path that will be used by traversal against the result of the route's *root factory*. See *Combining Traversal and URL Dispatch* (pp. 93) for more information on using this advanced feature.

request_type This value should be a *dotted Python name* string representing the *interface* that the *request* must have in order for this view to be found and called. The presence of this attribute is largely for backwards compatibility with applications written for `repoze.bfg` version 1.0. This value may be an HTTP `REQUEST_METHOD` string, e.g. ('GET', 'HEAD', 'PUT', 'POST', or 'DELETE'). Passing request method strings as a `request_type` is deprecated. Use the `request_method` attribute instead for maximum forward compatibility.

request_method This value can either be one of the strings 'GET', 'POST', 'PUT', 'DELETE', or 'HEAD' representing an HTTP `REQUEST_METHOD`. A view declaration with this attribute ensures that the view will only be called when the request's `method` (aka `REQUEST_METHOD`) string matches the supplied value.

> This feature is new as of `repoze.bfg` 1.1.

request_param This value can be any string. A view declaration with this attribute ensures that the view will only be called when the request has a key in the `request.params` dictionary (an HTTP `GET` or `POST` variable) that has a name which matches the supplied value. If the value supplied to the attribute has a = sign in it, e.g. `request_params="foo=123"`, then the key (`foo`) must both exist in the `request.params` dictionary, and the value must match the right hand side of the expression (`123`) for the view to "match" the current request.

> ⓘ This feature is new as of `repoze.bfg` 1.1.

containment This value should be a *dotted Python name* string representing the class that a graph traversal parent object of the *context* must be an instance of (or *interface* that a parent object must provide) in order for this view to be found and called. Your models must be "location-aware" to use this feature. See *Location-Aware Model Instances* (pp. 165) for more information about location-awareness.

> ⓘ This feature is new as of `repoze.bfg` 1.1.

xhr This value should be either `True` or `False`. If this value is specified and is `True`, the *request* must possess an `HTTP_X_REQUESTED_WITH` (aka `X-Requested-With`) header that has the value `XMLHttpRequest` for this view to be found and called. This is useful for detecting AJAX requests issued from jQuery, Prototype and other Javascript libraries.

> ⓘ This feature is new as of `repoze.bfg` 1.1.

accept The value of this attribute represents a match query for one or more mimetypes in the `Accept` HTTP request header. If this value is specified, it must be in one of the following forms: a mimetype match token in the form `text/plain`, a wildcard mimetype match token in the form `text/*` or a match-all wildcard mimetype match token in the form `*/*`. If any of the forms matches the `Accept` header of the request, this predicate will be true.

> ⓘ This feature is new as of `repoze.bfg` 1.1.

header The value of this attribute represents an HTTP header name or a header name/value pair. If the value contains a : (colon), it will be considered a name/value pair (e.g. `User-Agent:Mozilla/.*` or `Host:localhost`). The *value* of an attribute that represent a name/value pair should be a regular expression. If the value does not contain a colon, the entire value will be considered to be the header name (e.g. If-Modified-Since). If the value evaluates to a header name only without a value, the header specified by the name must be present in the request for this predicate to be true. If the value evaluates to a header name/value pair, the header specified by the name must be present in the request *and* the regular expression specified as the value must match the header value. Whether or not the value represents a header name or a header name/value pair, the case of the header name is not significant.

> This feature is new as of repoze.bfg 1.1.

path_info The value of this attribute represents a regular expression pattern that will be tested against the PATH_INFO WSGI environment variable. If the regex matches, this predicate will be true.

> This feature is new as of repoze.bfg 1.1.

custom_predicates This value should be a sequence of references to custom predicate callables (e.g. dotted.name.one dotted.name.two, if used in ZCML; a *dotted Python name* to each callable separated by a space). Use custom predicates when no set of predefined predicates do what you need. Custom predicates can be combined with predefined predicates as necessary. Each custom predicate callable should accept two arguments: context and request and should return either True or False after doing arbitrary evaluation of the context and/or the request. If all callables return True, the associated view callable will be considered viable for a given request.

> This feature is new as of repoze.bfg 1.2.

70.2 Examples

Registering A Default View for a Class

```
1  <view
2      context=".models.MyModel"
3      view=".views.hello_world"
4  />
```

Registering A View With a Predicate

```
<view
    context=".models.MyModel"
    view=".views.hello_world_post"
    request_method="POST"
/>
```

70.3 Alternatives

You can also add a *view configuration* via:

- Using the `view.bfg_view` (pp. 428) class as a decorator.

- Using the `configuration.Configurator.add_view()` (pp. 374) method.

70.4 See Also

See also *Views* (pp. 105).

Part V

Glossary and Index

GLOSSARY

ACE An *access control entry*. An access control entry is one element in an *ACL*. An access control entry is a three-tuple that describes three things: an *action* (one of either `Allow` or `Deny`), a *principal* (a string describing a user or group), and a *permission*. For example the ACE, (`Allow`, `'bob'`, `'read'`) is a member of an ACL that indicates that the principal `bob` is allowed the permission `read` against the context the ACL is attached to.

ACL An *access control list*. An ACL is a sequence of *ACE* tuples. An ACL is attached to a model instance. An example of an ACL is [(`Allow`, `'bob'`, `'read'`), (`Deny`, `'fred'`, `'write'`)]. If an ACL is attached to a model instance, and that model instance is findable via the context, it will be consulted any active security policy to determine wither a particular request can be fulfilled given the *authentication* information in the request.

Agendaless Consulting A consulting organization formed by Paul Everitt, Tres Seaver, and Chris McDonough. See also http://agendaless.com (http://agendaless.com) .

application registry A registry of configuration information consulted by `repoze.bfg` while servicing an application. An application registry maps model types to views, as well as housing other application-specific component registrations. Every `repoze.bfg` application has one (and only one) application registry.

authentication The act of determining that the credentials a user presents during a particular request are "good". Authentication in `repoze.bfg` is performed via an *authentication policy*.

authentication policy An authentication policy in `repoze.bfg` terms is a bit of code which has an API which determines the current *principal* (or principals) associated with a request.

authorization The act of determining whether a user can perform a specific action. In bfg terms, this means determining whether, for a given context, any *principal* (or principals) associated with the request have the requisite *permission* to allow the request to continue. Authorization in `repoze.bfg` is performed via its *authorization policy*.

authorization policy An authorization policy in `repoze.bfg` terms is a bit of code which has an API which determines whether or not the principals associated with the request can perform an action associated with a permission, based on the information found on the *context*.

Chameleon chameleon (http://chameleon.repoze.org) is an attribute language template compiler which supports both the *ZPT* and *Genshi* templating specifications. It is written and maintained by Malthe Borch. It has several extensions, such as the ability to use bracketed (Genshi-style) `${name}` syntax, even within ZPT. It is also much faster than the reference implementations of both ZPT and Genshi. `repoze.bfg` offers Chameleon templating out of the box in ZPT and text flavors.

configuration declaration An individual method call made to an instance of a `repoze.bfg` *Configurator* object which performs an arbitrary action, such as registering a *view configuration* (via the `view` method of the configurator) or *route configuration* (via the `route` method of the configurator). A set of configuration declarations is also usually implied via the use of a *ZCML declaration* within an application, or a set of configuration declarations might be performed by a *scan* of code in a package.

configuration decoration Metadata implying one or more *configuration declaration* invocations. Often set by configuration Python *decorator* attributes, such as `view.bfg_view`, aka `@bfg_view`.

configurator An object used to do *configuration declaration* within an application. The most common configurator is an instance of the `configuration.Configurator` class.

context An object in the system that is found during *traversal* or *URL dispatch* based on URL data; if it's found via traversal, it's usually a *model* object that is part of an object graph; if it's found via *URL dispatch*, it's an object manufactured on behalf of the route's "factory". A context becomes the subject of a *view*, and typically has security information attached to it. See the *Traversal* (pp. 61) chapter and the *URL Dispatch* (pp. 73) chapter for more information about how a URL is resolved to a context.

Context Finding The act of locating a *context* and a *view name* given a *request*. *Traversal* and *URL dispatch* are the context finding subsystems used by `repoze.bfg`.

CPython The C implementation of the Python language. This is the reference implementation that most people refer to as simply "Python"; *Jython*, Google's App Engine, and PyPy (http://codespeak.net/pypy/dist/pypy/doc/) are examples of non-C based Python implementations.

declarative configuration The configuration mode in which you use *ZCML* to make a set of *configuration declaration* statements.

decorator A wrapper around a Python function or class which accepts the function or class as its first argument and which returns an arbitrary object. `repoze.bfg` provides several decorators, used for configuration and return value modification purposes. See also PEP 318 (http://www.python.org/dev/peps/pep-0318/).

Default view The default view of a model is the view invoked when the *view name* is the empty string (`''`). This is the case when *traversal* exhausts the path elements in the PATH_INFO of a request before it returns a *context*.

distribution (Setuptools/distutils terminology). A file representing an installable library or application. Distributions are usually files that have the suffix of `.egg`, `.tar.gz`, or `.zip`. Distributions are the target of Setuptools commands such as `easy_install`.

Django A full-featured Python web framework (http://djangoproject.com).

dotted Python name A reference to a Python object by name using a string, in the form `path.to.modulename:attributename`. Often used in Paste and setuptools configurations. A variant is used in dotted names within *ZCML* attributes that name objects (such as the ZCML "view" directive's "view" attribute): the colon (`:`) is not used; in its place is a dot.

entry point A *setuptools* indirection, defined within a setuptools *distribution* setup.py. It is usually a name which refers to a function somewhere in a package which is held by the distribution.

event An object broadcast to zero or more *subscriber* callables during normal `repoze.bfg` system operations during the lifetime of an application. Application code can subscribe to these events by using the subscriber functionality described in *Using Events* (pp. 185).

Forbidden view The *view callable* invoked by `repoze.bfg` when the developer explicitly raises a `exceptions.Forbidden` exception from within *view* code or *root factory* code, or when the *view configuration* and *authorization policy* found for a request disallows a particular view invocation. `repoze.bfg` provides a default implementation of a forbidden view; it can be overridden. See *Changing the Forbidden View* (pp. 202).

Genshi An XML templating language (http://pypi.python.org/pypi/Genshi/) by Christopher Lenz.

Google App Engine Google App Engine (http://code.google.com/appengine/) (aka "GAE") is a Python application hosting service offered by Google. `repoze.bfg` runs on GAE.

Grok A web framework based on Zope 3 (http://grok.zope.org).

imperative configuration The configuration mode in which you use Python to call methods on a *Configurator* in order to add each *configuration declaration* required by your application.

interface A Zope interface (http://pypi.python.org/pypi/zope.interface) object. In `repoze.bfg`, an interface may be attached to a *model* object or a *request* object in order to identify that the object is "of a type". Interfaces are used internally by `repoze.bfg` to perform view lookups and other policy lookups. The ability to make use of an interface is exposed to an application programmers during *view configuration* via the `context` argument, the `request_type` argument and the `containment` argument. Interfaces are also exposed to application developers when they make use of the *event* system. Fundamentally, `repoze.bfg` programmers can think of an interface as something that they can attach to an object that stamps it with a "type" unrelated to its underlying Python type. Interfaces can also be used to describe the behavior of an object (its methods and attributes), but unless they choose to, `repoze.bfg` programmers do not need to understand or use this feature of interfaces.

Jinja2 A text templating language (http://jinja.pocoo.org/2/) by Armin Ronacher.

JSON JavaScript Object Notation (http://www.json.org/) is a data serialization format.

Jython A *Python implementation <http://www.jython.org/>* written for the Java Virtual Machine.

lineage An ordered sequence of objects based on a *"location -aware"* context. The lineage of any given *context* is composed of itself, its parent, its parent's parent, and so on. The order of the sequence is context-first, then the parent of the context, then its parent's parent, and so on. The parent of an object in a lineage is available as its __parent__ attribute.

location The path to an object in an object graph. See *Location-Aware Model Instances* (pp. 165) for more information about how to make a model object *location-aware*.

METAL Macro Expansion for TAL (http://wiki.zope.org/ZPT/METAL), a part of *ZPT* which makes it possible to share common look and feel between templates.

middleware *Middleware* is a *WSGI* concept. It is a WSGI component that acts both as a server and an application. Interesting uses for middleware exist, such as caching, content-transport encoding, and other functions. See WSGI.org (http://wsgi.org) or PyPI (http://python.org/pypi) to find middleware for your application.

mod_wsgi mod_wsgi (http://code.google.com/p/modwsgi/) is an Apache module developed by Graham Dumpleton. It allows *WSGI* applications (such as applications developed using repoze.bfg) to be served using the Apache web server.

model An object representing data in the system. If traversal is used, a model is a node in the object graph traversed by the system. When traversal is used, a model instance becomes the *context* of a *view*. If url dispatch is used, a single *context* is generated for each request and is used as the context of a view: this object is also technically a "model" in repoze.bfg terms, although this terminology can be a bit confusing: see *BFG Uses "Model" To Represent A Node In The Graph of Objects Traversed*.

multidict An ordered dictionary that can have multiple values for each key. Adds the methods getall, getone, mixed, and add to the normal dictionary interface. See http://pythonpaste.org/webob/class-webob.multidict.MultiDict.html (http://pythonpaste.org/webob/class-webob.multidict.MultiDict.html)

Not Found view The *view callable* invoked by repoze.bfg when the developer explicitly raises a exceptions.NotFound exception from within *view* code or *root factory* code, or when the current request doesn't match any *view configuration*. repoze.bfg provides a default implementation of a not found view; it can be overridden. See *Changing the Not Found View* (pp. 201).

package A directory on disk which contains an __init__.py file, making it recognizable to Python as a location which can be import -ed.

Paste Paste (http://pythonpaste.org) is a WSGI development and deployment system developed by Ian Bicking.

PasteDeploy PasteDeploy (http://pythonpaste.org) is a library used by `repoze.bfg` which makes it possible to configure *WSGI* components together declaratively within an `.ini` file. It was developed by Ian Bicking as part of *Paste*.

permission A string or unicode object that represents an action being taken against a context. A permission is associated with a view name and a model type by the developer. Models are decorated with security declarations (e.g. an *ACL*), which reference these tokens also. Permissions are used by the active to security policy to match the view permission against the model's statements about which permissions are granted to which principal in a context in order to to answer the question "is this user allowed to do this". Examples of permissions: `read`, or `view_blog_entries`.

pipeline The *Paste* term for a single configuration of a WSGI server, a WSGI application, with a set of middleware in-between.

pkg_resources A module which ships with *setuptools* that provides an API for addressing "resource files" within Python packages. Resource files are static files, template files, etc; basically anything non-Python-source that lives in a Python package can be considered a resource file. See also PkgResources (http://peak.telecommunity.com/DevCenter/PkgResources)

predicate A test which returns `True` or `False`. Two different types of predicates exist in `repoze.bfg`: a *view predicate* and a *route predicate*. View predicates are attached to *view configuration* and route predicates are attached to *route configuration*.

principal A *principal* is a string or unicode object representing a userid or a group id. It is provided by an *authentication policy*. For example, if a user had the user id "bob", and Bob was part of two groups named "group foo" and "group bar", the request might have information attached to it that would indicate that Bob was represented by three principals: "bob", "group foo" and "group bar".

project (Setuptools/distutils terminology). A directory on disk which contains a `setup.py` file and one or more Python packages. The `setup.py` file contains code that allows the package(s) to be installed, distributed, and tested.

Pylons A lightweight Python web framework (http://pylonshq.com).

PyPI The Python Package Index (http://pypi.python.org/pypi), a collection of software available for Python.

Python The *programming language <http://python.org>* in which `repoze.bfg` is written.

renderer A serializer that can be referred to via *view configuration* which converts a non-*Response* return values from a *view* into a string (and ultimately a response). Using a renderer can make writing views that require templating or other serialization less tedious. See *Writing View Callables Which Use a Renderer* (pp. 109) for more information.

renderer factory   A factory which creates a *renderer*. See *Adding and Overriding Renderers* (pp. 114) for more information.

Repoze   "Repoze" is essentially a "brand" of software developed by Agendaless Consulting (http://agendaless.com) and a set of contributors. The term has no special intrinsic meaning. The project's website (http://repoze.org) has more information. The software developed "under the brand" is available in a Subversion repository (http://svn.repoze.org).

repoze.catalog   An indexing and search facility (fielded and full-text) based on zope.index (http://pypi.python.org/pypi/zope.index). See the documentation (http://docs.repoze.org/catalog) for more information. A tutorial for its usage in `repoze.bfg` exists in *Using repoze.catalog Within repoze.bfg* (pp. 351).

repoze.lemonade   Zope2 CMF-like data structures and helper facilities (http://docs.repoze.org/lemonade) for CA-and-ZODB-based applications useful within `repoze.bfg` applications.

repoze.who   Authentication middleware (http://docs.repoze.org/who) for *WSGI* applications. It can be used by `repoze.bfg` to provide authentication information.

repoze.workflow   Barebones workflow for Python apps (http://docs.repoze.org/workflow) . It can be used by `repoze.bfg` to form a workflow system.

request   A `WebOb` request object. See *Request and Response Objects* (pp. 143) for information about request objects.

request type   An attribute of a *request* that allows for specialization of view invocation based on arbitrary categorization. The every *request* object that `repoze.bfg` generates and manipulates has one or more *interface* objects attached to it. The default interface attached to a request object is `interfaces.IRequest`.

resource   Any file contained within a Python *package* which is *not* a Python source code file.

resource specification   A colon-delimited identifier for a *resource*. The colon separates a Python *package* name from a package subpath. For example, the resource specification `my.package:static/baz.css` identifies the file named `baz.css` in the `static` subdirectory of the `my.package` Python *package*.

response   An object that has three attributes: `app_iter` (representing an iterable body), `headerlist` (representing the http headers sent to the user agent), and `status` (representing the http status string sent to the user agent). This is the interface defined for `WebOb` response objects. See *Request and Response Objects* (pp. 143) for information about response objects.

reStructuredText A plain text format (http://docutils.sourceforge.net/rst.html) that is the defacto standard for descriptive text shipped in *distribution* files, and Python docstrings. This documentation is authored in ReStructuredText format.

root The object at which *traversal* begins when `repoze.bfg` searches for a *context* (for *URL Dispatch*, the root is *always* the context).

root factory The "root factory" of an `repoze.bfg` application is called on every request sent to the application. The root factory returns the traversal root of an application. It is conventionally named `get_root`. An application may supply a root factory to `repoze.bfg` during the construction of a *Configurator*. If a root factory is not supplied, the application uses a default root object. Use of the default root object is useful in application which use *URL dispatch* for all URL-to-view code mappings.

route A single pattern matched by the *url dispatch* subsystem, which generally resolves to a *root factory* (and then ultimately a *view*). See also *url dispatch*.

route configuration Route configuration is the act of using *imperative configuration* or a *ZCML* `<route>` statement to associate request parameters with a particular *route* using pattern matching and *route predicate* statements. See *URL Dispatch* (pp. 73) for more information about route configuration.

route predicate An argument to a *route configuration* which implies a value that evaluates to `True` or `False` for a given *request*. All predicates attached to a *route configuration* must evaluate to `True` for the associated route to "match" the current request. If a route does not match the current request, the next route (in definition order) is attempted.

router The *WSGI* application created when you start a `repoze.bfg` application. The router intercepts requests, invokes traversal and/or URL dispatch, calls view functions, and returns responses to the WSGI server on behalf of your `repoze.bfg` application.

Routes A system by Ben Bangert (http://routes.groovie.org/) which parses URLs and compares them against a number of user defined mappings. The URL pattern matching syntax in `repoze.bfg` is inspired by the Routes syntax (which was inspired by Ruby On Rails pattern syntax).

scan The term used by `repoze.bfg` to define the process of importing and examining all code in a Python package or module for *configuration decoration*.

setuptools Setuptools (http://peak.telecommunity.com/DevCenter/setuptools) builds on Python's `distutils` to provide easier building, distribution, and installation of libraries and applications.

SQLAlchemy SQLAlchemy' (http://www.sqlalchemy.org/) is an object relational mapper used in tutorials within this documentation.

subpath A list of element "left over" after the *router* has performed a successful traversal to a view. The subpath is a sequence of strings, e.g. `['left', 'over', 'names']`. Within BFG applications that use URL dispatch rather than traversal, you can use `*subpath` in the route pattern to influence the subpath. See *Using *subpath in a Route Path* (pp. 101) for more information.

subscriber A callable which receives an *event*. A callable becomes a subscriber via *imperative configuration* or the `<subscriber>` ZCML directive. See *Using Events* (pp. 185) for more information.

template A file with replaceable parts that is capable of representing some text, XML, or HTML when rendered.

thread local A thread-local variable is one which is essentially a global variable in terms of how it is accessed and treated, however, each *thread* `<http://en.wikipedia.org/wiki/Thread_(computer_science)>` used by the application may have a different value for this same "global" variable. `repoze.bfg` uses a small number of thread local variables, as described in *Thread Locals* (pp. 227). See also the *threading.local documentation* `<http://docs.python.org/library/threading.html#threading.local>` for more information.

traversal The act of descending "down" a graph of model objects from a root model in order to find a *context*. The `repoze.bfg` *router* performs traversal of model objects when a *root factory* is specified. See the *Traversal* (pp. 61) chapter for more information. Traversal can be performed *instead* of *URL dispatch* or can be combined *with* URL dispatch. See *Combining Traversal and URL Dispatch* (pp. 93) for more information about combining traversal and URL dispatch (advanced).

Triad The three bits of information used by *view lookup* to find "the best" view callable for a given circumstance: a *context* type, a *view name* and a *request*.

URL dispatch An alternative to graph traversal as a mechanism for locating a *context* for a *view*. When you use a *route* in your `repoze.bfg` application via a *route configuration*, you are using URL dispatch. See the *URL Dispatch* (pp. 73) for more information.

view Common vernacular for a *view callable*.

view callable A "view callable" is a callable Python object which is associated with a *view configuration*; it returns a *response* object . A view callable accepts a single argument: `request`, which will be an instance of a *request* object. An alternate calling convention allows a view to be defined as a callable which accepts a pair of arguments: `context` and `request`: this calling convention is useful for traversal-based applications in which a *context* is always very important. A view callable is the primary mechanism by which a developer writes user interface code within `repoze.bfg`. See *Views* (pp. 105) for more information about `repoze.bfg` view callables.

view configuration View configuration is the act of associating a *view callable* with configuration information. This configuration information helps map a given *request* to a particular view callable and it can influence the response of a view callable. `repoze.bfg` views can be configured via *imperative configuration*, *ZCML* or by a special `@bfg_view` decorator coupled with a *scan*. See *Views* (pp. 105) for more information about view configuration.

View Lookup The act of finding and invoking the "best" *view callable* given a *request*, a *context*, and a *view name*.

view name The "URL name" of a view, e.g `index.html`. If a view is configured without a name, its name is considered to be the empty string (which implies the *default view*).

view predicate An argument to a *view configuration* which evaluates to `True` or `False` for a given *request*. All predicates attached to a view configuration must evaluate to true for the associated view to be considered as a possible callable for a given request.

virtual root A model object representing the "virtual" root of a request; this is typically the physical root object (the object returned by the application root factory) unless *Virtual Hosting* (pp. 181) is in use.

virtualenv An isolated Python environment. Allows you to control which packages are used on a particular project by cloning your main Python. virtualenv (http://pypi.python.org/pypi/virtualenv) was created by Ian Bicking.

WebOb WebOb (http://pythonpaste.org/webob/) is a WSGI request/response library created by Ian Bicking.

WSGI Web Server Gateway Interface (http://wsgi.org/). This is a Python standard for connecting web applications to web servers, similar to the concept of Java Servlets. `repoze.bfg` requires that your application be served as a WSGI application.

ZCML Zope Configuration Markup Language (http://www.muthukadan.net/docs/zca.html#zcml), an XML dialect used by Zope and `repoze.bfg` for configuration tasks. ZCML is capable of performing different types of *configuration declaration*, but its primary purpose in `repoze.bfg` is to perform *view configuration* and *route configuration* within the `configure.zcml` file in a `repoze.bfg` application. You can use ZCML as an alternative to *imperative configuration*.

ZCML declaration The concrete use of a *ZCML directive* within a ZCML file.

ZCML directive A ZCML "tag" such as `<view>` or `<route>`.

ZEO Zope Enterprise Objects (http://www.zope.org/Documentation/Books/ZopeBook/2_6Edition/ZEO.stx) allows multiple simultaneous processes to access a single *ZODB* database.

ZODB Zope Object Database (http://wiki.zope.org/ZODB/FrontPage), a persistent Python object store.

Zope The Z Object Publishing Framework (http://zope.org), a full-featured Python web framework.

Zope Component Architecture The Zope Component Architecture (http://www.muthukadan.net/docs/zca.html) (aka ZCA) is a system which allows for application pluggability and complex dispatching based on objects which implement an *interface*. `repoze.bfg` uses the ZCA "under the hood" to perform view dispatching and other application configuration tasks.

ZPT The Zope Page Template (http://wiki.zope.org/ZPT/FrontPage) templating language.

INDEX

www.ingramcontent.com/pod-product-compliance
Lightning Source LLC
Chambersburg PA
CBHW060955210326
41598CB00031B/4830